ARTIST
AND
AUDIENCE

Reproduced on the cover: Honoré Daumier. *Visitors in an Artist's Studio.*
Watercolor, 12¾ × 12¼″ (32 × 31 cm). Walters Art Gallery, Baltimore, Maryland.

ARTIST AND AUDIENCE

Terence Grieder

University of Texas at Austin

Holt, Rinehart and Winston, Inc.

Fort Worth   Chicago   San Francisco   Philadelphia   Montreal
Toronto   London   Sydney   Tokyo

Publisher   **Charlyce Jones Owen**
Acquisitions Editor   **Janet Wilhite**
Developmental Editor   **Anne Boynton-Trigg**
Manager of Production   **Tad Gaither**
Senior Project Manager   **Françoise Bartlett/Spectrum Publisher
Services, Inc.**
Photo Researcher   **Marion Paone Geisinger**
Interior Design and Cover Design   **Gloria Gentile**
Layout Design   **Connie Szcwciuk-Cree**
Composition and Color   **York Graphic Services, Inc.**
Printing and Binding   **R. R. Donnelley and Sons Company**

Library of Congress Cataloging-in-Publication Data

Grieder, Terence.
    Artist and audience / Terence Grieder.
       p.   cm.
    Bibliography: p.
    Includes index.
    1. Art—Psychology.   2. Communication in art.   3. Art and society.
    I. Title.
    N71.G685   1990   89-35356
    7C1'.1—dc20   CIP

ISBN 0-03-014199-0

Requests for permission to make copies of any part of the work should be mailed to: Copyrights and Permissions Department, Harcourt Brace Jovanovich, Inc., Orlando, Florida 32887.

Address Editorial Correspondence To: 301 Commerce Street, Suite 3700, Fort Worth, TX 76102

Address Orders To: 6277 Sea Harbor Drive, Orlando, FL 32887
                    1-800-782-4479, or 1-800-433-001 (in Florida)

Printed in the United States of America

   1 2 3   039   9 8 7 6 5 4 3 2

Photographic credits are on page 480.

Preface

Artist and Audience is an introduction to art for college students and the general reader. It puts the reader in touch with the concerns of the "art world" as they are experienced by artists, collectors, critics, and historians. Few of us become professional artists, but all of us—even those who become artists—will be members of the audience for art. This book aims to educate students for intelligent participation in the audience.

Recent criticism has emphasized the decisive role of the audience in determining what art is and what it means. In most cases we can never discover the artist's intentions. As we examine older art we discover that it brings to our minds many things which could never have been known to the artist. The awareness of a long history, conditioning our interpretation of all art, is a distinctive feature of our period and one of the premises on which the Post-Modern point of view rests. The audience's understanding of the world is constantly changing and giving rise to new interpretations of earlier art.

Artist and Audience is a new book in all senses. The Post-Modern outlook which informs it has the virtue of openness to many points of view, those found in other periods of our own history as well as in other cultures today. Works of art by African, Asian, and Native American artists are based on the same elements and principles as modern American and European art and appear in this book on an equal footing. Non-Western arts are part of the general body of art discussed throughout the book, which features special sections on Chinese, Japanese, African, and Islamic art.

Traditional art appreciation books often ask observers to pretend for a while that they are artists, but *Artist and Audience* seeks to balance the creative roles of those who send the messages with those who receive and interpret them. More traditional books often summarize art history texts, or choose a random selection of historical examples to make points. This volume focuses each section on an aesthetic, technical, or historical question and analyzes works of art concerned with those specific matters. Part of the Post-Modern aesthetic is the unity of the arts—the equality in artistic potential of ceramics and painting, for example—and the assurance that functional arts such as architecture or interior design have a philosophical expression comparable to that of any other art form.

A thoughtful selection of examples is intended to bring the reader a gradually expanding acquaintance with the great classics of Western art and the great masters who produced them. Major works are discussed in detail, and major figures are reconsidered in light of other aspects of their careers. Michelangelo, for example, is shown as a painter and draftsman, then as a sculptor, and seen again in a brief biographical sketch of his early training as an artist. Matisse, Pollock, Picasso, Cassatt, and Goya are among the many artists who are considered in several aspects. Biographical information is given throughout the text, allowing the reader to make the acquaintance of a variety of art world personalities.

Many of the 614 illustrations, over 200 of them in full color, have never appeared before in a general introduction to art. A symbolic figure by German Post-Modernist Anselm Kiefer, an interior by the Parisian Israeli painter Avigdor Arikha, a Japanese classic by Sotatsu, and a self-portrait in pastel by Liotard are a sample of the new range of images.

Along with new and unfamiliar works which may become the accepted masterpieces of the future, there has been a conscious effort to bring together images that are basic components of an educated mind. This book tries to familiarize the student with those works of art, which range from the ancient paintings in Lascaux Cave to the environmental sculptures of Christo, and from Michelangelo's frescoes to Hokusai's *Thirty-six Views of Mt. Fuji*. Although we are exposed to art throughout our lives, for many this book and the course of study it accompanies will be their only systematic study of these masterworks and the traditions that produced them.

Plan of the Book

The book is divided into five parts. Part I introduces the galleries and museums where art is seen and discusses the special role played by the audience in the interpretation of art. Part II builds the skills of interpretation by analyzing the elements and principles of art as the artist's tools of expression. Part III describes the various mediums, from graphic through painting and sculpture. Contemporary studio practice informs the point of view, but the artist's technical practices take second place behind the general understanding a collector or member of the audience needs to interpret the significance of the art. Part IV surveys the vast field of applied design in architecture, city-planning, interiors, clothing, and industrial design. Developments in technology and structure have played major roles in the applied arts. Historical comparisons help make these developments clear.

Part V is a selective history of art styles, concentrating on those of special contemporary interest, including ancient American, Classical and Hellenistic Greek, Renaissance, and Baroque. The entire history of art cannot be accommodated in an introductory book, but the history of style can be discussed with selective examples. Part V is concerned with style as message, revealing the attitudes and concerns of people at a particular time and place, including our own time and place. After reading Part V a student should feel more confident about interpreting the art of many of the world's societies—the only intentional extant messages from many ancient and nonliterate civilizations. This understanding of another culture's artistic heritage promotes the sense of the unity of humankind and the possibilities of communication among peoples which are such strong features of our age.

Set apart from the main text are features under the headings "A Point in Time" and "In Detail." Each amplifies the text, with illustrations and biographical details to give immediacy to the problem-centered discussion in the main text. The discussion of bronzecasting, for example, leads to a feature on Benvenuto Cellini's famous description of the casting of his sculpture *Perseus with the Head of Medusa*. A feature based on Paul and Jean Hanna's account of their experience as clients of Frank Lloyd Wright expands the discussion of Wright's architecture.

Newcomers to art are often baffled by foreign names and terms. This text features a simplified pronunciation guide for names and terms at their first appearance. Students will also find the glossary's short definitions of terms useful. The historical and geographical foundations of art are clarified by the full-color time lines which put periods and movements into chronological order, with dates for many of the major figures, and the set of full-color maps of cultural regions. At the end of each chapter is a summary of the main points in the chapter. Notes for each chapter, collected at the end of the book, will assist students in finding sources. A bibliography of suggested readings for each chapter is appended at the end of the book.

Teaching Aids

To make learning and teaching more effective an invaluable and comprehensive teaching package is available. An *Instructor's Manual* provides a course outline of the text, with reading assignments, illustration lists, an analysis of basic ideas and key words, and the educational objectives of each section. Discussion and test questions are provided in several formats (multiple choice, matching, true-false, essay), ready for classroom use, with answers separately. The Test Bank is available for Apple or IBM computers. A set of color slides is part of the teaching package, to provide a ready resource for classroom lectures and discussions. *Highlights from World Art,* a guide to finding the work of any major artist, school, or period of art, is included.

Acknowledgments

The author would like to thank the many individuals who have contributed to the making of this book: first, of course, the many artists whose work has enriched his life and provided so much stimulation and then the many students who have shared the pleasure of art over more than thirty-five years of teaching.

This book has benefited from the careful reading and thoughtful criticism of a group of expert reviewers, all professionals in the art world. The author thanks Kenneth Burchett, University of Central Arkansas; Patricia Covington, Southern Illinois University; J. David Diller, James Madison University; Robert Fisher, Yakima Valley College; Darrell Forney, Sacramento City College; James Hagenbuckle, St. Petersburg Junior College; Eugene Hood, University of Wisconsin–Eau Claire; Ralph Jacobs, Mankato State University; John Linn, Henderson State University; Roger Lintault, California State University–San Bernardino; Noyes Long, Appalachian State University; Lynn Mackenzie, Northern Illinois University; Helen Merritt, Northern Illinois University; Laurin Notheisen, Western Kentucky University; Helen Pullen, Towson State University; David Sharp, Eastern Michigan University; Michael Stone, Cuyahoga Community College; Barbara Swindell, Kennesaw College; Harold Wassell, Colorado State University; Donald Widen, Fullerton College; Frederick J. Zimmerman, SUNY–Cortland.

The author acknowledges the indispensable editorial help of Anne Boynton-Trigg and Françoise Bartlett, and the work of Marion Paone Geisinger in gathering the illustrations. Karen Dubno, who saw potential in the idea for this volume, and Janet Wilhite, who encouraged the author to persevere, deserve special thanks and acknowledgment.

Austin, Texas   *T.G.*
December 1989

Contents

ARTIST
AND
AUDIENCE

Part I
Communicating in a World of Art

When you step out into a dark night, you can look up into a sky filled with stars, a sight contemplated with wonder by all the generations of people. Those of us alive now are the first to understand that those shining points of light are a few planets of our solar system, many suns in our Milky Way galaxy, and billions of other galaxies like our own. Looking at the night sky we can understand, as earlier generations (which had not seen travel in space) could not, that the Earth is one small place with one connected history.

Some people say that contemplating the heavens makes them feel small and insignificant, but our new generations, who have seen the power of the invisible atom and the microscopic gene, know that size and significance have no connection. Although we cannot tell what is significant on a galactic scale, we can speak with assurance of that which exists on a human scale. The ancient Roman playwright Terence wrote, "Nothing human is foreign to me," which might stand as the motto of these times.

Art, which we see now as one of the basic expressive powers of all human beings, has seemed to be immune to progress, at least in qualitative terms. The artistic expression of early Stone Age art seems to be equal to anything that has come since. But in the *understanding* of art there has been considerable progress in recent years. To critics and historians of some

earlier periods art seemed to exist in a spiritual realm apart from the daily lives of the people who made it, purchased it, and enjoyed it. Art became something almost religious in that view. In current thought art may be about sacred things, but it is the product of the cultural interactions of people living their normal lives.

Despite the seemingly infinite variability of people and their ways of life, there are basic capacities and needs we all share. The only way to understand ourselves and our own future is to see ourselves in comparison with others. At this moment in other places there are people planning a future based on conditions and expectations we cannot imagine, but which are revealed and examined in their art. In earlier times people lived and planned but did not know what the future held for them. It is fascinating to look back at those times, knowing what was the future for them. Most poignant of all is to look at the expressions of our own recent past, knowing what came after. This is the beginning of that education recommended by the ancient inscription at the Oracle of Delphi: "Know thyself."

Although we live in a period when no part of the globe is more than a few hours away and the cultural barriers that separate nations and individuals are weakening more and more every day, still we find differences of language and tradition are obstacles to understanding. Art, which people value for the pure pleasure it brings, is also a medium of communication which can break through barriers and overcome obstacles. In his effort to make pictures that communicate, Anselm Kiefer (b. 1945) returns to old symbols that are shared by many people: a mountain, a robed figure with wings [1]. From very ancient times divine power has been imagined as inhabiting mountain tops. Divine messengers, imagined as winged humans, bring inspiration. Although hardly any artists of our day mix their paint on an oval palette with a thumb hole, such as the one carried by the winged figure, most people have seen pictures of such antique palettes. Kiefer does not explain his painting, but relies on us to figure out that it shows us the divine inspiration of the artist. Communication in this case depends on thick paint on a heavy canvas, a very material experience. The world of art is composed of people involved in that paradox of intellectual and spiritual communication in solid, material form.

1. Anselm Kiefer. *The Painter's Guardian Angel.* 1975. Oil on canvas, 4'3" × 5' (1.3 × 1.5 m). Collection A. and G. Gercken, Hamburg, West Germany.

This book begins with an analysis of the roles people play in the creation and interpretation of art, with emphasis on the role of the audience, the one role that everyone plays. Relative to the active role of the artist, the audience has generally been considered merely a group of passive spectators. Reconsidering the relationship between the artist and the audience, we can see that the audience plays a more active and important role in art than has been thought. We will also trace art from its origin with the artist, through the dealers and collectors to the museums where the public finds it. In the second chapter we will begin to consider what we the audience must know to play our role as interpreters of art, paying special attention to subject matter and originality.

Art is not the capricious invention of a few geniuses, but one of the most basic and ancient communication mediums of the human race. Just as people remain basically the same yet are constantly changing, so art has common threads through time and yet is always new. The aim of this book is to find old things that still speak to us as strongly as ever and also to explore the new conditions in which art exists today.

The Art World

A human society is bound together by its shared way of life. It is hard to explain a way of life—it is so all-encompassing—but we all try in our own ways to make it intelligible, to discover or invent symbols for the realities of life for us. Those symbols are our arts, messages we send back and forth among ourselves about life, truth, imagination, and all the other things we want to share.

When you look closely at the way some important works of art have come into existence you begin to notice that a lot of people were involved, all doing different things. We usually think of art as being something made by an artist, with no significant help from anyone else. In the literal sense we are correct because that is usually the contribution of the artist: to make the work. But someone else may have asked the artist to make it, may have made more or less detailed requests and suggestions, and may even have refused to pay for it until certain changes were made. Another person may write an article about it, discussing its importance or advising the reader that it is not worth the cost of parking to see it. Finally, there are all of us who do, after all, go to see it, pay for parking, discuss it with our friends, and remember it later as somehow part of our way of life.

Artists, driven by their expressive powers, are constantly at work in their studios, and if you ask them they will tell you that they paint or carve only to please themselves. But that is simply to protect themselves from unkind comments from the audience and critics as they seek a sympathetic audience to receive their message. Many works of art—most, perhaps—are never seen by anyone but the artist and disappear from the historical record. The works of art that make up what we call our culture have entered the social life of the community by being products of many individual efforts. The artist, the patron, the critic, and the audience must all play their parts or the work slips away into that limbo of undelivered messages.

It is for that reason you are right if you insist that everyone participates in the art world. Your friends who would not be caught dead in an art museum cannot escape commercial art and design. They are part of its audience and they are usually not timid about expressing their opinions about advertisements, clothes, or cars and all the other things that are not merely objects, but also symbolize in their design the way of life of their users. Thus they are part of the audience for commercial art. Your friends may not recognize themselves as part of the audience for the visual arts, but they almost certainly admit to being part of the audience for certain kinds of music.

Audiences at musical events are more conscious of themselves as an audience because they must all come together at one time, often pay admission, sit together, and experience and react in unison. Performers, critics, and the audience themselves all rate the quality of the audience just as they do that of the performing artists. Sometimes we read that the audience was "sophisticated and enthusiastic," other times "ignorant and unworthy of the performers." Musical understanding can be greatly improved by study and experience. The same is obviously true of the visual arts.

2. Honoré Daumier.
The Connoisseurs. c. 1858.
Black chalk, wash,
and watercolor
on paper; 9¾ × 7⅛"
(24.8 × 18.4 cm). The
Museum of Art,
Cleveland, Ohio
(Dudley P. Allen Collection).

We expect artists to be highly trained, but we usually forget that it takes as much education to understand a message as it does to send it. Artists and their audiences are almost always closely matched. You can find out a lot about yourself by examining critically the things for which you are a member of the audience. Honoré Daumier (pronounced *doe-MYAY*)(1808–1879) painted a watercolor, *Visitors in an Artist's Studio* [cover], which shows ideal relationships in the art world. The noble old artist, wearing his beret and holding his mahlstick (to rest his hand on while painting), stands back as a patron or critic examines the work on the easel. Other friends look attentively at the work and a mood of cordiality and pleasure prevails. Rarely do we have the opportunity to visit an artist's studio; usually we are on our own with the artist's work [2].

These four roles—artist, patron, critic, and audience—are the most important of the varied roles that make up the art world. The term **art world*** refers to "all the people whose activities are necessary to the production of a particular kind of art."[1] There is a large category of support people—those who manufacture paint, sell canvas and sculpture tools, keep accounts for patrons, set type

_____

* Terms in boldface are defined in the Glossary.

for critics' writings, guard museum displays, and carry out literally thousands of other activities without which our experience of art would be different; the contribution of these people will not be discussed here, despite its importance. But this widespread pattern of cooperation must be kept in mind when we think of art in society.

Most of the time the art world operates smoothly, and it is hard to distinguish the contributions of all the participants. But when things go wrong it is easier to analyze the parts. It is like your car: you don't think about the engine until you begin to hear strange noises. Two famous American art projects in which the machinery of the art world did make strange noises are revealing demonstrations of the art world in operation.

Two Case Histories

The Vietnam Memorial

Between 1979 and 1984 a project to build a memorial in Washington to the dead and missing of the Vietnam war produced so much controversy that it seemed for a while as if everyone in the country would eventually be one of the artists, patrons, or critics, leaving no one as simply audience. But finally the audience was massive: more than 100,000 veterans and their families attended the dedication on Veterans Day in 1982, with the project still not entirely finished, and hundreds of millions saw it in the news media [3].

The project started with Jan Scruggs, who served in the U.S. Army Light Infantry Brigade in Vietnam in 1969–1970.[2] Scruggs was among the wounded in a company of which half were killed or wounded, and upon his return to the United States he became deeply involved in veterans' problems. In 1979 he organized the Vietnam Veterans Memorial Fund (VVMF), whose only purpose was to erect a national monument honoring those who had died in the war. The monument was to be paid for by private contributions and was to be nonpolitical. Congress voted to provide land between the Washington Monument and the Lincoln Memorial, and President Jimmy Carter in 1980 signed a bill authorizing the project, informing the VVMF that the design would have to have the usual approvals of the National Capital Planning Commission, the Commission

3. Dedication of the Vietnam Veterans' Memorial, Veterans' Day, 1982.

of Fine Arts, and the Department of the Interior. Texas millionaire H. Ross Perot contributed $160,000 to launch a competition to design the memorial to be open to all U.S. citizens over eighteen.

In his recent book *Art Worlds,* Howard Becker defined an art patron:

> Patrons pay, and they dictate—not every note or brush stroke, but the broad outlines and the matters that concern them. They choose artists who provide what they want. In an efficient patronage system, artists and patrons share conventions and an aesthetic through which they can cooperate to produce work, the patrons providing support and direction, the artists creativity and execution.[3]

You can see right off that there were many different organizations and individuals who considered themselves the patrons of the Vietnam memorial: Jan Scruggs and his VVMF, many members of the U.S. Congress, several governmental bodies, and H. Ross Perot. They all wanted to dictate, but they disagreed about the broad outlines and the matters that concerned them.

The VVMF, which was still in charge of the project, set just two basic requirements for the design: (1) the names of all 57,939 Americans who died or were missing in Vietnam had to be engraved on the memorial; (2) the design had to fit harmoniously with the Washington Monument and the Lincoln Memorial. These requirements meant that a wall for the names had somehow to be part of the design and that the memorial had to be low enough not to compete with its tall neighbors. A prize of $20,000 was offered and drew a large response: 1,421 designs were entered. A jury of eight well-known architects, sculptors, and landscape designers judged the entries, which were presented anonymously, and the VVMF promised to accept their choice. You can see that the jury also played one of the roles assigned to the patron.

The jury's choice was a very simple design of two 10-foot (3-meter)-high polished black granite walls set at a 125-degree angle, each 250 feet (76 meters) long, set into a slight rise in the lawns. The names of the dead were to be engraved, not alphabetically, but in the order in which they had been killed; the designer planned that observers would see their own reflections in the polished stone [4]. The design may have been chosen for its simplicity and modesty, but it provoked tremendous controversy.

4. Maya Ying Lin. Vietnam Veterans' Memorial. 1982. Granite, each wall 250' (76 m) long, 10' (3 m) high.

Communicating in a World of Art

5. Maya Ying Lin.

Everyone was surprised to discover the artist was a 21-year-old Chinese-American, Maya Lin, an art student at Yale, who had made the design as a class project **[5]**. The Commission of Fine Arts met on October 13, 1981, with Maya Lin to discuss the choice of granite. A surprise visitor to the meeting was Tom Carhart, a wounded veteran and member of VVMF who had helped raise money for the monument. He had even entered the design competition with the first art work he had ever attempted. An interested party in several different ways, Carhart was upset by the chosen design, calling it a "degrading ditch"; he demanded a white memorial. That was the opening gun of sixteen months of argument between those who favored the Lin design, which had been legally accepted and could not be withdrawn, and those who wanted at least to add a sculpture of realistic figures with a flag, more like the Marine Corps War Memorial, a sculpture based on a news photograph of Marines raising the flag on the island of Iwo Jima during World War II **[6]**.

6. Felix W. de Weldon. Marine Corps War Memorial, Arlington, Virginia. 1954. Cast bronze, over life-size.

7. Frederick Hart. Original model, soldier group, Vietnam Veterans' Memorial. 1984. Cast bronze, 8' (2.4 m) high.

Anyone who believes that art is meaningless has a hard time explaining this controversy. Everyone involved was certain that they understood the art and that it meant something definite. Both sides saw the Lin design as anti-war, and those who had favored the war wanted a monument that would emphasize the glory of the cause. The bitter controversy that the war aroused in the American public and the hostile treatment many veterans received on their return made it almost impossible to get widespread agreement on a memorial.

Finally, bowing to pressure from Perot and a group of powerful members of Congress, Scruggs and the VVMF concluded a separate agreement with the sculptor Frederick Hart, whose design for a monument with realistic figures had placed third in the original competition. Some hoped to place his contribution, with a flag, at the junction of Lin's walls, thereby reducing them to a background, but the government agencies overseeing the project ruled that Hart's figures could not be visible from the walls. His sculpture, an 8-foot (2.4-meter) bronze group of three soldiers, was finally set in place in 1984, with the flag, at the entrance to the monument [7]. Hart's sculpture, though traditional in style, is not heroic, for the young soldiers stand quietly, and their expression has been described as "stunned" or "bewildered."

The attention of the public and critics has centered almost entirely on Maya Lin's black-walled memorial. A columnist who visited it alone shortly before it was dedicated found it too depressing: seeing the names of so many dead, "the feeling of waste and emptiness would not leave me," he wrote.[4] A colleague of his who attended the dedication a week later wrote:

> I think it is one of the most impressive memorials I ever saw. . . . In the crowd we looked at each other, deeply moved. . . . Some have said they think the Memorial is too negative; perhaps they have spoken before seeing its powerful effect on visitors. Crowds increased each day at the dedication ceremonies. Officials agreed to add a conventional sculpture of three soldiers next year. They can do nothing, I think, to increase its impressiveness.[5]

Veteran William Broyles, Jr., probably spoke for many: ". . . this memorial is not a monument to the abstract ideal of war, to glory and victory or even to a cause. It is a reminder of the cost of war. . . . Like the war itself, the memorial is less than the dead deserved." The deepest meaning of the war, he wrote,

> is in the fate of those who fought there. The veterans gave the war that meaning, and they and their families quickly, and spontaneously, did the same for the memorial. Through countless acts of pure emotion they completed a monument that seemed incomplete. It invited them, somehow, to make it their own. They propped roses beside it, set photographs of dead sons and brothers on it, bedecked it with wreaths, touched it constantly and washed it with tears [8].

Communicating in a World of Art

8. Offerings at the Vietnam Veterans' Memorial.

As I stood in front of the polished granite I saw the names, but I also saw my own reflection. It fell across the names like a ghost. "Why me, Lord?" we asked ourselves in Vietnam. It was a question that came back as I stood there: "Why them?" It was a terrible sadness that brought the tears. But also, beneath it, there was a deep relief tinged with guilt: my name isn't on the wall.[6]

After Maya Lin's walls had been dedicated, a *Washington Post* editorial writer concluded: "The argument over the memorial dissolves the moment you get there." Most of the members of the audience, it seemed, had decided that Maya Lin's conception was art enough. In this very imperfect world, those stark walls gave people a chance to add whatever they felt was missing to make the monument complete. Three years later, with Frederick Hart's three soldiers and the flag in place on the hill nearby, all points of view seemed to find satisfaction.

The Rockefeller Center Mural

If the controversy over the Vietnam Memorial represented sincere differences over a tragic theme, an earlier controversy has some lighter elements. In 1932 the great Mexican painter Diego Rivera (1886–1957) **[9]** was commissioned

9. Diego Rivera. *Self-Portrait*. 1930. Lithograph, 15⅞ × 11⅛" (40 × 28 cm). Harry Ransom Humanities Research Center, University of Texas at Austin.

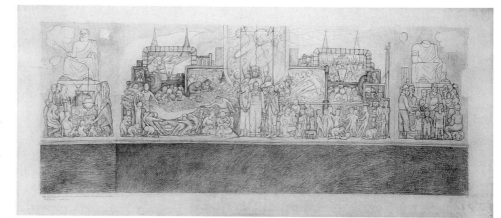

10. Diego Rivera. Study for *Man at the Crossroads*. 1932. Pencil on brown paper, 2'7" × 5'11" (.8 × 1.8 m). Museum of Modern Art, New York.

below: 11. Diego Rivera. *Man at the Crossroads* (unfinished). May, 1933. Fresco, central wall 19' × 40'10" (5.8 × 12.5 m). Destroyed 1934.

below right: 12. Diego Rivera. *Portrait of America.* 1933. Fresco panels, 6' × 5'10" (1.8 × 1.8 m), foreground heads life-size. New Workers' School, New York. Property of ILGWU, Unity House, Forest Park, Pennsylvania. Destroyed by fire February 28, 1969.

by John D. Rockefeller, Jr., to paint a mural in the newly completed Rockefeller Center in New York. Although Rivera was an outspoken communist, he was still willing to paint murals commissioned by wealthy capitalists in San Francisco and Detroit, including a fine series on the auto industry under the patronage of Edsel Ford. Rivera submitted designs **[10]** to Rockefeller for approval on the theme *Man at the Crossroads* and set to work on the wall, with a large group of politically aware assistants. As the painting began to emerge **[11]**, it became clear that the "crossroads" was between the capitalist and communist worlds, with a portrait of Lenin on the communist side (to the right of the central figure, between the ellipses). The artist claimed that Lenin's portrait was in the sketches that had been approved and, besides, was an indispensable part of the design, but if you compare the approved drawing **[10]** with the mural that was beginning to appear on the wall **[11]**, you will see that Rivera had revised the design considerably.

It is obvious that cooperation had broken down between artist and patron. When Rivera refused to change the mural, he was paid for his work and locked out of the building. This dispute quickly became a popular cause. To understand the situation, you have to remember that in 1933 the United States was at the depths of the worst depression in its history; it really looked as if the country was at a political and economic crossroads. There was a natural tendency to see a very wealthy person as a villain and an artist as the representative of freedom of

expression. But it is also obvious that Rivera was less than open with Rockefeller and was treated as well as he deserved. Rivera, working in the politically agitated environment of New York City, discovered, perhaps after the designs were already approved, that he had to make a political statement to retain his reputation as a radical. He also planned to return to Mexico, which had just elected a new, liberal president, and it was important to Rivera to prepare a hero's welcome for himself in his own country. Mexico was beginning the dangerous process of regaining control of its oil fields—of which Rockefeller companies were major owners—and the Mexicans feared U.S. intervention. It is clear that Rivera intentionally destroyed the cooperative relationship between artist and patron to keep his own political position; the result was that the unfinished mural was scraped off the wall. Rivera quickly found a more sympathetic patron in the New Workers' School in New York, for which he did a series of movable mural panels entitled *Portrait of America*. One panel included a sarcastic caricature of the senior John D. Rockefeller with workers carrying an anti-Rockefeller sign [12]. Back in Mexico in 1934, Rivera arranged to paint *Man at the Crossroads* again in the Palace of Fine Arts [13].

In the end the work came into existence with a new patron, the government of Mexico. Critics have accepted it as one of the standard works of the artist, and it has been widely reproduced. In the more than fifty years since it was painted the capitalist and communist worlds have been in competition, but it would be hard to find American workers who see themselves at a "crossroads" between them anymore. Not a passionate statement of principle, the mural still stands as a perceptive, but biased, comment on the political and intellectual history of this century. The other crossroads, between the microscopic and the astronomical, where Rivera placed his worker operating a colossal machine, was a better prediction of events in the next half century.

13. Diego Rivera. *Man at the Crossroads.* 1934. Fresco, 15'10" × 37'7" (4.9 × 11.5 m). Palace of Fine Arts, Mexico City.

If you were to trace the "life history" of a work of art you might find it was born in the mind and hands of an artist, passed on to the gallery of an art dealer, was purchased by a collector, inherited by his or her child, and donated to a museum, which will keep it and care for it, presumably forever. This typical scenario offers opportunities for a variety of characters to play the roles of artist, dealer, collector, and museum director. In this section we will examine both people and institutions: the personality and education of the artist, the work of the critic and the art dealer, the nature and role of the audience, and finally a few of the great museums.

The Artist

There is an old controversy: are artists born or made? Are artists those few individuals born with unusual gifts, or is art something that can be learned by anyone with sufficient motivation? According to the philosopher Suzanne Langer, "the average person has a little talent"; it is genius which is "the mark of the true artist." She continues:

> Talent is special ability to express what you can conceive; but genius is the power of conception. Although some degree of talent is necessary if genius is not to be stillborn, great artists have not always had extraordinary technical ability; they have often struggled for expression, but the urgency of their ideas caused them to develop every vestige of talent until it rose to their demands.[7]

Langer comes down on the side that says artists are born with special gifts, although she admits that "a small amount of genius is not a rare endowment," which suggests that a great many people have potential as artists. That accords with experience, for all of us know many people who are good at art, but only a few who are driven by the urgency of their ideas to develop their talent to its highest possible level. Considering the wide variety of visual art forms, from weaving to designing buildings and painting murals, probably almost everyone has some talent in at least one of those forms of art. What the audience is looking for in artists is that spark of originality that produces new conceptions, which Langer calls genius.

Jackson Pollock (1912–1956), one of the most respected American artists, was described by his teacher Thomas Hart Benton as having "little talent." But, Benton continues,

> I sensed that he was some kind of artist. I had learned anyhow that great talents were not the most essential requirements for artistic success. I had seen too many gifted people drop away from the pursuit of art because they lacked the necessary inner drive to keep at it when the going became hard. Jack's apparent talent deficiencies did not thus seem important. All that was important, as I saw it, was an intense interest, and that he had.[8]

Pollock was the youngest of five brothers, all of whom showed serious interest in art, inspired by their mother. The Pollock family is evidence that the early influence of a parent or role model has a powerful effect in directing a child's expressive powers toward art. At seventeen, having been expelled from his California high school, Pollock wrote a letter to one of his brothers: "As to what I would like to be. It is difficult to say. An artist of some kind. If nothing else I shall always study the Arts."[9] About a year later he arrived in New York and enrolled in the Art Students League, where a brother had studied and where Benton was teaching.

Those with talent, genius, and inner drive seek out ways to develop their abilities by studying. In earlier times artists learned the craft of art by apprenticeship, usually from about the age of ten to sixteen, helping the master with the preparation of paints and canvases or the other materials of the master's art and finally learning to carry out complete works on their own. Apprenticeship

A POINT IN TIME: Goya on Studying Art

In his later years Francisco Goya (1746–1828) was the director of the Royal Academy in Madrid, but he had very unacademic ideas about how an artist should be educated. His own experiences as a student and young professional contributed to those ideas, for he had a hard time gaining a success. At seventeen and again at twenty he entered competitions sponsored by the national academy, but failed to get the vote of even one judge. At 25 he entered a competition sponsored by an Italian academy. In academic fashion, the subject, "Hannibal Crossing the Alps," was given in great detail. The ancient general was to be shown "lifting the visor of his helmet and turning toward a Spirit, who takes him by the hand and points out the beautiful plains of Italy, lying at his feet and stretching into the distance." Goya came in second, the judges commenting, "If its coloring had been truer to life and its composition had followed the subject laid down more closely," then Goya might have won. Goya tried to meet the academic requirements and finally was accepted, but he was always inclined to give his imagination free rein.

Goya painted *The Crockery Seller* [14] when he was 33, but it was not intended as a finished painting. It was to be used as the pattern for a tapestry to decorate the Royal Palace, so academic requirements were not so strict. A scene from contemporary life was acceptable, and the color and drawing were more personal and imaginative than academic rules would permit. Goya wrote a letter describing his idea of educating artists:

> Academies should not be restrictive. . . . There are no rules for Painting. . . . To make everyone study the same way and follow the same path compulsorily, seriously impedes the development of those young people who practice this difficult art. . . . I know of no better way to advance the arts . . . than by . . . allowing students of art to develop their own abilities in their own way, without forcing them to go in one particular direction, and without making them adopt a particular style of painting if it is against their inclination.

Both Goya's ideas about the education of artists and his style of painting have been accepted by later generations. *The Crockery Seller* is now one of the most popular paintings in the Prado museum in Madrid, but the tapestry based on it is not considered very important. In our time we admire not only the conception, which is still present in the tapestry, but the brushmark left by the artist's hand.

Quotations from Nigel Glendinning, *Goya and his Critics* (New Haven: Yale University Press, 1977) 45–46.

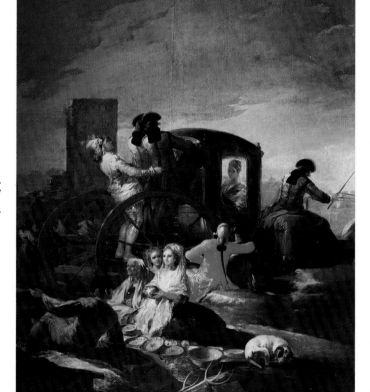

14.   Francisco Goya. *The Crockery Seller*.
       1779. Oil on canvas, 8'6" × 7'3"
       (2.6 × 2.2 m). Prado, Madrid.

trained the hands more than the mind and it is not surprising that patrons had little confidence in the ability of artists to imagine great subjects.

Only in Renaissance Italy, where the first art academies were founded, were artists accepted among the educated and considered capable of expressing themselves, instead of merely acting as craftsmen carrying out the ideas of better educated patrons, who were usually members of the nobility or clergy. The academies taught art as a science capable of being mastered by intellectual effort. Along with years of practice in drawing, there were required studies of mathematics, geometry, perspective, architectural design, and anatomy. An academic artist specialized in conception—the part requiring genius, as Langer says—and left the execution to artisans whenever it was dirty or laborious. The artisan, who had been apprenticed in a shop, may have been talented, but the definition of art as an intellectual discipline raised the social rank of artists in a society that considered manual work demeaning.

The Art Students League in New York, the school where Jackson Pollock studied and Thomas Hart Benton taught, was founded in 1875 in rebellion against the strict order of studies traditional in European academies. There are no entrance requirements and students take the classes as they please; the instructors are professional artists who come in to give criticism and discussion twice a week. Benton wrote of his teaching:

> Looking back, I can see that I was not a very practical teacher, especially for novices. . . . After indicating in a general way the directions I thought it profitable to pursue, I expected the members of my class to make all their own discoveries. I never gave direct criticisms unless they were asked for and even then only when the asker specified what was occasioning difficulty.[10]

This is the opposite of apprenticeship, for the student has to learn the craft pretty much alone, from books or from other students. Benton, who was a typical instructor, concentrated on criticizing composition and style, the expressive and intellectual side of art. This fulfills Goya's demand that students be allowed to "develop their own abilities in their own way."

Since the 1930s American colleges and universities have begun to offer education in both the practice of art and its history and criticism, and many of the independent art schools have become attached to local colleges. Currently most of the artists working in the United States have studied art in a college or university. The usual diploma showing completion of studies as an artist is the Master of Fine Arts (M.F.A.). Typically, students are selected by submission of a portfolio of previous work, and about sixty semester hours of studies (in theory about two years, but usually lasting longer) are required, with some form of examination and an exhibition of completed work at the end. Artists in our time are much better educated than ever before, especially in general studies designed to improve their power of conception. That kind of education fits with the contemporary audience's preference for expressions of genius, which shows in the ideas and design, over talent, which shows in skillful use of materials. An advanced art student studying at one of the modern art schools will learn some of the craft skills once taught by apprenticeship along with the intellectual disciplines found in the academies. In the end, it is not the artist's education that counts most, but the inner drive to express ideas.

The Art Dealer

In the second stage of its life history, a work of art is offered to the gallery of an art dealer. This is usually where the artist, the patron, the critic, and the audience first meet and interact. Galleries are the places where the deepest values of our culture, such as beauty and truth, are translated into market value, which is determined by how much money someone is willing to pay. It is a surprisingly large business. The greatest centers for art sales at the present time are New York City and London. In New York the Manhattan telephone directory

Communicating in a World of Art

A POINT IN TIME: Watteau Paints a Shop Sign

The oil painting called *Gersaint's Shop Sign* [15] was painted to fit into the arched storefront of the art dealer's shop, called Au Grand Monarque, at 35 Pont Notre-Dame in Paris. If you look carefully you can still see the original curve of its top from the upper right corner of the lowest painting on the right to one stone above the head of the boy on the left. More canvas and paint were later added by an unknown hand to make the painting into a rectangle, but that later artist very successfully matched the style of Watteau. The painting gives us a good idea of what an art dealer's shop looked like about 1721.

When Antoine Watteau *(wah-TOE or va-TOE)* (1684–1721) painted *Gersaint's Shop Sign*—his last work—he was only 37 years old, but he already knew he was dying of tuberculosis. The painting testifies to the close friendship between the painter and his dealer, Edmonde-François Gersaint *(zhair-SAn)*. Watteau was described as "timid, uneasy, and caustic with strangers."*

Gersaint later wrote: "I should have liked him to be occupied with something more solid," a theatrical or picnic scene, rather than a sign to be exposed to the weather,

> but seeing that it would give him pleasure, I agreed. It was all painted from models, and the poses were so truthful and relaxed, the arrangement so natural and the grouping so well understood that it caught the eye of passers-by, and even the most skillful painters came several times to admire it. It was the work of eight days, and even so he worked only in the mornings, his deli-

cate health, or rather his weakness, not allowing him to paint any longer. It is the only one of his works which he admitted being pleased with.

The shop is shown as if it were a stage, with the various activities of the shop being carried out before our eyes: the salespeople busy with customers on the right, the older man and woman scrutinizing a painting through their glasses, and shop assistants packing paintings, including a portrait of the king, into a shipping box delivered by the boy at the left.

When the painting was finished, Watteau retired to a country house Gersaint had helped him find, and there he soon died. The painting was removed from the doorway, expanded to a rectangle, and sold to a wealthy textile manufacturer, Jean de Jullienne, who already owned about forty paintings by Watteau. Jullienne was famous as a hard worker— he "awoke at five in the morning, even in winter, to attend to business"†—and he evidently enjoyed escaping in his imagination into Watteau's romantic scenes. This painting invites us to leave the daily world of the street, with its rough paving and flea-bitten dog, and follow the young couple on the left into an imaginary world of pleasure and fantasy. Later *Gersaint's Shop Sign* became a prize possession of several great collectors, and now it hangs in the State Museum in West Berlin.

_____
* Quoted in Kenneth Clark, *Looking at Pictures* (New York: Holt, Rinehart and Winston, 1961) 74–87 (author's translation).
† Donald Posner, *Antoine Watteau* (Ithaca: Cornell University Press, 1984) 271–277.

15. Antoine Watteau. *Gersaint's Shop Sign.* 1721. Oil on canvas, 5′4″ × 10′1″ (1.6 × 3.1 m). State Museum, West Berlin.

A POINT IN TIME: Durand-Ruel, the Impressionists' Dealer

We are all accustomed to the idea of a great artist, or a great patron, but a great *dealer* is something we rarely hear of. The dealer's role as middleman between the artist and a patron could develop only as the direct relationship between artist and patron broke down and artists began to produce work on speculation rather than on order. Thus dealers have existed as part of world art only in Western culture in the last three centuries.

Paul Durand-Ruel *(du-RONH-ru-EL)* (1831–1922) is one of the best-known dealers in the history of art because he acted on his convictions and was ultimately vindicated. "A true picture dealer," he said, "should also be an enlightened patron; that is, he should, if necessary, sacrifice his immediate financial interest to his artistic convictions, and prefer to oppose, rather than support, the interests of speculators."*

The son of an art dealer, Durand-Ruel made his first acquaintance with the young Impressionist painters in January, 1871, in London. Claude Monet *(mo-NAY)* (1840–1926) and Camille Pissarro (1830–1903), two of the leading Impressionists, were also in London and finding it hard to earn enough to survive. Durand-Ruel included paintings by both of them in a big exhibit in London, but he was unable to sell their work.

It is hard to imagine now that collectors were not interested in paintings like Monet's *The Thames*

Based on John Rewald, *The History of Impressionism*, 4th rev. ed. (New York: Museum of Modern Art, 1973).

* Quoted by Rewald 272.

and the Houses of Parliament, London [16], which was painted that year. But the English public was even more timid than the French, which depended on the annual exhibit of the Academy of Fine Arts in Paris, called "the Salon," to define what was acceptable. The Academy was dominated by the most conservative artists and the art public relied on the Academy for advice. The Impressionists were breaking the traditional rules by emphasizing color more than line, by painting outdoors, and by copying nature and ignoring the traditions of good taste—all of which resulted in bad art, in the opinion of the Academy.

Durand-Ruel operated differently from most of today's dealers. Rather than merely serving as an agent, he usually purchased paintings from the painters, then tried to sell them. In Paris in 1872 Durand-Ruel bought every painting that Edouard Manet *(mah-NAY)* (1832–1883) had available, about thirty canvases. Manet was a respectable artist of considerable reputation, but his Impressionist style made him a risky investment at that time.

After fifteen years of exhibition the Impressionists were still finding it hard to support themselves when Durand-Ruel decided in 1886 to experiment with an exhibit in New York. He took a large stock—about 50 Monets, 42 Pissarros, 38 Renoirs, 17 Manets, 23 Degas, 15 Sisleys, 9 Berthe Morisots, and others. The public in New York was less conservative, and Durand-Ruel already had a reputation for selling popular work by earlier artists. Those favorable factors were augmented by the praise of the leading American artists. A New York art journal summed up

lists 830 art dealers, and if you think of them as part of the business side of the art world they are just the tip of the iceberg. There are also 114 businesses selling art supplies, many commercial art studios, the art publishing business, and the art-related fields such as interior design and architecture. Even in a smaller American city such as Denver (population 1.25 million), 244 businesses advertise themselves as "art galleries, dealers, and consultants." We begin to see that the reality of art in the modern world is both much larger and somewhat different from what the word usually brings to our minds.

A commercial gallery has a permanent location to display the art it has for sale. The owner, usually called a "dealer," shows the work of a group of artists who are often called the dealer's "stable," as if they were racehorses. The race, of course, is for acceptance by an audience. An art dealer is similar to an impresario or a manager for musicians or other performing artists and plays an essential role in bringing art to an audience.

Another way art is bought and sold is by auction. Since prices paid at auctions are public knowledge, auctions are the way people keep track of market values in the business of art. In fact, high prices often are treated as newsworthy for the general public. You have probably seen newspaper articles featuring

Communicating in a World of Art

16. Claude Monet. *The Thames and the Houses of Parliament, London.* 1871. Oil on canvas, 18¾ × 25½" (48 × 65 cm). National Gallery, London.

the prevailing opinion: "New York has never seen a more interesting exhibition than this."†

The same year the Impressionist painters organized their last group show in Paris. The group was breaking up as styles changed and personal differ-

_____
† Unsigned article in *The Critic*, cited by Rewald 532.

ences developed, but success had arrived. Within a few years Durand-Ruel had earned back everything he had gambled on the Impressionists and had even opened a branch in New York. Monet, who had been desperately poor, could finally help his poorer friends with loans and purchases. Both Monet and Durand-Ruel had always known it was only a matter of getting the public accustomed to the new style.

huge sums paid for art, money that goes to dealers and often does not reach artists or their heirs. People in the art world are often reluctant to talk about the value of art because several different values get confused. There are three kinds of value, which must be kept clearly separate: intrinsic value, cultural value, and market value. Art ordinarily has little *intrinsic value,* which is the value of things which support biological life, such as food, clothing, and shelter. Those things have value regardless of what anyone might think of them—the opposite of cultural value and market value, which depend entirely on what people think.

Cultural value is what people mean when they speak of beauty. A branch of philosophy called **aesthetics** developed around the question of what is beauty, and we still hear of *aesthetic value.* Beauty is often said to be "in the eye of the beholder," which is another way of saying it depends on the tradition, or culture, in which you have been educated.

An expert on cultural value can tell you whether the art work you are thinking of buying is good or not, but may not be able to tell you whether the price is too high. *Market value* is the price a work of art will bring when it is offered for sale. Market value fluctuates much more widely and rapidly than cultural value. Keeping track of the fluctuations is the specialty of the art appraiser; it is also basic to the work of dealers. Works of art are often hard to convert into cash, but they are part of the basic wealth of a community, setting a standard of value somewhat the way a hoard of gold does. Although their market value changes, in general works of art tend to grow more valuable as they get older, which is another way of saying that units of money have a long-term tendency to decline in value. That is why, during periods of inflation when money is rapidly declining in value, many people buy art—they hope it will retain its market value.

The poverty of artists is legendary, but poverty is not a requirement in order to make good art. Some people think that any artist who earns money has "sold out"—become motivated by profit rather than quality. But artists need to earn enough to buy paint or stone, pay the rent on their studios, and feed their families. It is the business of art dealers to bring the artist and the audience together, and market value is fundamentally a way to keep this system of art creation and patronage in existence. While art has to pay well enough so that artists can continue to make it, money is not the basic need of the artists. Their basic need is for an audience.

The Patron

Earlier we defined patrons as those who pay for the work and dictate the general character of the work. It is hard to separate the contributions of the artist and the patron when we look at a finished work, but historical research can sometimes cast a revealing light on this relationship. In his analysis of the patrons of Rembrandt (1606–1669), Gary Schwartz showed that the subjects of Rembrandt's paintings reflect the interests of their patrons.[11] Patronage of his paintings also stimulated Rembrandt to be creative in drawing and printmaking. The desires of the patron are most obvious in portraits, such as the one of Frederick Rihel [17], who had himself depicted in a way usually reserved for a king or a victorious general. A wealthy bachelor businessman, Rihel kept fine horses and fine clothing, but the painting was meant to memorialize his participation in a visit of royalty to Amsterdam in 1660.

17. Rembrandt van Rijn. *Frederick Rihel on Horseback.* 1663. Oil on canvas, 7'10" × 6'2" (2.4 × 1.9 m). National Gallery, London.

We usually think of great painters, such as Rembrandt, as free agents in the choice of subjects, but their patrons had definite preferences for certain Bible stories, mythology, history, or portraits. Even Rembrandt had to consider the interests and desires of his patrons. The role of patron requires respect for the role of the artist and the realization that a patron cannot control the style and content, but only the subject, materials, and perhaps the general character of the art.

The Critic

An expert on cultural value we call a critic or an art historian. Those we call critics specialize in the art of their own time, while the art historian studies the art of earlier times and often of distant places.

The critic's role is to perform an interpretation which serves as a sample for the audience. Besides demonstrating an interpretation of new art, the critic also keeps older art "alive." In music and theater the performers constantly renew the art. A play by Shakespeare was spoken four hundred years ago in English very different from today's by actors dressed in the clothing of their day and acting in the style of the time. We bring the same play back to life by performing it in modern English, wearing modern clothing, and acting in the style of our time. The art critic provides that kind of interpretation, constantly reviving older works of art by acting as audience for them in the way appropriate to the times.

The Audience

The audience for any particular kind of art can be divided into three: a general audience of people who have a normal interest in their own culture, a serious audience of people who enjoy reading about art and who go out of their way to see new work, and students and professionals in art. The student and professional group are most interested in innovation and will tolerate boredom and confusion in the art if they think something new may turn up. By their presence at exhibits and by talking about what they have seen, the student and professional audience, as well as the critics, pass the word to members of the serious audience that there is something to see. Eventually the general audience learns through newspaper and magazine articles and television interviews that an art style or an artist is becoming interesting or fashionable.

All three sectors of the audience together are absolutely indispensable to the existence of art. If a hostess gives a party and nobody comes, it isn't a party; we can say pretty much the same for art. The whole audience decides what is art and what is not, usually with surprising independence of the critics. The professional audience is usually first to accept new work as art, but if that opinion is not eventually accepted by the members of the serious and general audiences, the work disappears from view. We sometimes look back and say that the audience was wrong or made a mistake, but such a statement is almost meaningless since every group of people defines art for themselves. The American writer and early patron of Picasso, Gertrude Stein, wrote that "nothing changes in people from one generation to another except the way of seeing. . . ."[12] The history of art is basically the history of the audience's way of seeing. As two psychologists of art have put it, "the value, estimation, fate, and survival of a work of art" are mainly determined by the audience.[13]

These arrangements among groups and individuals are so complicated you wonder how anything ever gets made. But even the Vietnam Veterans Memorial was actually built. All the wrangling was actually a necessary part of the process; perhaps we should call it negotiation. When you look at the finished memorial, with its parts in different styles, you discover they actually can live together. In the end everyone had to give up something to other groups in order to get what they wanted themselves.

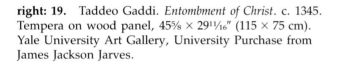

above: 18. Hubert Robert. *View of the Grande Galerie of the Louvre.* 1796. Oil on canvas, 3'9" × 4'9" (1.2 × 1.5 m). Louvre, Paris.

right: 19. Taddeo Gaddi. *Entombment of Christ.* c. 1345. Tempera on wood panel, 45⅝ × 29¹¹⁄₁₆" (115 × 75 cm). Yale University Art Gallery, University Purchase from James Jackson Jarves.

This is what happens in all art that finds a place in history. The artist has an idea and carries it out, hoping to find a patron and an audience. Sometimes the idea originates with a patron, who seeks an artist to bring it into existence as a work of art. In that case the patron must grant the artist liberty to carry out the work in a personal style. Both the artist and the patron have to grant the critic freedom to analyze its historical significance, and all three concede that the audience will decide whether it is good art or not and what it really means.

Art Museums

In the life history of a work of art the museum is its final home. Occasionally an artist will give a work directly to a museum; sometimes museums buy from the art dealers; often a collector will give or sell to a museum. Museums rarely sell works from the museum collection, a practice which sounds shocking to many in the art world, who think of museums as perpetual guardians of art. The ideal of the museum is to be the protector of the cultural values of its community. The modern form of the museum is a very recent development, and it is surely no exaggeration to say that we are living in the great age of museums.

When the Americans won their Revolution they won no palace full of art, but a different situation confronted the French only a few years later. When you have executed the king, what do you do with his palace and his art collection? In 1793 the revolutionary leaders proclaimed that the royal collections belonged to all citizens, and the Louvre *(LOOV-ruh)* Palace in Paris was opened three days a week to the public **[18]**. When Napoleon emerged as emperor of France, his conquests allowed him to loot most of the great collections of Europe, and even of Egypt, enriching the Louvre—now a public museum—on a legendary scale. Even though much of the loot had to be returned when Napoleon was finally defeated, the Louvre remained legendary.

When James Jackson Jarves, the Boston-born editor of Honolulu's first newspaper, visited the Louvre in 1851, he was so overwhelmed that he devoted the rest of his life to art. Jarves settled in Florence, Italy, and slowly formed a collection of Italian paintings [19] which he brought back to New York and, when he needed money, tried to sell. Educated taste was still too narrow to include the Gothic and early Renaissance paintings Jarves had purchased, so no buyer could be found. Finally Yale College reluctantly loaned Jarves $20,000 with the paintings as collateral. When Jarves was unable to pay, the college ended up with the collection, which is now a major attraction at the Yale University Art Gallery.

In 1871, when Yale tried unsuccessfully to auction the Jarves Collection, there were already movements afoot in New York and Boston to form art museums—the Metropolitan Museum of Art in New York and the Museum of Fine Arts in Boston were both founded in 1870. In a little over one hundred years the people of the United States have built hundreds of museums, by far the larger number devoted to art, some supported by federal taxes, others by state or local governments, and many of them by private foundations. A small guidebook to U.S. art museums lists 283, and covers only the most important ones.[14] Since 1950 this country has built the equivalent of fourteen Louvre museums, more than enough square footage to pave a six-foot-wide road from New York to California.[15]

Walking around a large American museum, with its collections of ancient sculpture, modern painting, reconstructed rooms from colonial houses filled with antique furniture, its bookstore and its restaurant, with busloads of school children sitting on the floor for lectures on weekdays and hordes of visitors thronging the galleries on weekends, you may well ask what is going on here. Even more is going on than is visible to the visitor: in a laboratory [20] works of art are examined, conserved, and restored; and an art conservator in a white coat is positioning a wooden sculpture for radiation to stop decay [21]; in a handsome office the director and his staff are discussing the insurance costs for shipping a painting; in a gallery a curator examines a painting borrowed for an exhibit; in a silent library one of the curators is trying to figure out the ceremony a Polynesian

below: 20. X-ray spectrometry analysis of pigment chemicals in a painting.

right: 21. A technician positions a wooden statue for nuclear radiation treatment.

sculpture was used in; and in a cool, shadowy storeroom a staff member replaces paintings on racks after a show is taken down. Is this a school? Or a community treasure house? Or a strange kind of church? Art museum professionals have asked themselves those questions for years, and the answer seems to be "All of the above."

You can visit your own local museum and judge for yourself what kind of institution it is, but let us take a look now at two famous museums in New York which embody very different ideas. The Frick Collection [22] is located in a mansion at 1 East 70th Street in Manhattan. The mansion was built in 1913 by Henry Clay Frick as a home, but with the museum it would become always in mind. Frick had nothing in his Pennsylvania farm background to nourish a love of art; he was apparently born with it. When he applied for a bank loan at the age of 21 in 1871, the banker thus evaluated him: "On job all day, keeps books evenings, may be a little too enthusiastic about pictures but not enough to hurt. . . ."[16] A millionaire coke and steel manufacturer by the time he was 30, his success unaffected by a notorious record as a strike-breaker, Frick could afford the best. He bought Rembrandt's *The Artist as a Young Man* and *The Polish Rider*, Vermeer's *The Music Lesson*, Velazquez' *King Philip IV*, and many others. Frick had the courage of his own taste and knowledge to buy the work of some artists who were not then popular, such as El Greco (1541–1614), whose *Saint Jerome* [23] was the first El Greco in a private collection in this country. The Frick Collection is a place to see a permanent collection of fine "old master" paintings in a quiet, elegant setting, and hear occasional chamber music concerts.

The Museum of Modern Art [24] was meant to be something entirely different when it was founded in 1929 by three wealthy women—Lillie P. Bliss, Abby Aldrich Rockefeller, and Mary Quinn Sullivan—over a lunch table. It attracted crowds from its first show and has been one of the most influential art institutions in the world [25]. Dedicated to showing the work of the most impor-

below left: 22. The living hall, The Frick Collection, New York.

below right: 23. El Greco. *Saint Jerome*. c. 1610.
Oil on canvas, 42⅛ × 34¼" (107 × 87 cm). The Frick Collection, New York.

Communicating in a World of Art

above left: 24. Cesar Pelli and Associates. Abby Aldrich Rockefeller Sculpture Garden, Museum of Modern Art, New York. 1984.

above right: 25. A panel of experts meets at the Museum of Modern Art in 1948 to discuss the state of modern art. On the wall are Picasso's *Girl Before a Mirror* and Yves Tanguy's *Slowly Toward North*.

tant living artists and their precursors in the Modern movement back to about 1875, it has also shown other kinds of art—African and American Indian, for example—which were of special interest to artists working in the Modern movement. It has gradually built up a first-class collection of its own, but it also shows temporary exhibits of work borrowed from other owners. It has an excellent library devoted to the history of modern art, a film library with regular showings, a photography department, and collections of industrial art and design. You can hear music at MOMA (its nickname, said as a word, not letters), as well as at the Frick, but it will probably be jazz. Even the building is different. While the Frick Collection is housed in an elegant low mansion, the Museum of Modern Art occupies part of a skyscraper.

Recent years have seen important new museums built all over the United States—Atlanta, Houston, Los Angeles, Denver, Fort Worth, among others—rivaling the great older museums of Chicago, Cleveland, Philadelphia, Kansas City, and others. There is most likely a museum within visiting distance of your home.

When you arrive at an art museum, the first thing is to examine a map of the building and look over parts with a quick walk-through just to see what is there. Then you may want to concentrate on a few things that especially interest you. At the information desk you may want to inquire about events such as concerts, films, or lectures, and the cost of membership and what privileges it gives. Since most museums have more work than they can pay for, you may wish to ask if there are any interesting jobs for unpaid volunteers that you might like to do. Most people go to museums too rarely, and when they go they feel obliged to stay too long. A break for lunch or a drink in the restaurant is a good way to give your eyes and feet a rest. It is important to remember that a museum is supposed to be a place for pleasure, for spiritual renewal; a visit should not be turned into a chore. Even though museums may serve as an educational resource for study of our culture and history, that must never interfere with our pleasure in using them.

26. The Tate Gallery, London.

The fact is that looking at pictures, and other kinds of art, seems to satisfy many different needs of all kinds of people **[26]**. An accountant in Boston said the following in an interview:

> It's been a long hard road for me, and I'm just 34. I'm the first in my family to graduate from college. . . . Once I stopped in at the Museum of Fine Arts myself, just on a lark. I was driving by, and I felt like breaking out of the rat-race for half an hour. So, I pulled over—I almost got in an accident, because I did it so suddenly. And I walked in, and I just moved along, from picture to picture. It was like being in another world. I couldn't believe it. All the worries left me. I felt like I was becoming—well, you know, a philosopher. I got some distance on my life. I came home and told my wife that it was better than beer, better even than a good movie; because you could be alone with yourself, standing there.[17]

Summary for Review

The art world is made up of all those whose activities are necessary to the production of art. The activities of the artist, the patron, the critic, and the audience are easy to distinguish, especially in public monuments. The patron's role may be played by groups or individuals representing the public, designated to choose the winner of a design competition, select materials, and control the amount of money spent. The artist may be creating art independently, but on commissions may have to work within guidelines laid down by the patrons. The critic's role is to formulate the philosophy of art and begin the discussion of works of art. Most important is the audience, which includes everyone but can be divided into a general audience, a serious audience, and a professional audience. The audience decides what it will accept as art and what the art means. The meaning of a work of art changes as the audience learns more or sees things differently. Art is a cooperative activity in which all parts of a society play a role.

The "life history" of a work of art often takes it from the studio of the artist, whose genius for imagining things and talent for making them bring the work into existence, to the gallery of the dealer, to the house of a collector, and eventually to a public museum. The training of artists has changed during the past five hundred years from apprenticeship, to the academy, to the art school, and, most recently, to the college. The dealer's gallery is where the living artist and the audience for contemporary art meet. Art dealers, who form an important part of the business world, must balance market values of art against cultural value. What we mean by "cultural value" is a particular society's concept of beauty. Public art museums, inspired by the Louvre museum in Paris, have a history of only a little more than a century in the United States, with tremendous expansion in the last thirty or so years.

Interpreting Works of Art

In the art world everyone has a job to do: the artist to create, the patron to support, the dealer to sell, the critic to discuss. Perhaps the hardest job belongs to the audience: to interpret the art. We take it for granted that a work of art is some kind of meaningful expression made by an artist and intended to be understood or experienced in a predictable way by spectators. The situation is actually more complicated than that. In the first place, it is very rare for an artist to explain a work of art in words. Artists rely on their work to speak for itself, and for them. But art is notoriously subject to different interpretations, the same sculpture or painting being explained in entirely different ways by different individuals or by people in different periods. Is there any way to be sure that your interpretation is more than a personal fantasy? And is there any way to evaluate the interpretations of others?

The great periods of art have been characterized by great audiences as well as great artists. Because it requires almost as much skill and understanding to receive and interpret a message as to send it, artists depend on their audiences for understanding. The interpretation of art is not mere fantasizing, but depends on powers of analysis which are improved by practice, like any other skill. In analysis the experience of art is divided into parts. Those parts could never exist by themselves, but it is convenient to discuss them separately. In this chapter we will concentrate on the relationships among the *subject* represented, the *material* of the work of art, and its *meaning*.

The Limits of Art

Art is one of the forms of symbolic expression. We human beings, it seems to us, are the only species that has the symbolizing power to make art. People have such a longing for symbolism that we tend to find it in nature and other places that no human created. However, the category "works of art" does not include nature, but only things which a human being made as the expression of an idea or symbol.

How do you react when you walk into a room [27] and find the floor covered with piles of waste cotton thread? On second glance you note that mirrors have been placed upright among the piles of thread, reflecting nothing but more cotton thread. Is it art? Is it symbolism? Robert Morris (b. 1931) gives you two clues that you are indeed to see this as art: it is installed in an art gallery, and the nearly invisible mirrors are set upright, clearly controlled and not accidental, as the placement of the thread appears to be.

To interpret such a work you have to know that in recent years artists have been especially interested in defining the term "work of art." Works that expand our ideas of art have been praised as original and have opened up new possibilities in form and content. Robert Morris' work of the 1960s and 1970s was mainly

27. Robert Morris. Untitled. 1968. Mixed media (waste cotton thread, mirrors), c. 26 × 20′ (7.9 × 6.1 m). Collection of Philip Johnson (as installed at the Whitney Museum of American Art, New York).

concerned with exploring the limits of our definition of art. So the idea in the thread-and-mirror piece could be stated as something like, "This stuff, too, disorderly as it appears, is a complex human product and is worth reflection (as in thought, as in a mirror)."

The location of Morris' thread-and-mirror sculpture in an art gallery suggests that art can be defined as "anything in an art gallery." Set outdoors such sculptures are hard to separate from the rest of the environment. Part of their meaning is the question, "Where is the line between art and the rest of the world?" It is easy to grasp that Mark di Suvero's steel and timber construction *Praise for Elohim Adonai* [28], in its parklike setting on the grounds of the St. Louis Art Museum, is symbolic. If we saw it in another setting—against an industrial background, for example—we might imagine it was the wreck of some utilitarian machine, impressive in its scale and balance but not obviously symbolic. Setting and other circumstances help us understand that a message is intended, even when the form of the message is unexpected. The audience often does not know exactly what symbolism the artist intended and must do its best to interpret the work without any words from the artist. But we can always be confident that the artist did intend the work to be symbolic; often that is all that can be said about the artist's intentions.

Form, Subject, Content

In Melissa Miller's (b. 1951) painting *Flood* [29] the **subject** is everything that is represented: a river in flood, two tigers and a crane taking refuge on a hill. The **form** is all the things that have actual material existence. It is the things that are *presented* rather than *represented*: the oil paint thickly applied with brushes to a linen canvas, the horizontal design with a strong diagonal (the river) interrupted by two vertical masses (crane on one side, tigers on the other). All the colors, lines, and shapes and the way they are organized into a composition are considered parts of the form. Both the form and the subject contribute to the **content**; art cannot exist without a material form which expresses meaning, which we call the content.

You immediately see the crane and tigers escaping the flood, which is the subject, but you probably feel there is more to be said. There is a feeling of

28. Mark di Suvero. *Praise for Elohim Adonai.* 1966. Wood and steel, 22 × 30′ (6.7 × 9.1 m). St. Louis, Missouri, Art Museum (gift of Mr. and Mrs. Norman B. Champ, Jr.).

powerful forces unleashed, of danger made amusing by being fantastic. Each of us would use different words to describe the painting, but we would probably agree on the mood of danger and mystery and the need to include the action and energy suggested by the strong colors, brush marks, and curving shapes. When you talk about art it is often easier to discuss the form and subject separately, but they join to produce meaning. Inexperienced observers sometimes think the form is merely the vehicle for the subject, just a way to make the subject visible. Looking at the pictures in this book should dispel that idea. The form can be so powerful that it gives meaning to subjects and ideas that seem trivial when described in words.

29. Melissa Miller. *Flood.* 1983. Oil on linen, 4′11″ × 7′11″ (1.5 × 2.4 m). Museum of Fine Arts, Houston, Texas (museum purchase with funds provided by Texas Eastern Corporation).

The subject of *The White Sugar Bowl* **[30]** by Paul Cézanne (*say-ZAHN*) (1839–1906) is nothing more world-shaking than some pears and a sugar bowl on a table, but the design and the way the paint has been applied make the painting important. Cézanne's subject is not exactly pears on a table, but *the shape and mass* of pears on a table. That makes the content a general statement about solid, spherical masses in space. The content of Cézanne's art has often been summarized by a remark the artist made: "You must see in nature the cylinder, the sphere, the cone."[1] He did not say, "You must see in nature the pear, the sugar bowl and the tablecloth." Those are specific examples of larger categories, categories which exist as pure geometry only in our minds.

Perhaps the hardest thing for many people to accept is that art is not, and never has been, pictures of things. It is a way of thinking and recording thought; *things* often appear in art because the artist is thinking about them, often using them as examples of *ideas.* Composing a design is a way of organizing our thoughts.

Thoughts, of course, are abstract in the sense that they are not objects. Organizing our thoughts often results in a design that is **abstract**, as in El Lissitzky's (1890–1941) *Composition* **[31]**, showing invented shapes that never existed anywhere except in Lissitzky's mind and in this painting. That makes the painting **non-representational**, since it does not represent anything that has a material existence. A synonym for non-representational is **non-objective**, meaning that no material object is represented. On the other side, there are **representational** paintings, which are depictions of things that do have a material existence in the world, such as Cézanne's white sugar bowl or Miller's tigers. When an artist represents material things as faithfully as possible, avoiding the expression of personal thoughts (if such a thing is possible), the style is called **naturalistic**. You might argue that naturalistic art *is* pictures of things and not a way of organizing our thoughts, but no one has ever figured out how to make a picture without *some* mental control. Just the decision to make a naturalistic art is a complicated symbolic act.

The Subjects of Art

Intention to find meaning is vital in both the artist and the audience. Although the artist may never have said a word, we in the audience have many

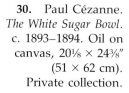

30. Paul Cézanne. *The White Sugar Bowl.* c. 1893–1894. Oil on canvas, 20⅛ × 24⅜" (51 × 62 cm). Private collection.

Communicating in a World of Art

clues to the artist's intention. One of the easiest to discuss is the subject matter the artist has chosen.

"What shall I draw?" Anyone who has taught a children's art class has heard that phrase and probably answered it by suggesting that there is an endless number of good subjects. The possibilities may be endless, but every culture has chosen just a few subjects which sum up its view of reality. Artists are constantly trying out new subjects, but only a few are accepted by the audience. Yet there are general themes which have a broad appeal that has lasted for centuries. We will look at five of them: portraits of individuals, the still life, the nude figure, the landscape, and the divine powers. There are other important themes, but these five illustrate traditional subjects of art.

The challenge to the artist is to put original, sincere feeling and thought into forms that are conventional enough to be recognized. The audience cannot receive a communication which is one hundred percent original. Robert Morris is so original that he risks such misunderstanding. Originality can be seen only as a contrast with its opposite, conventionality. A work of art is always trying to stay on that narrow path between the purely conventional, which everyone understands instantly and is soon bored with, and the totally original, which no one recognizes as art. Originality consists of a controlled variation on a well-known form expressing an independent point of view.

For these reasons, the traditions of subject matter are not boring old bins of exhausted ideas. They are well-worn paths, and at the end of them the audience waits for the artist to come out and say something original.

Portraits of Individuals

How do we remember other people? We need a face that can be named, or at least a face that is distinctive enough that we see a unique personality. Not all representations of people are portraits. Often artists have had other intentions that fall outside the conventions of the portrait; Michelangelo, for example, put generic faces on his memorials to two members of the Medici family, saying "In a thousand years who will care what they looked like?" Michelangelo wanted to represent the active and the contemplative ways of life in his figures, not individuals. But in the portrait we do care what the person looked like, and one of the pleasures of art is the cast of characters we meet. Here are just a few examples.

31. El Lissitzky. *Composition.* 1922. Oil and tempera on wood panel, 28 × 24¾" (71 × 63 cm). Museum of Modern Art, New York (The Riklis Collection of McCrory Corporation; fractional gift).

The name of the Roman [32] is unknown, but that hardly seems to matter. His face is so full of expression we feel we know the man. We can sense his personality and intelligence, almost hear his voice. This terra-cotta (fired clay) head is under life-size, but it is so natural that critics assume it was based on a life mask—that is, a plaster mold made of the living face. A life mask probably provided the basic structure of the face, but the significant parts of this face are the eyes and the mouth, where the expression is to be seen, and those had to be modeled by the sculptor. Among the many surviving portraits of people of the ancient world, this one is especially revealing of an individual personality. Romans kept such family portraits to fulfill some of the same needs the photo album fills for us: this portrait must have been a valued memento for the family, who were the main audience for such a work.

A more mysterious portrait is one from the Moche (*MO-chay*) kingdom of Peru [33]. No one knows exactly why it was made or who is represented. The Moche made many portraits of individuals, always as part of a pottery vessel to go into a tomb. The Moche were expert with molds, but this face is so thoroughly marked with hand-held tools that the use of a mold could have played little part. You can see the large, almost abstract forms which make up this powerful masculine face. Moche art was mostly concerned with religion and ritual, but all we know of this portrait head is that it was placed as an offering in a tomb, but not necessarily in the tomb of the person portrayed. That suggests the man portrayed here was a person of ritual or political leadership, meant to identify or protect the dead in the afterlife. Who might be the audience for art placed in a tomb is hard for us to understand, but ancient Peruvians seem to have considered the dead, who continued to exist in an afterlife, an important audience.

Portraits are often meant to tell us about the social position of the sitter, which sometimes seems more important than the individual's personality. Mary

Communicating in a World of Art

and Elizabeth Royall [34], daughters of one of New England's wealthiest families, were painted as a family memento, a common practice now largely replaced by photographs. Already a skilled portraitist when he was only twenty years old, John Singleton Copley (1738–1815) established the individuality of the girls by subtle differences in their expressions. Gowned and posed like young debutantes, the girls give reality to their luxurious setting by their lively expressions. In some ways, this is the most conventional of all these portraits, since it follows a well-established tradition of depictions of the European nobility. That, of course, was the message the Royall family wanted Copley to convey, and they definitely did not want him to be original. Within those boundaries, Copley managed to reveal the individual personalities of the girls. The result is sufficiently original and sincere to give life to the conventional subject. This portrait seems to be intended for the eyes of more than the members of the family; it was intended to establish forever the social position of Mary and Elizabeth Royall in the eyes of their social circle.

One of the reasons to paint a face is to try to understand it, to read its expression and fathom its message. When the face is the artist's own, the audience first examines the image to discover why it was painted. Is it an image of vanity and self-assertion, or one of self-discovery? In the case of Vincent van

34.
John Singleton Copley.
Mary and Elizabeth Royall.
c. 1758. Oil on canvas,
4'9½" × 4' (1.5 × 1.2 m).
Museum of Fine Arts,
Boston (Julia Knight Fox
Fund, 1925).

Gogh *(van GO)* (1853–1890) there can be no doubt that his self-portraits were painted for self-discovery [35]. They seem to be painful and searching answers to the question, "Who am I?" In this painting from the last year of his life, the body in its blue suit merges with the blazing blue and white pattern of the background. The face is strongly drawn in dark lines and modeled in blue and orange around the penetrating eyes. Despite its intensity, the figure has a tendency to slip away into the misty whirling space behind it—one can see the eyes willing the body into material existence against the background forces which threaten to carry it off. Fortunately, few self-portraits show such an effort to prove the question of existence; few of us have such a desperate need to reaffirm the fact of our being.

There are as many reasons to paint a portrait as there are people in the world, but the sitter and the painter have different reasons in every case. The sitter has a self-image that must be conveyed, and the artist sees a unique individual who must be revealed. Those two images are always different, unless the sitter and the painter are the same person. In such cases, the unity of intention makes self-portraits especially powerful and revealing.

The Still Life

Painters sometimes consider the **still life**—the name that covers a variety of paintings of all kinds of food and drink, table settings, and other household objects, as well as flowers—to be a kind of study or practice subject, since the models will sit patiently while the artist carefully examines the color, light, and composition. But still life is a very old subject with traditional meanings of pleasure, abundance, and security—it is the hedonistic subject.

In an ancient still life painted in **fresco** on the wall of a Roman house [36] peaches still on their leafy branch show the sweet gifts of nature, but the artist was also fascinated by the challenge of the transparent glass jar of water. Only a few still-life paintings from ancient times remain, but they were popular, especially with city people who liked to be reminded of nature and its abundant production of food.

In Detail: Van Gogh's Oleanders

Self-revelation is not limited to the self-portrait, for artists reveal themselves in all their work. Vincent van Gogh's *Oleanders* [37] gives the still life an intensity that belonged to the artist, not the flowers.

Vincent (which was the way he signed his work) was the son of a Dutch Protestant minister. At sixteen he went to work for art dealers, first in The Hague and later in London and Paris. An unsuccessful love affair plunged him into depression, and he decided to pursue a religious life, studying for the ministry. Though he failed the educational requirements, he became a missionary anyway, working among the poverty-stricken coal miners in the mining country of Belgium. His extreme identification with the miners shocked church officials and he was dismissed. At the age of 27, Van Gogh turned definitely to art, which he hoped would provide a way to serve humanity. In the remaining ten years of his life (1880–1890) he produced the hundreds of paintings that place him among the great masters.

The intensity of his temperament led to continual frustration in his love affairs and friendships. His closest friendship was with his younger brother Theo, who worked in a Paris art dealer's shop and supported Vincent throughout his later years; Vincent wrote wonderful letters to Theo describing his work. Vincent settled in Arles, in the south of France, hoping to form a colony of artists, but only Paul Gauguin joined him. Their relationship was stressful, and van Gogh's depression grew so severe that he committed himself to asylums, first near Arles and later at Auvers, near Paris. During these final years, 1888–1890, Van Gogh kept up a tremendous production as an artist and began to receive recognition, although he sold almost nothing. Finally, in despair over his severe depression and worried that his brother could no longer afford to support him, he shot himself. He died July 27, 1890, at the age of 37.

Considering his tragic life, it is surprising that Van Gogh was an important still-life painter, since still life is conventionally about the pleasures of life. In *Oleanders* Vincent reveals his knowledge of that traditional meaning by including in the composition a book by Émile Zola whose title is *La Joie de Vivre,* or "The Joy of Life." But the painting is so dramatic in its colors and in the spiky leaves of the plant that our conventional idea of pleasure is given a very original twist.

37. Vincent van Gogh. *Oleanders.* 1888. Oil on canvas, 23¾ × 29" (60 × 74 cm). Metropolitan Museum of Art, New York (gift of Mr. and Mrs. John L. Loeb, 1962).

The next two paintings [38] and [39] were made in the same period, but they contrast strikingly. Ambrosius Boschaert's *(BO-shart)* (1573–1621) *Bouquet in a Niche* [38] is one of the early paintings to concentrate on flowers, each of them portrayed as an individual specimen in a bouquet containing a surprising variety. Juan Sánchez Cotán's *(hwan SAN-chase ko-TAN)* (1561–1627) *Quince, Cabbage, Melon, and Cucumber* [39] has no flowers at all, but each fruit or vegetable is portrayed with hypnotic intensity. Sánchez Cotán joined a monastery in his native Toledo, Spain, and observers have always seen his still lifes as mystical. The dark space behind the shelf or window sill hints at an invisible presence which shows these living forms as evidence of its power. They hang in space like a demonstration of the planets, forming a descending arc.

Boschaert's flowers are so beautiful and the picture is so full that at first we may miss its message about the richness of nature. It is like a botanical study, including as many different flowers as possible, each one portrayed with scientific accuracy. Boschaert contrasts the delicacy of the flowers with the space beyond, the tiny with the vast. The nearly white space beyond the niche is sky with a distant landscape of mountains, and ocean at the bottom, which is the opposite of the darkness in Sánchez Cotán's painting. The power in nature which produced this abundance of flowers seems to be reasonable, even scientific, and willing to be seen in bright light.

William M. Harnett (1848–1892) had a successful career as a still-life painter in Philadelphia and New York between 1875 and his death in 1892. *After the Hunt* [40] is an American version of a type of painting very popular in Europe called "trompe l'oeil" *(trawmp loy),* or "fool-the-eye," that usually shows objects on shelves or tacked on a wall or door. The inspiration for Harnett's "sporting still lifes" was a set of black-and-white still-life photographs by Adolphe Braun printed from negatives that were 29½ by 22 inches (75 by 54 centimeters), an unusually large size that provides very fine detail [41]. With the advantage of color, Harnett was, and remains, popular for his "most natural-looking" pictures. The illusion is one of the pleasures of this kind of still life. But even in Braun's photographs and Harnett's paintings the illusion is not the only point—the dead game animals, the hunting horn, and so on, are symbolic, recalling the pleasures of hunting and the sense of the richness of nature from which this harvest was taken.

Modern still-life painting has that idea of natural abundance behind it, but it has turned away from the path pursued by Harnett. The style of Braun's photographs has survived mainly in advertising, glorifying the abundance of

our consumer products. The painters have used this subject as a way to work out compositions that carry over into other subjects. Paul Cézanne's *Pink Onions* **[42]** has such grandeur it could be turned into a landscape of rocks, trees, and a waterfall. One critic sees its cool color scheme of pinks and blues as "a harmony of sadness and disenchantment,"[2] a far cry from the feeling of pleasure traditional in the still life. Cézanne took the still life to its expressive limits, making it hint at larger, sometimes more tragic, ideas. His still lifes are as rich in meaning as his other subjects, including his figure paintings and landscapes.

42. Paul Cézanne. *Pink Onions.* 1895–1900. Oil on canvas, 26 × 32" (66 × 82 cm). Louvre, Paris.

left: 43.   Georges Braque. *The Round Table*. 1929.
Oil on canvas, 4'9¼" × 3'8¾" (3.7 × 2.9 m).
Phillips Collection, Washington, D.C.

above: 44.   Wayne Thiebaud. *Cake Window*. 1970–1976.
Oil on canvas, 4' × 4'11⅜" (1.2 × 1.5 m).
Private collection, New York.

Painters of the **Cubist** movement took off from Cézanne's work to make still life one of their basic subjects. Georges Braque *(brock)* (1882–1963), with his love of music and the Classical traditions of ancient Greece, remained closest to the old traditions of still life **[43]**. The guitar, sheet music, fruit, and bottle on a round table are things that must have been easily available in his studio. But they have been painted with a scale and soberness that suggests they are important things. Braque's paintings make us understand that nothing has more dignity than the objects surrounding us in daily life.

Pop Art of the 1960s and 1970s gave still life a new lease on life. The abundance Pop Art showed was not that of nature, but that made by cooks and bakers. *Cake Window* **[44]** by Wayne Thiebaud *(TEE-bo)* (b. 1920) was painted from memories and the imagination, not from life, but the cakes are meant to be everyday objects. "I'm interested in the dignity of the thing, the object, so long as it has some sort of genuineness," Thiebaud has said. "When my students worry about what to paint I tell them what James Joyce said—that any object deeply contemplated may represent a window on the universe."[3]

The audience for Cézanne, Braque, and Thiebaud has always understood that a theme of natural abundance lies behind their still lifes, but their originality lies in the ways they have departed from the conventional idea. Their work has appealed especially to educated observers seeking new ways to see reality. Originality is especially easy to see in subjects in which the conventions are firmly established, as they were in still life.

The Nude Figure

You might think that one naked person is, symbolically, pretty much like any other naked person, but the figures of men and women unclothed have entirely different meanings in art. That is apparent, first of all, in the fact that male nudes are practically always doing something, such as throwing a spear **[45]**, while female nudes are not doing anything. Usually they are simply standing or sitting and seem to suggest that they are just existing.

Communicating in a World of Art

45. Greek Classical. *Zeus.* 460–450 B.C. Bronze, height 6'10" (2.1 m). National Archaeological Museum, Athens.

That traditional difference is summed up in *Fête Champêtre (fet shawm-PET-ruh)* by Titian *(TI-shun)* (1477–1576) **[46]**, long attributed to Giorgione *(jor-JO-nay)* (1478?–1511). Here two clothed young men are playing music on a country hill-side, oblivious to two nude women, one holding a flute, the other dipping water from a fountain. One gets the impression that the women are invisible to the young men, that they are imaginary, or symbolic, in a way that the men are not. The shepherd with his flock, the lush landscape, and the lute we are supposed to hear in our minds bring a vision of the simple, sweet pleasures of country life.

46. Giorgione and Titian. *Fête Champêtre (Pastoral Concert).* c. 1508. Oil on canvas, 3'7½" × 4'6¼" (1.1 × 1.4 m). Louvre, Paris.

47. Hellenistic. *Aphrodite of Kyrene.* c. 100 B.C. Marble, height 4'8" (1.4 m). Museo Nazionale Romano, Rome.

The ancient Greeks set poetic stories about that kind of life in the region called Arcadia; this painting still speaks to us of "arcadian" pleasures. The arcadian life is lived under the patronage of female nature spirits—Mother Nature, we would say. The women in Titian's painting occupy the foreground because they are the most important figures, the supernatural ones who rule this happy country of natural pleasures.

Titian's women show no sign of shyness about their nakedness; it seems to be their natural condition. Most of us in such a situation would feel naked, a word that implies we are accustomed to appear in public wearing clothes. The word "nude," however, belongs to art and refers to human figures which were never clothed and which represent the eternal idea of the human body.[4] The men in Titian's painting are placed at a certain time in history by their clothing, but the women are timeless. For that reason we are shocked when we look at nude portraits of real people. Both George Washington and Napoleon were portrayed by sculptors who had the misguided notion that they could be represented in the nude, like Greek gods. But both men belonged to a particular time in history, and we expect to see them in the clothes of their period.

The Greeks had a different attitude to nakedness than we do today. For men it was the normal way to engage in sports or war, but women were usually more sheltered. It was always considered proper to portray men naked in war and athletics, as well as male gods as nude figures [45]. Thus later people inherited the tradition of the male nude as the hero, in war or sport. But centuries earlier, the Greeks had rejected the idea of the female nude in art and it was shocking to them when the sculptor Praxiteles (*prax-IT-uh-leez*) (c. 390–330 B.C.) revived the ancient image of a nude goddess to fulfill a commission for the people of Cnidos, so shocking that they rejected the sculpture. The power of the female nude depends only partly on the abstract beauty of its lines and shapes. For human beings the human body is a form full of symbolism and poetic meaning that surely derives from our nature as sexual beings. The unknown Hellenistic sculptor who carved the *Aphrodite of Kyrene* [47] knew that the sexual drive was given by the gods, that it was the motor for our ideals as well as for the continuation of our species.

When Renaissance artists began to revive ancient Greek and Roman subjects, the nude was among the first to return. An ancient poem describes Venus (Roman name for the Greek Aphrodite), the goddess of love, born from the sea, and those lines were the inspiration for a commission to Botticelli (*bot-tih-CHEL-lee*) (1444–1510). The result was the most famous nude of its period [48]. *The Birth of Venus* is a **tempera** painting, unusual in being on canvas and in the large size of about 6 by 9 feet (1.8 by 2.7 meters), with the soft pastel colors and linear style characteristic of that medium. The figure of Venus is mainly produced by a narrow brown line that outlines her body and, combined with yellow lines, forms the graceful flow of her hair. Her body is very lightly shaded, so we get a strong sense of her body as a flat shape, which increases her elegance and unearthliness. Because her body is almost entirely to the right of the supporting foot, she appears weightless, floating on her shell and blown by the winds. These things make her the most spiritual, least physical, of all the nude figures. The result is to change her meaning from the Spirit of Nature to the Spirit of Unearthly Beauty.

Rembrandt, who fluctuated between the earthy and the spiritual in his art, painted one nude which is the perfect combination of the two [49]. The model for this painting, entitled *Bathsheba*, was probably his faithful mistress Hendrickje, playing the role of King David's beloved in the Bible, whom the king saw bathing. A real woman with a plump body and practical hands and feet, not an imaginary ideal, Bathsheba has an expression that is so full of thought, doubts and regrets that her whole story (told in chapters 11–12 of the Book of Samuel) is summed up in her face. Natural as Bathsheba is, she is treated by Rembrandt as a timeless figure, not a portrait of an historical person.

Communicating in a World of Art

above: 48. Botticelli.
The Birth of Venus. c. 1485.
Tempera on canvas,
6'7" × 9'2" (2 × 2.8 m).
Uffizi Gallery, Florence.

left: 49.
Rembrandt van Rijn.
Bathsheba. Oil on canvas,
4'8" (1.4 m) square.
Louvre, Paris.

50. Pablo Picasso. *Woman in an Armchair.* 1929. Oil on canvas, 6′4¾″ × 4′3⅛″ (2 × 1.3 m). Musée Picasso, Paris.

With the rise of **Modernism** at the beginning of the 20th century the nude entered a new chapter. Modern artists were trying to overthrow all the traditions, which surely included the nude as an ideal. On the other hand, they wanted art based on creative imagination, not on copying the visible world. It turned out that many of the most important Modern paintings included nude figures because one of the forms found in every imagination is the human body. *Woman in an Armchair* **[50]** by Pablo Picasso (1881–1973) is a Modern version of the nude which rejects tradition. Those earlier nudes, Picasso seems to say, are idols I no longer worship. The body can make other expressions—it can scream, for example. Critics have commented on the pain and agony the figure conveys, not only by the pose and expression but also in the red and green colors and the brushwork, which are harsh.

The Landscape

Although the first views of natural scenes began to appear in Mediterranean art in the 1st century B.C., the common way to represent nature and her moods in ancient Western art was by **personification**, by a human figure representing the goddess of nature. In China, however, old religious and philosophical ideas led to the development of views of natural scenes to express some of their deepest beliefs. Landscape began to play an important part in Chinese art by the 6th century A.D. and has remained the supreme category in Chinese painting. The most distinctive Chinese style, which developed in the Song Dynasty (A.D. 960–1279), was monochrome paintings in black ink on paper or silk mounted as vertical hanging scrolls or handscrolls, to be unrolled between the two hands. *Travelers on a Mountain Path* **[51]** by Fan Kuan *(fahn kwahn)*, is one of the few original paintings by a known artist to have survived from that period. A hanging scroll nearly 7 feet (2.1 meters) tall, it presents a scene of wild mountains and cascading streams only made grander by the tiny mule train approaching the ford. Chinese philosophies suggested that nature has a moral dimension: "Nature is vast and deep, high, intelligent, infinite, and eternal," as one Confucian tract says.[5] Those are exactly the qualities Fan Kuan sought to convey, but he painted the rocks and trees realistically, without the personification that might be indicated by attributing intelligence to nature, and also without the stylization and abstraction found in the work of his many followers. Later painters developed the style of Fan Kuan into a very conventional scene of rocks and streams, losing much of the dignity and power conveyed by his attempt to show nature as it appeared. His seriousness about representing rocks and trees convinces us that he saw a moral significance in nature that could be expressed only by a faithful depiction.

Another hanging scroll painted about three hundred years later by an unknown artist, *Landscape with Flight of Geese* [52], shares several features with *Travelers on a Mountain Path*. Foreground and background, which are sharply separated by a misty lake in Fan Kuan's painting, are still separate despite the later artist's effort to unite them by reedy banks and a flight of geese. The later painter (a very fine artist, though anonymous to us) did not follow a conventional design, but, like Fan Kuan, was inspired by experience of nature. Yet the effect of the later painting is quite different from Fan Kuan's, much milder and more intimate. The use of some color along with the black ink, as well as the smaller size, make the later painting charming, rather than powerfully imposing, as the older painting is.

The glories of Chinese landscape painting were unknown in Europe until the 18th century, by which time the Europeans had developed landscape paint-

left: 51. Fan Kuan. *Travelers on a Mountain Path.* c. 1000. Ink on silk; hanging scroll, height 6'9¼" (2.1 m). National Palace Museum, Taipei, Taiwan.

below: 52. Chinese. *Landscape with Flight of Geese.* c. 1300. Ink and color on silk; hanging scroll, 25½ × 15" (65 × 38 cm). Art Institute of Chicago.

ing of their own. By the 16th century the old tradition of the female nude as Mother Nature began to take a new form. The moods of nature which had been personified in the goddess began to appear as seasons and weather in depictions of scenes from nature, with the human figure confined to the role of providing scale for nature, as in the Chinese paintings.

Landscape [53] by Claude Lorrain (1600–1682) is the ideal landscape: animals in a green pasture, noble trees, ruins of a classical building, and a distant view of the sea and sky. Classical gods still appear—here it is Mercury bribing the cowherd to forget he saw the theft of Apollo's cattle—but the ancient story serves only as a reminder that the earth goddess is somewhere nearby. Claude's drawings and paintings of such scenes were accepted by artists and the public alike as the new conventional version of nature as the expression of divine creation. Claude (Lorraine, in France, was his birthplace; Gellée was his real last name) made his career in Rome and spent much time sketching in the countryside. Drawings such as *Landscape* are the result of these sketching trips and are closer to the natural scenes than the oil paintings Claude produced later in his studio. More than any other artist, he defined the standards for Western landscape painting.

The English painter John Constable (1776–1837) studied Claude, whom he described as "the most perfect landscape painter the world ever saw,"[6] but in *The White Horse* [54] we see that it is nature alone—its light, water, and vegetation—which expresses his sense of the sacred, with no Classical gods to be seen. "Every tree seems full of blossoms of some kind & the surface of the ground seems quite living," Constable wrote in a letter;"—every step I take & whatever object I turn my Eye that sublime expression in the Scripture 'I am the resurrection & the life' seems verified about me."[7] Paired diagonals spreading left and right from the sky-reflection in the water show careful composition, but Constable's intimate knowledge of his country dominates the geometry. He shows an actual place on the Stour River where the bargemen loaded their towing horse into the bow of the barge to be poled to the opposite bank where the towpath continued. The gestures of the bargemen and our sense of the barge moving into the scene enliven the natural setting.

After Constable the picturesque (meaning "like a picture") frequently became the quality most sought in landscape, an aim almost guaranteed to produce a conventional result. But a radical change was soon to emerge with **Impressionism** in the last quarter of the 19th century. Camille Pissarro's *Place du*

53. Claude Lorrain. *Landscape*. 1663. Brown ink on blue paper, 7¾ × 10" (20 × 26 cm). British Museum, London.

Théâtre Français, in the Rain [55] is an extreme example: wilderness has given way to the creations of people. Cityscape had existed as a category in earlier times (as works by Butteri and Canaletto in this book show), but its aim had been to glorify the life of the community, not represent the natural world. In his later years Pissarro gave up outdoor painting and would rent a room and paint the view from the window, which permitted him to paint even on rainy days. The results truly reflect the world most of us inhabit: great streets full of traffic,

56. Neil Welliver. *The Birches*. 1977. Oil on canvas, 5' (1.5 m) square. Metropolitan Museum of Art, New York (gift of Dr. and Mrs. Robert E. Carroll).

massive buildings, a smoky sky, and imprisoned trees struggling for survival. Pissarro's *Place du Théâtre Français* is that modern creation, the completely secular landscape. Pissarro knew this landscape as intimately as Constable knew his corner of England, and probably loved it as much, but we can hardly imagine him saying "the surface of the ground seems quite living." The aim of landscape painting had changed to the authentic representation of personal experience, rejecting any philosophy or convictions which were not based purely on sense experience. Pissarro's Impressionist colleagues shared that attitude.

At the present time landscape is emerging from a period when **abstract** or non-objective art took its place. Post-Modern landscape painters look at recent abstractions (by such artists as Mondrian, Pollock, or De Kooning) as their antecedents, not Claude or Constable. Neil Welliver's (b. 1929) *The Birches* **[56]** has a lively pattern over its whole surface which calls our attention to the flatness of the canvas, as in many non-objective paintings. Yet Welliver says, "I am very interested in the idea of the spectator entering a picture, being able to, in fact, not see the picture as an object but really actively entering into it."[8] The 5-by-5-foot (1.5-by-1.5 meter) size of *The Birches* is large enough to seem to envelop a viewer standing close to it.

Those contrary aims of wanting the painting to look both abstract and representational coexist in Welliver's art, as in the work of many of the leading contemporary artists. This is a new version of the contrary aims which have stimulated landscape painters, from Fan Kuan and Claude to our own time: to combine the actual and the ideal. For Welliver the ideal is geometry and abstract marks on a flat canvas; that is the intellectual realm in which the eternal is found now. The actual is the natural environment, which for Welliver has been rural Pennsylvania, where he grew up, and rural Maine, where he has lived for 25 years. To combine those contrary aims, as Welliver says, "I look very hard, then I make it up as I go along."[9]

The Divine Powers

Each religion has its own set of subjects which focus on God's manifestation as a human teacher, or on other human teachers and prophets: Moses,

Jesus, Mohammed, and Guatama Buddha. But there are still more universal religious subjects in which people have sought a way to express the idea of the Creator, or God the Father.

People have always sensed that behind the confusing richness of the experiences of daily life there is some hidden order. If the world has an order and meaning there must be a universal intelligence behind it which human beings can contact. The most ancient religions divided up the powers of nature into a kind of bureaucracy, controlled by many gods, each with its own special powers. Only later did monotheism—the idea that all of these are just aspects of one universal spirit—begin to emerge.

Among the oldest images of the divine powers in nature are masks used in the initiation of children into adult life, such as a mask [57] from the Papua (*PAH-puh-wah*) region of New Guinea, which follows a very ancient tradition. It is made of bark cloth on a wooden frame, painted in red and black, with the huge eyes and small open mouth being the main features. This is just one of a large group of masks worn by men impersonating the wild spirits that control nature, who are fierce and unpredictable, as people know nature to be. Masks were invented to give a face to the invisible. Even a terrifying face can be dealt with more easily than the invisible.

It is a great leap from the New Guinea mask to the bronze figure of a Greek God [45]. No one is certain whether it represents Zeus, ruler of the heavens, or Poseidon, god of the sea, but there is no question that a supernatural being is portrayed. The nude figure stands balanced to throw a spear, tense and concentrating on his aim. It is hard to imagine that this Greek god would have time to listen to human prayers; he looks preoccupied with his own activities. Yet we sense in this figure the majesty and momentous power of nature.

Christian art sought a more kindly image of divine power, following the teachings of Jesus. *The Ghent Altarpiece* [58], painted by Jan van Eyck (*yan van IK*, rhymes with "like") (1370–1440?) and his brother Hubert, sums up the whole

57. Papuan Gulf, New Guinea. Eharo mask of nature spirit. Late 19th–early 20th century. Bark cloth and cane, height 30¼" (77 cm). Museum of Cultural History, University of California, Los Angeles.

58. Jan and Hubert van Eyck. *The Ghent Altarpiece*. c. 1425–1432. Oil on wooden panels, 11'5¾" × 15'1½" (3.5 × 4.6 m). Cathedral of St.-Bovan, Ghent, Belgium.

heavenly power on a grand scale. The dozen panels focus on a youthful, bearded God the Father in the top center, robed in red with pearl borders and wearing a triple crown. In the panel below is his symbol, the Fountain of Living Waters, and above, the metaphor for Christ, the self-sacrificing lamb. In the sky above the lamb is the dove representing the Holy Spirit. Devout pilgrims gather from all directions, while above, Adam and Eve look on, a choir sings to organ music, and Mary and John the Baptist flank the supreme figure.

An early oil painting on wooden panels, *The Ghent Altarpiece* is one of the high points of painting, but not just because it is so well painted. The variety of its subjects, which is all-encompassing, and the solemnity and richness of its depictions make a very convincing vision of the supernatural personalities ruling the universe. God the Father is majestic, but he looks at us and raises his hand in a gesture of teaching or blessing. It has been suggested that as humans have gained more control over their surroundings, the divine powers of nature begin to seem more kindly. The Europeans of Van Eyck's time actually were in reasonably good control of their environment, and the feeling that nature is not an overwhelming threat is communicated in this very orderly and systematic painting.

El Greco's large painting of *The Trinity* [59] was originally set at the very top of a tall altarpiece, which explains the setting of the figures in the clouds. El Greco (meaning "The Greek," the nickname of Domenikos Theotokopoulos) shows God the Father as a distinguished old man holding the powerful, athletic body of the dead Christ, as God the Son. Both these figures are different from those in *The Ghent Altarpiece* and were invented as subjects of art during the century and a half after *The Ghent Altarpiece* was painted. The white dove was a traditional symbol for the Holy Spirit, just as in *The Ghent Altarpiece*.

The mood of *The Trinity* is much more emotional than in any of the earlier examples. The Father holds the Son tenderly and looks with loving sadness down into his face as mourning angels surround them. The idea that the universe is ruled by a power which can understand and experience human emotions is one that had not been much seen before. The worshipper with the Greek Zeus sculpture in mind would approach the altar in quite a different frame of mind from one who had been looking at El Greco's painting, which might suggest that God would pay attention to prayers.

Iconography

The **content**, or meaning, of a work of art is the marriage of the **subject** and the **form**. Both subject and form have an objective material side and an expressive symbolic side. Looking at the subject, we see there is something represented in the picture, but it symbolizes something beyond itself. The study of the symbolism of subjects is called **iconography** *(ikon-OG-raf-e)*. But form also has an expressive side, in which the craft of the drawing and designing, as well as the materials used, become meaningful. That expressive side of form we call **style**. We must postpone the study of style to the end of Chapter 4 and Part V, after we have examined the elements and principles which contribute to it. But we should pause here to look at iconography, the symbolism of subjects.

Frida Kahlo's *(KAH-lo)* (1907–1954) *The Little Deer* [60] brings together a group of objects, some obviously symbolic, but others with hidden meanings. Although it may not seem like a portrait at first glance, it is part of Kahlo's lifelong examination in art of herself and her life. Only by studying her life can we interpret the symbolism of the painting. Her face, sensitive but expressionless, appears on the wounded deer leaping over a fallen branch. Perhaps it is significant that she kept a deer as a pet and perhaps identified with it, but more important are the arrows, which surely refer to Kahlo's own wounds.[10] She suffered polio as a child and was slightly lame, but much worse was a bus

left: 59. El Greco. *The Trinity*. 1577. Oil on canvas, 9'10⅛" × 5'10⅛" (3 × 1.8 m). Prado, Madrid.

above: 60. Frida Kahlo. *The Little Deer*. 1946. Oil on masonite, 8¾ × 11¾" (22 × 30 cm). Collection of Jorge Espinosa Ulloa, Mexico City.

accident in which she was nearly killed at sixteen, surviving with a smashed pelvis and her back broken in several places. Those injuries finally killed her at the age of 44, but for about fifteen years she lived very intensely, married to the mural painter Diego Rivera, and producing great paintings of her own. The little deer is surely fatally wounded and, like the broken branch, is sure to die. The forest of thick tree trunks, solidly rooted in the earth, offers no shelter for the deer, which, like the branch below, seems rootless and vulnerable.

It is fascinating to learn to read the iconography of works of art, but it takes patience. All artists have a personal language of symbols, as Frida Kahlo did. What we would call their private iconography can be interpreted confidently only when we know the artist's life story and have examined several works. Artists living in the same period may share a set of symbols, but that will be the subject of Part V of this book.

Summary for Review

A work of art has a material form, which is given expressive meaning by the artist's style, and a subject, whose meaning lies in the symbolism of the things represented. The content, or meaning, of the work of art is the product of the form and subject together. The intention to find meaning in forms is what brings the artist and the audience together and defines their roles. The artist may reveal intentions by choosing a conventional subject which has a traditional meaning. The originality of an artist is only perceptible by contrast with conventions, a sincere personal expression in a traditional subject. The study of the symbolism of subjects is called iconography. Art made in the same period may share symbolism, but modern artists, especially, often use a personal iconography, which must be learned before the work can be understood.

Part II

Analyzing Works of Art

Pieter Bruegel (c. 1525–1569) shows us **[61]** the artist with his audience looking over his shoulder. Showing us people of an earlier time, he is clearly amused by the fantastic old artist he has invented. Looking at the difference in the two faces we can hardly doubt that the two will interpret differently the work of art emerging under the sharp eyes and large brush of the artist. But the spectator peering through his glasses is pleased—in fact, he is putting his hand in his purse. The drawing suggests that a real understanding between these two may be impossible, but in the end it will be the spectator who carries the work away, to be interpreted by himself and his friends.

To interpret a work of art the piece must be considered from several different points of view. In Part II we will concentrate on two aspects of art. Chapter 3 examines the work of art as a set of marks made by the artist with a brush, chisel, or any other tool. Lines, shapes, textures, and other **elements of art** are the result of these marks with a tool. In Chapter 4 we will consider how the **principles of design** define relationships among these marks in compositions. The elements of art and the principles

of design depend on each other and cannot exist separately, but to analyze a work of art we must divide it into its components and consider them separately.

The artists under consideration here choose to use materials, marks, and designs that appeal to the eye. To understand these marks and designs the members of the audience have to learn to read their language. Art is a form of symbolic expression. As far as human beings know, we are the only species that has the symbolizing power to make art. The meaning of symbols is not constant; they change slowly all the time. That is why one of the common themes of our conversations is, "What does [she, he, or it] mean?"

In this part we will discuss ways in which symbols are given form and the way that form, in lines, shapes, compositions, and so on, contributes to the content, or meaning. Form is the constant feature of art, one that observers in all periods have had to confront as they struggled to understand the symbols of their own time. Dealing with art form, we constantly feel we are looking over the artist's shoulder as marks emerge on the canvas or stone.

61. Pieter Bruegel the Elder. *The Painter and the Connoisseur.* c. 1565.
Pen and brown ink, 9¾ × 8½" (25 × 22 cm). Albertina, Vienna.

The Elements of Art

A work of art must be composed of something. In music it is notes or tones; in art it is lines, shapes, masses and spaces, size and scale, light and dark, texture and color. For the artist the problem is to use those things in an expressive way, just as a musician must use tones in an expressive way. These elements have unusual independence in James Havard's (b. 1937) painting *Posted Mimbres Forest* **[62]**, in which a green and white background tone is a stage where lines and shapes, masses and colors play their parts. Notice that the thick orange lines have sufficient mass that they cast shadows on the background, creating an illusion of space, despite the abstraction of the elements.

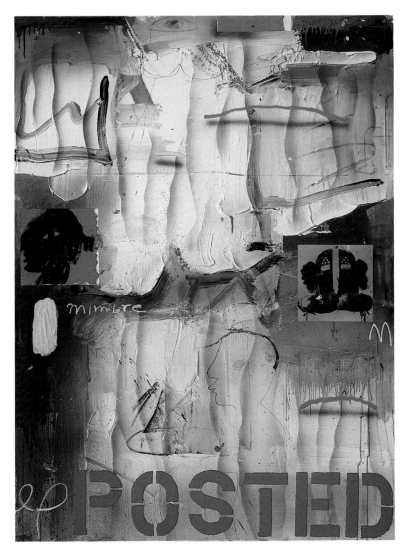

62. James Havard. *Posted Mimbres Forest.* 1986. Acrylic collage on canvas, 6′½″ × 5′5½″ (1.8 × 1.7 m). Elaine Horwitch Galleries, Santa Fe, New Mexico.

63. Varieties of lines: (a) line of gesture or action with open ends; (b) lines as arrows to imply movement beyond their own ends; (c) line as the edge of a two-dimensional surface—the boundary of a shape—and line as texture; (d) lines as contours of a mass and as hatching and crosshatching for shading; (e) lines as contours of a mass; (f) variations in line quality: direction and curvature, weight and width.

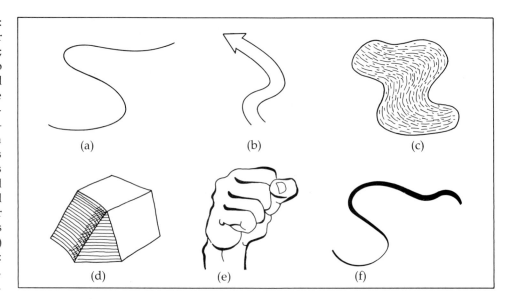

The most basic fact about art is that it exists in the material world; it doesn't count if it exists only in your mind. The reason there are pictures in this book is to keep our minds focused on concrete examples. Although we will look at the work of a number of artists, we will return several times in this chapter to the work of the French artist Henri Matisse (*mah-TEECE*) (1869–1954). He made the kind of deep analysis of the elements of art that people think of when they speak of scientific research. Although Matisse has been dead for nearly forty years, artists right now are especially interested in his work because his balance of subject matter and abstract form is one they also are seeking.

Line

There are no lines in nature; they are products of the human mind. One can imagine that the first **line** was a circle drawn in the earth by a magician to divide a sacred space from the everyday world outside. All later lines have something in common with such an act, being human marks placed in an environment. They serve as traffic signs for our eyes and our minds, showing patterns of movement like the lines on roads, the edges of surfaces, and the boundaries of solids. We will examine line in its primary uses—as a sign, as a gesture or energy, as the boundary of a shape or the contour of a mass, and finally as having qualities of length, direction, strength, and variability of its own **[63]**.

"Each thing has its own sign," Henri Matisse said. "The importance of an artist is to be measured by the number of signs he has introduced into the language of art."[1] Matisse had an unusual criterion for evaluating the importance of artists, but in the photograph **[64]** we can begin to see what he meant. Working on the symbols to ornament the walls of a chapel he designed in southern France, Matisse uses lines as signs. When we write with the alphabet we are making such signs, but they stand for sounds rather than things. Writing in Chinese is more like Matisse's signs, since Chinese ideograms developed from pictures rather than from sound symbols **[65]**.

One might disagree with Matisse about the importance of an artist being measured by the number of signs he has introduced, but it is one of the commonest uses of line. Signs are the simplest possible mark with a specific meaning. Matisse arrived at this very simple way of drawing after years of practice—he is 82 in the photograph. It is not easy to find the line that is the absolute sign for something. You can probably think of the logo of a company which aims to be the memorable identification of the company and its product. Company logos are the carefully considered work of artists, but all of us who open a bank ac-

Analyzing Works of Art

64. Henri Matisse drawing a medallion of the Virgin and Child for the chapel at Vence, France, about 1950.

count have to provide our own personal logo, our signature, which is a linear sign that stands for us.

A line is the product of an action or gesture, and it always retains that active appearance. "Drawing," Matisse told his students, "is like making an expressive gesture with the advantage of permanence."[2] With modern technology we can make permanent what were once fleeting gestures such as those Picasso made with a flashlight **[66]** before an open camera lens. Lines have direction, as gestures do, and they exert psychological pressure in the direction of their imagined motions—or actual motions in Picasso's case—swinging outward toward the horizon or shooting skyward.

above: 65. Chiang Yee. Chinese ideogram for "house."

right: 66. Gjon Mili. Pablo Picasso drawing with light, 1950.

above: 67.
Vincent van Gogh.
Grove of Cypresses.
1889. Reed pen and ink
over pencil on paper,
24⅝ × 18″ (62 × 46 cm).
Art Institute
of Chicago (gift of
Robert Allerton).

above right: 68.
Henri Matisse.
*Dancer Resting
in an Armchair.*
1939. Charcoal
on paper,
25¼ × 18¾″
(64 × 48 cm).
National Gallery of
Canada, Ottawa.

To be perceived as energetic a drawn line must have open ends, not be closed into a shape. Line plays a special role in the expression of energy and mass, lines with free ends being an important way to express energy, and lines with their ends joined to form shapes a way to indicate the existence of masses. The quality of the lines—their direction, smoothness, variability, and the apparent speed with which they were drawn—controls the amount and kind of energy or mass and gives meaning to the action or shape.

Vincent van Gogh's drawing *Grove of Cypresses* [67] is mostly composed of short curving lines with free ends. It would be hard to imagine a more energetic design. Most of the lines end in space and do not close into shapes. That increases the feeling that they represent a gesture rather than a boundary. Many of the things represented in the drawing are solid masses—tree trunks, a farmhouse, the surface of the earth—but Van Gogh used mostly unclosed lines to represent them, which reduces their massiveness. The gestures of his hand are clear in the short curving or spiraling marks, which show a strong motion and no hesitation. Van Gogh is letting us see that the trees seem to him more important for the growing life they embody and the agitation of their leaves than for their solidity and permanence.

Dancer Resting in an Armchair by Matisse [68] has such powerful, swiftly drawn lines, lines that retain so much energy, that we hardly believe the dancer is resting. The springy curves, opposing each other on the inside and outside of the legs, and widening to form the arms, suggest a rising, opening movement like a dancer leaping up. The lines just barely join to make shapes; they weaken where they are about to join the next line at the waist, neck, and shoulder. Matisse joined the lines so loosely to tell us that it was the energy of the dancer that impressed him, not the restfulness.

The style of drawing for which Matisse is most famous is that seen in his portrait of Louis Aragon [69], in which simple lines try to tell us everything. Many of the lines have free ends, suggesting the energy of the man. Yet the lines

69. Henri Matisse.
Louis Aragon. 1942.
Pen and ink on paper,
20¾ × 15¾"
(53 × 40 cm).
Fondation Capa, Sutton
Manor Arts Centre,
Hampshire, England.

are long enough that we begin to see shapes. The outline of the head is almost entirely closed, even though it runs off the page, and that helps us see it as a solid and the area outside the line as space. The effect of solids and spaces is strong enough that we see the right hand, especially, as overlapping the body and coming forward. This is another use of line, as the contour of a mass. A contour line, the ancient Roman Pliny wrote, "should appear to fold back, and so enclose the object as to give assurance of the parts behind, thus clearly suggesting even what it conceals."[3] These lines do not show us what we would call "the shape of a hand," but they suggest its mass as viewed from a particular angle.

Madame Matisse Among Olive Trees [70] shows patterns of short lines used to suggest the textures of surfaces and the forms of masses. Shapes are not the

70. Henri Matisse. *Madame Matisse Among Olive Trees.* 1905. Pen and ink on paper,
8 × 10½" (20 × 27 cm).

A POINT IN TIME: Classical Line

A particular style of drawing with long, even contour lines has been associated with classical style for more than two thousand years. Drawings done with this kind of line, even by a 20th-century artist, bring with them echoes of ancient Greece. Line drawing was the basis of ancient Greek painting, especially as we see it on Greek vases, which are almost the only surviving paintings from that period. In the battling warriors [71] painted on a wine cup by an artist named Psiax (active c. 520–515 B.C.) we see the controlled lines which the Greeks admired.

Line is even the subject of legend. The Greek painter Apelles of Kos went to the island of Rhodes to visit the famous painter Protogenes, whom he had not met. He called at Protogenes' house, but an old woman guarding his studio told him the artist was out. Seeing a large panel on the easel ready for painting, Apelles snatched up a brush and painted a single fine line across the panel; then he left. When Protogenes returned he examined the line on the panel and concluded that Apelles must have visited him, for no one else could have drawn such a line.

That kind of precise drawing was admired in Roman times and has been revived repeatedly over the centuries, down to our own times. It is always associated with the idea of classicism, or an intellectual, controlled kind of art in which line and shape are more important than color. In the Renaissance this style was used by Botticelli. In the 19th century, Jean Auguste Dominique Ingres (*ANG-gruh*) (1780–1867) not only used the style but thought everyone else should too. Since he was the most influential person on the committee choosing artists to receive

71.   Psiax. Greek warriors in battle, on a red-figured cup (kylix).
c. 515 B.C. Painted pottery, height 4⅜" (11 cm).
Metropolitan Museum of Art, New York (Rogers Fund, 1914).

subject; no line is completely closed, saying "This is the shape of this thing." Yet these sketchy lines strongly suggest a world of texture. The lines in *Louis Aragon* [69] and *Madame Matisse* [70] look quite different, a difference we summarize with the word *quality*, which can be defined as differences of length, width, color, solidity, spacing, and direction of lines. They all affect line quality, and consequently the mood and meaning of the drawing.

above left: 72. Jean Auguste Dominique Ingres. *Portrait of Merry Joseph Blondel.* 1809. Pencil on white paper, 7 × 5½″ (18 × 14 cm). Metropolitan Museum of Art, New York (bequest of Grace Rainey Rogers, 1943).

above right: 73. Pablo Picasso. *Sculptor, Crouching Model and Sculpted Head.* 1933. Etching, 10½ × 7⅝″ (27 × 19 cm). Museum of Modern Art, New York.

government commissions and fellowships, his intolerance of styles that were freer or more emotional became a controversial issue—an issue that lasted, in fact, for about a century.

In spite of Ingres' intolerance, his own drawings are still much admired. His portrait drawing of Merry Joseph Blondel [72] is typical of his work. He was one of the early artists to draw with graphite pencils (what we usually call "lead pencils"), which permitted shading and gray tones that the Greek vase painter could not achieve. But Ingres allowed himself only very limited effects of light and shadow, preferring to concentrate on a very pure line.

Pablo Picasso drew in almost every possible style, including the classical. Some of his most classical drawings were done on copper plates and printed as **etchings** (see Chapter 5 for a discussion of etching). In *Sculptor, Crouching Model and Sculpted Head* [73] we see the sculptor and his model—perhaps they are ancient Greeks, but the mood, like the style, is really timeless. The purity of the lines gives the picture a dream-like quality which would be lost in a style with contrasts of light and dark or heavier textures and illusions of mass. Classical line drawing, we can be sure, will always find artists to use it and audiences to appreciate it.

Line quality is especially affected by the speed with which the line was drawn. Artists often call a rapidly drawn line "free" and a slowly drawn line "tight." One is not better than the other, but in different periods the audience may strongly prefer one or the other. Matisse and most modern artists draw with a fast free line, but in the time of Rogier van der Weyden (*RAH-ger van der VI-den*) (1400–1464) a slow, controlled line was preferred. Rogier's drawing *Saint*

Mary Magdalene **[74]** has firm outlines and lighter patterns of lines as shading, every line placed exactly right. The lines give a sense of propriety, even primness, that fits this subject but would have been out of character for Louis Aragon **[69]**.

Pablo Picasso's *An Anatomy* **[75]** shows the use of lines to make shapes. These strange human-like constructions seem to have no energy at all, and it is not just because they are made out of boards and pillows. All the lines which represent them have been carefully closed. A simple line passes behind the figures, interrupted by their legs, and it too makes the edge of a shape, which is the floor. Short parallel lines, called **hatching**, have been used to shade the shapes and indicate shadows on the floor, a way to give the shapes a third dimension, or mass. In this way, line, which is one of the least massive of the elements, can be used to describe mass.

The uses of line are vast and varied, and it is especially in line that we see the human mind in contact with the world of experience. "My line drawing is the purest and most direct translation of my emotion," Matisse said.[4]

Some Uses of Line in Sculpture

Before we leave the element of line we must go to the other extreme, from lines drawn to lines carved, modeled, and constructed in sculpture. Boundary lines of shapes and contour lines of masses exist also in three-dimensional

74. Rogier van der Weyden. *Saint Mary Magdalene.* c. 1450. Silverpoint on ivory prepared paper, 6¾ × 5" (18 × 13 cm). British Museum, London.

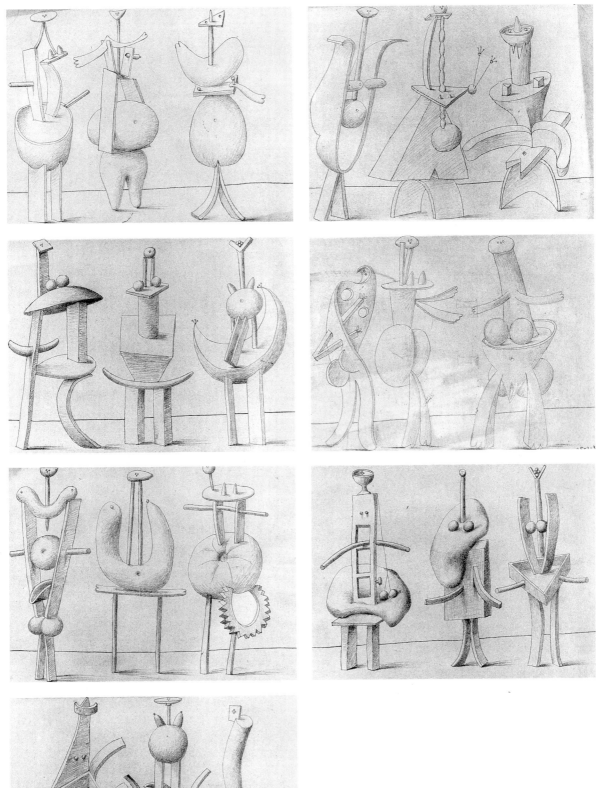

75. Pablo Picasso. *An Anatomy.* 1933.
Pencil on paper, Musée Picasso, Paris.

forms. In Matisse's *The Back IV* [76] the deeply cut angles where the body meets the background and the hair overlaps the back are seen as lines enhanced by contrasts of light and shadow. These smooth continuous lines serve to emphasize the shapes, just as they would in a drawing, the light and texture turning the shapes into masses. The earthiness of mass is the dominant expression; the function of the lines is to define the shapes and masses.

The unknown sculptor who carved the figure called *Saint Theodore* [77] saw his problem differently: how do you represent the soul in stone? All artists face that problem to some degree—how to use materials such as paint or stone to represent the immaterial—the spirit, or thought. This artist did not have the opportunity to choose a less massive material because his sculpture was part of the decoration of a Gothic cathedral and had to be made of stone. Yet he did everything possible to help us see the soul within the stone. The man is slender, with a long face, which helps us believe he is not given to such earthly vices as gluttony. Even more important, though, is the long tunic which is almost flat near the shoulders and falls into a dense pattern of shallow folds which make vertical lines, many of them ending in spear-like shapes at the top. These unclosed lines are not only vertical, leading our eyes heavenward, but they maximize energy and minimize mass. We might doubt that the saint had the strength to be a soldier if we could not see his arms, their solidity and breadth emphasized by the texture of the chain mail over them. The sculptor avoided horizontal lines, which would recall the horizon and the earthly world, and indeed gave the saint such a heavy sword that even his belt is dragged down to a steep diagonal. Along with the sword and spear, the belt adds to the pattern of rising lines. Here line played an important part in opposition to the massive character of the stone.

In 1977 the American sculptor Carl Andre (b. 1935) made a sculpture for the German city of Münster consisting of, as the title says, *97 Steel Line* [78]. A work of art always changes its surroundings by its presence, but this line of steel plates incorporates its surroundings and makes them become art along with it. The lake and distant steeple become lines and shapes by the force of the line pointing to them. This is not an imaginary line—we will examine the compositional uses of imaginary lines later—but a material reality. It is an open line, which makes it active, like the gesture of pointing or the motion of walking. Its separate plates suggest stepping stones, drawing us into a quick measured movement along its length. Since the grass remains the same on both sides, it is not a boundary or a contour. It seems miraculous that such a simple thing could unify everything within the horizon, but that is the power which the elements of art have, to give form and meaning to the random experience of the world.

Shape

In our common language we use the word **shape** for both two- and three-dimensional forms—we speak of "the shape of a car," for example. But artists usually use the word "shape" mainly for two-dimensional forms and speak of three-dimensional forms as "forms" or "masses" because for artists there are great differences between the two- and three-dimensional arts. This section will be concerned with two-dimensional shapes. Three-dimensional shapes will be discussed under the heading "Mass and Space."

A **shape**, then, is a two-dimensional surface with a boundary or edge—the basic way we represent a thing. As small children we move from scribbling toward drawing and begin to make circles that stand for everything—people, animals, houses, trees. A five-year-old [79] even shows the teeth of a saw as circles, not thinking of them as shapes but merely as signs for "thing."[5] Later we

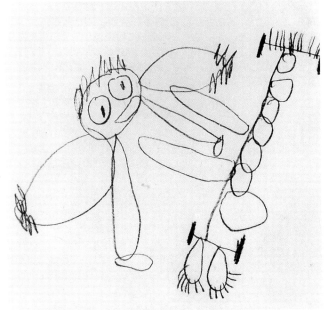

left: 78. Carl Andre. *97 Steel Line.* 1977. Steel plates, environment. Landesmuseum für Kunst, Münster, West Germany.

below: 79. Five-year-old. *Man with a Saw.* c. 1960. Crayon on paper.

80. Henri Matisse.
Blue Nude I. 1952.
Cut paper, paint;
45⅝ × 30¾"
(116 × 78 cm).
Beyeler Gallery, Basel.

learn how to make more different shapes, but even as adults we diagram things by drawing simple shapes, showing one category by circles, another by squares. In other words, generalization about conceptual or visual reality starts with shapes. Still, shapes are remote from earthly experience because there are no two-dimensional things in nature. Perhaps it is that "purity" that gives shape its elegance for us. Just as lines express action and textures hint at mass and strength, shape expresses a state of existence divorced from gross material.

Matisse frequently used cut-paper shapes as a way of designing paintings, but in his later years he began to make cut-paper designs in powerful colors as finished works of art. *Blue Nude I* [80] is one of those, cut from paper which had been painted a brilliant blue. Matisse used scissors, not trying to hide the cuts or blend them into a smooth line, but cutting freely and directly. Just as he often used line to arrive at a "sign," in this cut-paper design he uses shape for the same purpose, to arrive at the simplest possible expression of the subject, one that seems inevitable and unchangeable, to which nothing need be added or taken away.

Matisse's blue nude is seen as a figure against a white background. It demonstrates the idea of *figure-ground relationship* which artists must keep in mind as they work with shapes. The relationship of a line to the paper on which it is drawn is often uncertain: is the line the edge of an imaginary shape, or perhaps a cut in the paper? As soon as the line is closed into a shape we see the shape surrounded by a background surface or space. The background is the **ground**, the shape the **figure**. It is usually easy to make the figure (shape) stand out against the ground; it is harder to keep the two closely related by color, texture, or additional shapes to preserve the unity of the design.

The moment a second shape is added the design grows much more complex. Armando Morales (mor-AH-lace) (b. 1927) reminded us over and over that his *Study of a Figure* [81] was made of shapes, with no depth despite the overlapping parts and the angle of the wall suggesting space. A brown triangle in the lower left seems to be a folded corner, hinting that the figure is just a drawing on a piece of paper. Artists use the term "negative shape" for places in a design where the ground shows between elements of figure, which might be called "positive shapes." Morales takes that concept to an extreme, seeming to cut out a part of the leg of the figure, leaving shadowy emptiness. *Study of a Figure* is psychologically disturbing because it presents a shape that is solid enough to cast a shadow, but has no thickness, and whose positive human shape is invaded by a negative shape suggesting this is not a human figure but merely abstract shapes.

For the artist the most important feature of shape is its expressive potential. We observers identify with those expressions, as if the shapes were actors dramatizing them for us. We identify instinctively with the restfulness of horizontal lines and shapes and their relation to the earth, with the dignity and alertness of the vertical, and the energy and action of diagonal lines and shapes. We understand without being told that curving shapes are like our bodies and other living things, whereas angular shapes relate to inorganic, mental, or manufactured things.

Value

Our eyes are sensors of light; without light we cannot see color or shapes, or anything else, and in that respect light is the most basic attribute of the visible world. For the artist representation of light and shadow grows out of the effects

81. Armando Morales. *Study of a Figure.* 1969. Oil on canvas, 5'3¼" × 4'3½" (1.6 × 1.3 m). Huntington Art Gallery, University of Texas at Austin (Gift of Mary Brewster McCully, 1969).

In Detail: Collage

The style called Cubism, which one would expect always to emphasize cubical masses, turned in its later years (about 1912) to an emphasis on shapes and textures, leaving the cubical aspect for the viewer to imagine. The flatness of the shapes was intensified by the new invention **collage** (*ko-LAZH*; French for pasting), which means cut and pasted paper, or other things, added to the painted surface. In Picasso's *Violin and Guitar* [82] it is the double curve with a printed wood grain which is pasted on.

No one considers Matisse's *Blue Nude I* a collage because it is purely cut paper, without the combination of painting or drawing, but it is obviously related to collage. Matisse and Picasso were part of a generation of artists who were trying to revolutionize art by giving the form more prominence; in this case, emphasis was on the element of shape. One way to do that was to focus the observer's attention on the **picture plane** (the actual surface of the paper or canvas), rather than on the illusion of space within it. The cut and pasted parts are very obvious shapes which set a standard of flatness which the remaining parts of the design play up to. In *Violin and Guitar* none of the shapes, even those with heavy surface texture, are quite as definite as shapes as the wood-grained shape with the double curve that was pasted on. Collage is a very effective way to focus attention on shape, and on the picture plane, which is another shape, a surface without real depth. The pasted materials, like a famous actor playing a surprising role, remain themselves—a piece of newspaper or a segment of wallpaper—but adopt a new shape to fit the new design.

An artist whose name is especially identified with collage is Kurt Schwitters (*SCHVIT-terz*) (1887–1948), though he called his collages by another name, trash-pictures (*Merzbild* in German). Collage was already a well-established technique for making abstract art when Schwitters took it up in 1919, considering it an ideal way to express the anguish and disillusionment of World War I. The **Dada** movement, of which he was a part, felt that the horrors of that war invalidated all reason and that the only valid art must be irrational, absurd, and made of humble materials of everyday existence, as we see in *Cherry Picture* [83], made of things the artist scavenged from his environment. Many of the Dada artists later became members of the **Surrealist** group, which emphasized the psychological in art and also promoted collage as a way of finding unexpected and irrational connections.

For Dada and Surrealist artists collage was a way to bring objects from the real world into the picture, and their shapes often were not the point. That approach was different from Picasso's; for him collage was a way to strengthen the power of the shapes. It was no accident that musical instruments were common subjects in Picasso's collages, such as *Violin and Guitar,* since music is disembodied in a way he wanted his new style to be. Shape is unearthly, much as music is. By using angular and geometric shapes Picasso expressed an idea that music is intellectual and inorganic, more like a crystal than like a plant.

84. Jan Vermeer. *The Guitar Player.* 1671. Oil on canvas, 21 × 18¼" (53 × 46 cm). Iveagh Bequest, Kenwood, London.

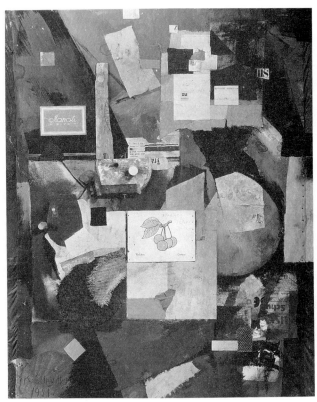

above left: 82. Pablo Picasso. *Violin and Guitar.* 1913.
Oil and pasted paper on canvas, 35 × 25″ (90 × 64 cm). Philadelphia Museum of Art
(Collection of Mr. and Mrs. Walter C. Arensberg).

above right: 83: Kurt Schwitters. *Cherry Picture.* 1921.
Collage and gouache on cardboard, 36⅛ × 27¾″ (92 × 70 cm). Museum of Modern Art, New York
(Mr. and Mrs. A. Atwater Kent, Jr., Fund).

of **value**, which in this case means not market or cultural value, but the range from black through an infinite gradation of grays to white. You can get an idea how that works by examining *The Guitar Player* **[84]** by Jan Vermeer (1632–1675). Bright white light pours in from the upper right on the young woman, grading across the cream-colored wall from very dark brown below the window to nearly white at the far left. The side of the woman away from the light is in dark values, the side toward the light, in light values. Her hair and flesh, the yellow of her coat, and the green of her skirt all change value dramatically depending on their illumination. If we extract a slice of the painting **[85]** and look at it in black and white we can see the full range of values used by Vermeer, an infinite gradation of tones from black to white.

The use of light and shadow to produce illusions of mass and space was a subject of careful study by artists of the Renaissance in Europe. The Italian word **chiaroscuro** (*kee-aro-SKOO-ro:* light, chiaro, and shadow, oscuro) is still used to refer to a kind of drawing popular in the Renaissance. It was done in black and white on colored paper, as we see in Hans Baldung's (1484–1545) spooky draw-

85. Section across the middle of Vermeer's *The Guitar Player* to show value relationships.

The Elements of Art —————— 65

ing, *Death and the Maiden* [86]. The black acts as shadows, the white as highlights, and the color of the paper is the middle tone. Chiaroscuro drawings were done on paper of various colors—brick red or brown, gray-green or gray-blue—but as long as the paper was a medium value, comparable to a gray, the result was a convincing illusion of mass. The extreme contrast of light and dark in such drawings also heightens the drama. Works in which the value range is very limited tend to have a cooler emotional tone, while high contrasts give a stronger expression.

Punchinellos [87] by Giambattista Tiepolo (*jahm-bah-TEES-tuh tee-AYP-o-lo*) (1696–1770) was drawn with a pen and dark brown ink and shaded with a brush, the ink being thinned with water to modulate the shadows. Notice that the figure on the left casts a shadow on the floor and that his face is in shadow, except for his gigantic nose. You can see clearly that the light source is on the left. Although the background is plain white, each form is not only outlined but shaded with tones to give it roundness. The lines drawn around the figures do not exist in nature, but the play of light and shadow is powerful enough that we believe in the illusion of solid figures in a brightly lighted space.

Artists often make use of light and dark values that do not refer to visible light and shadow. A bowl painted by a Mimbres (*MIM-bres*) Indian [88] is a good example of this use of abstract values. That is, the white does not represent light and the black does not stand for shadows. Two mountain lions follow each other around the interior of the bowl, each of them marked by a great zigzag *S*. The painting is in black on white, all the paint the same solid black with no transitional tones of gray. The absolute contrast of value harmonizes with the confidence the artist demonstrated in the drawing. His—or very likely her—hand never shook or hesitated, and the two animals are amazingly alike. Even in painting on pottery it is possible to thin the paint and make a gray tone, but the artist wanted an effect of total black on pure white. Visually we do experience gray tones in the areas of hatching, where sets of black lines are separated by exposed lines of the white background.

Modern book designers and illustrators have to consider abstract value because it appears in the text. To harmonize with a text (in Latin), Aristide Maillol (*my-OL*) (1861–1944) made a woodcut design of two wild forest spirits

88. Mimbres Indian. Bowl with mountain lions. c. 950–1150. Painted pottery, 5½ × 11¾" (14 × 30 cm). Private collection.

[89] in solid black and white. Notice how similar the printed marks of the figures and background are to the printed marks of the text. Yet the picture is easy to understand, and we do not confuse it with the writing.

The Chinese ink painting by Shen Chou (jo) [90] also harmonizes writing and picture, but the whole range of values appears, from white through grays to

left: 89. Aristide Maillol. Title page for *Carmina* by Q. Horatius Flaccus. c. 1928. Woodcut print on paper, 7½ × 5½" (19 × 14 cm).

below: 90. Shen Chou. *Poet on a Mountain.* c. 1500. Brush and black ink on paper, 15 × 23¾" (38 × 60 cm). Nelson-Atkins Museum of Art, Kansas City, Missouri (Nelson Fund).

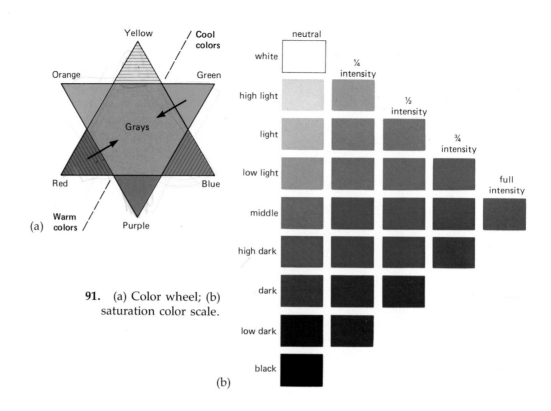

91. (a) Color wheel; (b) saturation color scale.

black. The poem in the upper left tells us: "White clouds encircle the mountain waist like a sash, Stone steps mount high into the void where the narrow path leads far." The painter wanted the mountains to recede from near to far, as the poem suggests, so he used strong contrasts to show the nearer parts and pale grays for the more distant ones. Still, we cannot tell whether the sun is shining and the poet casts no shadow.

Color

For the artist *color* is usually light reflected from a surface, but it may be a beam of light from an electric source or a sunbeam through a prism. Whatever the source, the color will have a certain hue, an intensity, and a value. **Hue** is the named color, such as red, defined scientifically as light of a certain wave length. **Intensity** (sometimes called saturation or chroma) describes the purity of the color. **Value** is the amount of black or white mixed with the color. Intensity is naturally reduced by the addition of black (which makes a **shade** of the color) or white (which makes a **tint**).

Artists working in different mediums think of color in somewhat different terms. A painter thinks of colors as paint in a tube or can which take their color from a **pigment**, a mineral or organic powder. Every painter knows that the three basic colors—called **primary colors**—from which all the other colors can be mixed are red, blue, and yellow. For an artist working in video, or in any medium in which color is cast by a bulb or electric source rather than reflected from a colored surface, color is a beam of light and the primary colors are red, blue, and green. Light reflected from a surface and cast light mix in surprisingly different ways.

Here we will consider color from the standpoint of the artist using paint or pastels. Color relationships are diagrammed on a **color wheel**, usually drawn as a six-pointed star **[91a]** made of opposed triangles. The first triangle has the three *primaries* (red, yellow, blue) at its points. The second has the *secondary* colors: orange between red and yellow, green between yellow and blue, and purple between blue and red. Each of the secondary colors is made by mixing its neighboring primaries. Between all of these points is an infinite variety of *tertiary* (third-stage) colors, such as blue-green and red-orange, made by mixing primaries and secondaries together.

The color wheel places primaries opposite secondaries: red and green opposite each other, yellow opposite purple, blue opposite orange. Those pairs are called **complementary colors**. If you mix complements in equal measure, you get a neutral gray in which the intensity of each color is canceled by that of its opposite. The mixture of complements produces the least intense reflection of light from the painted surface. If a color in your painting is too intense, too radiant—you may say it is "too bright"—then you can add a few drops of its complement to gray it. You can also use black to reduce the intensity of a color by making a shade, or dilute it with white to make a tint. **[91b]**.

One of the reasons painters must rely on experiment when they work with color is that our eyes produce afterimages in complementary colors. You can try this by staring for a few seconds at any intensely colored surface and then quickly looking at a plain white surface. You will see the shape of the colored area but in the complementary color. Such optical effects inevitably occur when we look at paintings, and the artist must simply look and change colors until the intended effect is achieved.

Richard Diebenkorn's (b. 1922) *Ocean Park No. 21* **[92]** is a subtle study in color on a canvas so large (7 feet 9 inches by 6 feet 9 inches; 2.4 by 2.1 meters) that it seems to surround you with color as you stand before it. At the upper

92. Richard Diebenkorn. *Ocean Park No. 21.* 1969. Oil on canvas, 7'9" × 6'9" (2.4 × 2.1 m). The Art Museum, Princeton, New Jersey (on loan from the Schorr Family Collection).

above: **93.** Persian, Herat School. *Bahram Gur in the Turquoise Palace on Wednesday.* 16th century. Book illustration, miniature. Metropolitan Museum of Art, New York (gift of Alexander Smith Cochran, 1913).

above right: **94.** Pablo Picasso. *The Old Guitarist.* 1903. Oil on panel, 4'1½" × 2'8½" (1.2 × 0.8 m). Art Institute of Chicago (Helen Birch Bartlett Memorial Collection, 1926.253).

center are tiny strips of red and blue, and a larger strip of yellow. Those primary colors orient your eyes, give a solid base from which you can float off into mixtures and grays. Moving downward, you enter a green that has been grayed with red (and also lightened with white), and then a red that has been grayed with some green. Off to the left you find grayed yellows, with tiny areas and lines of blue, and a border of an intense red, its shade darkening toward the top. Right of the center are large areas of very grayed blue; that is, orange has been added, along with white to make a tint. The painting is about color. The primaries are each presented once; then they reappear in mixtures which reduce their intensity. Such a description sounds very scientific, but the result is not cold-blooded. It could be compared to a muscial theme and variations or a deliciously seasoned dish.

Bahram Gur in the Turquoise Palace on Wednesday [93], a Persian book illustration, shows a decorative use of color. For the Persian artist each color belongs to the surface or thing represented, quite a different attitude from Diebenkorn's, in which color belongs only to the painting. Color represents tile walls and floors, plants in the garden, sky, and clothing, but which color is chosen for each part is dictated by the artist's experience of such scenes and by decorative considerations. The natural color of the things shown gives the artist a general hue, but each color appears at a high intensity, undiluted by shades for shadows and white highlights. Flat color, in which color areas do not vary, gives extra emphasis to color, which we enjoy for its beauty.

Color is the most emotional part of art, and in that sense the most like music. We use color names for our moods—feeling blue, seeing red, for example—and artists consider carefully the emotional affect of their color schemes. Picasso's *The Old Guitarist* [94] is painted all in blues and grays; it is a composition about sadness. Picasso was about 22 when he painted this, one of a

A POINT IN TIME: The Impressionists' Color

"Never paint except with the three primary colors and their immediate derivatives!" That was the advice of Camille Pissarro to his friend Paul Cézanne. All the browns and black, for a long time among the basic colors for the painter, had been eliminated from Pissarro's palette.

If brown and black are eliminated, how can shadows be represented? The **Impressionist** painters believed in working outdoors, with their landscape and figure subjects before their eyes. By experience they learned that shadows were not merely black, but had colors of their own. They began to color the shaded areas with the complement of the local color; that is, the shadows on a red skirt would be painted by mixing green with the red, the shadows on yellow drapery would be purple. The best test of color in nature, they found, was in snow scenes in which the ground was white, not brown, and the surrounding colors reflect on the snow.

Pierre Auguste Renoir (*ruh-NWAHR*) (1840–1919) once commented on a snow scene by another painter, giving a lesson on Impressionist color:

White does not exist in nature. You admit that you have a sky above that snow. Your sky is blue. That blue must show up in the snow. In the morning there is green and yellow in the sky. These colors must also show up in the snow when you say you painted your picture in the morning. Had you done it in the evening, red and yellow would have to appear in the snow. And look at the shadows. They are much too dark. . . . Shadows are not black; no shadow is black. It always has a color. Nature knows only colors. . . . White and black are not colors.

Although in theory Impressionist painters believed in recording only their "impression" of what was actually before their eyes, in practice that was not always convenient or possible. Renoir's painting *Blonde Bather* [95] shows the adaptation of Impressionist ideas about color to a subject which was only partly before the eyes of the painter. The model who actually posed was his wife, Aline, but the scene of a sea coast was imagined. Shadows in flesh are purple, and orange hair turns toward blue in the shadows. The background is yellow in the highlights, purple in the shadows. Black is confined to an accent in the eyes. Although Renoir did not follow strict Impressionist theory in imagining the background, his color was entirely Impressionist.

———
Quotations from notes taken by Dr. Ernest L. Tross, quoted in J. Rewald, *The History of Impressionism,* 4th ed. (New York: Museum of Modern Art; distributed by New York Graphic Society, Greenwich, Conn., 1973) 210.

95. Pierre Auguste Renoir. *Blonde Bather.* 1881. Oil on canvas, 32³/₁₆ × 26″ (82 × 66 cm). Sterling and Francine Clark Art Institute, Williamstown, Massachusetts.

left: 96. Michelangelo. *Nude Figure from the Back.* 1496–1500. Pen and ink on paper, 16½ × 14¼" (42 × 36 cm). Casa Buonarroti, Florence.

above: 97. Frank Lloyd Wright. Living room, Taliesin, Spring Green, Wisconsin. 1925.

series of pathetic subjects he painted then all in blue. Though that was a hard period for the young painter, who was very poor, his blue paintings do not necessarily mean he was feeling gloomy. The painting is *about* feeling sad and full of regrets; that was the artist's theme, but painting itself requires work, and work requires a reasonably energetic and optimistic mood in the painter.

There is no reliable way to predict how color will behave in a composition, and all we can do is look carefully. Blue, you might predict, will look sad, but a vivid blue may remind you of the sky on a sunny day, or a bright day at the seashore. Picasso made sure his blue guitarist would be sad by using a variety of gray-blue shades with black and white. It does not require a mental effort to receive the emotional message of color; we experience color and its mood spontaneously and passively.

Texture

Whether rough or smooth, there is no surface that lacks texture. The word *texture* refers to our experience of touch, either actual roughness or smoothness or illusions produced by value contrasts such as we see in Michelangelo's (1475–1564) drawing **[96]**. Modern life tends to sensitize us to visual experience and make us somewhat indifferent to touch, but texture is one of the important resources of the artist. Most people find soft or rough textures, with their strong appeal to the sense of touch, relaxing and pleasant, and for that reason they are often used in interior designs for homes and environments meant to be restful. The rough stone walls of Frank Lloyd Wright's (1867–1959) own home, called Taliesin, in Wisconsin **[97]** are an unusually rugged example of interior use of texture, relieved by the smooth ceiling with its rafters and the soft pillows and rugs. The naturalness of the materials and their soft colors enhance the sense of escape from the industrial world of work in which most of us spend much of our lives.

In arts in which representation is absent or relatively unimportant the real texture is always a major factor. Textile arts always appeal to us for their texture, even when they are used for pictorial tapestry. When the textiles are used for our clothing we pay special attention to texture. Mariano Fortuny's (1871–1949) famous pleated silk dresses [98] were always in a solid color to allow the shining pleated texture its full impact, unrivaled by color changes. Real texture is a basic consideration in all the things we use in our daily life—clothing, furniture, the interiors of our houses and cars, the settings of our tables—and we can treat them as art or not, yet they express our way of life even when we think of them as purely utilitarian.

Even in the representational arts, real texture plays another role which we have not yet considered. This is the texture of the marks made by the artist, which form a kind of screen through which we experience the world of his or her creation. As soon as you have become accustomed to Vincent van Gogh's rugged texture of brush strokes in *Starry Night* [99] you accept it unconsciously and "see through it" to the subject. The texture of brush strokes performs two functions: it unifies the various separate parts of the design into one composition (the paint texture is the only thing every part has in common with every other part), and it reminds us that the painting was made by an individual who made this distinctive texture as a personal mark, like a signature.

Representational artists have the problem of placing shapes on a background—the **figure and ground** relationship mentioned earlier. We think of the figure as solid and textured and the ground as empty space without a texture. Artists rarely have any difficulty in making figures stand out from the ground; it is more difficult to keep them sufficiently unified to provide a single artistic experience that fills the whole canvas or paper. Textured surfaces are also perceived as closer than empty surfaces and that reinforces the tendency of textured surfaces to separate from empty ones. To keep the figure and ground unified, to keep them from separating too much, Van Gogh employed his heavy brushstroke over the whole canvas, for solids and spaces alike.

left: **98.**   Mariano Fortuny. Delphos gown. 1907–1949. Pleated silk.

below: **99.**   Vincent van Gogh. *Starry Night.* 1889. Oil on canvas, 29 × 36½″ (74 × 93 cm). Museum of Modern Art, New York (Lillie P. Bliss Bequest).

Edwin Smith's (1912–1971) black-and-white photograph *In the Chestnut Avenue, Croft Castle, Herefordshire* [100], is a composition in light and dark, but it is also a study in texture. It is doubtful that we would be able to appreciate illusions of texture, such as that of the chestnut trees in the photograph, if we had never been able to experience such textures with our fingers. Knowing real textures permits us to understand the illusions of texture which play important parts in the two-dimensional arts. The shapes and masses in a work of art all have textures, and the artist must take into account not only the real texture but also the represented texture. The chestnut trees in the picture have rough textures, but the photograph has a smooth texture, and the viewer experiences both. Often we are unconscious of one of these textures—most often of the real texture of the work, since we take it for granted—but they both influence our understanding. It is strange, but generally we pay more attention to illusions of texture perceived with our eyes than to real textures perceived with our fingers.

Mass and Space

With mass and space we enter the third dimension: *mass* is solid material, *space* is the emptiness between solids. Real masses and spaces belong to sculpture, architecture, and the applied design fields such as furniture, clothing, and automobiles. *Illusions* of mass and space play an important part in the two-dimensional arts; they will be discussed below, after we have examined the uses of real mass and space.

Mass and space cannot exist separately, but artists have often tried to emphasize one and minimize the other. An Aztec sculpture in stone of the ancient god Quetzalcoatl (*KET-zal-CO-atl*, meaning Feathered Serpent) [101] is one in which space plays a small part, mainly as the space required by the observer. The masses of the body, somehow both human and serpent, bulge out as if growing from some central kernel. The figure looks up into the sky, which was

below: 100.
Edwin Smith.
*In the Chestnut Avenue,
Croft Castle,
Herefordshire.* 1959.
Photograph.

below right: 101.
Aztec. Feathered
serpent (Quetzalcoatl).
c. 1500. Gray lava,
height 10¾″
(27 cm). Cleveland,
Ohio, Museum
of Art (purchase
from the J.H. Wade
Fund, 41.46).

Analyzing Works of Art

Quetzalcoatl's domain (he appeared as the morning star), but he seems unaware of the space around him occupied by mere humans. Despite his heavenly powers, this Aztec spirit is represented as powerfully massive.

Several of our senses work together to help us appreciate mass and space. We can walk through spaces, touch masses, but mostly we rely on our eyes to show us spaces and the masses that shape them. Our eyes are dependent on light; it is only by light and shade that we can see masses and interpret the form of the spaces between them. All artists working with mass and space learn how to help the audience see mass by providing textures and controlled light; those two elements are indispensable for the perception of mass and space.

When Michelangelo began to plan a sculpture he made drawings in pen and ink in which hatching and crosshatching suggest the rough surfaces of masses seen in light [96]. Those pen lines were not imaginary, but represented the parallel grooves cut in the surface of the stone mass when Michelangelo used a flat chisel with comb-like teeth to refine the masses of his sculptures [102]. That texture intensifies the effects of light and shade, helping us see the masses of the torso more clearly. Our hands can detect the presence of mass without the aid of light or texture, but those elements are essential for our eyes to perceive mass. When variations of light and texture are present in a drawing we perceive an illusion of mass even in that non-massive art form.

Sculptural Mass and Space

When Michelangelo was working, four hundred years ago, sculpture was thought of as an art concerned with masses. Spaces were considered more a problem for the architect. But modern sculptors have claimed spaces as part of their art. In Matisse's bronze *The Serpentine* [103] the audience's space surrounds the figure and penetrates into it. The spaces between the body and the pedestal, the legs, and the arms and the body, seem to have as much form as the masses; they appear designed.

below left: 102.
Michelangelo. Detail of unfinished *Bearded Slave*. 1530–1534. Marble. Accademia, Florence.

below: 103.
Henri Matisse. *The Serpentine*. 1909. Bronze, height 22¼" (57 cm). Museum of Modern Art, New York (gift of Abby Aldrich Rockefeller).

In Detail: The Primordial Couple

If you step up close to the *Primordial Couple* [104], you can see the bench or stool they are sitting on. From a distance you might think the legs of the stool are simply irregular, like a crankshaft, but each of them is actually a crouching human figure. Stools like this are carved separately as sculptures in their own right. You might think they were furniture, but no living person ever sits on them.

On one stool [105] each leg is a figure very much like the larger figures of the *Primordial Couple,* the eight legs forming four more couples. In Dogon belief those four couples were the first human ancestors of the Dogon people and were descendants of the larger gods shown seated on a similar stool [104]. These ancestral couples that form the legs of the stool stand between two disks, the lower one symbolizing the earth, the upper the sky. If this little stool stands for the world, then the *Primordial Couple* sculpture represents the universe, with the divine creator couple seated on the world, which is supported by the first generations of people.

The balance of masses and spaces in the larger couple is true also of the stool. The log from which it was carved is still clear in its general form, but the sculptor has carved away about half the wood, especially the inner core, leaving the small figures as slender angular supports. Notice that the sculptor is not satisfied to create just masses and spaces, but uses also patterns of incised lines both on the figures and on the base and seat. Those lines and textures emphasize the massiveness of the forms, partly by contrast of decorated with plain areas, but also by letting us see lines and patterns in perspective, getting smaller as they recede in space. Dogon sculptors were not concerned about a slick finish, but they were sophisticated about their art. They used all the elements of art which contribute to sculptural form. Dogon sculpture was once considered "primitive," a word which suggests it is very ancient (= primary) or crude in technique or in expression. Probably all Dogon sculpture was actually carved in the last three hundred years, and it is still made today. It is admired both as good sculpture and as an expression of profound thought.

left: 104. Dogon, Mali. *Primordial Couple.* 19th century. Wood, height 29″ (74 cm). Metropolitan Museum of Art, New York.

above: 105. Dogon, Mali. Sacred stool. 19th–early 20th century. Wood, height 14¾″ (38 cm). Lester Wunderman Collection.

Such interdependence of spaces and masses has been especially interesting to sculptors in this century, inspired by the study of African sculptures in which those abstract relationships are especially important. Matisse was the first modern artist in Paris who was known to have purchased an African sculpture. *Primordial Couple* **[104]** by a sculptor of the Dogon (*DO-gahn*) nation, in the modern country of Mali, balances masses and spaces in a way modern European and American artists were trying to do. The sculpture represents the couple who were the first divine ancestors of human beings, the Dogon nation's Adam and Eve. The slender angular masses, rigid and vertical, tell us that these are not merely human beings. The open spaces are larger than in natural human figures, which is meant to suggest that these beings are especially spiritual. Matisse's *The Serpentine* and the African *Primordial Couple* have in common a near equality between masses and spaces. *The Serpentine*, while not a religious figure, has a spiritual quality also in that it seems to be deep in thought.

As the balancing of masses with spaces has become of interest to sculptors, their work has developed a closer relationship with architecture, as we can see in Henry Moore's (1898–1986) sculpture *The Arch* **[106]**. The artist stands beyond the opening of the natural-looking rocky gateway (actually this is a fiberglass cast). The opening is clearly part of the sculpture, perhaps the most important part. Moore's sculpture plays with the relation between masses and spaces in a way we usually associate with architecture—the name *The Arch* shows that Moore recognizes that fact. The visible interior space of *The Arch* reveals Moore's desire to emphasize the elements of mass and space for their own sakes.

Some younger sculptors have taken over a different kind of space, space quite unlike Moore's preferred outdoor settings, where the unlimited space of nature flows around and through his work. Judy Pfaff's (b. 1946) *3-D, 1983* **[107]** was built into a room 22 by 35 feet (6.7 by 10.7 meters) and about 12 feet (3.7 meters) high, and that is all the space it allows itself. As with *The Arch*, you can enter the space of the sculpture. "Peripheral vision is and always has been cru-

above left: 106.
Henry Moore.
The Arch.
1963–1969. Fiberglass
to be cast in bronze,
approximately 20' (6 m)
high. The Henry Moore
Foundation, London.

above: 107. Judy Pfaff.
Detail of 3-D, 1983.
1983. Installation using
mixed materials,
22 × 35'
(6.7 × 10.7 m).
Holly Solomon Gallery,
New York.

cial to my work," Pfaff says. "If you can look and see it all at once—then there is a false sense that you know it. I think that if half the work is in back of you, you'll never be coaxed into believing you know or see it all." That can only happen in sculptures which have spaces that can be entered by the audience. But Pfaff says, "I tried to include all the things that were permissible for painting, but absent in sculpture."[6] Line and color, which are important in her work, are elements that have traditionally played a larger part in painting than in sculpture; the room becomes a kind of three-dimensional canvas—we have entered inside the imaginary space of an abstract painting. The design of such complex works as Pfaff's is usually done now on a computer, which allows the artist to see on the screen an illusion of the space with all its shapes and masses. Computer programs permit the artist to rotate the design, move the masses around, and finally print the exact specifications. The final work is constructed by hand, but the computer serves as a sketchbook.

Illusions of Mass and Space

Illusions of mass and space play an important part in all the two-dimensional arts. Artists must know how to create illusions or avoid them when they want a flat two-dimensional appearance. As mentioned above, texture and light and shadow can be used to represent mass and space in two-dimensional arts, but in this section we will consider the effects of size and scale, perspective systems, and color in the representation of masses and spaces. Artists use these elements both to create illusions and to avoid illusions, depending on the content they wish to express.

Size and Scale

In shape and color everything in René Magritte's (*mah-GREET*) (b. 1898) *The Personal Values* [108] is just as we would expect to see it in our daily experience. If you concentrate on one item at a time, they are all faithfully depicted.

108. René Magritte. *The Personal Values.* 1952. Oil on canvas, 31½ × 39" (80 × 100 cm). Collection of Jan-Albert Goris, New York.

left: 109. Yves Tanguy. *The Extinction of the Species II.* 1938. Oil on canvas, 36¼ × 28¾" (92 × 73 cm). Patricia K. Matisse Collection. New York.

above: 110. *The Buddha's First Sermon.* Gandhara style, Kushan Dynasty, Pakistan. c. A.D. 200. Stone, height 26⅜" (67 cm). Freer Gallery of Art, Washington, D.C.

But even if we admit that someone might have a realistic sky painted on the bedroom walls, this is still a very strange room indeed because the sizes of things do not have the usual relationships. The simplest way to explain this is to say that Magritte wanted to startle us. Such variations from natural scale make us wonder, imagine symbolism, and look at our surroundings to make sure that nature truly remains as we thought it was.

Every artist who ever made a picture or sculpture had to make decisions about *size* and *scale*—size being the actual measurements of the work of art and of things presented or depicted in it and scale being the relationships of size among things. Decisions about size are straightforward and depend on the circumstances, but decisions about scale are a different matter. Scale is a graduated series of steps or degrees. In Magritte's painting the bar of soap, the match, and the comb are all size 1, followed by the shaving brush and glass, size 2, and the bed, cabinet, and rugs at 3—quite a different series of steps from those we see in daily life.

As we try to see Magritte's painting as natural, we may suggest to ourselves that the bed and cabinet must be farther away, but the locations of the comb and shaving brush prevent us from explaining the scale as produced by distance. *The Extinction of the Species II* **[109]**, by Yves Tanguy (*eve tahng-GHEE*) (1900–1955), demonstrates the power of scale to represent distance. Without a horizon line or any natural object whose size is known, Tanguy convinces us that we see a limitless plain populated by weird forms. Cast shadows and some thin white lines contribute to this impression, but the main factor is the size and position of the forms, all the smaller ones being higher on the canvas. *The Extinction of the Species II* is organized by size and position, but not in linear perspective (see the next section), of which size and position are just parts.

A graduated series of steps may be a perspective based on distance, or it may represent something entirely different, such as importance. *The Buddha's First Sermon* **[110]** shows the Buddha much larger than the other figures to represent his significance, although in life he was the same size as other people. If we

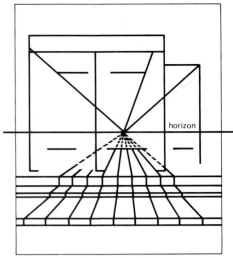

horizon

left: 111. Lorenzo Ghiberti. The Isaac panel, doors of Baptistery, Florence Cathedral. c. 1435. Bronze relief, 31¼" (79 cm) square.

above: 112. The perspective scheme in Ghiberti's Isaac panel **[111]**.

look back at Magritte's *The Personal Values* **[108]** with this idea in mind, the title becomes more meaningful: some things have more personal value to the painter than others and are shown larger. Grooming and habits (drinking, smoking) rank above furniture in his scale of values, and thus in size.

Four Systems of Perspective

We will examine four important systems of **perspective**: linear perspective, isometric perspective, an Oriental system of perspective, and aerial (or color) perspective. Each of these systems has something in common with our experience of the natural world, but in each case it is something different. Linear perspective, for example, shares with vision the factor of things diminishing in size as they are farther away from the observer. Oriental perspective shares the feeling that we are at the center of our own experience and that the world expands outward from where we stand. Isometric perspective conforms to our knowledge that parallel lines are parallel, whatever they may look like from any particular position. And aerial perspective places colors in relationships that conform with our experience of nature. Each of these systems is true to nature in its own way and untrue in other ways.

Linear Perspective.   *Linear perspective* is a system for representing masses in space using a scale in which size represents distance, closer things being larger than farther. Linear perspective seems so natural that it is hard to imagine that it needed to be invented, but it was, and the inventor was the Italian architect and sculptor Filippo Brunelleschi (*BROO-nuh-LESS-kee*) (1377–1446) in about 1430. Artists had been experimenting with scales of size based on distance for more than a century, but Brunelleschi discovered the vital principle in the system: that the scale of sizes had to reach zero at one point on the horizon (or eye level, which is the same thing), called the **vanishing point**.

One of the earliest examples of linear perspective (dated about 1435) is Lorenzo Ghiberti's (*ghee-BARE-tee*) (1378–1455) bronze relief of the story of *Isaac* [111]. Even though Ghiberti does not show the horizon line, you can easily find its location by extending all the lines that seem to be receding: the tops of the walls and the edges of the floor tiles [112]. Where those lines meet—and they must meet at one point—is on the horizon line, and it is the zero point of the scale, the vanishing point. You notice that the building is seen straight from the front; all the walls that do not recede are exactly parallel to the picture plane (that is, the actual surface of the bronze relief). This is very natural-looking but rather limited, since we cannot see any building from a corner view in this system. The kind of perspective Ghiberti used here is sometimes called *central perspective* [113], since the vanishing point is in the center, or near it. It is also called *one-point perspective* to distinguish it from *two-point perspective* [114], in which we see a corner view and the receding lines meet at two vanishing points at the outer edges of the horizon line. The more vanishing points used, the more natural the representation. Tall buildings, for example, diminish upwards, or, if we are on top looking down, downwards.

The most extravagant use of linear perspective was in **Baroque** churches and palaces, where it was used to make large buildings even larger by adding the illusion of still more space. Andrea Pozzo (*POT-so*) (1642–1709) painted on the flat ceiling of the Church of Saint Ignatius in Rome a scene symbolizing the

113.   Central perspective or one-point perspective.

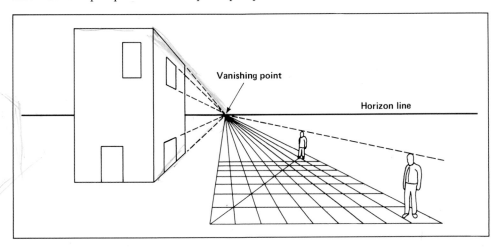

114.   Two-point perspective.

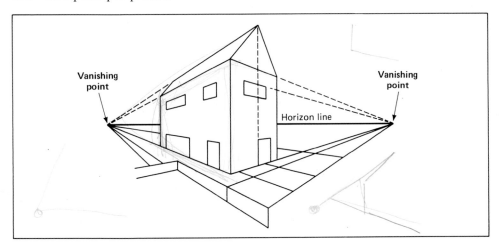

missionary work of the Jesuit Order [115]. The vanishing point is in the center of the ceiling, where Jesus accepts the saint into heaven. Everything that ascends toward the sky grows smaller as it approaches that point. At the edges of the photograph you can see the windows and arches of the real architecture of the building, but above the windows all the architecture is pure illusion. The flat ceiling acts as the picture plane, with the elaborate classical architecture vanishing upward through it evenly from all four walls.

Linear perspective has always fascinated people. The illusions can be very convincing because what it shares with our experience is one of the basic parts of vision: that more distant things appear smaller. The scale works best when everything in the picture is angular, such as buildings, railroad tracks, and roads, and it provides only general guidance in landscape paintings of hills and trees. Ghiberti made no attempt to fit the small area of landscape into his perspective scheme [111], beyond making the figure and the tree of a size approximately correct for their positions, and Pozzo relied on the architecture, not the clouds and the human figures, to create the illusion of space opening through the ceiling.

Oriental Perspective Systems. The Chinese painter Guo Xi (old style Kuo Hsi) (*gwo-shee*) (1020–1090) advised landscape painters: "There are three sizes for things. The mountain is bigger than the trees, and the trees are bigger than the men. If the mountains are not several dozen times larger than the trees, they are not considered big." He also described three types of views of mountains, which may be translated as "perspectives": "Looking up from below is called the high perspective; looking from the rim at the interior of mountains is called deep perspective, and looking toward the distance is called level perspective."[7] It is obvious that this does not refer to what Westerners mean by perspective, and when we look at Guo Xi's paintings, such as *Clear Autumn Skies over Mountains and Valleys* [116], we can see both the three sizes of things and the

115.   Andrea Pozzo. *Triumph of Saint Ignatius Loyola*, Church of Saint Ignatius, Rome. 1691–1694. Ceiling fresco.

Analyzing Works of Art

above: 116. Guo Xi. *Clear Autumn Skies over Mountains and Valleys*. c. 1060. Ink on silk; detail from scroll, 10¼ × 6'9⅜" (0.26 × 2.1 m). Freer Gallery of Art, Washington, D.C.

left: 117. School of Chou Wen-chu. *A Palace Concert*. 10th century. Ink and colors on silk, 19 × 27" (48 × 69 cm). Palace Museum Collection, Taichung, Taiwan.

different kinds of mountain views. Guo Xi also understood that mountains, trees, and men or houses appeared smaller if they were farther away, but neither he nor any other Far Eastern artist defined in writing a scale for representing things as they receded in the distance.

Yet when we look at Chinese and Japanese paintings we often find that a viewpoint was used in which the observer seems to be standing on the focal point of the scene and the world seems to expand outward from that point. That feeling is especially appropriate in landscape paintings, such as the one by Guo Xi [116]. When Oriental artists represented buildings or furniture, such as the table in *A Palace Concert* [117], they usually showed them with the parallel sides drawn parallel but on a diagonal, in what we shall see below is called an isometric view. But even in architecture artists sometimes used a perspective in which parallel lines actually spread apart as they recede into the distance, as shown by the sides of the platform used by a maker of rectangular floor mats (*tatami*) in a

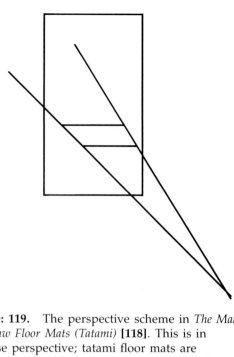

above: 119. The perspective scheme in *The Maker of Straw Floor Mats (Tatami)* **[118]**. This is in reverse perspective; tatami floor mats are rectangular, and this appears to be larger the farther away it gets.

118. Japanese. *The Maker of Straw Floor Mats (Tatami).* c. 1600. Watercolor and ink on paper, from a six-panel folding screen, *The Occupations*; each panel 21⅞ × 12" (55 × 30 cm). Art Museum of Greater Victoria, British Columbia, Canada.

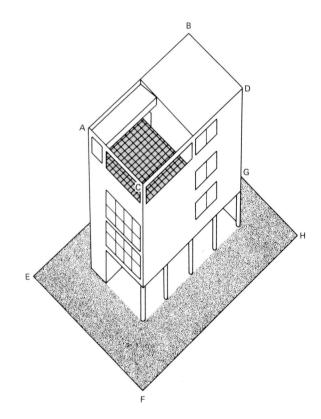

right: 120.
Isometric perspective.
Based on a house design by
Le Corbusier.

panel of a Japanese screen showing *The Professions* **[118]**. If you extend the sides of the rectangular platform, and walkways, they meet in the foreground **[119]**, harmonizing with that tendency we see in Oriental landscapes to suggest that the world expands to infinite size in the distance, rather than contracting into a single point, as Western linear perspective suggests.

When the horizon is shown in Oriental paintings it is usually a vast stretch of mountains or water, spreading into an infinity of space. "As to landscapes," wrote Zong Bing (Tsung Ping) (who lived from 375 to 443), "they exist in material substance and soar into the realm of the spirit."[8]

Isometric Perspective.   **Iso** (equal) **metric** (measure) means that the lengths of equal lines in nature remain equal in the drawing; the result is that parallel lines remain parallel and things do not get smaller as they get more distant. This system of scale is especially useful for technical and architectural drawing, so that with a scale ruler it is possible to measure every line and get the actual dimensions without worrying about their distance from the observer. The drawing **[120]** shows an isometric perspective. It is the angle view from above which is called isometric. The observer is, theoretically, at an infinite distance from the house, so parallel lines remain parallel. Three views (top and two sides) are combined in an isometric drawing, all their lengths in proper scale, but the angles distorted; you can see that the posts of the house are not drawn at right angles to the line of the floor, though we know they must be at right angles in reality. Lines AB and CD are parallel in the drawing as they are meant to be in the house, and the same is true of lines EF and GH. In linear perspective those sets of lines would be drawn meeting at a vanishing point or points.

Isometric perspective has been used in much drawing and painting, but for a different purpose. When Henri Matisse painted *Pink Nude* **[121]**, it was not his purpose to provide us with this woman's measurements. You must remember

121. Henri Matisse. *Pink Nude.* 1935. Oil on canvas, 26 × 36½" (66 × 93 cm). Baltimore, Maryland, Museum of Art (Cone Collection).

that Matisse's audience in 1935 was familiar with linear perspective. In traditional painting a figure would seem to recline on a surface which receded according to linear perspective. For that effect the white lines on the blue background should be focused on a vanishing point on the horizon. Matisse denied that he was making illusions; like a good Modernist, he was making only a painting.

Although linear perspective produces a superior illusion of natural appearance, it has the limitation of narrowing our view of the world down to a few specified points where all lines must focus. The vanishing point is defined as infinity in that system. The concept of infinity is important in both the other systems of scale, too. In Oriental perspective the whole horizon is infinity. In isometric perspective the position of the observer is defined as infinity, where we see the truth about parallel lines, not the accidental distortions produced by seeing things from a particular place. There are good reasons for using each of these perspective systems.

Aerial Perspective. Color has its own system of perspective, traditionally called **aerial perspective**. It is also sometimes called "color temperature," since it is based on what are called "warm" and "cool" colors. What we see is not really temperature, but the apparent relative distance of the paint surface from the viewer's eyes. This natural phenomenon began to be considered seriously only when landscape painting first became popular; the name "aerial perspective" was given it because things in the distance look more blue because we see them through more air. Now we know the explanation is not so simple. Each surface that reflects light appears to be a certain distance away from the viewer. Painters have learned that areas of different color on the same flat surface appear to be slightly different distances away from the viewer. The relative distances of those areas can be changed by changing the colors, so that one which seemed farther away can be made to appear closer. As a general rule, red, orange, and yellow—the so-called warm colors—appear a little closer than they are, while blue, purple, and green—the cool colors—appear to be a little farther away. But that general rule is only a very rough guide, for the positions of the colors are always related to their neighbors. Light and dark also have an effect, but it is even less predictable than the effect of warm and cool colors. For example, white may seem closest of all, or it may be the most distant.

Annibale Carracci (*ah-NEE-bah-lay kah-RAH-chee*) (1560–1609) was one of the early landscape painters. His *Landscape* [122] has deep yellows and browns in the foreground, with rough-textured dark brown tree trunks and detailed patterns of leaves. The middle ground is green, blue-green in the water, with grayed browns and greens on the left. In the background, around the pale gray-yellow of the cityscape, are blue-gray mountains and pale blue and purple hills. This pattern of colors, from warm (yellow, brown) in the foreground, through cooler greens in the middle ground, to very cool (pale gray blue) in the background, follows the system of aerial perspective. Carracci seems to have considered this system mainly useful for landscape painting and the result of seeing through air into deep distances. In more recent times it has become clear that aerial perspective is not an effect of the air, but is a feature of the colors and their interrelationships. That means that solid forms can be represented in painting as if they were sculptural solids by coloring nearer parts warm and farther parts cool. The colors then act as a kind of perspective.

Composing pictures on the basis of color was the special obsession of the French painter Pierre Bonnard (*bo-NAR*) (1867–1947). Color has become the main element in Bonnard's *Interior with Woman at Her Toilette* [123]. We are in a small dressing room with bright yellow walls, a tile floor in red, white, and blue, a mirror, and a white dressing table. Through an open door (note the doorknob) we see into a shadowy room where a woman can be seen bending over a wash basin. The pattern on the floor of the farther room intrudes into the area of the

122. Annibale Carracci. *Landscape.* c. 1590. Oil on canvas, 2'10¾" × 4'10¼"
(0.9 × 1.5 m). National Gallery of Art, Washington, D.C.
(Samuel H. Kress Collection).

dressing room; the walls and floors suggested by the shapes are confusing and
give us little help in figuring out the shape of the rooms. Bonnard intended us to
rely on the color. The large area of intense yellow is relatively close compared
with the bluer and purpler areas through the door. Notice that some of the

123. Pierre Bonnard.
*Interior with Woman at
Her Toilette.*
1938. Oil on canvas,
4'1¾" × 4'1¼"
(1.3 × 1.3 m). Yale
University Art Gallery,
New Haven,
Connecticut
(Katharine Ordway
Collection).

farthest parts and some of the closest are both white. What is the effect of that spot of blue on the white dressing table? Does it make the dressing table seem closer or farther? If you block it from your vision you can see that it plays an ambiguous, but very important, part in the composition by making a cool accent in a predominantly warm area, by tying the yellow side more closely to the shadowy room with its bluer tones, but also by making the spatial position of the white table uncertain relative to the yellow walls. Bonnard accepted the ambiguity, letting the dressing table slip back in space about even with the walls. Really convincing illusions of space were not part of his artistic intentions, even though his composition relied on the apparent distance of the colors in relation to each other. At first it looks as if the Persian illustration [93] might have a lot in common with the Bonnard, but their aims in the use of color were entirely different. The color is the most important element in both paintings, but for Bonnard each color belongs to a position in space within the painting, while for the Persian artist each color belonged to a thing portrayed.

There is more to color than its spatial expression. Although color provides much of the beauty and emotional expression we enjoy in art, understanding how an artist uses color demands some active mental effort. The artist has to think intelligently about color and may use it for its decorative beauty or its emotional effect, but also to create illusions of masses and spaces, or to remind us of the atmospheric effects of nature.

Time and Movement

We can perceive the passage of time, which has been called the fourth dimension, only by change. Most commonly the changes which suggest time are movements, like the movement of the hands of a clock, but they can just as well

124. Nancy Holt. *Sun Tunnels*, Utah. 1973–1976. Four concrete conduits; each: diameter 9′ (2.7 m), length 17′ (5.2 m).

be changes of light or color. We think of time as a regular continuous stream, but our sense of its passage is very irregular. One of the powerful effects of a work of art can be to stop time as we become absorbed in the details of the work before our eyes.

Yet change goes on ceaselessly in the natural world. Nancy Holt (b. 1938), like the builders of such ancient monuments as Stonehenge, in which the movements of celestial bodies dictated the plan of the temple, has designed modern sculptures which dramatize the passage of time in nature. Her *Sun Tunnels* **[124]** is composed of four concrete conduits 9 feet (2.7 meters) in diameter and 17 feet (5.2 meters) long, aligned to the sunrise and sunset at the solstices. The passage of time, measured by the movement of the sun, is an important part of their meaning. ''I'm interested in conjuring up a sense of time that is longer than the built-in obsolescence we have all around us,'' Holt says.[9] The slow, regular rhythms of the sun and seasons may be the basis of all our sense of time and change.

In recent art there has been considerable interest in actual movement of parts of the art. Earlier artists sometimes brought real movement into art using water in fountains, but in recent times **kinetic art,** or art that really moves, has been most often powered by wind or electricity. Alejandro Otero's (b. 1921) *Delta Solar* **[125]**, which stands beside the National Air and Space Museum in Washington, is unusual in that it is powered by sunlight, which hits the very light-weight reflecting sheets with sufficient force to keep them in rippling motion. Their movement is reflected in the pool, which also reflects the play of light from the structure, which seems about to take off into space. Like Holt's *Sun Tunnels, Delta Solar* is tuned to the sun, its motion and reflections turned on by sunlight and turned off by darkness, as time and motion occur in the universe.

Modern people seem to grow constantly more aware of time and motion. Surely those elements will play parts in our future art which we cannot even imagine now.

125. Alejandro Otero. *Delta Solar*, National Air and Space Museum, Washington, D.C. 1977. Stainless steel, 46'8½" × 27' (14.2 × 8.2 m). Gift of the people of Venezuela to the people of the United States on its Bicentennial.

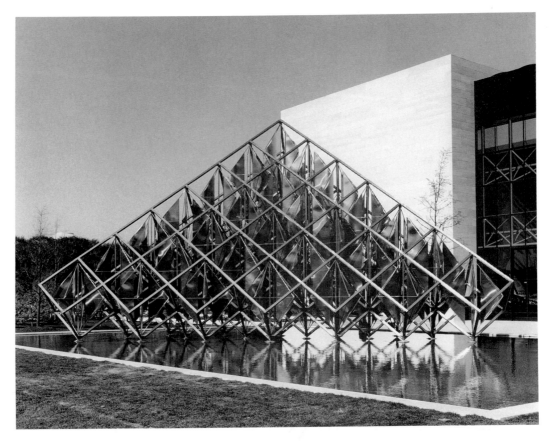

Summary for Review

The artist's problem is to make a material thing that is expressive. The **elements of art** (**line**, **shape**, **value**, color, mass and space, texture, size and scale) are the things and qualities the artist uses for expression. **Line** can be the sign for something, a gesture, the edge of a shape or the contour of a mass, and it has length, direction, and quality. **Shapes** are two-dimensional surfaces whose character is given by the line features of their edges and the color, value, and texture of their surfaces. Like lines, shapes exist in their pure forms only in our minds—there are neither lines nor any two-dimensional objects in our three-dimensional natural world—so they convey abstract ideas, lines expressing energy, shapes expressing an ideal elegance. Light and dark are called **value** and can be used to show illumination (or **chiaroscuro**) or as abstract tones. Color appeals to us for its beauty and emotional expression, but it has rules for mixing and the power to make spatial illusions with aerial perspective. *Mass* and *space* are the three-dimensional elements used mainly in sculpture, architecture, and many applied design fields (clothing, furniture, etc.). *Texture* is a basic feature of real materials. In the two-dimensional arts (drawing, painting, etc.) *illusions* of mass and space are important. They are created by *light and dark, texture,* and by systems of scale called **perspective** systems. We have considered four systems: *linear perspective, Oriental perspective,* **isometric perspective,** and **aerial perspective.** Each of them is true to nature in some ways and false in others. *Time,* a fourth dimension, is expressed by *movement,* often by movement powered by such natural forces as sunlight or wind.

Understanding Design

Our minds require that certain conditions be fulfilled before we understand a work of art, or anything else. These conditions are called the **principles of design**. The human mind operates on a set of rules—a kind of owner's manual for the mind—which reflect our need for pattern or order in our thinking. The way we fulfill that need we call "design." Since the mind is our main tool for dealing with the universe, we naturally see the universe as designed. That fact has given rise to most of the world's great religions and philosophies. Art, which is a product of the mind, is also organized by those same principles of design so that it can be grasped by other minds.

Works of art are designed by putting together the elements of art we looked at in Chapter 3, just as a writer puts together words and a composer puts together sounds. Various authorities define these principles differently, but everyone agrees on the fundamental idea, that design makes creative acts understandable by others. These are the major principles:

1. The Principle of **Unity**. The work must be understandable as a coherent unit. The audience must be able to tell what is the work and what is unrelated environment.
2. The Principle of **Variety**. The work must have enough variability to sustain the viewer's attention. The human eye moves constantly and is attracted by contrasts, so the work must appeal to the eye's need for change.
3. The Principle of **Balance**. The parts of the work must be in equilibrium. Since we observers are balancing ourselves against gravity, we identify with things in our environment which do the same. While we enjoy things that are precariously balanced, we will not look long at things that are disturbingly unstable.
4. The Principle of **Rhythm**. There must be an orderly pattern of movement through the work for our eyes, or in the case of city plans and buildings, for our bodies. Order is given to movement by rhythm, which is repetition according to a rule.
5. The Principle of **Emphasis**. Relationships among the parts of a composition reflect their relative power or significance. One part may be emphasized by a design which draws the observer's attention to that part, or the design may give equality to all parts.
6. The Principle of **Proportion**. The parts must be related according to a plan based on the artist's intentions. Proportions are affected by function and by meaning; the height of a chair is proportioned to the size of the people who will use it, and the size of the hands in a painting of a person depends on their importance to the meaning.

Designers and artists do what looks right to them, paying little conscious attention to the principles of design. These principles were discovered when people began to try to explain what qualities are shared by the works of art they

126. Egypt. The priest Niajj and his wife obtaining food and drink from the tree goddess. c. 1310 B.C. Painted limestone relief from Abu Sir, 22 × 23½″ (56 × 60 cm). Kestner Museum, Hanover, West Germany.

like best. Both works of art from ancient Egypt and by the younger American artists have unity and variety; they look balanced, and we find that our eyes move around them in a controlled pattern, as much in one as the other. All this means is that the human mind operated according to the same principles back in ancient Egypt, four thousand years ago, as it does today. You can easily imagine an ancient Egyptian artist reminding his apprentices, "You must not confuse your audience with too much variety, but, on the other hand, you must not bore them with too much unity."

When you look at the painted limestone relief [126] of the priest Niajj and his wife you see how an Egyptian artist actually expressed those principles. To understand the relief you need to know that the Egyptians believed that one of the possibilities of life after death was to return to the world of the living during the day as a bird and be fed by the tree goddess. The priest and his wife appear twice, once kneeling before the tree goddess, who blesses them with water and food (including even a roast duck), and again as human-headed birds. The design on the square slab of limestone is complete, so we can make an accurate judgment about the composition.

Only two carving styles were used on the Egyptian relief, a very low relief for all the pictorial parts, and narrow incised lines and shapes for the hieroglyphic writing. The writing and the picture tend to separate, but the way the picture overlaps the panels of writing in the streams of water and the woman's headdress keeps them joined. The nearly vertical and horizontal shapes in the tree, its arms, tray, and platform, and the straight backs and arms of the couple join the two parts of the composition, which is also tied together by the streams of water. All those features contribute to the unity of the design.

The contrast of the writing and pictures, of the pleated clothing with the large round shapes of the food and the small shapes of the leaves, contribute to variety. The design balances around the center formed by the man's head and hands. His head is set apart and emphasized by his collar or neck ornament. There are a series of repetitions which produce rhythm: branches and leaves, pleats and locks of hair, to name only the most obvious. Our eyes tend to move from the priest's head down to the bird-people, up the tree, down the streams of water to the couple, especially to the woman, and are led by their legs back to the bird-people again. The proportions tell us that the people are important, but dependent on the power of the tree, which is a little larger. The bird-spirits are smaller and not the real form of these people; the proportions make it clear that Niajj and his wife remain human beings.

Speaking to his painting students, Henri Matisse told them, ''What you are aiming for, above all, is unity.''[1] In *Artist and Goldfish* [127] we can see the strong unity Matisse sought, achieved by color as well as by shapes. An earlier version of the same subject [128] helps us understand what natural forms Matisse took as the source: a small table before a window which has an ornamental wrought-iron screen. The large areas (in 127) of white at the bottom, upper right, in the fishbowl, the top of the wrought iron, and the block at the right (probably the end of a couch), with the pale blue sky, form a unifying background, firmly joined by black shapes and lines. Variety is introduced with red and raspberry-colored fish, yellow and orange fruit, green leaves, maroon table legs, and some red areas on the right margin. The wrought-iron curls are important variations from the dominant straight lines. While the earlier painting seems intimate and cozy, this one has large, severe rhythms like powerful drumbeats (the black areas), and its vertical proportions and large plain shapes in black and white make it dignified and serious.

The Egyptian relief and the painting by Matisse help us see how the six principles work together, but it is also useful to examine each of the principles separately.

below left: 127.
Henri Matisse.
Artist and Goldfish.
1915. Oil on canvas,
4'9½" × 3'8"
(1.5 × 1.1 m). Museum
of Modern Art, New
York (Florence M.
Shoenborn and
Samuel A. Marx
Collection).

below: 128.
Henri Matisse.
Interior with Goldfish.
1914. Oil on canvas,
4'8¾" × 3'2⅝"
(1.4 × 1 m). Musée
Nationale d'Art
Moderne, Paris.

Unity

A work of art must appear to be one thing, easy to distinguish from its background and complete in itself. When the parts cooperate there is unity, but that also means there must be identifiable parts with their own identities. Unity is produced when the parts share something; it may be a color or texture, a shape, or any of the elements.

In *Night Sea* **[129]** Agnes Martin (b. 1912) uses one kind of line, two shapes, and two colors to compose a very highly unified work. The grid pattern of metallic gold lines establishes such a powerful unity that our eyes seek variation. It becomes important to us that the rectangles of the grid do not repeat the shape of the canvas and that the gold of the lines contrasts with the blue of the shapes. Martin is aware that the relationship between unity and variety is important in the meaning of her work. "My formats are square," she has said, "but the grids are never absolutely square, they are rectangles a little bit off the square, making a sort of contradiction, a dissonance, though I didn't set out to do it that way. When I cover the square surface with rectangles, it lightens the weight of the square, destroys its power."[2]

In Edward Hopper's (1882–1967) *Room in New York* **[130]** the content is the isolation of people from each other, but Hopper still had to bring the man and woman together in the composition. He accomplished it with rectangles: pictures on the wall, panels in the door and exterior wall, and the shape of the window we look through. That dark-framed box, with its many boxes, dramatizes the situation of two people, with nothing to say to each other, shut up together in a small space.

Instead of using similarity of shape to unify the design, as Hopper did, Georges Rouault *(roo-OH)* (1871–1958) used powerful black lines and thick crusts of oil paint to unify the design of *Three Clowns* **[131]**. The tight clustering of the figures unifies them, but it is the massive appearance of the paint and the heavy dark lines and areas which unify the figures and the background.

Unity is a primary consideration in composition and it is always based on repetition of some element or attribute in various parts of the work of art. Once unity has been established, then the artist must start worrying about introducing enough variety to keep the audience from getting bored.

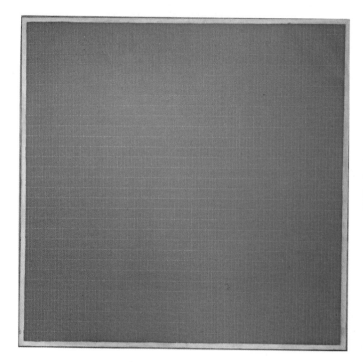

129. Agnes Martin. *Night Sea.* 1963. Gold leaf and oil on canvas, 6' (1.8 m) square. Collection of Mr. and Mrs. S. I. Newhouse, New York.

Analyzing Works of Art

above: 130. Edward Hopper. *Room in New York.* 1932. Oil on canvas, 29 × 36" (74 × 91 cm). Sheldon Memorial Art Gallery, University of Nebraska, Lincoln (F. M. Hall Collection).

left: 131. Georges Rouault. *Three Clowns.* 1930s. Oil on paper, 41½ × 29½" (105 × 75 cm). Private collection.

Variety

If we say that unity is based on similarities among the elements, then variety is produced by differences. Any of the elements—line, color, shape, etc.—can be varied, but not every element can vary without destroying unity, which must be dominant at the end.

In Michael Gallagher's (b. 1945) *Shuffling* [132], the paint shapes, most of them made with a single broad stroke, are so varied in size, shape, color, direction, and placement in space that a flat grid of squares is needed to unify them into a single picture. Even so, the feeling of explosive energy is so strong that the picture is barely held together. The shadows cast by these blobs of paint show us that they are in the air above that gridded background, and some cast shadows on others, making a series of levels in space. This is a wonderful demonstration of the idea that variety is a matter of form, not really a question of having varied *things* in the picture.

One of the most varied art experiences ever presented to the public was *Ruckus Manhattan*, a walk-through portrait of the city of New York built in 1975 by Red Grooms (b. 1937), Mimi Gross, and about twenty helpers. It was constructed mainly of metal, plastic, wire, and paint in twelve large sections, of which *Subway* [133] is one. About two hundred thousand people walked through this sculpture that year, and probably all of them were overwhelmed with its variety in somewhat the same way they were overwhelmed by the chaos of the big city that inspired it. Yet, like the city, there was a fundamental unity given by the materials, the scale (from life size to miniature), the exaggerations and distortions, and the similarities to real life in the city. Those things gave the unity necessary for the audience to feel they had had one identifiable experience. Still, the differences between sculpture and flat painted scenes, and the irregular ups and downs of all the surfaces, combined with the bright color, gave the observer a sense of the genuine variety of the big city. It was both funny and scary.

Variety always has to be subordinated to unity, but it gives art its flavor. It is in variety that the artist's personality and the special tastes of the moment can have free rein.

below: 132.
Michael Gallagher.
Shuffling. 1980.
Acrylic on paper,
42¾ × 31″
(109 × 79 cm).
Collection of the artist.

below right: 133.
Red Grooms
and Mimi Gross.
Subway (detail of
Ruckus Manhattan). 1976.
Mixed media (metal,
plastic, etc.),
9′ × 18′7″ × 37′2″
(2.7 × 5.7 × 11.3 m). As
installed at
Marlborough Gallery,
New York.

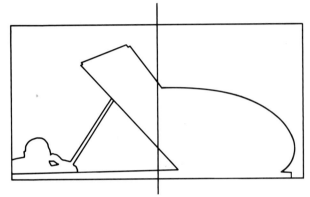

above: 134. Arnold Newman. *Igor Stravinsky.* 1946. Photograph. Collection of the artist.

left: 135. Diagram of the balance of Newman's *Igor Stravinsky* [134].

Balance

Since we live in a world of gravity, against which we must balance ourselves every minute, we become very conscious of the way in which the things around us maintain their balance. We can usually tell at a glance whether an object is stable or dangerously unstable, or just barely balanced in some exciting way. We often enjoy balancing games, and the feeling of being unstable for a moment is either terrifying or exhilarating. Art tells us things by the way it is balanced. Buildings, which share our space and must stand up to gravity just as we do, are especially expressive of balance.

To consider the balance of anything we start with two ideas: a vertical line or axis in the center, which is directly in line with the force of gravity, and the areas on both sides of that axis, which must have equal weight in a visual or psychological sense. When Arnold Newman (b. 1918) made a portrait photograph of composer Igor Stravinsky [134] he took 26 pictures, tackling the problem of balancing the composer and his piano. Newman began the session by placing Stravinsky's head in the center of his pictures, giving a symmetrical balance, but as he worked the photographer began to realize that an asymmetrical balance centering on the notch in the piano lid was more interesting. Like children on a seesaw, balance required placing the heavier (the great black swirl of the piano lid) nearer the center, and the lighter (the small triangular shape of the composer) farther from the center. That process of adjustment is easy to do with designs in two dimensions, in which the image—in the camera's viewfinder or in the printing—can be moved around until the invisible center of gravity is in the center of the paper [135].

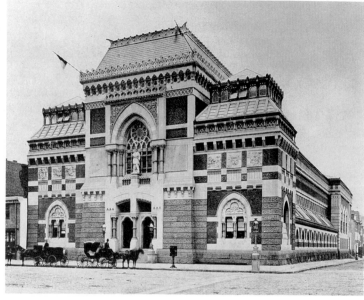

left: 136.   Greek style, Apulia, southern Italy. Volute krater; Nike in a four-horse chariot on neck, gods observing a battle between Greeks and Amazons on body. c. 330 B.C. Terra-cotta, height with handles 41⅝″ (106 cm). Metropolitan Museum of Art, New York (Fletcher Fund, 1956).

above: 137.   Frank Furness. Pennsylvania Academy of Fine Arts, Philadelphia. 1880.

The artist in charge of the decoration of the tall jar, called a krater [136], knew that his painting could have variety and movement because the form of the vase is so perfectly balanced. The design of the krater is **symmetrical**—the two halves are identical. Even if we saw it from an angle we could understand its symmetry, which is not simply visual, but is something we understand about its organization: that it has a center and the parts are set around it in perfect balance. The painted decoration in a late classical Greek style shows Nike, goddess of victory, in a four-horse chariot on the neck, and on the body of the vase four gods observing a battle between Greeks and Amazons. The flat black background and the brick red color of all the figures unify the design, and the eye contact, overlapping and gestures of the figures help bring them together. But the unity of the bands of ornament and the symmetrical balance of the three-dimensional form of the vase are most important in forming a stable framework for the complicated painting.

A symmetrical design, in which the two halves are alike, has such a simple and powerful balance that it can make almost any amount of variety stable and unified. Frank Furness (1839–1912) proved that with his design for the Pennsylvania Academy of Fine Arts in Philadelphia [137]. Two colors of brick and two colors of stone, and an amazing variety of architectural forms and decorative elements are controlled by the matching of the two sides of the front of the building.

Asymmetry, in which the two halves are different in measure or size, can also be balanced. The portrait of Stravinsky [134] is a good example of asymmetric balance, but we find it commonly in architecture as well. Frank Furness balanced tall against wide and advancing against receding in the Rhawn House [138]. The tall section on the right has a part which advances toward us, balanced by the wider part on the left which has a deeply shadowed porch. Although the two halves of the design are about as different in form as they could

138. Frank Furness. Exterior from south, William H. Rhawn House ("Knowlton"), Fox Chase, Pennsylvania. 1879–1881.

be, they balance in a satisfactory way. Furness avoided the varied color and decoration which he felt a symmetrical design could control. Asymmetry is interesting by itself, and hard enough to balance, without additional ornament.

Balance is not simply a matter for art. The bankers who had a billboard-like symmetrical **pediment** (the gable of a Classical Greek temple) put up in front of their mobile-home bank **[139]** were joking, but not entirely. Banks have often been designed to look like Greek temples because that style has the perfect balance, stability, and seriousness you want your banker to have, even if his office is a mobile home.

139. Anonymous. Security State Bank, Madison, Wisconsin. c. 1971.

140. Antonio Gaudí. Crypt of the Güell Chapel, Barcelona, Spain. 1908–1915.

We have been looking at buildings in which the walls and columns all stand vertically, demonstrating very clearly that they oppose the force of gravity. It is rare to find buildings which seem intentionally to be giving in to gravity. One of those is Antonio Gaudí's (*gow-DEE*) (1852–1926) Güell Chapel **[140]** in

below left: 141. Early Classic Maya. Figure of dignitary or priest. 6th–9th centuries A.D. Wood, height 14⅛" (36 cm). Metropolitan Museum of Art, New York (Michael C. Rockefeller Memorial Collection, bequest of Nelson A. Rockefeller, 1979).

below right: 142. Kenneth Snelson. *Free Ride Home*. 1974. Aluminum and stainless steel, 30 × 60 × 60' (9.2 × 18.3 × 18.3 m). As installed at Waterside Plaza, New York, 1974. Collection of Storm King Art Center, Mountainville, New York.

Analyzing Works of Art

Barcelona, Spain. Even seen directly from the front, many of the columns and parts of the vaulted ceiling seem about to collapse. But they do not collapse. Gaudí was an expert structural engineer and built this design on purpose. It seems to suggest to the worshipper that earthly things are very precarious and held up only by the power of God, a reasonable idea to present in a chapel. This is how the terror and exhilaration of teetering on the edge of balance can take a religious turn.

Traditionally, sculptors have used symmetrical balance to show the spiritual or ritual, rather than daily life in this world. The small sculpture of a priest, or perhaps a dignitary [141], is one of the few sculptures of wood to survive from the ancient Maya kingdoms in the damp jungles of southern Mexico and Central America. Originally the arms rested on some plaque-like object set on the thighs, but even so the posture was very erect, rigid, and evenly balanced. Those ancient societies lived more ceremonious lives than we moderns; it is hard to find a modern sculpture so formal as this.

More characteristic of our times are the sculptures made of aluminum pipe and steel cables by Kenneth Snelson (b. 1927). His *Free Ride Home* [142] is described by the artist as "a force diagram in space."[3] Supported only at a few points at each end, with none of the tubes touching each other, Snelson's sculptures are best seen outdoors against the sky where they vibrate in the wind, seeming to vault across space. What kind of balance is this? Perhaps it has ancient sources in the string game called cat's cradle, but mostly it is based on modern knowledge of the forces of compression (in the pipes) and tension (in the cables), and it is literally those two forces which are in balance, rather than weights in the usual sense.

In two-dimensional art there is far greater freedom in composing for balance since the picture will not fall off the wall even if it is unbalanced, while a building or a sculpture may actually fall down. One of the great inventors of compositions was the Spanish painter and printmaker Francisco Goya (1748–1828). His etchings show scenes of bullfighting as it was done in about 1800. In one [143] a nobleman with a pack of mastiffs is fighting the bull, evidently in an arena. The bull's dark head is just left of the center of the picture, surrounded by the dogs, some of whom it has already injured. The nobleman rides away in the right background, turning his back on the carnage. This can be compared with the portrait of Stravinsky [134] in that the two main areas are set at a distance from the center commensurate with their visual weight. This asymmetrical bal-

143. Francisco Goya. *Tauromaquia: The Dogs.* 1816. Etching, 7⅝ × 11⅝" (19 × 29 cm). Bibliothèque Nationale, Paris.

144. Francisco Goya. *Tauromaquia: Death of the Mayor of Torrejon at Madrid.* 1816. Etching, 7⅝ × 11⅝" (19 × 29 cm). Bibliothèque Nationale, Paris.

ance is sometimes called **occult balance** (meaning "hidden balance") because at first glance it is not obvious how the design is stabilized. It requires some careful observation to notice that the man and the injured dog play the part of the composer in the Stravinsky photograph, while the bull is playing the role of the piano. This is a more complicated composition because all the figures are moving, while Stravinsky and the piano sat still and the man faced us directly.

But what can we say about *The Death of the Mayor of Torrejon in Madrid* **[144]**? The title suggests that Goya is presenting this as if it were a news photograph, a quick snapshot taken on the run, and that its unbalanced design shows that it was not composed carefully at leisure. That, surely, is part of the meaning of this strange design. Yet we know it was really composed, and if we examine it carefully we notice that several of the people are scrambling along the bleachers toward the empty left side. The railing, which marks the center of the design, also slants strongly toward the left. The small box on the left side becomes very important, acting like the head in the Stravinsky portrait. Still, the design is unbalanced; Goya broke the rule on purpose to make us see that the subject too is breaking all the rules. The bullfight, which traditionally was meant to dramatize the struggle between the dark forces of nature (the bull) and the powers of reason and order (the human), has resulted in the victory of the forces of nature. Our attitudes toward animals are different, and as animal lovers we may have trouble grasping Goya's message, but the sharp point of the horn emerging through the mayor's back should help us understand what he meant. The unreasoning power of nature rules in Figure **144**. In Figure **143** balance is visible to show that human reason is dominant, although it is equally cruel.

Rhythm

Rhythm is repetition of some element (in art most commonly line, shape, or color) according to a rule. The rule might require a shape to be repeated at least three times with equal spaces between, or a line to be repeated with uneven spaces. To succeed as rhythm the repetition must be obvious. Rhythmic repetitions in still compositions suggest movement, but actual motion, as of a motorized sculpture, must be controlled by the design according to a rule, which is rhythm.

It is rare to find an art movement devoted to the expression of a single principle, but it is no exaggeration to say that the **Futurist** movement, founded in Italy in 1909, was concerned mainly with rhythmic movement. They didn't call it "rhythmic movement," but "dynamism," and they were thinking more of machines—racing cars, motorcycles, and trains, especially—than they were of human movement. Still, one of them painted a dancer [145], not the smoothly flowing movements of classical dance, but the staccato action of a popular tap dancer. The painter, Gino Severini (1883–1966), repeated arms and hands, eyes and curls of hair, so we feel as if we are seeing the dancer by strobe light. The visual arts are mostly still and must resort to repetition or elongation of forms to convey natural movement. Severini chose several different shapes which he standardized and repeated over and over—the semicircles in the skirt, strips and curves in the arms, painted ribbons with real sequins attached to them, and broad angular areas in the background. He repeated colors as well, to emphasize the repetition: blue in the semicircles of the skirt, tan in the arms, blue with sequins in the ribbons, gray in the background shapes. As your eyes jump from shape to shape and color to color they absorb the quick, snappy rhythm of the dance, like the beats in the music.

145. Gino Severini. *The Blue Dancer.* 1912. Oil on canvas, with sequins, 24⅛ × 18¼" (61 × 46 cm). Private Collection, Milan.

146. Umberto Boccioni. *Unique Forms of Continuity in Space*. 1913. Bronze, height 43½" (110 cm). Museum of Modern Art, New York.

147. Umberto Boccioni. *Muscular Dynamism*. 1913. Pastel and charcoal on paper, 34 × 23¼" (86 × 59 cm). Museum of Modern Art, New York.

The most famous piece of Futurist art is Umberto Boccioni's *(bah-CHO-nee)* (1882–1916) bronze sculpture entitled *Unique Forms of Continuity in Space* [146]. To have called it "Man Running" would have sounded too simple and would have brought the wrong kind of sculpture to mind. Boccioni did a charcoal drawing [147] before he made the sculpture. It shows the use of lines with open ends to express the gesture. The drawing has a somewhat chaotic movement because the rhythm of the movement is not clear; the dominant curvilinear lines are interrupted by short straight lines that break the rhythm. But in the sculpture almost all the lines are long curves. Boccioni criticized his drawing and made changes which enhanced the rhythmic movement as he turned it into sculpture. Its movement is expressed by the elongation of the forms into long pointed shapes which are repeated throughout the design.

But rhythmic movement is part of pictures that do not represent any actual motion. Aside from three small human figures, there is nothing in Grant Wood's (1892–1942) *Young Corn* **[148]** which is moving, and the painting conveys a feeling of calm and stillness entirely different from the frenetic action of Severini's *The Blue Dancer*. The rhythmic movement in *Young Corn* is the movement of the observer's eyes—or perhaps we should say the observer's attention—moving over the shapes in the painting. Wood, too, repeats standardized shapes which lead the attention through the design. We enter along the rows of young corn at the bottom, and its lines lead us back to the large tree on the left and the pattern of green lines in the center, or to the road and the house on the right. The gentle curves of the hills at the bottom are echoed by the hills at the top, and our eyes are attracted by that similarity, just as the round shapes of the trees lead our eyes around the design by their repetition. Between lines (of corn plants, harvested grain, fence posts, and so on) and shapes (hills, bushes, trees), Wood controls the movement of the audience's attention.

Rhythm cannot be separated from our sense of time and movement, but the basic design problem for the artist is controlling the movement of the observer's eyes and attention. Merely adding real moving parts does not solve the problem; it may make it more complicated.

Emphasis

Often artists emphasize one part of a composition, designing the composition so the viewer's attention is drawn irresistibly to that part. Unlike unity and variety, emphasis is not required by the human mind, but it is used when the

148. Grant Wood. *Young Corn.* 1931. Oil on masonite panel, 23½ × 29½" (60 × 75 cm). Cedar Rapids, Iowa, Art Association, Community School District Collection.

149. Benin kingdom. The Oba (king) mounted with attendants. 16th–17th centuries. Bronze plaque, 19½ × 16½″ (50 × 42 cm). Metropolitan Museum of Art, New York (Michael C. Rockefeller Memorial Collection, gift of Nelson A. Rockefeller, 1965).

meaning of the design requires it. The bronze plaque **[149]** from the palace of the Oba (king) of Benin (part of modern Nigeria) shows the Oba himself in the center on horseback, with two attendants holding up his hands and two more shading or fanning him. There can be no doubt about which figure is the important one in the design, and in Benin society. The Oba is larger, is in the center,

150. Edgar Degas. *The Dancing Class.* c. 1871–1872. Oil on wood, 7¾ × 10⅝″ (20 × 27 cm). Metropolitan Museum of Art, New York (bequest of Mrs. H. O. Havemeyer, 1929; The H. O. Havemeyer Collection).

and receives the service of the other figures in the picture, just as he was the "biggest" and in the center of real life in the kingdom. The emphasis on the Oba expresses the most important idea in this sculpture, which is the importance of the king.

Usually human figures act as the point of emphasis, sometimes called "the center of interest." As human beings we are naturally interested in our own kind. But in Edgar Degas' *(duh-GAH)* (1834–1917) *The Dancing Class* **[150]** it is the mirror which receives the emphasis, in spite of the interesting figures that surround it. It occupies the same position as the Oba of Benin, in the top center, its dark value and its central position enhanced by the violin case in the foreground. Degas further stresses the mirror by placing the violinist's bow so it points to the mirror, and the gestures of the dancers seem to point to or be directed toward the mirror. The ballet, this design suggests, is about appearances, in the same way the Benin sculpture suggests that life in Benin revolves around the Oba.

We could go back to Agnes Martin's *Night Sea* **[129]** for a design in which emphasis is not used, but that might suggest that such unstressed designs belong in landscape or abstraction, as opposed to scenes with human figures. Jan Vermeer's *The Little Street* **[151]** is evidence to the contrary; it is a very natural scene of a Dutch town that does include four small figures. And yet there is no center of emphasis. If our eyes are attracted to the arched doorway we find it closed and move to the open passage with the figure of a woman, which leads us on to the larger woman sewing in the doorway, back to the children playing on the narrow tiled porch, to the green shutters, to the various dark windows. All of these things seem to be about equally important: one person is not more

151. Jan Vermeer. *View of Houses in Delft*, known as *The Little Street*. c. 1658. Oil on canvas, 21⅜ × 17⅜" (54 × 44 cm). Rijksmuseum-Stichting, Amsterdam.

important than another and the people are not more important than the houses; it is from these relationships that we extract the meaning of the scene, which is that life is a harmony of modest equals in this town.

Emphasis reveals relationships of meaning or power among the parts of a work of art. Those relationships always reflect, often in very subtle ways, relationships in the artist's real world. Power in Benin was concentrated in the person of the Oba, as the artist saw it, but all the elements in *The Little Street* were equal in power and meaning to Vermeer.

Painters always use proportions to make their point, sometimes in subtle ways. Perhaps the most subtle painter was Diego Velázquez (vay-LAHS-kes) (1599–1660), court painter to the king of Spain. He was officially ranked with the royal barber in the very snobbish court society, but he was a close friend of the king and felt he was as good as anyone. Besides, as an artist he knew that art was the highest calling. The problem was to suggest these things when he could not say them out loud (without losing his head, at least). In the great painting called *The Maids of Honor* [**152**], Velázquez shows himself working on a very large painting, but since we see it from the back we cannot tell what its subject is. It might be the little princess in the center, accompanied by her maids of honor and her dog, or it might be a double portrait of the king and queen, who are reflected in the mirror on the back wall. As you stand before this painting (in the Prado museum in Madrid), the painter and most of the faces in the picture look directly at you, as if you were posing, not they, and you are in the place occupied by the king and queen, as the mirror tells us.

But in the painting as it really exists, the painter has a very strong position, rivaled only by the little princess. Historians who have studied this painting believe that the large paintings depicted on the back wall can be identified among those in the royal collection and that their subjects are myths telling how the Greek gods invented the arts. Diego Velázquez made a subtle but strong claim here, that his art was a sacred activity descended from the ancient gods and that, in the world of art, at least, even kings and queens are tiny compared with him. Surrounded by snobbish courtiers, it must have done his heart good to show this, in the only way open to him.

This painting shows people in a variety of sizes, which makes us consider their relative proportions. They include adults and children, men and women, full-grown and dwarfs, and even a large dog. Velázquez, standing at his easel on our left, sets a stan-

dard for adult size in the middle of the room. We compare him with the very small man in the doorway, whose smaller size we take as an indication of distance since he appears to be a full-grown adult. The five figures across the front of the scene present a different problem. The small blond person in the center [**153**] is a child, judging by her size compared with the painter and her soft features and small hands. Historians identify her as Princess Margarita, about five years old in this painting. Flanking her are two young women—their hands tell us they are grown, even if the one on our left is shown no taller than the princess; the fold in her skirt informs us that she is kneeling. But on our right is a woman who looks like an adult but is the height of the princess; thus, she must be a dwarf, and the boy with her looks very small, also. The dog, on the other hand, looks very large. The names and careers of all these people are known. The dwarf woman on the right, for example, was a German woman named Maribárbola who lived at the Spanish court for many years until 1700, when she returned to Germany.

153. Detail of Princess Margarita from Velázquez's *The Maids of Honor.*

opposite: 152. Diego Velázquez. *The Maids of Honor (Las Meninas).* 1656. Oil on canvas, 10′5¼″ × 9′¾″ (3.2 × 2.8 m). Prado, Madrid.

Proportion

The size of things and their placement in relation to each other are the problems of proportion. The audience is quick to criticize works of art on the basis of proportion—odd proportions are something we can all spot instantly. But it is rare for an artist to make a real mistake in proportion; however odd it looks, it is usually what the artist really meant. In fact, proportions, along with emphasis, are among the main ways an artist can express ideas and attitudes.

154. Henri Cartier-Bresson. *New York.* 1947. Photograph. Collection of the artist.

Photographs are the easiest way to see expressive use of proportion, since we usually know how big the objects in the picture really are. Henri Cartier-Bresson's *(car-TYAY bruh-SONH)* (b. 1908) photograph called *New York* **[154]** shows not much more than a cat, a man, and the walls of buildings. Our first thought in proportion is always that big things are more important than little things—it is often not true in life or in art, but that is the starting point. In *New York* the extreme difference in the size of the buildings and the two living creatures immediately makes us question the meaning of that difference. We begin to wonder if perhaps the relationship between the cat and the man is really bigger than the buildings. The fact that we accept photographs as true to life makes them very powerful comments on real life.

Every work of art is designed in a system of proportion. The expressive use of proportions is especially clear in photographs and representational paintings, but proportional systems are not based on nature. Proportion is a basic way of expressing the meaning of the work of art and it belongs only to art. One of the first considerations in designing a composition is the proportions of the parts in relation to each other. *Size* and *scale* are closely related to proportion, but while scale leads to considerations of perspective and the representation of distance, proportion is mainly concerned with solid forms and the relationships between their parts. Whether the artist thinks actively about a system of proportion or just does what seems natural, a system of proportion will find its way into the work. This is a good place to look at a couple of systems which have been influential over the centuries, one for dividing up the picture plane and one for constructing the human figure.

The Golden Mean

A proportional system called the **Golden Mean**, or Golden Section, was used by the ancient Greeks and Romans and revived by the Italian mathematician Lucas Pacioli (1450–1520). It proposed that the most beautiful division of a line is into segments in which the shorter is to the longer as the longer is to the whole line, which results in a proportion of approximately 8 to 13. Many artists, among them Leonardo da Vinci and Albrecht Dürer, experimented with compositions based on the Golden Mean. In the United States great interest in such proportional systems was stimulated by Jay Hambidge (1867–1924) in the 1920s, under the name Dynamic Symmetry. Hambidge taught that the square was the basis of proportional composition and that it was converted into satisfying proportions by using the diagonal as a radius which gave the base of a new rectangle, which he called a "root 2 rectangle." The diagonal of the root 2 rectangle would produce a root 3 rectangle, and so on [155, above]. The shape called the Golden Mean rectangle [155, below] is a development from the root 5 rectangle; its sides have that approximate 8-to-13 proportion (more accurately 1 to 1.618).

The shape of the canvas in George Bellows' (1882–1925) *On the Porch* [156] is a root 2 rectangle, and the pattern of the green framing of the screened porch can be analyzed into various Golden Mean rectangles and diagonals. Bellows was impressed by the proportional system taught by Hambidge and used it as a starting point for many compositions.

The Canon of Human Proportions

The Egyptians and Mesopotamians, and later the Greeks, were all fascinated by geometry and the mathematical analysis of nature. That led them to develop systems of proportion, especially for the human figure. The system which has had the longest popularity derives from the sculpture of Polyclitus, a Greek sculptor of the 5th century B.C. who specialized in idealized portraits of athletes. Polyclitus created a sculpture of a spearbearer called *The Canon*, meaning the standard or rule, because it embodied his system of proportions. Both

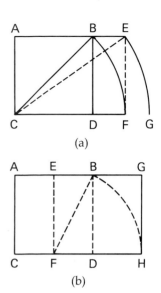

(a)

(b)

155. The Golden Mean. (a) The square is converted to a root 2 rectangle by using the diagonal of the square as the length of the long side. The diagonal of the root 2 rectangle gives the length of the long side of a root 3 rectangle. (b) The Golden Mean rectangle has sides related 1 to 1.618, a proportion of about 8 to 13.

156. George W. Bellows. *Children on the Porch* (or *On the Porch*). 1919. Oil on canvas, 30¼ × 44″ (77 × 112 cm). Columbus, Ohio, Museum of Art (museum purchase, Howald Fund).

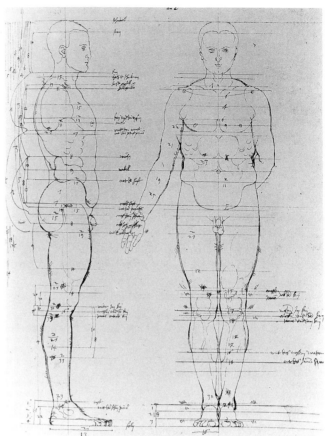

the original sculpture and the essay Polyclitus wrote about it have been lost over the centuries, but the sculpture was copied several times **[157]** by later Roman sculptors, and the essay was quoted by later writers. This became the basic system of proportion for the human figure among many later artists: the whole figure is seven and a half heads tall, divided at the chin, nipple, navel, crotch, and above and below the knee. Actual human beings vary from these proportions, of course, but they make a useful starting point for artists.

Polyclitus gave his figure proportions which are strong but not very elegant, and other artists often lengthened the legs to make a figure whose height was eight times the height of the head. Albrecht Dürer did a study of human proportions, making many detailed measurements to try to find the ideal proportions **[158]**. His figure is about eight heads in height, which is still a common proportion for the ideal figure.

Intuitive Proportions

No artist has ever exceeded Piet Mondrian *(peet MON-dree-ahn)* (1872–1944) in the study of proportion from the artist's point of view. His compositions were inspired not by mathematics but by mystical philosophy, and were calculated by eye. A friend once analyzed his paintings to show they were based on the Golden Mean and showed the calculations to Mondrian. "This is very interesting," Mondrian said, "but it is not how I paint." In an article on abstract art, Mondrian wrote that "the apparently mathematical must be consciously expressed."[4]

Composition Gray-Red **[159]** has one perfect square (the gray upper left), but all the other shapes were designed intuitively, by moving strips of tape until the design was satisfactory. Mondrian then painted in the heavy white background and the black lines, and finally the color areas. This very cool and intellectual looking art was, for Mondrian, full of human feeling. "The importance of purely abstract painting is . . . showing the richness and fullness that are expressed in and are requisite to the joy of living," Mondrian wrote.[5]

Proportion is a basic question in composition; it is concerned with how the parts of the design fit together. Whether the answer is arrived at by geometry, by a traditional system or a new personal invention, or is achieved by contemplating each design problem intuitively, an answer must be found. How big, how long, how dark, and many of the other questions that the artist ponders during the making of art are questions of proportion.

The artist consciously considers the principles of design, but there is no set order or system in applying them. Each one contributes, balancing the others. Unity has to be one of the first considerations, so the audience will see the work as an object, and the artist will not call the work finished until unity has been achieved. The observer's attention is always considered: variety attracts and sustains attention, which is satisfied by the order and balance of the design. The observer's attention moves through the work in a controlled, rhythmic way and finally draws conclusions based on proportion, as well as on the way all those other principles are expressed. These principles are the point at which the mind of the audience and the work of the artist meet and interact.

Composing Designs

Three geometric patterns—the circle, the square, and the triangle—lie behind composition. Artists consciously plan their compositions in these geometric patterns, choosing the pattern that helps convey their ideas.

The Circle and the Square

Paul Klee *(clay)* (1879–1940) believed compositions based on the circle and the square depended on our knowledge of nature, and he provided diagrams

159. Piet Mondrian. *Composition Gray-Red*. 1935. Oil on canvas, 22⅜ × 21⅝" (57 × 55 cm). Art Institute of Chicago (gift of Mrs. Gilbert W. Chapman, 1949).

Understanding Design _____ 113

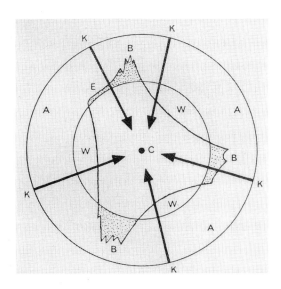

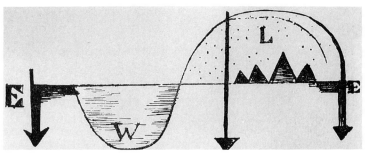

left: 160. Paul Klee. *The Earth as We Know It to Be.* 1923. Pen and ink. From *Paul Klee Notebooks*, Vol. II. *The Nature of Nature*, 1973.

above: 161. Paul Klee. *The Earth as We Experience It.* 1923. Pen and ink. From *Paul Klee Notebooks*, Vol. II. *The Nature of Nature*, 1973.

based on that point of view. In one [160] he shows us the shape we know the earth to have—a massive sphere with a gravitational center and an enveloping atmosphere. This suggests a composition of concentric circles which expresses the power of the center, a useful pattern when the composition is meant to emphasize something in the center. In another drawing [161] Klee shows us how we experience our natural surroundings: the earth is a horizontal plane and gravity pulls vertically. That suggests a composition of verticals and horizontals, and these lead to the square or the checkerboard grid used for compositions in which emphasis is spread over the whole picture and no single part is dominant.

Klee used both these compositions in his own work. *Hunting Tree* [162] is based on concentric circles, but the center point is not marked. Each curving line departs from the circle, but is close enough to its curve that we sense the grow-

162. Paul Klee. *Hunting Tree.* 1939. Oil on canvas, 39⅜ × 31½" (100 × 80 cm). Kunsthaus, Zurich.

163. Paul Klee. *Highway and Byways.* 1929. Oil on canvas, 32⅝ × 26⅜″ (83 × 67 cm). Museum Ludwig, Cologne.

ing form of the tree as it presses outward into the air from an invisible center. The painting is clearly about the tree and its pattern of growth, and the circular design promotes that concept subtly, hiding the circle and leaving its center unmarked. In *Highway and Byways* **[163]** the squares and rectangles have been scaled to recede into the distance, but it is clear that a grid of vertical and horizontal lines was the starting point of the composition. Klee still wanted some emphasis even in this design, which he achieved by permitting the center "highway" to be the only one whose sides run straight back to the horizon. Even so, it remains less dominant in its design than the tree in the other because the vertical and horizontal grid diffuses, or spreads out, the dominance of the center.

The circle and square also have a very long association joined together to make a design called a **mandala** *(MAHN-da-la),* an ancient symbol of the universe. The circle represents the sky, the square or grid the earth's plane. Leonardo da Vinci (1452–1519) placed a man in the center of that ancient pattern

[164], the best illustration of the saying that "man is the measure of all things." Leonardo was drawing an old proportional system described by a Roman writer showing how the human figure relates to the circle and the square. But many people of earlier times would have considered Leonardo's drawing too proud, since the center of a mandala should be occupied by a divine figure, one who rules the universe, not a mere human. Buddhist painters in Nepal and Tibet have specialized in painting mandalas showing Buddhist divinities at the center, with the four directions of the world represented by gateways and with saints and divinities around the heavenly circle, as we see in the Mandala of Vairocana (vi-RO-chah-nuh), the Buddha at the center of the universe. In the mandala [165] the circle's emphasis on the center is more powerful than the square's diffusion of the stress.

Although there are differences between compositions made by people in different cultures, there are also many points in common. It is interesting to look at compositions by the contemporary American artist Jennifer Bartlett (b. 1941) that were done during the fifteen months after December, 1979. During that time she exchanged homes, sight unseen, with an acquaintance—her New York studio for his house in southern France. She grew tired of sightseeing, the weather was bad, and she found it hard to carry on her work, but one day she sat down by the large dining room window and began to draw the view, which she described as "the awful little garden with its leaky ornamental pool and five dying cypress trees."[6] In 1981, 197 of her drawings were exhibited under the title *In the Garden,* and they were subsequently published. Among those drawings one finds a wide range of compositional approaches based on the square and the circle.

below: 164.
Leonardo da Vinci.
*Study of
Human Proportions
According to Vitruvius.*
c. 1492. Pen and ink,
13⅛ × 9⅝″ (33 × 24 cm).
Accademia, Venice.

right: 165. Tibetan.
Mandala of Vairocana.
17th century.
Gouache on cotton,
31 × 28″ (78 × 72 cm).
Museum of Fine Arts,
Boston (gift of
John Goelet).

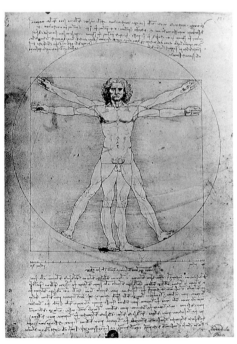

Analyzing Works of Art

above: 166. Jennifer Bartlett. *In the Garden, Number 154.* 1980–1981. Brush and ink on paper, 26 × 19¾″ (66 × 50 cm). Charles Saatchi Collection, London.

above right: 167. Jennifer Bartlett. *In the Garden, Number 191.* 1980. Pencil on paper, 19¾ × 26″ (50 × 66 cm). Private collection.

right: 168. Jennifer Bartlett. *In the Garden, Number 176.* 1980. Gouache on paper, 19¾ × 26″ (50 × 66 cm). Hillman R. Holland Collection, Atlanta.

Number 154 **[166]**, in brush and ink, gives an easily understandable picture of the garden as seen from the window: a lawn, a rectangular tiled pool with a statue of a small boy urinating into it, and a border of trees. This composition is clearly based on the grid, taking the tiles of the pool as a point of departure. The value division between the lawn and the trees is nearly horizontal, and the verticals of the cypresses and the dark band on the right margin reinforce the rectangularity of the grid pattern. The small statue acts as a center, but there is little emphasis on it.

In *Number 191* **[167]** the grid reappears, but the pool is repeated in each of ten squares, being isometric in the two lower corners but receding in perspective in all the others. To give the grid more movement diagonal lines and shapes have been added, using the shape of the pool and the dark slanting shape of the cypress trees in the background. The center is not stressed, although the darker values move around the margin to give some variety to the grid. The grid provides strong unity, but variety and emphasis can be introduced only by departures from the grid.

In *Number 176* **[168]** Bartlett turned to a circular composition, done in two versions on the same piece of paper. The center is emphasized by a red oval from which all the other shapes radiate. The circular composition, with its stress

169. Jennifer Bartlett. *In the Garden, Number 136*. 1980. Pastel on paper, 26 × 19¾″ (66 × 50 cm). Amerada Hess Corporation Collection.

on the center, led her to draw in the radii running out to the corners. Those straight lines give variety to this design, whose fundamental source is the circle in the center.

Number 136 **[169]** is an example of the complexity that can occur as these basic patterns merge and interact. This softly toned pastel places the small turquoise rectangle of the pool at the bottom, with gigantic cypress trees on the left and a swirl of oval and diamond shapes rising on the right, appearing to radiate from a center whose position, somewhere just left of the pool among a group of oval shapes, is most strongly indicated by the curves of the upper right corner. The slight emphasis Bartlett allows in this design is on the red line representing the little statue.

Jennifer Bartlett's *In the Garden* series is a good example of the power of art to create meaning using subject matter which, in itself, has no meaning. When you scan these four compositions it is clear they are all "saying" different things about reality and the way a human mind interacts with a place. The content of art is not something the artist finds in the subject; it is in the composition. The lines, shapes, colors, and so on create a mood and a vision of the world, each composition creating a new and entirely different mood and vision. These works of visual art can be translated into words no more easily than a piece of music can be recreated in words.

The Triangle

The geometric pattern which provides the greatest stability is the triangle or, in three dimensions, the pyramid. The ancient Egyptian pyramids **[170]** were designed not only to be eternally stable but also to look eternally stable—their

170. The Pyramids at Gizeh, Egypt. c. 2530–2460 B.C. Stone, height of highest originally 480' (146 m).

shape clearly tells us that. Even designs that are full of action are often stabilized by a triangular composition. Emanuel Leutze's (1816–1868) *Washington Crossing the Delaware* [171] is composed on a triangle with the boat as its base and the flag as its apex. Leaving the right side of the triangle open gives the design more energy, making it an arrow moving left. Pablo Picasso's mural about the destruction of the town of Guernica [172] seems at first to be violent and frenzied, but

right: 171. Emanuel Leutze. *Washington Crossing the Delaware.* 1851. Oil on canvas, 12'5" × 21'3" (3.8 × 6.5 m). Metropolitan Museum of Art, New York (gift of John Stewart Kennedy, 1897).

below: 172. Pablo Picasso. *Guernica.* 1937. Oil on canvas, 11'6" × 25'8" (3.5 × 7.8 m). Prado, Madrid.

173. Dosso Dossi. *Circe.* c. 1512–1520. Oil on canvas, 5′9⅜″ × 5′8⅝″ (1.8 × 1.7 m). Borghese Gallery, Rome.

the composition is stable: a triangle at the center with a vertical rectangle on each side (see pages 129–131 for more on this work).

The triangle has always been especially useful for compositions of seated figures. A good example is Dosso Dossi's (1479?–1542) painting of *Circe (SIR-see)* [**173**], the witch in *The Odyssey* who turned men into animals. This exotic figure is so glamorous that we can easily imagine the attraction which lured the human-looking dog to his fate. The artist's design reminds us that the idea of the *femme fatale* is as eternal as the pyramids. The figure of Circe is not simply a triangle, but suggests a pyramid with the foot in the lower right corner marking a corner of the base and the form receding in space up the skirt toward the face of the seated figure. Circe seems tied to the ground, like a pyramid. For this reason triangular and pyramidal shapes are used for figures whose stability or earthliness are important to their meaning.

When we consider composition and the principles of design it is easy to lose sight of the main point, which is that all these organizational considerations are meant to help us express ourselves and understand the expressions of other people. These geometric designs are tools that may be combined, or ignored in favor of some more personal or more natural composition. But many artists have been sure that geometry is the basis of design, in somewhat the way nouns and verbs are the basis of sentences.

Personal Style

In Chapter 3 and this chapter we have been examining the elements of art and the principles of design, but the work of individual artists often looks so different that it is hard to imagine they started with the same elements and principles. That difference we call **style**, which is defined as an emphasis on *particular* elements of art and principles of design for the sake of expression. The elements and principles come together in style.

It is fascinating—and often upsetting—to discover that we really do not understand what is going on in other people's minds. Even when we are sure we know what our friends think, they often surprise us. In art this variation among individuals shows up as personal style. We usually think of personal style as characteristic of artists, but it is found in all of us in whatever we do. Each artist emphasizes line or color, unity or variety, partly consciously but also driven by unconscious preferences which are entirely personal. Later, in Part V, we will look into the fact that people who live in the same place at the same time tend to have similar personal styles—which we call **period style**.

As you look at a lot of art you gradually begin to recognize the personal styles of individual artists. The next three illustrations are major paintings by famous artists, each with a strongly individual personality. It is easy to recognize the paintings of Paul Gauguin *(go-GAN)* (1848–1903), the French painter best known for his paintings of Polynesian subjects. *We Hail Thee, Mary* [174] is a traditional Christian subject set in Tahiti, with the Virgin and Child transformed into Polynesians. But it is not only the Polynesian setting that tells us the artist was Gauguin; we also recognize his style. We soon learn to identify Gauguin's color: the purple path, the brown strip of bushes behind the path, the pink field behind Mary. Those areas of color change very little from part to part, but stand as areas and seem nearly flat despite the small marks of the brush. Color areas are also outlined in narrow black lines, which makes them even flatter. Other artists use bright, flat colors and black outlines, but their work looks different from Gauguin's.

174. Paul Gauguin. *We Hail Thee, Mary (Ia Orana Maria).* 1891. Oil on canvas, 44¾ × 34½" (114 × 88 cm). Metropolitan Museum of Art, New York (bequest of Sam A. Lewisohn, 1951).

Max Beckmann (1884–1950) painted *Actors* **[175]** in 1942 when he was a refugee from Nazi Germany. That may account for the desperate mood, totally different from the peacefulness of Gauguin's painting. Like Gauguin, Beckmann painted in flat, strong colors outlined in black. Beckmann surely learned from the work Gauguin did fifty years earlier, but still their styles are different. Beckmann's paintings are full of people and things, their proportions adjusted to their importance in the composition, while Gauguin's figures are in natural scale to each other and to a wide environment. In *Actors* the black outline around shapes and colors has expanded and taken on an importance that Gauguin never allowed it to have. For Gauguin the color was the main thing, but for Beckmann the black line drawing was most important. Style is the emphasis put on certain selected elements of art or principles of design.

The personal styles of Beckmann and Gauguin are easy to tell apart, but they were both Europeans of modern times. Their work has as much in common as we might expect, and we would not be surprised to find that the work of an artist from a different time or place would be very different from that of both of them.

The Averoldi Altarpiece **[176]** by the Italian painter Titian has something in common with both the Gauguin and the Beckmann paintings. It is on a religious subject, as is Gauguin's, and it is composed of several panels, like Beckmann's. (*Actors* we would call a **triptych** *[TRIP-tick]*, meaning it has three panels; *The Averoldi Altarpiece* is a **polyptych** *[pah-LIP-tick]*, the term for any number over three.) But in style it is very different, which is accounted for partly by differences in temperament among the individuals, but mainly by the long lapse of time between them (370 years between Titian and Gauguin and 420 between Titian and Beckmann). Titian was not thinking mainly of the color, or of the line, and certainly was not trying to make the shapes appear flat. Titian's brush strokes do not show unless one examines the painting up close. Light and dark was Titian's main concern—he took the trouble to illuminate all five panels from the upper left, which gives them unity. All Titian's figures cast shadows; some of Beckmann's do, but they are inconsistent; none of Gauguin's do. Light and dark bring out the three-dimensional solidity of Titian's figures; he made sure we would understand that the figures are solid enough to cast shadows. His

175. Max Beckmann. *Actors.* 1941–1942. Oil on canvas, triptych; center 6′6½″ × 4′11″ (2 × 1.5 m), wings 6′6½″ × 2′9⅜″ (2 × 0.8 m). Fogg Art Museum, Harvard University, Cambridge, Massachusetts (gift of Mrs. Culver Orswell).

176. Titian. *The Averoldi Altarpiece.* 1522. Oil on wooden panels; center panel 9'1½" × 4' (2.8 × 1.2 m), upper side panels 31 × 26" (79 × 65 cm), lower side panels 6'6" × 2'2" (2 × 0.7 m). Church of Saints Nazario and Celso, Brescia, Italy.

representation of light and its effects unifies the separate panels by suggesting a continuous space filled with massive bodies and lighted from a single source.

These three artists are much admired, not because they recorded nature accurately, but because they used the elements and principles of art to "speak" in a personal way about their thoughts and their experiences. Each of them created a complete world in which their style is simply "reality." As you look at *Actors* it is hard to imagine another way for this scene to appear, and the same is true of other successful works of art. The emphasis and viewpoint of a style are the expression of a mind and personality living within a particular set of historical circumstances.

Summary for Review
Unity, **variety**, **balance**, **rhythm**, **emphasis**, and **proportion** are the principles, or features, which our minds seek in a design. They are produced by the relationships the artist gives the elements of art. Unity allows the observer to perceive the work as a single thing; variety makes it interesting. Balance may be **symmetrical** or **asymmetrical**. **Rhythm** is repetition according to a rule, used to control the movement of the observer's attention through the work of art. **Emphasis** reveals relationships of power or meaning in a composition. **Proportion** always expresses ideas. Systems of proportion have been invented for the shapes of buildings and all objects (the **Golden Mean**) and for the human figure, but proportions may also be designed intuitively. Compositions have traditionally been designed geometrically based on the *circle*, the *square* or grid, and the *triangle* or pyramid, given uniqueness by their combinations. **Personal style** in art is the emphasis placed on selected elements of art and principles of design. Personal style is the outcome of a unique personality interacting with the conditions of life in a particular time and place; features of style shared by artists of one place and time we call **period style**.

Part III

Art Mediums

The talent we attribute to artists is mainly evident in their skill in using materials and tools—the brushes, chisels, paints, cameras, papers, stones, and all the other innumerable things we find in the studio. As members of the audience we must develop enough knowledge about the tools and materials of the artists so that we can understand their effect on the meaning of the work. As we have seen earlier, artists are distinguished by their drive to express their ideas and feelings in a visual form. That leads them to seek ways to apply the technology of their time to expression. Art mediums are exactly that: technology which has many other uses, but which artists have figured out ways to use for expression.

Thomas Hart Benton (1889–1975) sits sketching beside a river in Missouri [177]. The paper and pencil he uses could be used for many other things; you could make a shopping list or write a business plan. The same could be said of a camera or a computer, which can record scientific experiments and analyze the results, but which can also be used to make art. The question is not, "What are the materials and tools of the artist?" It is more accurate to ask, "How does the artist use the technology of the culture to make art?"

We hardly think of pencil marks on paper as technology because they are so simple; but for the art collector, the marks that Benton put on the paper are of special interest and value. They are unique and completely personal. As an intimate record of Benton's thought and personality there is nothing that beats a pencil drawing. From the collector's standpoint, such a drawing has the disadvantage of being expensive to purchase because it is unique. However, a drawing that could be duplicated as a set of perfect copies could be sold much more cheaply and have a much larger audience. The challenge is to produce a set of identical drawings without losing intimate contact with the personality of the artist.

That, of course, is what printmaking was invented to do. One of the important developments in technology during the last five hundred years has been the invention of many different ways to make series of identical pictures, first by means of the woodcut and most recently by means of videotape and electronic digital recording. But it all starts with Tom Benton sketching with his pencil beside the river.

The following three chapters discuss the artist's materials and tools used for the graphic mediums, painting, and sculpture. That order is based on the common order of development of a private art collection. Collecting usually begins with prints—etchings or serigraphs, for instance, which are relatively inexpensive. The collector, now seriously interested, will proceed on to the purchase of drawings and paintings, which are one of a kind (that is, unique). Sculpture is usually the last step in art collecting, a step taken by collectors with plenty of space to show their purchases.

From the standpoint of the collector, as well as the artist, the thing one wants to know about each of these mediums is how it can be made to express individual ideas and feelings. That is what makes the product art and separates it from all the other applications of these tools and materials.

177. Anonymous. *Thomas Hart Benton Sketching*. Photograph. Missouri Division of Tourism.

The Graphic Mediums

The word *graphic* refers to all the symbolic marks we make in drawing, writing, or printing, whether on paper, film, or a computer screen. Painting is often considered to be among the graphic arts, but we will set it aside for the next chapter. Here we will discuss drawing and the many ways drawings can be produced in multiple copies or replaced by photographic or electronic imagery. All the arts serve for research and development in technology, but the graphic arts are in the forefront of technical progress, and there is intense competition to find new ways to make and record marks. Some of the oldest techniques are still useful and have changed very little, while other ways of drawing and printing have been superseded and forgotten. It might be imagined that electronic methods will completely supersede chemical or mechanical methods, but that is not the case because each method produces a particular appearance, and thus a particular range of expression. The audience's taste for a particular appearance and artists' desires for certain kinds of expression dictate the methods that are popular. Technical progress responds to those tastes and desires in very unpredictable ways.

Drawing

Drawing may be the oldest of the arts, but it is more alive than ever because it is the purest record of the human mind in action, rivaled only by spontaneous speech. Drawing and speaking are the natural expressive activities of each of the two halves of our brains. Research on brain function has shown that language abilities are largely located in the left hemisphere of the brain, while the synthesizing, relational abilities which control drawing are largely located in the right hemisphere. Just as speaking has its codes, which we call languages, each with its grammar and vocabulary, so does drawing have its codes, which we call styles, each with its materials, intentions, and emphases. That is why it is impossible to concentrate on drawing and talk at the same time. The pictures in this book challenge you to turn off, for just a moment, the left hemisphere of your brain which reads the text, to allow your right hemisphere to take in the pictures. But the left hemisphere also has to work on the pictures, taking the design apart and analyzing the meaning part by part. Art, both in the making and in the understanding, is a whole-brain activity, both synthesizing to see the whole design and analyzing to appreciate the significance of the parts.

Vincent van Gogh's drawing *View of Arles* [178] shows what a code in drawing can look like. Van Gogh started with paper, brown ink, a brush, and probably two pens of different widths. He had in mind a set of marks that could be made with those tools: narrow and wide lines, either short or long, straight or curving, parallel or radiating; spots of solid ink, of various sizes; shapes made of lines with empty centers. Each kind of mark stood for an identifiable material in the natural scene, large spots and open shapes for irises, small dots and close-set lines for different plants in agricultural fields, close-set dots and lines for the

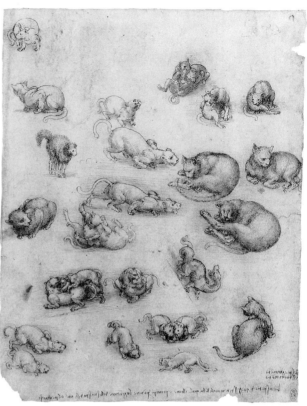

above: 178. Vincent van Gogh. *View of Arles.* 1888. Ink on paper, 17 × 21½" (43 × 55 cm). Museum of Art, Rhode Island School of Design, Providence.

right: 179. Leonardo da Vinci. *Sketches of Cats.* c. 1506. Pen and ink over black chalk, 10⅝ × 8¼" (27 × 21 cm). Royal Library, Windsor Castle, England.

trees and walls of the town. Beginning students of drawing often hope to reproduce exactly the appearance of the scene before their eyes, but in the end they must consider the set of marks they can make and what each one can represent. Language and drawing are both descriptive codes, each with its own powers and limitations. To draw and to understand drawings requires a realistic idea of both the powers and the limitations of the medium.

The Sketch, the Study, and the Finished Drawing

There are three reasons for making a drawing, and the result in each case has its own name. Since they have different uses, they also have different appearances. Those three reasons are:

1. To make a note of an idea or something seen, which results in a **sketch**.
2. To plan for another work, which results in a **study**. The word **cartoon** is also used for studies done full size, usually for a large work such as a mural; its meaning has expanded to include humorous or satirical finished drawings, which belong in the next category.
3. To make a work of art in its own right, which results in a **drawing** or, to distinguish it from other kinds of drawings, a **finished drawing**.

The reason is important only to the extent it is reflected in the appearance of the drawing, but those reasons also bring to our attention the role of drawing in our thinking, from first thoughts, to planning future activities, to making final statements.

Leonardo da Vinci's sketches of cats [179] show his eyes stimulated by the poses and activities of living cats. But this sheet also shows his mind stimulated by the cats' movements—a kind of stream of consciousness that led him to think of lions and even a dragon. Leonardo had no reason to make sketches of cats except that they interested him.

One of the most famous series of studies is that for Pablo Picasso's mural *Guernica*. When the government of Spain commissioned Picasso to paint a mural for its pavilion at the Paris World's Fair to open in the fall of 1937, he had about eight months to complete the project. During the first four months he did no drawings, but he was surely considering how the mural could express the struggle for survival of the democratic Spanish government against an overpowering attack by Fascist armies. Then on the sunny Monday afternoon of April 26 the defenseless city of Guernica was attacked by the German air force, employed by the Spanish rebels. In three and a quarter hours of bombing and strafing the city was destroyed, the first time in history that a city was destroyed by aerial bombing. Like Hiroshima later, Guernica (*gare-NEE-kah*) became a symbol of brutality and the senseless destruction of war. Within the week Picasso was at work on his mural, the theme clear in his mind.

Of the hundreds of studies made for the mural we will examine just three. The first **[180]**, in pencil on blue paper, dated Saturday, May 1, 1937, shows Picasso's first thoughts: a bull and horse, a Pegasus crouched on the bull's back, ruins in the background, and a scribble at the upper right that will turn into a woman holding a lamp. Interpretations of these symbolic creatures vary, and there is no right, or wrong, interpretation; Picasso was wise enough to make only a few ambiguous remarks and, as we know, it is the right and duty of the audience to make such interpretations. To me, then, the horse and bull are the actors in the drama of the bullfight, a subject Picasso frequently depicted. The bull represents the powers of nature, brute force, or darkness; the horse is the ally of the human bullfighter, who represents the powers of civilization, humanity, and enlightenment. Pegasus, or victory, alights on the powers of darkness.

The design developed rapidly as Picasso continued to draw. On Sunday, May 2, he did another drawing of the plan for the whole mural **[181]**. The Pegasus has disappeared, the bull leaps triumphantly over the fallen horse, the woman in the upper corner is nearly in final form, and the scrawls in the foreground of **[180]** have turned into a dead warrior and woman, of which only the warrior will be retained in the final mural, and then turned into a statue.

below left: 180.   Pablo Picasso. *Study for Guernica*. May 1, 1937. Pencil on blue paper, 10⅝ × 8¼" (27 × 21 cm). Prado, Madrid.

below right: 181.   Pablo Picasso. *Study for Guernica*. May 2, 1937. Pencil and gouache on gesso wood panel, 23⅝ × 28¾" (60 × 73 cm). Prado, Madrid.

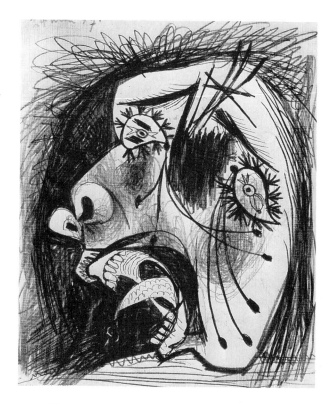

182. Pablo Picasso.
Head of Weeping Woman.
May 24, 1937. Pencil, color
crayon, and oil on canvas;
21⅝ × 18½″ (55 × 47 cm).
Prado, Madrid.

The head of a weeping woman **[182]** is a study for the head of the woman in flames on the right of the mural, a figure not part of the earlier studies and one which was taking on an independent existence as the sole subject of Picasso's other paintings. Even here, on May 24, as he was painting on the Guernica mural, this study was becoming a painting in its own right, since it is done in pencil, crayon, and oil paint on canvas.

As early as May 11 the canvas had been stretched, its dimensions 11½ by 25⅔ feet (3.5 by 7.8 meters), and the figures drawn in. But over the next few weeks all the figures except the woman with the lamp underwent drastic changes **[183]**. Picasso continued to draw, on paper, on other canvases, and on the mural itself, which even as a finished work is nearly pure black, white, and

183. Pablo Picasso. *Guernica.* 1937. Oil on canvas, 11′6″ × 25′8″ (3.5 × 7.8 m). Prado, Madrid.

gray, more like our idea of a drawing than a painting. The absence of color makes the painting more stark and somber and more like a newspaper photograph and deprives us of any pleasure we might find in color. Although it is a large oil painting, *Guernica* still has the spontaneous appearance that we associate with drawings. Since Picasso had planned the painting carefully in many preliminary studies and it was not really a spontaneous production, that appearance was clearly Picasso's intention.

But, of course, there is no rule that drawings must appear to be spontaneous. Many finished drawings are as thoroughly planned and as carefully executed as paintings. Georges Seurat's *(suh-RAH)* (1859–1891) portrait of Edmond-François Aman-Jean [184] is as large as many paintings (a little over 24 by 18 inches, or about 61 by 46 centimeters) and very carefully finished. Seurat was famous as a painter in the Post-**Impressionist** style of **pointillism**, using dots of pure color, but in this black crayon drawing on textured white paper the style shifts to dots of pure value (black to white range). Although we might think we see lines, Seurat was careful to work only in areas of value tone, all of them perfectly modulated to create a perception of lighted masses, some of them solid black and light absorbent, in a dusky space.

The Tools and Materials of Drawing

It is hard for us to realize how modern an art drawing really is. Before paper was available and inexpensive it was hard to find a surface to draw on, and most of the surfaces that were used were hard to preserve. People drew in the sand and on cave walls, on clay tablets, and on animal hides, all surfaces which were very inconvenient by our standards. The Egyptian invention of papyrus paper was a tremendous breakthrough, producing a smooth sheet which was easily transportable and more durable than most modern paper. Although it never became inexpensive, it was used for many fine ancient drawings and paintings, though few have survived to our day. Paper, made of pulverized organic fiber, was supposedly invented in China in A.D. 105, replacing ancient bark paper. It was first made in Europe in the 13th century, but it did not become common until the Renaissance. Villard de Honnecourt, whose sketchbook survives from the 13th century, drew on parchment and vellum, made from animal hides [see **458**]. The surface, or **ground**, on which drawings are made is particularly interesting now because we are in the midst of another

184. Georges Seurat. *Portrait of Edmond-François Aman-Jean.* 1882–1883. Black conté crayon, 24½ × 18¾" (62 × 48 cm). Metropolitan Museum of Art, New York (bequest of Stephen C. Clark, 1961).

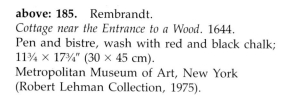

above: 185. Rembrandt.
Cottage near the Entrance to a Wood. 1644.
Pen and bistre, wash with red and black chalk;
11¾ × 17¾" (30 × 45 cm).
Metropolitan Museum of Art, New York
(Robert Lehman Collection, 1975).

right: 186. Edgar Degas. *The Morning Bath*. 1887–1890.
Pastel on off-white laid paper mounted on board,
26 × 17½" (66 × 44 cm). Art Institute of Chicago
(Potter Palmer Collection, 1922).

revolution much like that caused by the invention of paper; the new surface is the cathode ray tube computer screen, which we will examine later.

As soon as a good drawing surface was easy to obtain, the next problem was to find a tool that made a mark. There were several tools which had been known since ancient times, used by scribes, manuscript illustrators, and artists. Pencils made of real lead or silver, which make pale marks on a white surface; pens made of a bird quill (usually from a goose), which produce a flexible, cursive line, or from a reed, which produce a strong, angular line; brushes; and ink (usually brown or blue-black); and chalks of various colors (usually brick red, black, or white) had all been known since ancient times.

Rembrandt's *Cottage near the Entrance to a Wood* [185] shows the use of a mixture of these traditional mediums. The main dark areas and shadows were laid in with a brush and brown ink, with wide variations in its tone. Then a reed pen was used to draw details on the cottage and the foreground areas of trees, logs, and ground. The blunt, stiff lines show the nature of the reed pen. Finally red and black chalks were used to reinforce some darks and add a brightening warm touch.

Colored chalks, or **pastels** (made by mixing colored pigments with glue formed in sticks), and crayons (pigments mixed with wax or grease) were popular new mediums in the 18th century and led to important art. In the 19th and 20th centuries pastels have been considered an ideal medium for impressionistic effects of light and color, since the pastel stick can be very soft (with little glue) to give rough spots of color without sharp edges, as well as hard (more glue and less pigment) to give sharp detail. Edgar Degas was one of the great practitioners of pastel drawing, as we see in *The Morning Bath* [186]. Pastel drawings are very close to paintings, and Degas' pastels are close to his Impressionist paintings in

In Detail: The Pastel Portraits of Liotard

Jean Étienne Liotard *(leo-TAR)* (1702—1789) was advised by his art teacher in Paris to take up pastels, the newly popular colored chalks, as his medium. It was a fortunate choice for the young Swiss artist from Geneva, for he became one of the most successful portrait artists of his century, traveling from one royal court to another most of his life. But his finest portraits were of himself [187]. He shows himself (at about age 42) with a tremendous gray beard and dressed in a fur hat and fur-collared coat, a costume he adopted while working in Turkey. A stick of pastel is held delicately in his fingers as he draws himself. The precision of the style is quite different from what we now expect of a pastel drawing, but it is found in most of the pastels of the 18th century. The background tones are softly blended, as are the changes from light to shadow on the face, but sharp lines are drawn on top of those tones to give detail to the features, to add gray and white curls to the beard and spiky hairs to the collar and hat.

Liotard was working in Rome, where he did pastel portraits of Pope Clement XII and several cardinals, when the English Lord Duncannon offered his patronage for a trip through Greece and Turkey (1738—1742). Those were the most exciting years of Liotard's life. He enjoyed drawing Turkish musicians and commoners, probably a relief from portrait commissions. When he traveled on to Austria in 1743 to make portraits of the Empress Maria Theresa and her court, his Turkish outfits earned him the nickname "the Turkish artist." From this self-portrait we can see what a striking figure he must have been. We can also see why his work was admired by noble patrons from one end of Europe to the other.

187.   Jean Étienne Liotard. *Self-Portrait.* c. 1744. Pastel, 27¾ × 18⅜″ (71 × 47 cm). Staatliche Kunstsammlungen, Dresden, East Germany.

their use of color. But chalk and crayon can also be done in the light and dark of monochrome, as we see it in Seurat's drawing [184].

The first really new drawing tool to be added to the artist's kit was the graphite (mineral carbon) pencil, introduced a little before 1800—what we usually call a "lead" pencil. It was an improved version of the old lead pencil, which

left: 188. Salvador Dalí. *Cavalier of Death.* 1934. Pen and black ink on paper, 33½ × 22⅜" (85 × 57 cm). Museum of Modern Art, New York (gift of Miss Ann C. Resor).

above: 189. Michelangelo. *Resurrection.* 1532–1533. Black chalk on paper, 12½ × 11⅛" (32 × 28 cm). British Museum, London.

was made with real lead, or the silverpoint, both of which were rather faint and could not be easily erased.

Although tools and materials play important roles in the artist's expression and often inspire the artist to make a particular kind of drawing, from the audience's point of view the artist's creativity is revealed in more subtle ways. Drawing, like speaking, reveals the mind of the artist, and the audience is looking to see the mind in spontaneous action. Like our minds in dreams, drawings are very literal; what is shown is "there" and everything shown has symbolic meanings. Salvador Dalí *(dah-LEE)* (1904–1989), in his *Cavalier of Death* **[188]**, tried to gain access to a dream-like state-of-mind by making ink blots like a psychological Rorschach test, which he then interpreted in his drawing. Both the horse and its rider are skeletal, the rider gloomy, but the horse laughing triumphantly. Although it is not really an ink-blot test, it has a strangeness and richness of symbolism that really are like a dream.

Pentimenti (Italian for "repentances") are changes of mind visible in a drawing (or painting). At first thought it might seem that such "mistakes" and corrections would ruin a drawing, but the audience has never felt that way about them. On the contrary, they are of special interest since they reveal the mind of the artist in action. Michelangelo's black chalk drawing *Resurrection* **[189]** shows ghostly ideas for figures on the left and right and in the center foreground, none of them brought to completion. They involve the observer in the action of drawing, making us speculate on why Michelangelo tried them and then rejected them and forcing us to visualize the drawing as it might have been.

To leaf through an artist's sketchbook is just about as intimate a contact as we have with another person, like reading someone's diary. That intimacy is both the special appeal and also the limitation of drawings—each one is unique and can have only one owner. So it was natural that, as drawings became more common, the question of duplicates arose.

Printmaking

Quickly following paper from Asia to Europe was its use to make multiples of a drawing, which we call an **edition**. Like paper, printmaking had a long history in Asia; techniques were known in India at least as early as the 7th century and in Japan by 770, when an edition of a million prints of the Buddha was stamped from wood blocks.

Editions of prints vary tremendously in size, and that is one of the reasons prints may vary in price. A wooden block used for a woodcut is fragile compared to a copper plate used for an etching and will simply wear out. But the copper plate also wears out after a few hundred trips through a heavy press. Fine-art prints are usually made in editions of a few hundred, each print requiring special care and handling. Photolithography used for magazine illustrations can produce thousands of excellent pictures in the time required to make a few prints, but the hand-made prints still set the standards for quality in printing.

Relief Prints: Woodcut and Linocut

Japanese woodcuts are part of a long tradition which is independent of Western art. Hokusai *(HO-koo-si)* (1760–1849), in the early part of the 19th century, revolutionized the tradition by introducing landscape subjects, most famously in his series *The Thirty-six Views of Mount Fuji*. One view of the volcano **[190]** is between two stores in Edo (now Tokyo). The Mitsui Store, on the right, whose sign reads ''Dry Goods, cash payment, fixed prices,'' is having its roof repaired, one man flinging packets of tiles up to the roofers. The tall roofs, the flying kites, and the gestures of the workmen make a pattern of nearby elements to contrast with the spacious sky and distant peak. Like all Japanese printmakers, Hokusai made the original design and the printing was done by a team of specialists. Each color required a separate block, which was carefully registered so that its print fitted exactly with the other blocks to form the complete image in color. Gradations of color, such as we see in the sky, were made by uneven inking of the blocks.

190. Hokusai. *The Thirty-six Views of Mount Fuji: The Mitsui Store at Suruga-machi in Edo.* 1823–1831. Color woodcut on paper, 9¾ × 14½'' (25 × 37 cm). Metropolitan Museum of Art, New York.

left: 191. Albrecht Dürer. *The Vision of the Seven Candlesticks.*
1498. Woodcut on paper, 15¼ × 11" (39 × 28 cm).
National Gallery of Art, Washington D.C.
(gift of Philip Hofer).

above: 192. Paul Gauguin. *Te Atua (The Gods).* c. 1893–1895.
Color woodcut on paper, 8 × 13¾" (20 × 35 cm).
Art Institute of Chicago (Clarence Buckingham Collection, 1948).

 Woodcuts and linoleum cuts (sometimes called **linocuts**) are the common methods of making relief prints, in which the artist cuts away the negative areas, leaving the positive parts in relief to catch the ink and print on the paper. We are all familiar with rubber stamp impressions, fingerprints, tire tracks in the mud, and so on, all of them relief prints. Woodcuts were first made in Europe for humble uses, such as playing cards, but soon came to the attention of serious artists.

 Albrecht Dürer (1471–1528) accepted the challenge of duplicating the style of Renaissance pen drawings in woodcut. You can judge his success in one of a series of prints on the Apocalypse **[191]**, or the end of the world as seen in a vision by John the Evangelist, who kneels at the lower left. John recorded his vision in Revelation, the last book in the New Testament. Dürer interpreted John's words (1:12–16) literally: "I saw seven gold lampstands, and among them a being like a man, wearing a long robe, with a gold belt around his breast. His head and hair were white as wool, as white as snow; his eyes blazed like fire. . . . In his right hand he held seven stars; from his mouth came a sharp double-edged sword, and his face shone like the sun at noonday." It is hard to believe that those fine lines were printed from lines left on a block of wood as the white areas were cut away.

 Woodcut (done on the length of the board, which has grain) and wood engraving (done on the end of the board, which has no grain) remained in use, mainly for commercial illustration, until photography took over in the 1890s. But just at that point, woodcut was revived in a totally unexpected way by Paul Gauguin, working in the Polynesian Islands. He was inspired by his romantic view of Tahitian life and his knowledge of Asian, especially Indonesian, art. *Te Atua (The Gods)* **[192]** shows that Gauguin was not trying to reproduce a drawing, but thinking more in terms of a painting, with printing in both black and tan, each color from a different block of wood, and yellow, orange, and green added with a brush, probably using stencils. Dürer's prints impress us with their absolute control; Gauguin's give an impression of technical freedom and spontaneity. All modern printmaking has been influenced by Gauguin's woodcuts; relief printing as a technique was brought back to life by his example.

Edvard Munch's *(moonk)* (1863–1944) woodcut *The Kiss* **[193]**, done in 1902, shows how quickly the understanding of Gauguin's prints spread among artists. The main idea was to take advantage of the natural character of the materials—in this case the grain of the plank of wood. Two blocks were used; one coarse-grained block, probably from weathered wood to let the grain show, was printed lightly to create an atmosphere, and a separate heavily inked block (still the plank but finer grained and inked so heavily that the wood grain does not show) was used for the lovers.

Intaglio Prints: Engraving and Etching

Albrecht Dürer realized that a finer line could be made by cutting it into a surface than by cutting away the background around it. The result would be a more durable printing surface, since very thin lines in a woodcut have a tendency to break under the pressure of printing. As the son of an armor maker, Dürer learned the crafts of intaglio at his father's knee, for engraving and etching were used to put ornamentation on fancy armor. In **intaglio** *(in-TAL-yo)* the lines which will print are cut into the surface of the plate or block (usually a copper plate), the ink is rubbed into the cuts, and the plate surface is rubbed clean of ink, though ink remains in the cuts. Then the plate is laid on the steel table (called the "bed") of a press, dampened paper is laid over it, and together they are subjected to heavy pressure from the press rollers. The ink from the cuts is pressed onto the paper; the wider and deeper the cuts the more ink they hold and the darker the line. In **engraving** the cuts in the copper plate are made by hand with a small hardened steel chisel called a **burin**. In **etching** the cuts in the copper plate are made with acid. In other respects the two techniques are similar. An intaglio print is always identifiable by the *plate mark* where the edge of the copper plate was embossed into the paper by the hundreds of pounds of pressure from the rollers of the press. The design, of course, was also embossed and would show up even if it contained no ink.

A view of a printmaker's studio in the 17th century **[194]** shows three men hard at work printing intaglio plates. In the left background a man applies ink to a plate which already has an engraved or etched design. The nearer man on the left is wiping the surface ink from a plate. He would have started with cotton waste (the rag in his left hand) to get most of the ink off, but the final wiping is done with the heel of the hand, which is hard enough that it leaves ink in the cuts but wipes the surface clean. On the right the third man has laid an inked plate on the bed of the press, laid paper over the inked plate, and covered them

both with felt blankets. The final step is cranking the bed of the press through the heavy rollers of the press. Then the blankets will be thrown back, the paper peeled from the plate and hung on a wire to dry.

Dürer was one of the first artists to print by these methods, and one of the greatest. *The Knight, Death, and the Devil* [195] was part of a pair on a favorite Renaissance topic; the difference between the knight's active life in the world and the quiet life of study, represented by a saint. The knight rides through a dangerous world of wild forests and mountains, threatened by Death and a grotesque devil, but neither he nor his horse nor his dog shows any fear. Renaissance people, such as Albrecht Dürer, took their images of lifestyles from the Middle Ages, from the monastery and the medieval warrior, but even today we can identify with the ideas this print expresses. The picture is composed entirely of lines cut into a copper plate with the burin. Dürer's working method was to cut a strong line around the main shapes in one part of the design, then add details until that part was finished before going on to the next part. Variations in values were made by **hatching** and **crosshatching**; all the gray and black areas were made by overlapping lines.

Dürer sometimes used etching, but he seems to have preferred engraving, which gives a sharper, stronger appearance to the design. The etcher can simply sketch lightly on the copper plate, which is covered with a soft asphalt surface, called the **ground**, which resists acid. Wherever the sharp steel tool (called an etcher's needle) scratches through the ground the acid will cut a line. The depth of the cut is controlled by removing the plate from the acid bath at intervals and "stopping out" by varnishing the lines that are deep enough. Rembrandt was one of the great etchers, and his *The Three Trees* [196] shows the atmospheric effects he attained, with deep dark areas, heavily etched, and cloud areas with the finest patterns of line.

Etching remained the most popular medium for art printing through the 19th century, the black-and-white tones serving very well the desire for atmospheric effects and a passionate mood so characteristic of that century. Charles

left: 195. Albrecht Dürer. *The Knight, Death, and the Devil.* 1513. Engraving on paper, 9¾ × 7½" (25 × 19 cm). British Museum, London.

above: 196. Rembrandt. *The Three Trees.* 1643. Etching on paper, 8¼ × 11" (21 × 28 cm). Rijksprentenkabinet, Amsterdam.

197. Charles Meryon. *The Morgue.* 1854. Etching on paper, 9 × 8" (23 × 21 cm). British Museum, London.

Meryon (*mare-YOn*) (1821–1868), the most admired Parisian etcher, had about five years of work before madness ended his career. His views of Paris often contain strange figures. In *The Morgue* [197] a drowned man is carried from the river by his friends, and mourned by his wife and child as a policeman directs them to the morgue. The dark windows, tall houses, smoking chimneys, water-pipes, and enigmatic figures create a mood well suited to the etching medium, which allows heavy darks and irregular sketchy marks that express more emotion than the tightly controlled engraved line.

Lithography

Unlike the older print techniques, whose origins are lost, the invention of lithography is a well-known story of genius and obsession. Alois Senefelder (*ZEN-uh-fel-der*) began to write plays and music when he was eighteen, in 1789, and wanted to publish them himself inexpensively. The printing press using movable type had been invented long before (by Gutenberg about 1450), but it did not offer a method for printing music, which was still copied by hand. Senefelder was mixing his ink on a piece of smooth limestone and by accident discovered that a greasy liquid he planned to use as a ground for etching his writing onto copper could be used to mark on the limestone. It took nine years of experimenting before he could obtain a patent for his new method of printing, which was quickly adopted as a way to print pictures, often with text (as in advertising), as well as music. Senefelder's method of making "chemical prints," as he called them, quickly spread to other countries. As early as 1802 a young French artist received a patent from the French government on the technique, and in 1809 a manual on lithographic printing was published. The technique spread around the world within a quarter century and began the surge of printing developments which historians in future centuries are sure to see as one connected story from **lithography** to photography and electronic printing.

Senefelder's invention consisted of drawing with a grease crayon on a smooth limestone, which gave the medium its name (litho = stone, graphy = marking). The drawing on the stone is treated with a very weak nitric acid solution ("etched") to make the grease of the drawing penetrate the stone and to make the areas without drawing more receptive to water. For printing, the stone is kept damp so that it repels the ink everywhere except where the greasy crayon has left its residue. Paper is laid over the inked stone and it is passed through a press under moderate pressure. Artists soon learned that lithography had the potential for printing color, using a separate stone for each color. The design on each stone must be carefully fitted (or "registered") to its place in the design, but the process is identical except that colored ink is applied to the stone for printing. The process is sufficiently complicated that most artists have their lithographs printed by specialists.

Two French artists brought lithography to unsurpassed levels. Honoré Daumier used it for rapid black-and-white drawings and cartoons and Henri de Toulouse-Lautrec *(ahn-REE duh too-looz-lo-TREK)* (1864–1901) perfected the large multicolor poster. Both these artists worked in what were considered commercial arts, which were printed on short-lived papers and expected to have a short life as art. Looking back at their work now we see clearly that it is of a standard we consider fine art, which we hope will endure.

Daumier's print of the famous photographer Nadar making the first aerial views of Paris from a balloon was published in the magazine *Le Boulevard*, May 25, 1862. It was entitled *Nadar Raising Photography to the Level of Art* **[198]**. (The photographer returned the favor by making the best-known portraits of Daumier.) Nadar actually had a huge, propeller-driven balloon made for aerial photography, and we see him precariously perched in a tiny gondola (surely it was larger!) high above the city, which seems to consist entirely of photographers' studios. During most of his life Daumier was terribly poor, working as a lithographic illustrator from the age of fourteen, and once jailed for six months for cartoons attacking the government. The pressure to produce drawings every day resulted in the free, sketchy style we see in this print. To Daumier these were crayon drawings. The lithographic medium, used in this way, is a very direct way to make editions of drawings.

198. Honoré Daumier. *Nadar Raising Photography to the Level of Art.* 1862. Lithograph on paper. Metropolitan Museum of Art, New York (Harris Brisbane Dick Fund, 1925).

199. Henri de Toulouse-Lautrec. *Napoleon*. 1895. Lithograph on paper, 23⅜ × 18″ (59 × 46 cm). Metropolitan Museum of Art, New York (gift of Mrs. Bessie Potter Vonnoh, 1941.

If one had to choose the supreme masters of lithography, Henri de Toulouse-Lautrec would certainly be among them. He is famous for posters that give us a vivid picture of Parisian entertainment of the 1890s. Lautrec did studies for the lithographs, usually as drawings in charcoal, but sometimes as paintings in **gouache** (water-base paint) or oil on cardboard mounted on canvas. His print *Napoleon* **[199]** was done in 1895 for a competition to choose a poster to publicize a biography of Napoleon, but since another (less interesting) print won, Lautrec's remains without lettering. It gives a good sample of his way of working. The main lines of the study done in oil paint were transferred to the stone. Lautrec placed tracing paper over the stone to try out colors, about which he was very particular, mixing the inks himself to get subtle shades. He drew in the outlines with black crayon, then dramatized parts with a brush, especially on the horses and the French general on the right. Napoleon's horse was left as a shape in the natural color of the paper, with the background around it spattered with color dots, a technique invented by Senefelder, but one that Lautrec liked so well he sometimes claimed he invented it. The radiating pattern of the riders, the contrasts of shape, texture, and color, and the somber but human mood of Napoleon—all make this an unusually interesting print, a lesson in lithographic art.

Serigraphy

Silkscreen printing, called **serigraphy** *(suh-RIG-ra-fee)* as an art technique, had a long history as a commercial and industrial stencil technique before it began to be used as a fine-art medium in the United States in the 1930s. Since that time it has become very popular, partly because it is relatively inexpensive to do and the basic processes are easy to learn.

The screen is a wooden frame with silk cloth stretched over it. Placed over a piece of paper, the screen receives the printing ink and spreads it evenly as a scraper, or sqeegee, is run across it. To make a design a stencil may be cut and attached to the silk, or glue may be painted onto the silk and allowed to dry to

above left: 200. Andy Warhol. *Campbell's Soup Can.* 1964. Silkscreen on canvas, 35¾ × 24″ (91 × 61 cm). Leo Castelli Gallery, New York.

above right: 201. Timothy High. *Rebel Earth, Ramath-Lehi.* 1983. Silkscreen print, 40 × 26″ (102 × 66 cm). Collection of the artist.

prevent the ink from passing through parts of the silk. It is in the stencil, of course, that the art is composed. Serigraphy is easily used for color printing: a separate stencil or a separate screen is used for each color, and often twenty or more screens are printed on the same piece of paper, making prints which rival paintings in the complexity of their color.

Serigraphy has been used by many well-known American artists. Andy Warhol (1931–1987) and other members of the Pop Art movement of the 1960s found silkscreen printing the ideal medium because of its strong connection with popular commercial culture since it was often used for posters and advertising. The cool, impersonal precision of its shapes and the flat color tones it naturally produced were considered desirable qualities in prints such as Warhol's *Campbell's Soup Can* **[200]**. At first it was considered an insult to art and art lovers, but it has become a famous image of its period.

Silkscreen has the power to print both the flat color areas and sharp edges we expect in a poster or the personal brush stroke and modulated color more typical of painting, and contemporary printmakers are exploiting a range of such effects. Timothy High (b. 1949) used three basic techniques in *Rebel Earth, Ramath-Lehi* **[201]**: photo-posterization, hand-reduction, and split-fountains in printing. The jawbone (with which Samson killed a thousand Philistines) and darts in the foreground were made by photo-posterization, using five black and white photographic negatives—each exposed for a different range of values—to make five stencils to represent the full range of values. The rest of the picture was drawn by hand with a maplewood stylus and glue-like liquid methyl cellulose "block out" to fill the pores in the silk for eighty-three runs of color. Hand-reduction begins with the stencil with the largest area open for ink and the lightest value. Areas that are to remain that light value and that color are then blocked out, and the next value and color is applied. The screen is gradually filled with block-out, dot by dot or area by area, until at last the darkest value is printed. High's print includes areas—such as the sky—in which color blending appears. That was achieved by split-fountains, in which the screen is charged (or filled) with two or more colors that blend as they are dragged across the screen with the squeegee. These complicated processes result in great variation of color and detail. In this print High symbolizes the conflict between pagan powers represented by the ancient Peruvian dolls with their dart weapons and Samson's Old Testament God, who met in battle at Ramath-Lehi ("Jawbone Hill").

This combination of handwork and photographic processes was used in Melissa Miller's print *Ablaze* [202]. Miller painted twenty-one clear acetate sheets with black acrylic paint, each sheet representing a color or value of ink. Each acetate sheet was converted to a stencil by printing it photographically on a silk screen coated with photo-emulsion, which acted as a negative, leaving openings in the screen where the black paint had been brushed on. Printing with colors resulted in a print notable not only for its variety of colors and values but especially for its exact recording of the artist's brush stroke. Each of the fifty prints in the edition is an original, and preserves much of the individuality of brush stroke that we would expect in a one-of-a-kind painting.

Like High's *Rebel Earth, Ramath-Lehi,* Miller's *Ablaze* is an image of spiritual conflict. The viewer identifies with the panther, standing like a human being, beset by demonic spirits in the forms of skeletons, howling masks, glowing ectoplasm, and leaping enemies.

202. Melissa Miller. *Ablaze.* 1988. Silkscreen print, 40 × 30″ (102 × 76 cm). Texas Gallery, Houston, Texas.

203. Seymour Chwast. *Nicholas Nickleby* poster. 1981–1983. Graphic design for four-color lithography. Collection of the artist.

Graphic Design and Illustration

A main source of Andy Warhol's Pop Art style was graphic design, which is the work of artists applied to illustration, publicity, or advertising. Graphic designers produce most of the art we see, printed and on television. Perhaps the graphic designers' most useful knowledge is in ways to use the print and electronic mediums which produce the final prints of their work. One of the best-known American designers, Seymour Chwast (b. 1931), told an interviewer:

> I love working with the media, working with printing papers, finding new methods of printing. . . . My work as a commercial artist, seen by millions, gives me joy and satisfaction that "fine" art cannot supply. Besides, since the sixties there have been so many crossovers in artists and the ways artists work that the line between fine and applied art has become blurred. The only real difference between them is intent.

That intent, as Chwast says, is, "The client's message must be presented in the most clear and accessible manner possible."[1]

The difference between fine and applied graphic art is especially blurred in the field of illustration, in which the artist must invent or choose a style that is right for the assigned material. For example, in August, 1981, Chwast was commissioned to design the poster for the Mobil Showcase television series of Charles Dickens' *Nicholas Nickleby*, to be shown in January, 1983. The project began with a briefing by Sandra Ruch, art director for Mobil Oil, followed by research in English cartoons and prints of Dickens' period. Then Chwast began to draw. One of the early drawings, with a full-length figure of the hero under a ladder full of other characters, was published as a teaser advertisement, so Chwast had a chance to criticize and revise his design. He decided on a stronger contrast of scale, with only the head and shoulders of Nickleby and the ladder perched on his shoulders **[203]**. That design, drawn in black-and-white line with colors indicated by paste-on transparent color sheets as a guide for the printer, became the poster, the album cover, and the cover of the paperbound companion edition of the book. The outlines drawn black in Chwast's line drawing were printed blue, which indicates that the final work of art was produced in the printing, not in the artist's studio. The figures on the ladder were separated and took on a life of their own in animated film advertisements.

Chwast, like all graphic designers, is a member of a team of highly specialized artists and artisans. We often speak of our age as one in which the visual rivals or exceeds the written expression of information and ideas. The clarity and power of widely disseminated visual information depend on the work of these teams of artists working in graphic design.

Photography

We think of photography and its descendants in film and video as *the* 20th-century mediums, but their roots go back at least to the 10th century and an empty room in Cairo, Egypt, that had a round hole in one wall. By some process which the medieval Egyptians found hard to explain, on sunny days the image of the scene viewed through that hole was projected upside-down on the opposite wall of the dark room. We may still find that hard to explain, but we have gotten accustomed to it, and have learned to make images that are even harder to explain.

The Latin words for "dark room" are "camera obscura"; that term is still used, and from it we get also the word "camera." The room in Cairo was a camera without the film, which remained absent for about eight hundred years. But lack of film did not keep artists from using this kind of camera. Eventually they put a lens in the hole, mounted paper opposite it, and drew the image projected through the lens. Such a filmless camera used for drawing is still called a **camera obscura [204]**; it was frequently employed by artists before the invention of photographic film. For example, Frederick Catherwood (1799–1854) drew his detailed rendering of Mayan architecture at Uxmal **[205]** by means of a camera obscura. In the final lithographic print he added figures from his imagina-

above: 204. Camera obscura stamped with the name of Canaletto. 18th century. Glass lens, ground-glass plate 7½ × 8¼" (19 × 21 cm) in wooden box. Correr Museum, Venice.

right: 205. Frederick Catherwood. Part of La Casa de las Monjas, Uxmal, Mexico. 1844. Lithographic print from camera obscura drawing, 16¼ × 11⅝" (41 × 30 cm). From *Views of Central America, Chiapas, and Yucatan.*

206.
Philippe Halsman.
Dalí Atomicus. 1948.
Photograph.
© Yvonne Halsman,
1989.

tion. The value of the camera obscura was in the exactness and accuracy of the drawings, the best possible before photographic film existed.

Photography and the other art mediums have always had a close relationship, fertilizing each other with new ideas. Philippe Halsman's (1906–1979) *Dalí Atomicus* [206], showing Salvador Dalí in an "atomic" environment, is an amusing attempt by a photographer to rival the imaginative fantasies of Dalí himself. Photographers, the moment they think of their pictures as art, begin to show the influence of paintings and sculptures. On the other side, painters and sculptors use photography as a sketching tool and a source of inspiration. Before photography, artists often used "pattern books" of engravings of parts of the body, architecture, and of every detail an artist might suddenly need as a model. Photographs have largely taken over the job of showing us what the world looks like.

The feature that sets photography apart from the other visual arts is its objective recording of appearance. Since our eyes are our most important source of information, and photography serves as a tremendous extension of our eyes, photography is certainly more important as a source of information than it is as

below: 207.
William Henry Jackson.
*War Dance at Zuñi
Pueblo.* Photograph.
Colorado State
Historical Society,
Denver.

below right: 208.
Lewis W. Hine.
Carolina Cotton Mill.
1908. Gelatin-silver
print photograph.
Museum of
Modern Art,
New York.

an art medium. That is to say, the feelings and ideas of the artist and audience are in the long run less important than the fact that the information is recorded. Photography allows expression and interpretation, but it is alone in making possible an objective record.

From about 1870 to 1895, William Henry Jackson (1843–1942) traveled on foot, with an assistant and a mule heavily loaded with photographic equipment, all over the western United States. His thousands of photographs were among the documents that showed Americans the frontier lands of the West. *War Dance at Zuñi Pueblo* [207] is a wonderful record of that Indian town when white settlers were just beginning to invade its territory. The artist's feelings are impossible to ascertain from the photograph, and surely that is one of its great advantages. Such photographic records have been made of other countries, wars and political events, astronomical and experimental data in science—all extending our knowledge of the world in ways we now take for granted.

Some of the great photographers manage to combine the objectivity of the medium with their subjective intentions. A famous example is Lewis Hine (1874–1940), a sociologist who began about 1905 to take research photographs showing people at work. Using a large camera with 5-by-7-inch (13-by-18-centimeter) negatives, he took some of the early open-flash pictures using explosive magnesium powder, which extended the photographer's range into dark places and night times. *Carolina Cotton Mill* [208] was one of Hine's pictures which convinced the public that children were being exploited in American factories and mines. Its power to convince comes from the fact that Hine did not intrude and dramatize—he showed the scene as his eyes saw it.

Photographic technology has improved so much that it is hard to imagine taking pictures with the equipment W. H. Jackson or Lewis Hine used, even though we still admire their work. High-speed film, electronic flash, and small and miniature cameras have made it possible to take pictures under almost any conditions. Sports, in which humans are stretched to the limits of their strength, have always had a strong attraction for both photographers and their audiences. It is hard to imagine the sports pages of the newspaper without photographs— many sports pictures are among the most dramatic images we see. The picture of speed skater Bonnie Blair [209] by an Associated Press photographer is typical of the fine images we almost take for granted in the daily newspapers and in magazines.

Brett Weston's (b. 1911) *Century Plant* [210] is the kind of photograph which is obviously intended as a work of art, not a record of an event. If you could

above left: 209.
Associated Press photographer. Bonnie Blair winning the Women's 500 Meter World Cup speed-skating championship, Butte, Montana. 1987.

above: 210.
Brett Weston. *Century Plant.* 1977. Photograph. Collection of the artist.

A POINT IN TIME: Berenice Abbott
Recording New York

To photograph New York City means to seek to catch in the sensitive and delicate photographic emulsion the spirit of the metropolis, while remaining true to its essential fact, its hurrying tempo, its congested streets, the past jostling the present. . . . Already many an amazing and incredible building which was, or could have been, photographed five years ago has disappeared. The tempo of the metropolis is not of eternity, or even of time, but of the vanishing instant.

Berenice Abbott wrote those words in 1935, during a period of ten years dedicated to photographing the city.

Nightview [211] was taken about that time on a large view camera that accepted 8-by-10-inch (20-by-25-centimeter) negatives, with an exposure of fifteen minutes. To catch the windows lighted Abbott had to take the picture after dark but before offices closed at 5:00, which gave her about half an hour in the early darkness of December. She wrote about taking this photograph: "In this case I was at a window, not at the top of the building; there would have been too much wind outside. It was, of course, hard to get permission [to photograph in the building]. They always thought you wanted to commit suicide and superintendents were always tired, lazy and annoyed. They usually had to be bribed." We see the

seemingly endless expanse and depth of the city as an organism pulsing with light and life. Abbott always had, from her earliest work, the ability to understand and capture on film the significant truth about what could be seen. *Nightview* is a good example of Abbott's conviction that in photography interpretation is achieved by the artist's understanding of the subject, not by darkroom manipulation of the negative. Abbott's only change in her negatives was to crop them, which means to print only part of the negative.

Abbott, who was born in Springfield, Ohio, in 1898, learned photography when she got a job as laboratory assistant to the American photographer Man Ray in Paris in 1921. She moved in 1961 to Maine, where she lives in a restored inn which has become a mecca for those interested in photography. In the 40 years between she made every kind of photograph: portraits, revealing views of experiments in physics, and documentary pictures. For many years her work was largely ignored, but she practiced her art with a legendary selfless dedication which has been rewarded by recognition in her later years.

Quotations from Hank O'Neal, *Berenice Abbott, American Photographer*, with commentary by Berenice Abbott (New York: McGraw-Hill, 1982) 2.

examine the original print, rather than the reproduction in this book, it would be still more evident that it is a work of art, for Weston specializes in a very refined printing process that gives a fine-grained, silvery tone to the prints. It must not be forgotten that the original print of a photograph, like any other original print,

212. Jerry N. Uelsmann. *Kudzu House.* 1982. Photograph. Collection of the artist.

211.
Berenice Abbott.
Nightview.
c. 1935.
Photograph.

is the work of art. Reprintings in books and magazines are simply reproductions.

Jerry Uelsmann (YULES-man) (b. 1934) has written, "For me the darkroom functions as a visual research laboratory."[2] The idea that the photographic image is a product of visual research done in the artist's studio (darkroom) is one that some photographers disagree with, arguing that the photographer should print only what the camera records in one exposure. Uelsmann has been one of the leading photographers to take the view that photographic images are starting points for artistic composition. *Kudzu House* **[212]** was constructed of four negatives: one of the kudzu vines, one of an abandoned building, another of an ocean beach, and finally one of a small human figure. The sharp detail and the objectivity which we associate with the photographic medium give this image a strong psychological realism, like a vivid dream. We know that all these things exist in the natural world, but they come together as they do in our imaginations. Uelsmann's work is so clearly art—rather than science or journalism, for example—that it helps us see that other, more objective photographs are also art.

Color Photography

From the earliest days of photography color was considered the goal. The separate stones for each color in lithography was one of the hints which inventors had in their minds, and the craft of the artist was very much in the minds of early photographers. Not until 1907 was a form of color photography put on the market, the Autochrome, using a glass plate coated with starch grains dyed orange, green, and violet, each of which absorbed light of its complementary color and allowed its own color to print. This French process had a dotted "impressionistic" appearance, which may be more than mere coincidence. Yet the Autochrome dots are invisible—a million per square centimeter, a much finer grain than a television screen. Léon Gimpel's Autochrome *Family of Acrobats, Paris* [213] gives an idea of the soft, natural color of this method. The long exposure it required (one second in bright sunlight) was too much for two of the children, who moved slightly.

With modern color film, which came on the market in the late 1930s and the 1940s, the technical limits of color photography have disappeared. Now the limits are mental, spiritual, and artistic, the same as in any other art. In this most competitive international field, we are slowly beginning to be able to distinguish art from expertness.

Hideki Fujii's brilliant blue-and-yellow bathing suit picture [214] makes full use of the power of color and the power of shape, to the point that we nearly forget that a three-dimensional body is inside the suit. Powerfully contrasted colors, printed flat without highlights and shadows, produce a design of pure shapes that exceeds that made by Matisse by cutting plain blue paper [80]. It could be compared with the Japanese kimono designs [519, 520], which manifest the same abstract design sense, an important part of the Japanese tradition in art.

Although color photography offers a great temptation to make gorgeously colored abstractions, it also has the power to record the real world objectively. The color picture [215] taken by Susan Meiselas of a mass demonstration in Nicaragua in memory of a murdered young woman comes from the real world of pain and struggle. Yet it is a fascinating work of art, too, that turns that moment

below: 213. Léon Gimpel. *Family of Acrobats, Paris.*
c. 1910. Autochrome color photograph.
Collection de la Société Française
de Photographie, Paris.

right: 214. Hideki Fujii. Untitled. 1985. Color
photograph.

215. Susan Meiselas. *Nicaragua.* 1978. Color photograph. Collection of the artist.

into a symbol of all struggles of people for justice. The presence of the dead woman herself, in an enlarged black-and-white photograph, a beautiful face dreaming above the angry crowd, reminds us of the uses and powers of photographic images in our lives, both public and private.

Computer Graphics

Developments in electronics in the 20th century have given us several new mediums in the graphic arts. As we have seen earlier, drawing and printmaking have been in a constant state of evolution, sometimes at a speed more properly called a revolution. Electronic graphics are the latest development in this story. They are based on about two centuries of technical development in two fields which started out as quite separate: photography and electronics.

Compared with a pencil and paper, a computer is a very complicated instrument, one which few of us know how to make or repair. But with a few lessons, all of us can learn to operate it more quickly than we can learn to draw, paint, or carve manually. While the earlier technologies made pictures abundant and cheap enough that the size of the audience and the number of collectors expanded, the computer, like the camera before it, has made the craft of the artist easier to master. Just as the camera expanded the number of participants in visual art, the photo-electronic revolution is again democratizing the world of art.

The computer's production of still images has already made important contributions to art. Design in almost all its many aspects is mostly done on the computer screen. The architect and those who draft the plans for buildings can use the computer's power to quickly change scale and perspective, rotate designs to see other views, and repeat elements on command. Designers can try out colors and patterns, change them, and give logical commands whose appearance is unpredictable (such as "color higher elevations blue"). Images can also be made to move at rates coordinated to other effects such as music, so film animation is now done electronically.

We see computer graphics so often and in so many mediums that we have a hard time realizing that the same tool was used. Television and all the film mediums are especially adapted to computer graphics, but any medium which can make use of photographs can be adapted to computer manipulation. Until recently the obstacle to electronic art was the production of "hard copy"—the picture on paper which can be hung on the wall. One of the common solutions has been to make color photographs directly from the computer screen [216]. Martin Maguss's *Rex Goes on Vacation* is a large Cibachrome color photograph made from a computer screen. The photograph converts the **pixels** (a word coined from "picture element," meaning a dot of light or darkness on the screen) of the electronic medium to the smooth color fields of the chemical medium of photography. Light and shadow are convincingly suggested to give a fantastic realism to this funny picture, full of incompatible things such as lightning in a starry sky, the floor in isometric perspective and the chair in central perspective, not to speak of the dinosaur in the swimming pool.

The development of digital imagery brings together drawing, photography, and video into one compatible system, a system which will soon be within the budget of the average consumer. A photograph, video image, or drawing can be digitized (all its variables coded in a numbering system in the computer) and brought up on the computer screen. The artist can then change it or add to it and finally print it on a standard computer printer. The limitations on this system are the same kinds of limitations we found in any other print medium—the limits of the tools. From the point of view of art printing, the basic character of computer printing is the electronic "grain" (or pixels) of the image on the screen and in the resulting print. Actually, in currently available computers and

216. Martin Maguss. *Rex Goes on Vacation.* 1987. Cibachrome photograph (created on a Genigraphics 100D computer, several multiple exposures), 20 × 30" (51 × 76 cm). Collection of the artist, San Francisco.

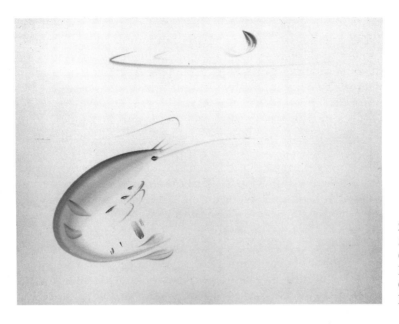

217. Steve Strassmann. *Shrimp and Leaf.* 1986. Computer graphic. MIT Media Lab, Cambridge, Massachusetts.

printers very subtle color transitions can be printed, with more than 1000 dots per square inch.

Even the challenge of "brushmarks" has been accepted by software designers, and we can see the kinds of results achieved in 1986 in Steve Strassmann's *Shrimp and Leaf* **[217]**, done at the MIT Media Lab. The model on which *Shrimp and Leaf* is based is an Oriental brush drawing, made with a tool which is extremely responsive to the artist's hand. As in the field of artificial intelligence, it is the most purely human which is the highest challenge to the electronic mediums. Strassmann proves that technology has reached a point that the main limits on electronically generated prints are human limits.

Video

Video art is the adaptation of the television medium, which we ordinarily think of as the expression of large corporate bodies, to individual expression. Video art has a history of about thirty years, during which all aspects of the video form have been used by artists. The first element of video to become available was the television set, or *monitor*, which is used as one object in an assembled complex of forms. About 1965 the portable video camera became available, permitting simultaneous recording and display of the image, as well as delayed display or taping. From the first, video has had strong connections to performance arts, social criticism, and experimental art.

Video is unusual in its ability to involve the viewer in the image— "interactive video." Bill Viola's *He Weeps for You*, made in 1976, was one example. This was a subtle application of interactive video requiring a viewer, a source of water falling in drops onto a toy drum, a video camera, and screen projection of the video image 4 feet (1.2 meters) high. The drops of water reflected the viewer and were recorded highly magnified by the zoom lens of the camera. The viewer saw his or her own image on the screen as reflected in the magnified drops and heard the amplified sound of the drops as they hit the drum.[3] Interactive video has no fixed form, but provides certain conditions within which the viewer's activity produces an image.

The first artist to make a name in video art was Korean-born Nam June Paik *(pike)* (b. 1932), who bought thirteen used television sets in 1963 for use in his art. He has used television in several ways: the monitor is part of a sculpture, sometimes "preparing" it by taking it apart or manipulating the screen image with magnets, and more recently by making videotapes. *TV Buddha* [218], done in 1974, consists of three parts: the antique Buddha statue of wood, the video camera, and the screen which projects instantly what the camera records. In this case the camera records the Buddha meditating on his own image on the screen. Although not an interactive image in the usual sense, *TV Buddha* dramatizes the interactive principle of video art.

Paik, who has an advanced education in musical composition, has given performances of his own avant-garde music in which the use of the tape recorder and electronic sound are vital, but he also wanted to expand the *visual* expression of music. Video, music, and performance combine in some of Paik's best-known work, done in collaboration with cellist Charlotte Moorman. In *TV Cello* [219] Moorman plays a cello made of three video monitors with their casings removed, larger screens on top and bottom to suggest the shape of a cello. The screens show Moorman, a camera recording the event and projecting it as it occurs. She also wears *TV Glasses*, invented by Paik, in which she sees herself.

Paik has been inventively exploring the medium, emphasizing its involvement with time—as a still object (the monitor), a mirror of the present, or record of the past for future projection, or any combination of those—projecting abstract designs made by electronic and magnetic means, as well as showing images from the real world. His work has gradually shifted from mainly sculptural forms to an increased use of videotape.

Guadalcanal Requiem [220], made during the 1970s, is Paik's most complex videotape, the latest version running 29 minutes. The central imagery focuses on Charlotte Moorman playing the cello on the beach of Guadalcanal Island, in the

below left: 218.   Nam June Paik. *TV Buddha*. 1974. Video camera, monitor, antique statue of Buddha. Stedelijk Museum, Amsterdam.

below right: 219.   Nam June Paik. *TV Cello* and *TV Glasses*. 1971. Video camera, three monitors, glasses; life-size. Collections of Charlotte Moorman, New York, and the artist, New York. © 1971 by Peter Moore.

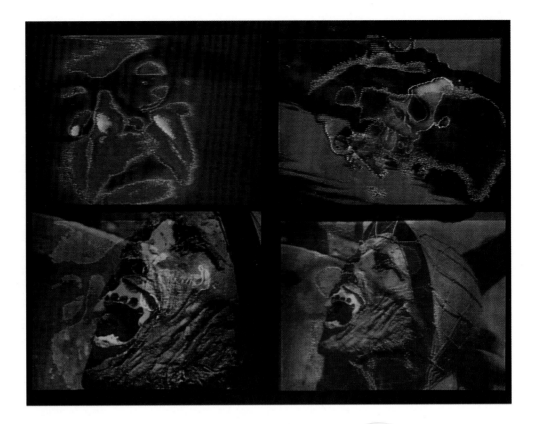

South Pacific, surrounded by wreckage of the great battles fought there in 1942. The subject has both a present and a past. It is also pictorial and abstract, as Paik presents it, and has both a purely visual effect and an anti-war message. Videotape allows Paik greater complexity than attainable in his sculptural video art because it represents much that cannot really be present and it permits time to see a variety of images.

Paik is concerned about the worldwide effects of television. "Video has immeasurable magical powers," he has written. "This means that the Eskimos' ancient traditional culture is in danger of being rapidly crushed by the bulldozers of Hollywood. The satellite's amplification of the freedom of the strong must be accompanied by the protection of the culture of the weak. . . ."[4] As a person who has bridged the Oriental and Western cultures and the traditional and avant-garde arts, Paik sees both the danger that electronic mediums will bring us boring similarity around the world and the opportunity that these mediums will bring peace and understanding. His work is his statement that artists, as well as commercial entrepreneurs, must be involved in the development of electronic mediums.

Cinema

Cinema, films, motion pictures, or movies—whichever term we use, this medium when compared to video has a different relation to time and to abstraction. The camera, the projector, and the screen have never taken an obvious part in the work of art as the video monitor has. They have always been considered supports for the art, comparable to the wall on which a picture is hung. The art of cinema is what is on the film and, like any other art, its content can be analyzed from two aspects, the form and the subject. The form is the film, the camera, and all the lights, dollies, microphones, projector, screen, and other equipment that help put the image and sound track on the film. But it is also the planning of shots and the editing into a continuous series of images. The subject

220. Nam June Paik. *Guadalcanal Requiem.* 1977. Videotape, 29 minutes. Distributed by Electronic Arts Intermix, New York.

221. D. W. Griffith. *Birth of a Nation.* 1915. Film still; panorama of battle with "iris effect" blocking outer edges of scene.

is the story. The content is the meaning, both emotional and intellectual, of the story.

The early directors, such as D. W. Griffith (1875–1948) in the United States and Abel Gance *(gawnse)* in France, saw the movies as a chance to produce dramas on an epic scale that was impossible on the stage. The camera could record immense panoramas, with a cast of thousands. *Panning* (from the word "panorama"), in which the camera turns across a scene, converted the whole surrounding environment into a stage. Although he had begun as a playwright, Griffith learned how to take advantage of the epic possibilities of cinema that differentiated it from stage drama. *Birth of a Nation* **[221]**, filmed in 1914 in nine weeks (which was considered a long time) for $125,000 (a record amount at the time), was the culmination of Griffith's film-making. He had learned the art of cinema by trial and error, making more than four hundred short films between 1908 and 1913. Two of the many things he learned were the usefulness of varied shots and the importance of editing, both basic differences from staged theater. The shot (a piece of film in which the camera appears to have run without stopping[5]) that was commonly used for a whole picture when Griffith began his work was what is now called the "full shot" or "far shot," showing the full figures of the actors within a stage-like environment. Griffith began to move the camera closer or farther away, to pan by turning the camera to follow action, and even to use "tracking shots" by moving the camera on a track. Then in editing these varied shots were combined to tell the story. The drama of *Birth of a Nation* focused on a Southern family (the Camerons) and a Northern family (the Stonemans) who struggled and suffered through the Civil War but were finally united by a marriage. The colossal theme of the war and Reconstruction called for panoramic scenes of battles and politics, but the intimate life of the families had to be portrayed in closer, more intimate, psychological form. Griffith laid the groundwork in film technique for both those aspects of cinematic art.

Today, perhaps even more than in Griffith's day, editing remains at the core of the art of film-making. Carol Littleton edited her first Hollywood film in 1974 and has since been the editor of a long series of notable movies, among them *Body Heat, The Big Chill, Places in the Heart, Silverado,* and *Brighton Beach Memoirs.* In an interview published in 1987, Littleton discussed her work, describing the process of learning by doing, learning the tools of a complicated technical skill. An editor, she said, has to have "a good mixture of an analytical approach—understanding characterization, structure, and so forth—and an

Art Mediums

A POINT IN TIME: Mickey Mouse

Walt Disney, then 26 years old, and his collaborator, Ub Iwerks, were faced with a crisis: the hero of their animated cartoons, a small black animal with a white face and big ears named Oswald the Lucky Rabbit, was legally the property of their film distributor, and he wanted to cut Disney out of the company. In self-defense Disney and Iwerks invented Mickey Mouse, who debuted in 1928, when sound film was brand new. Mickey had to have a voice, and after many auditions it was decided that only Walt Disney himself could speak Mickey's lines in the proper falsetto. Disney spoke for Mickey Mouse for 25 years. *Steamboat Willie*, Mickey Mouse's first film, was the first sound cartoon and *The Band Concert* (1935) [**222**] was one of the early films in Technicolor. Sound and color film were not Disney inventions, but he was responsible for a style of film animation which has so thoroughly dominated that art that we can hardly imagine there is another way to do it. Strangely enough, Walt Disney never drew a figure himself after about 1926, leaving the drawing of the thousands of figures and scenes required for animation to a huge crew of hard-working artists. But Disney knew exactly what he wanted and worked very closely with the animators.

The action in film animation is achieved by a series of pictures ("frames") which show transitions in the movement. This is done now largely by computer programs, but in Disney's time every picture was entirely drawn by hand. Disney's artists understood the active power of the curved line; if we look at Mickey [**222**] we see almost nothing but curves, each one ready to expand into motion as the frames pass through the projector, the more transitions shown, the smoother the action. Cartoons were action comedies. In *The Band Concert* Mickey conducts the town band in "The William Tell Overture" but finds his music interrupted by a swarm of bees, a street vendor (played by Donald Duck) playing "Turkey in the Straw" on his harmonica, and finally a tornado. Almost every line drawn for the thousands of frames of the short cartoon had a springy curve. The Disney style took such complete advantage of the curving action line that it is difficult for animators to find an action style that does not appear to derive from Disney.

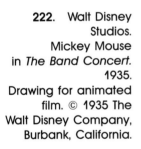

222. Walt Disney Studios. Mickey Mouse in *The Band Concert*. 1935. Drawing for animated film. © 1935 The Walt Disney Company, Burbank, California.

emotional approach—being able to let yourself go and enjoy the movie. . . . as a member of the audience. . . ." The biggest problem, she said, is time pressure from producers who count the cost of a film in hours of work. "But it doesn't work that way," Littleton insisted. "We're not manufacturing tires. We're not stamping out cookies. It's so much more than a mechanical process." Editing is "truly collaborative," she explained. "I have a role to play as an editor. I am not doing my own movie; I am interpreting the director's movie. There's a great deal of myself in it, undoubtedly, but I need to understand the director's point of view—what he or she needs to do—and execute it as best as possible."[6]

Nam June Paik, commenting on "the painstaking process of editing" his videotapes, mentions that editing is a simulation of the brain function of changing the time structure of real life experience, cutting from one shot (or memory) to another, shortening or lengthening the time in terms of its emotional meaning.[7]

We have all grown so accustomed to the horizontal rectangle of the projected movie image that we never think how different it is from the shape of other art forms, which are often vertical rectangles or three-dimensional forms of space or solid. But there are several good reasons for the shape of the image (which we usually call the screen) in a horizontal rectangle. First, it conforms to our natural visual field, which is about twice as wide as it is high. Second, it provides stable horizontal and vertical margins for the changing and moving viewpoint of the camera's shots. The commonest proportions for the screen are 1:1.33, or three units high to four wide.[8] That is a compromise between the natural visual field, which is much wider, and our desire to look closely at details, especially details of faces, which are called "close-up shots" (close-ups, for short). Experiments with wide-screen movies show that they are most effective in showing landscape. They show too much irrelevant background in the close-ups and thereby reduce the effect of psychological drama. And it is in psychological drama that the film excels.

It is not only the close-up and the dramatic story that contribute to the psychological power of the film, but also the fact that the audience experiences movies as a group. The group reinforces and enhances the mood and meaning experienced by each individual in it, a factor ordinarily absent from our experience of other arts, in which each member of the audience is alone with the work of art.

The 1987 film *Blue Velvet* [223] is a gripping psychological thriller based on two traditional story types: the coming-of-age and the Freudian version of the Greek myth of Oedipus *(ED-i-pus)*. The screenplay was written by its director, David Lynch. The film was photographed by Frederick Elmes and edited by Duwayne Dunham. On the surface it is the story of a romance between Jeff, just back from college, and Sandy, the pretty high school senior. But from the opening scenes, which descend from a typical American small town into the lawn

223.   David Lynch, director. *Blue Velvet*. 1987. Still from color film (actors: Kyle MacLachlan as Jeff and Isabella Rossellini as Dorothy). De Laurentis Entertainment Group.

224. Bill Lundberg. *Nocturne*. 1984. Color film with sound, projected on headboard of bed. Collection of the artist, Austin, Texas.

where insects struggle violently beneath the grass, we know that we are to penetrate beneath surface appearance. It is Jeff's subconscious mind we penetrate, not through close-ups but by a dream-like drama played by symbolic characters in symbolic settings. Jeff is surrounded by characters in pairs: his father and the insane villain Frank, his mother and the night club singer Dorothy. The dark red walls and curving entrance of Dorothy's apartment create a womb-like sensuality for scenes played between Jeff and Dorothy. By the end of the film, when Jeff has had an affair with Dorothy and killed Frank, he is liberated from his psychological conflicts, and the reward for his coming of age is Sandy (whose story should be told in another film.)[9] The impact of the film is as much in its dark and mysterious colors as in the spoken dialogue, for the words are often conventional but the colors used in the film are unusual and convey their messages to our subconscious minds.

Not all films are the expensive products of an industry. *Nocturne* [224] was made in 1984 by Bill Lundberg as an individual artist. The film, in color with a sound track of footsteps and birdsongs, is projected on the semicircular headboard of an old iron bed. It shows "a night-time trip down an anonymous country road," Lundberg has said. "This surreal vision just above the pillow was meant to entice visitors to lie down on the bed and enter into the fantasy. Whether anyone did or not I don't know."[10] Film becomes part of a sculpture in Lundberg's work, with the element of time introduced by the movement of the filmed image, but without the story which dominates in many cinematic works of art.

Film has no rivals in its power to tell stories, but it can also introduce movement, time, and interaction with the viewer in ways that video and cinema are currently exploring.

Summary for Review

The graphic arts are **drawing**, *printmaking*, *graphic design and illustration*, *photography*, and the related electronic mediums of *computer graphics*, *video*, and *cinema*. These mediums have always served as communication arts and especially today bring art to a vast audience. Drawing is one of the basic expressions of creativity; its tools are anything that makes a mark. There are three reasons for drawing: to record an idea or something seen **(sketch)**, to prepare the design of another work **(study)**, or for its own sake **(finished drawing)**. Printmaking began as a way of reproducing drawings in an **edition**, but the qualities of each medium are valued for their own beauty. **Relief** printing is done by **woodcut** or **linocut**. **Intaglio** printing is done by **engraving** or **etching**. *Stencil* printing is done by **serigraphy**, or silkscreen print. **Lithography**, or printing from stone, depends on chemical opposition of grease and water on a flat surface. *Graphic design illustrations* are designed for reproduction by industrial printing. *Photography*, a chemical process, was the first duplicating process that did not depend on drawing. Black-and-white and color photography show the interaction of the artist's consciousness with the objective visible world. Both drawing and photography have been adapted to electronic signals which can be manipulated by the artist in *computer graphics*, *video*, and *cinema*. Animation, now done by computer, permits drawing in these mediums, although photography is basic. Video has been used both as sculpture and as a film medium. Psychological drama is the special strength of cinema.

Painting

The novelist Oscar Wilde wrote of a painted portrait of Dorian Gray that aged horribly as Gray lived his wicked life, while the man remained unchanged, as if he were a painting. There is something magical about paintings. If you show people a painting and ask "What is this?" most people will not say, "It is a painting." They are likely to answer, "A vase of flowers" or whatever the subject may be. As you look back at the recorded comments of the critics and audience in earlier times you will find an amazing variety of painting styles described as absolutely lifelike. That is merely testimony to the complementary facts that painters try to represent things as they see them and that the audience learns to see the world through the eyes of the painters.

Given the mystique that surrounds painting, it may be a good idea to look at it very materialistically. Artists and collectors are those most likely to answer, "It's a painting." Neither of those groups can afford to be mesmerized by the mystique, but they must know how a painting is made, how to care for it, and how to pick out the better ones. That does not mean they get less out of the subject—more likely the opposite.

There are five major painting mediums: fresco, watercolor, tempera, oil, and acrylics and other synthetic resins. Each of those mediums is distinguished by its use of a different kind of glue, called the **binder**, to hold the colored pigments together and to attach them to a surface. **Pigment** is colored powder, usually made of minerals (which sets paint pigment apart from a dye or stain, which usually has color from plants). Ultramarine, for example, is a blue pigment now made in chemical laboratories, but which used to be made by grinding up the semi-precious stone lapis lazuli. To make paint, pigments are thoroughly mixed with a binder, which is the most important part in the sense that its chemical characteristics require certain methods of painting. Each binder requires a different **solvent** or thinner, and each one can be applied to a different group of **grounds**, or surfaces. Each may require a different set of painting tools and different techniques. The painting may be able to survive outdoors, or it may need to be protected from bright light, depending mainly on the binder. The term **medium**—the plural is either *mediums* or *media*—refers to any system which carries communications or expressions. In painting, the word is used for the whole process in which a specific solvent, binder, and ground are used together. In some the medium takes its name from the solvent (watercolor), in others from the binder (oil).

We will examine those five major mediums, but you should remember that there are others which are less commonly met. **Encaustic**, for example, uses pigments mixed with melted wax, the solvent being heat. That technique was commonly used for decorating Egyptian mummy cases [225], and it is still used occasionally. From time to time you are certain to encounter mediums that are new to you, since artists are constantly experimenting with new materials. The basic problem for the artist and the collector is to find out the characteristics of the medium, how it can be used effectively, and what kind of care paintings in that medium need.

225. Egypt. Portrait on mummy case of Artemidorus. 1st century A.D. Encaustic on wood. Metropolitan Museum of Art, New York.

A POINT IN TIME: Jasper Johns'
First Show

226. Jasper Johns. *Flag.* 1955.
Encaustic, oil, collage on fabric; 3'6¼" × 5'5⅝" (1 × 1.5 m). Museum of Modern Art, New York
(gift of Philip Johnson in honor of Alfred H. Barr, Jr.).

In 1958 the New York art dealer Leo Castelli presented a show by the 29-year-old painter Jasper Johns which not only sold out but changed the direction of American art. A reviewer called Johns "the brand-new darling" of the art world. Castelli recalls that he was introduced to Johns by the painter Robert Rauschenberg. "I walked into the studio and there was this attractive, very shy young man, and all these paintings. It was astonishing, a complete body of work. It was the most incredible thing I've ever

Fresco

The ancient medium of **fresco** has been given up for dead every few centuries, but whenever there are good solid walls to paint on it comes back to life. It was practiced by the ancient Greeks and Romans, was largely ignored by Gothic artists, who made stained-glass windows instead, was brought back to glorious life in the Renaissance, was given up for dead in the 19th century, and revived again in modern Mexico. It grew out of a simpler technique of painting on dry plaster walls called "fresco secco," a name meaning dry fresco. It appears that some painter must have been in a hurry and painted on a lime plaster wall that was still wet, later discovering that those parts were much more durable than seen in my life." Among the unusual features of Johns' work was his use of encaustic, in which the pigment is mixed with hot wax and troweled on with a palette-knife. What led up to this show, and where did it lead?

Johns, born in Augusta, Georgia, in 1930, studied at the University of South Carolina, then served in the Army, and in 1953 went to New York, intending to finish college. He had been painting for several years and planned to study art. After one day of classes he dropped out, took a job in a bookstore, and kept on painting. A year later he destroyed all his art work. He explained, "Before, whenever anybody asked me what I did I said I was going to become an artist. Finally I decided that I could be going to become an artist forever, all my life. I decided to stop *becoming*, and *to be* an artist." So he started over from scratch.

The New York art world of the early 1950s was dominated by the **Abstract Expressionist** style, a style that called for large, dramatic expressions of individual personality. Johns has said, "If I could do anything I wanted to do, then what I wanted to do was find out what I did that other people didn't, what I was that other people weren't." It turned out that there were several things he did that were unusual. Among them were painting with encaustic, building up a heavy, rather sculptural-looking surface; another was casting in plaster; and a third was making paintings of such things as the American flag [226], targets, and numbers and alphabets incorporating plaster casts of faces. These were the paintings that amazed the art world in 1958. Johns, along with several other artists, was considered a major figure in the new **Pop Art** movement, with the idea that such things as flags and targets were public (*pop*ular) themes, not private symbols invented by the artist. No one had seen this kind of art before, even though the subjects were things everyone had seen many times.

The art historian Leo Steinberg wrote about his reaction to Johns' show: "My own first reaction was

227. Jasper Johns in 1959.

normal. I disliked the show. . . . I was angry at the artist, as if he had invited me to a meal, only to serve something uneatable." That kind of reaction was common, but the originality and skill of the work were unmistakable, and collectors and museums flocked to buy.

Johns' own reaction was perhaps not what you would expect. For a young artist who has just sold out a show and become the darling of the art world, he looks very somber in a photograph taken at the time [227]. Johns says he "liked the attention," but during the next year he changed from the style which was so successful. *False Start* was the title he gave to a painting in his next style, an abstraction in bright splashy colors painted in oil paint. A very private person, Johns appears to have been bothered by his sudden celebrity. It might almost seem as if he wanted to destroy all his work again and start anew from scratch. In spite of this sensitivity and his rejection of personal celebrity, Johns has remained one of the most productive and original artists of his time.

the parts painted on dry plaster. Fresco ("fresh") uses the wet lime plaster as the binder, the pigments being mixed only with water. As the plaster sets, calcium carbonate forms a protective coating on the surface. Fresco is naturally used to decorate buildings, since the plaster is too heavy and fragile to be easily used for an easel picture. Thus it is appropriate for us to look at two decorated buildings.

Although we see few frescos in the United States, there are many great examples in world art, including several of supreme importance—the "superstars" of world art. Michelangelo's Sistine Chapel Ceiling is at the top of that list, and we should look also at a modern fresco series, Orozco's murals in the Cabañas Orphanage in Guadalajara, Mexico. Between those two great series we can learn most of the potential of the fresco medium.

left: 228. Michelangelo. Ceiling of the
Sistine Chapel, Vatican, Rome. 1508–1512.
Fresco, 44 × 128′ (13.4 × 39 m).

above: 229. Michelangelo. *Noah's Ark and the
Flood*. Detail of ceiling of the Sistine Chapel,
Vatican, Rome. 1509. Fresco.

Michelangelo's Sistine Chapel Ceiling

The Sistine Chapel [228], built by Pope Sixtus IV, was used for the private
devotions of the papal court and as a meeting place for the College of Cardinals,
and served as the nerve-center of Christendom of its time. Its side walls already
had fresco murals of an earlier generation of artists, including Botticelli, when
Pope Julius II in 1508 asked Michelangelo to paint the ceiling. The Pope's idea
was to paint the Twelve Apostles, but Michelangelo objected to the design. In
later years Michelangelo remembered the Pope telling him to paint anything he
liked, but the vast theological story embedded in the paintings presupposes the
presence of a scholar as Michelangelo's adviser. That adviser was almost certainly Cardinal Marco Vigerio, a close associate of Pope Julius II.

Work began on stories from Genesis telling of the beginnings of the world,
with hundreds of drawings, in which the artist invented figures and compositions to express the great theme. Then the **cartoons**—the full-scale drawings—
were made. Ready to begin painting, Michelangelo instructed his mason where
to place the first patch of new lime plaster. Since painting could be done only on
fresh plaster that had not chemically set, the patch for one day's work would be
about a square yard or the size of one head, those being considered one day's
production. The cartoon would be held up over the fresh plaster and a sharp
point would be run over the main lines, pressing them into the soft plaster
(which explains why few cartoons survive). The torn remains of the cartoon
would be discarded and painting would begin on the smooth, damp plaster
surface.

Michelangelo began painting at the end farthest from the altar and with the end of the story, *Noah's Ark and the Flood* [229]. Michelangelo needed two tries on the first parts he painted because the plaster had the wrong composition. He was deeply depressed about his work. Looking at the Flood panels critically he realized that the scale of the figures had to be enlarged and the setting simplified to be seen effectively from the floor. Beginning with *The Temptation and Expulsion from Eden*, he enlarged the scale of the figures and simplified the scenes. He alternated wide panels with narrow panels framed by medallions and male nudes, added powerful athletes with no connection to the Bible story, then a band of illusionistic architecture and a series of enthroned Prophets and Sibyls, who had predicted the coming of Christ. All of these figures grew larger, more effectively lighted and colored, as Michelangelo gained experience with the fresco medium.

The most famous individual panel is *The Creation of Adam* [230], in which we see God transmitting the spark of life into the drowsy body of Adam. You can see the plain white plaster of the background, with cracks which have developed in the ancient building. You can see the lines pressed through the cartoon on the top of the bent leg [231]. At the end of the day the edge of the plaster was

230. Michelangelo. *The Creation of Adam.* Detail of ceiling of the Sistine Chapel, Vatican, Rome. 1511–1512. Fresco.

231. Michelangelo. Detail from *The Creation of Adam.* Detail of ceiling of the Sistine Chapel, Vatican, Rome. 1511–1512. Fresco.

above left: 232.   José Clemente Orozco. Cabañas Orphanage, Guadalajara, Mexico. 1939. Fresco.

above right: 233.   José Clemente Orozco. *Cortez and the Conquest*. Detail of ceiling of Cabañas Orphanage, Guadalajara, Mexico. 1939. Fresco.

carefully trimmed with a trowel and new plaster was put on at the beginning of the next day's work. Ordinarily, the painter tried to divide the work so he would not have to match colors from one day's work to the next. Those joints can be seen at the top of the outstretched arm and, very faintly, at the base of the neck and around the top of the head, that head being one day's work for Michelangelo.

Michelangelo's imaginative power rested on the Judeo-Christian conception that God created the human body "in His own image." Going far beyond his many drawings of the human figure, in the powerful figures of the Creator and Adam he gave that conception a form which has never been rivaled.

Orozco's Cabañas Orphanage

José Clemente Orozco *(o-ROS-ko)* (1883–1949) is widely considered the greatest of the modern Mexican painters and the Cabañas Orphanage his finest work **[232]**. The 200-year-old chapel with a high dome forms the entrance to a group of orphanage buildings in the city of Guadalajara, in western Mexico.

Orozco spent seven years in the United States in the late 1920s and early 1930s, painting important murals at Pomona College and Dartmouth College and taking part in New York art life. In 1934 he was attracted back to Mexico by commissions from the Mexican government, but his terrific, pessimistic murals would hardly be called government propaganda. Between 1936 and 1940 he painted a large group of important murals in state government buildings in Guadalajara, about the same length of time it took Michelangelo to paint the Sistine Ceiling.

More than Michelangelo, Orozco was given independence to choose his own subjects, and he chose the history of the Americas as the general theme of the Cabañas murals. Not one to glorify ancient times as a golden age, he shows the gloomy and threatening gods of ancient Mexico, then the arrival of the Spanish conquerors as machine-men, literally heartless, inspired by a mechanical angel as they butcher the native people [233]. Mixed with these historical subjects are others of more general symbolism, such as the Apocalyptic horses charging across the sky above a Mexican village, the houses looking like rows of coffins, the invisible riders brandishing spears [234]. Around the base of the dome are armed workers climbing a rocky cliff, then symbols of the arts and professions, and, finally, above a ring of windows, the red-and-black composition *Man of Fire* in the dome [235]. Earth, Water, and Air, as gray figures of the material world, recline around the edge of the dome, while the dematerialized spirit of Fire disappears in steep foreshortening into the heavens.

Both of these mural series were strong examples for their times. Succeeding centuries continually returned to the ceiling of the Sistine Chapel as the supreme expression of Western art. Orozco's example has been followed less obviously; his most successful followers were not in Mexico, but in New York, where about ten years later his grand scale, slashing style of brushwork and personal expression were adopted for oil paintings by the Abstract Expressionists.

below left: 234.
José Clemente Orozco. *Apocalypse*. Detail of wall of Cabañas Orphanage, Guadalajara, Mexico. 1939. Fresco.

below: 235.
José Clemente Orozco. *Man of Fire*. Dome of Cabañas Orphanage, Guadalajara, Mexico. 1939. Fresco, diameter 30½' (9.3 m).

The two artists' techniques, being very different, show the range of possibilities in fresco. Michelangelo did not allow brushstrokes to show, turning each mark into a colored light or shadow and producing illusions of mass and space. Orozco never lets us forget that the picture was made by the movement of a human hand; each mark remains as a mark even though it forms part of a person or a horse. Orozco tried not to close his lines into shapes, since that would reduce their energy. Michelangelo, who always considered himself basically a sculptor, tried not to let lines show, but to blend them into the illumination of masses to make the figures as sculptural as possible. He relied on color and shapes to give spirit and energy to the design.

Watercolor

The binder for **watercolor** is the resin of the acacia tree, which is called **gum arabic**. The solvent, of course, is water. By about 1780 European painters in watercolor no longer had to mix the pigment and gum arabic themselves, but could buy cakes of paint ready-made at pharmacies; one English merchant advertised himself as "Superfine Water-Colour Cake Preparer to Her Majesty and the Royal Family." At the same time fine watercolor paper was invented and offered for sale. Thus all the ingredients were ready to launch a great period of watercolor painting: the paints, the paper, and the interest of a royal patron.

Pigments mixed with gum binders had been used earlier—for centuries in China, where watercolor was often applied to silk—but the inventor of transparent watercolor of the modern sort was Albrecht Dürer, who used it for sketching landscapes on a trip to Venice in 1494. It remained in use for painting miniatures and for tinting maps and drawings, but not until the 18th century did its delicacy and luminosity become fashionable and appealing to a wide audience.

It was in England that the best work in watercolor was done, and it was used mainly for landscape. It was part of the newly popular "sightseeing," the search for the picturesque ("like a picture"), the sublime and awe-inspiring, which accompanied the beginnings of the scientific study of nature. "The art of sketching is to the picturesque traveller, what the art of writing is to the scholar," said a writer of travel books in that period.[1] Despite the fragility of watercolor paintings, which will fade if hung in bright light, there was a large audience eager to purchase them, especially if they showed a famous or dramatic scene.

Two of the finest English masters of watercolor were born the same year (1775): Joseph M. W. Turner and Thomas Girtin. Girtin died at age 27, but Turner lived to be 76 and produced many more paintings, in oil as well as in watercolor. Turner's oils were criticized for looking like his watercolors, and there is truth to the charge; he tried to retain in oils the effects of light which are natural to watercolor. The watercolor, *The Burning of the Houses of Parliament* [236], was based on an actual event but was painted from memory and imagination. The atmosphere is enhanced by the varying strength of the color washes, and the agitation of the crowd is conveyed by the simple shapes and lack of detail. Gum arabic is such a weak glue that it can hold only a little pigment, so the brilliance of the color is enhanced by the light reflected from the white paper through the thin washes of color. It is this light reflected through color that is meant by the term "luminosity" in referring to watercolor. In fact, the power of color is a large part of the appeal of Turner's work. He used the medium with maximum freedom, scratching the paper to give white lines and dots and sometimes adding opaque white paint—a practice which proper English watercolor painters regarded as breaking the rules. Turner was not concerned with that rule, nor with the one that says no corrections should be made, since they inevitably show through the transparent color.

In *The Gorge of Wathenlath with the Falls of Lodore, Derwentwater* **[237]**, Thomas Girtin showed a famous tourist sight. A popular travel writer described a visit there: " 'Which way to Watenlath?' said one of our company to a peasant. 'That way,' said he, pointing to a lofty mountain, steeper than the tiling of a house."[2] The tangled crags and wooded gorge rise to the clouds, the trees blowing in the wind. No artist exceeded Girtin in bringing atmosphere into a painting, and no medium adapts so well as watercolor to wind, mist, clouds, and rain. The nature of the medium is ideal for landscape.

236.
Joseph M. W. Turner.
The Burning of the Houses of Parliament.
1834. Watercolor and gouache on gray paper,
11¾ × 17¾"
(30 × 45 cm).
Tate Gallery, London.

237. Thomas Girtin.
The Gorge of Wathenlath with the Falls of Lodore, Derwentwater, Cumberland.
c. 1801. Watercolor, pencil, reed pen on paper;
21 × 17" (8 × 7 cm).
Ashmolean Museum, Oxford, England.

238. Winslow Homer. *Woodsman and Fallen Tree*. 1891. Watercolor on paper, 14 × 20″ (36 × 51 cm). Museum of Fine Arts, Boston (bequest of William Sturgis Bigelow).

The American painter Winslow Homer (1836–1910) gave the watercolor technique and its subjects an American twist. Hunters, fishermen, and pioneers abound in his landscapes, such as *Woodsman and Fallen Tree* [238]. Homer was expert at retaining the paper as his white and at drawing freely but with perfect control. Watercolor, of all the mediums, is the one that demands an unhesitating hand. Homer's confident placement of shadows on the fallen tree, leaving the

239. Carolyn Brady. *Blueberry Jam*. 1979. Watercolor on paper, 39 × 28½″ (99 × 72 cm). Nancy Hoffman Gallery, New York.

white of the paper for the highlights, appears a simple matter, but can be achieved only by years of practice with the brush.

Contemporary watercolor painters are working on a scale earlier artists would have found hard to imagine. Carolyn Brady's (b. 1937) *Blueberry Jam* [239], which measures 39 by 28½ inches (99 by 72 centimeters), is a size that used to be considered appropriate for oil paintings but too large for watercolor, which was thought to be delicate, intimate, and properly small. Recent watercolors often reach sizes much larger than this example and often have a ruggedness that would be out of place on a breakfast table. The effects of light and the subtle variations of white used by Brady would be hard to match in any other medium. Those qualities, achieved so well in *Blueberry Jam,* are part of the natural luminosity of watercolor, produced by very faint washes of thin color on the white paper.

Tempera

The ancient medium of **tempera**, in which pigment is mixed with egg yolk, has been especially important in 20th-century American art. Tempera had been ignored for several centuries when the young Peter Hurd (1904–1984) began to experiment with it in 1930. He had recently married Henriette Wyeth (daughter of the famous illustrator N. C. Wyeth and sister of Andrew Wyeth) and moved back to his native New Mexico. Tempera appealed to him for its precision and detail and for the brilliance of the light reflected from the **gesso** (gypsum, or plaster of Paris) coating of the wood or masonite panel often used as the ground for this medium. In *El Mocho* [240] every brush stroke is revealed, since the paint dries almost instantly—notice the jacket. But Hurd was expert at modeling forms in light and shade by adding fine lines of the shading color; notice the hills. Oil paint is different from tempera because oil dries so slowly the painter can blend different colors together. In tempera that is not possible; the transitions must be made by feathery strokes, each slightly changing the color.

240. Peter Hurd. *El Mocho.* 1936. Tempera on panel, 30 × 25⅛" (76 × 64 cm). Art Institute of Chicago (Watson F. Blair Purchase Prize, 1937).

241. Andrew Wyeth, *Indian Summer.* 1970. Tempera on panel, 3'6" × 2'11" (1 × 0.9 m). Brandywine River Museum, Chadds Ford, Pennsylvania. © 1988 Brandywine Conservancy.

In the late 1930s Hurd taught both his father-in-law and brother-in-law to paint in tempera; it became the basic medium for Andrew Wyeth (b. 1917). A very talented painter in watercolor, Wyeth discovered he liked tempera because it did not allow any flashiness. As he has said, it put a brake "on my real nature—messiness."[3] *Indian Summer* [241] shows the detail accomplished with a small brush and the subtle textures and lighting which Wyeth gives to his temperas. It is painted in tones of brown, with each stroke making a tiny strip of light or shade.

Modern American tempera painters have used tempera in a way that is opposed to the basic nature of the medium, which favors large areas of flat color. The patience and expertise of Hurd and Wyeth and their many followers appeal to the American taste for seriousness and skill in art. Despite its long history, the tempera medium has never been used more successfully than by these American painters.

The history goes a long way back, for until oil paint was invented in about 1400, tempera was the basic painting medium. Egg yolk and its solvent, water, were easy to obtain, and it was a reasonably permanent and durable medium (if you have washed the breakfast dishes you know how firmly egg yolk can bind to a surface!). The eggs of birds or of sea turtles were used as paint binders by Australian Aboriginal painters, who used natural rock walls or sheets of bark as painting surfaces. Modern Aboriginal artists still use those binders, or the juice of plants like orchid bulbs or bloodwood leaves, for paintings in traditional style, such as Figure **242**. The illustrators of medieval manuscripts used tempera for decorated initial letters and symbolic designs [243], as well as for pictorial illustrations [244].

Notice that both **242** and **243** were made with linear designs in which each color remains unchanged. The artists were concerned with the natural local color of things or with the decorative effect, but they were not interested in the light and shadow that concerned Hurd and Wyeth. This technique using a generalized light is appropriate for subjects that are timeless, in which the light of

morning or the shadows of dusk play no part. *The Four Horsemen of the Apocalypse*
[244], painted by a Spanish monk in the early Middle Ages, is about the end of
the world, and no particular time of day or quality of light need be represented.
The powerful flat colors in tan, orange, yellow, and blue bands seem to have

above left: 242.
Namilgi.
*Sacred Rocks of Early
Dreamtime.* 1970.
Tempera on eucalyptus
bark, 18½ × 10½″
(47 × 27 cm).
Private collection,
Oenpelli, Australia.

above: 243. Irish.
Chi-Rho monogram
from *The Book of Kells.*
8th century. Tempera on
parchment. Trinity
College Library, Dublin.

244. Spanish. *The Four
Horsemen of the Apocalypse.*
Folio 135 of *The
Commentary of Beatus on
the Apocalypse of Fernando
and Sancha.* 11th century.
Tempera on parchment.
Biblioteca Nacional,
Madrid.

A POINT IN TIME: Jacob Lawrence's Tempera Series

Revival of the tempera medium by Hurd and Wyeth owed much to Renaissance painting; on the other hand, Vuillard's work belongs to an **Impressionist** style. Jacob Lawrence (b. 1917) has evolved a tempera style that grew out of **Cubism** and **Expressionism** of the 20th century. "I'm just interested in putting paint on paper," Lawrence says. "Since I have always been more interested in what I wanted to say rather than the medium, I just stayed with it. I know this medium so well that my thinking is in terms of the tempera medium. It's like a language—the better you know the medium, the better you can think in it."

The Migration of the Negro: In the church the migrants found one of their main sources of recreation and social activity [245] is the fifty-fourth in a series of 60 tempera paintings on panels painted during 1940–1941. Lawrence's parents had been part of the black migrations out of the South, and he grew up in Philadelphia and New York. "As a youngster, you just hear stories. . . . I didn't see the migration as an historical event, but people were talking about it." The Migration series was the result of research and many sketches and studies. "My work had always been flat, geometric. I didn't think in terms of Cubism, but later in my development I became more aware of it. Most people at that time worked cubistically without thinking about it." The steep, distorted perspective and strong contrasts of light and color give the style a powerful emotional content, which was Lawrence's main motive.

Pictures in a series has always attracted Lawrence. Each painting can stand alone, but together they tell a powerful story. The story of Harriet Tubman, who rescued hundreds of people from slavery in the middle of the 19th century, has inspired two sets of paintings by Lawrence. The second set, a series of seventeen, was done in egg tempera on panels and was published as a book for children, for which it was awarded a prize. *Daybreak—A Time to Rest* [246] shows Harriet Tubman with a rifle, resting with her refugees. A librarian complained that the artist had made Harriet look grotesque and ugly, as he here exaggerates her feet, on which she was traveling and which were the subject of the painting. Lawrence responded: "If you had walked in the fields, stopping for short periods to be replenished by underground stations; if you couldn't feel secure until you reached the Canadian border, you, too, madam, would look grotesque and ugly. Isn't it sad that the oppressed often find themselves grotesque and ugly and find the oppressor refined and beautiful?" The paintings, however, are refined and beautiful.

Lawrence's work illustrates a central purpose of art: the mediums and techniques of the artist and the style in which they appear are meant to be in the service of an idea and a meaning.

Quotations from E. H. Wheat, *Jacob Lawrence, American Painter* (Seattle: University of Washington Press/Seattle Art Museum, 1986) 190, 60, 62, 116.

247. French. *The Book of the Heart Possessed by Love.* 15th century. Tempera on parchment. National Library of Austria, Vienna.

above left: 245. Jacob Lawrence. *The Migration of the Negro; No. 54: In the church the migrants found one of their main sources of recreation and social activity.* 1940–1941. Tempera on hardboard, 18 × 12″ (46 × 31 cm). Museum of Modern Art, New York (gift of Mrs. David M. Levy).

above right: 246. Jacob Lawrence. Harriet Tubman series: *Daybreak—A Time to Rest.* 1967. Tempera on hardboard, 30 × 24″ (76 × 61 cm). National Gallery of Art, Washington, D.C. (gift of an anonymous donor).

been chosen for their richness and emotional effect. Notice that the corners are ornamented with interlace designs similar to those on the Irish ornamented initial **[243]**.

Effects of light and shade (that is, **chiaroscuro**) began to appear in tempera paintings at the end of the Middle Ages. The illustrations **[247]** for *The Book of the Heart Possessed by Love*, written by King René of Anjou, tell a symbolic tale in which the Knight Heart (the hero, naturally) is defeated by the Black Knight Trouble and has to be pulled from the river by Lady Hope. The painter who decorated the text in the lower half of the page added both white highlights and dark shades to give the floral pattern a hint of the third dimension, which it needs to harmonize with the very spacious scene above. In that scene you can easily distinguish the small brush strokes which model the colors. There are very few areas of flat color; the bright red horse at the left edge is one of the few. A common way to blend colors in tempera during this period was to use pure saturated color for the darkest parts, then add white little by little to make the lighter areas. This artist used that method on some parts of the landscape, and mostly on Lady Hope's blue gown (where there is also a very sparing use of black in the deepest shadows). That way of shading with pure color, instead of shading with black, gives the paintings a brilliant cheerfulness. You can easily imagine that such paintings as this were an inspiration to Peter Hurd when he was learning to paint in tempera.

248. Édouard Vuillard.
Under the Trees. 1894.
Gouache on canvas, 7'1½" × 3'2½"
(2.1 × 1 m).
Cleveland, Ohio, Museum of Art
(gift of the Hanna Fund).

Tempera is basically an opaque watercolor. Any paint made by mixing pigment with a water-soluble glue is similar to egg tempera, and all these paints can be applied to watercolor paper, wooden panels, or cloth coated with gesso. The "poster paint" or **gouache** (*gwash*) used in school art classes is of this type, with simple hide glue as the binder. Just because it is used in school doesn't mean it cannot be used for serious art. *Under the Trees* **[248]** was painted by Édouard Vuillard (1868–1940), who frequently painted with gouache. There is absolutely no shine on the surface of a painting in gouache—it looks much like a pastel—which makes the colors clear and soft, with no sense of depth or shadow in the darker colors. Vuillard liked that appearance, like a carpet, and covered his paintings with rug-like textures. Surely he also liked the fact that he could paint over and over, making endless changes and additions that completely hid whatever was there before. That is, of course, an advantage of opaque watercolor; no matter how much the artist reworks, it still looks fresh.

Oil Painting

Oil painting is a field in which the great battles about "what is reality?" are fought. There are two methods of painting in oil which are based on contrary ideas about representing reality. Even so, painters in both methods agree about the basics of grounds, binder, and solvents. The ground is canvas, linen being better than cotton because it expands and contracts less with changes in humidity, which helps prevent cracking of the paint surface. The canvas is tacked on a wooden frame (called a stretcher) and sized with a coat of glue to keep the paint from penetrating the canvas. Then it is given a first coat (a "prime" coat) of white oil paint whose binder is linseed oil and whose solvent is turpentine. These preparations keep the later paint film, which is the art, separate from the canvas that supports it. The paint film is much more durable than the canvas, and an old, rotting canvas can be reinforced (by a professional art conservator) by attaching a new canvas to the back with glue or wax, a process called "relining."

As noted, there are two methods of representation open to the painter in oils. The method most in use now is called **alla prima** (*ah-lah PREE-mah),* which can be translated as "all at once," which is to say there is just one coat of paint. An older method, which we can call the "glazing method," used many thin, transparent coats of paint. It was used by the inventors of oil paint. Although most painters use some elements of each method, it is useful to understand the principles behind each of them.

The original appeal of oil paint was its durability, since it resists moisture and abrasion better than tempera and watercolor. By 1400 some artists in northern Europe realized they could paint very thinly with linseed oil (from the flax plant) over their tempera paintings to give them a glossy durable surface. They also realized they could add colored pigments to the oil film, making something like colored glass, or what we call a **glaze** in contrast to an **impasto**, which is thick, opaque paint. The way of painting associated with the term "old master" uses impastos in the first coats, especially for white in highlighted areas where the thick coat of paint reflects more light than places where the thinner paint allows the canvas texture to absorb some light. When the impastos have dried (which may take weeks), colored glazes made of a little colored pigment in linseed oil thinned with turpentine are added to give color to the highlights and to vary and modulate the colors in other places.

Portait of a Carthusian Monk **[249]** by Petrus Christus (c. 1400–1473) was painted in that early phase, and it makes clear why oil painting became popular.

249. Petrus Christus. *Portrait of a Carthusian Monk.* c. 1446. Oil on panel, 11½ × 8" (29 × 20 cm). Metropolitan Museum of Art, New York (Jules Bache Collection, 1949).

250. Giovanni Bellini, and Titian.
The Feast of the Gods. 1514. Oil on canvas, 5'7" × 6'2" (1.7 × 1.9 m).
National Gallery of Art, Washington, D.C. (Widener Collection).

Petrus Christus had a valuable advantage in the market and, like other early oil painters, he tried to keep his formulas secret. The slow drying of linseed oil permitted the artist to blend colors for several days, getting very subtle gradations of light and shadow and amazingly lifelike textures of skin, hair, cloth, and metal. Petrus Christus even stoops to teasing his audience by painting a fly on the painted frame around the monk.

Although oil painting was invented in Flanders (modern Belgium), the secret was soon learned by the Italians. It became especially popular in Venice, where Giovanni Bellini (c. 1430–1516) founded an unsurpassed tradition of oil painting with works such as *The Feast of the Gods* **[250]**. That painting, which has additions by Bellini's great pupil Titian (the left half of the landscape and some changes in the figures), was the first of the "picnic" paintings, scenes of leisure and flirtation in a beautiful landscape. The atmosphere created by the soft blending of colors and light and shadows, the radiant colors that oil permits, and the variety of textures (earth, trees, cloth, flesh, metal) produce a mood of supernatural beauty. Bellini visualized a rather sedate party around Mercury (in helmet), Bacchus (drinking), Juno, and Jupiter, amidst a regular line of trees. Titian tried to liven up the party with a more dramatic setting and by revealing more nude bodies, but Bellini's mood remains supreme.

The sense of atmosphere in *The Feast of the Gods* was attainable only with oil paint, and such expressions of mood were an irresistible attraction to viewers. The glaze technique, with colors modulated by thin, transparent tones applied over earlier colors which had been allowed to dry completely, is the only way to get the effects we admire in Bellini's work.

A POINT IN TIME: John Brealey, Art Conservator

Art conservation has existed as a profession in the United States for only 60 years, but with the spread of museums and art collections it is becoming ever more important. John M. Brealey, chairman of the Department of Paintings Conservation at the Metropolitan Museum of Art in New York, is not only the most respected conservator working today but an important teacher of art conservation. Several doctoral students in art history and young conservators study with him and his assistants. Gisela Helmkampf, a professional conservator and Brealey's principal assistant, says it is important for the students "not to be terrified, although this *is* very scary work." You can imagine the heavy responsibility of working on a great painting, a unique and priceless national treasure. Brealey has had that responsibility, most famously in his successful work on Velázquez's *The Maids of Honor* [**153, 154**].

John Brealey grew up in England, the son of a portrait painter. "I wasn't interested in being a painter," he says, "in projecting my own personality. Tuning in—that's what interested me. The thrill of being associated with great minds." He did not go to college, but apprenticed himself to the best conservator in London and eventually opened his own laboratory. He has been at the Metropolitan since 1975. In 1987 Brealey described his work to interviewer Calvin Tomkins.

> We're here to serve the artist. The poor bloody artist long since deceased, and the grandeur of his creation looking like a messed-up jigsaw puzzle. . . . But you just do your damnedest to identify in the most servile way with the artist. To allow your personality to be eclipsed, as though you were standing behind the artist while he painted and following his thinking. His thinking happens to be expressed in visual terms, but it's thinking. . . . what we are dealing with is visual truths. If the visual aspect of a painting changes, the meaning changes—because the look *is* the meaning. . . . In a painting, somebody's personality and intellect are expressed by colored muds. Colored muds held together by a sticky substance—that's painting.

We see Brealey in the laboratory in front of two paintings he has recently cleaned and restored [**251**]: Ingres' portrait of the Countess of Haussonville, which belongs to the Frick Collection, and Lorenzo Lotto's *Venus and Cupid,* a recent purchase of the Metropolitan. Brealey's approach to conservation is cautious: "When in doubt, abstain," he has said. Gisela Helmkampf says of Brealey's special skill, "It is not in the hands. . . . it is all in the head. It is his way of seeing into pictures, and sensing what the artist is attempting to do."

Based on Calvin Tomkins, "Profiles: Colored Muds in a Sticky Substance," *The New Yorker* March 16, 1987: 44–70; quotations from pages 60, 49, 48, and 53–54; and Philip Jodidio, "L'homme qui a osé restaurer les ménines," *Connaissance des Arts* (Paris) July–Aug. 1985: 62–67.

251. John Brealey in his laboratory at the Metropolitan Museum of Art, New York, 1985.

252. John Sloan. *South Beach Bathers.* 1908. Oil on canvas, 25⅞ × 31⅞" (66 × 81 cm). Walker Art Center, Minneapolis, Minnesota.

South Beach Bathers **[252]** by John Sloan (1871–1951) is similar in subject to Bellini's *Feast of the Gods,* but of course brought down to earth in America. It is painted in the alla prima, or direct, technique. This technique is sometimes called painting "wet into wet" since a color can be modulated or changed only by applying more wet paint on top of a wet coat, which almost always causes some uncontrollable mixing of the colors. The freedom of the brushwork and the simple, strong areas of color seem more appropriate than subtle glazes for portraying average Americans at the beach.

Alla prima painting has been the dominant method for about two hundred years, not because it is necessarily the best method, but because it fits with our ideas of what is real and important. The illusions of solid masses and open space, which are the main results of glazing, have seemed less important than energy, immediacy, and spontaneity in our world in which change seems more normal than permanency. Alla prima painting is more quickly done, and looks quick and sketch-like, as we see in Sloan's painting.

Mark Rothko (1903–1973) painted in oils in a technique somewhere between the two general methods. *Number 10* **[253]** was painted on a canvas that had been toned a reddish brown tint on top of a thin white prime coat. That reddish tone shows through all the other colors to some degree. The blue, white, and yellow were painted in flat colors over the dry background. Rothko used a technique called **scumbling** to modulate and unify his colors. Like glazing, scumbling allows some of the background color to show through a later coat, but instead of being transparent it is opaque, fairly dry color which has been dragged with a brush over the slightly rough background color. Its incomplete coverage of the background permits the reddish tone to affect the other colors and act as a unifying element in the design.

For alla prima painters the slow drying of oil paint is no advantage; in fact, it is a disadvantage, and the impatience of modern painters led them to experiment with new paint mediums first developed for industrial work. That brings us to the latest developments in painting.

Synthetic Resin and Acrylic Paints

Synthetic resin and acrylic paints were developed by industrial chemists, not artists, and were intended for the protection of machinery, especially outdoors. A variety of carbon compounds similar to natural plant resins (such as

253. Mark Rothko. *Number 10.* 1950. Oil on canvas, 7'6¾" × 4'9⅛" (2.3 × 1.5 m). Museum of Modern Art, New York (gift of Philip C. Johnson).

above left: 254. David Alfaro Siqueiros. Unfinished murals in Chapultepec Castle, Mexico City. 1957. Synthetic resin paints.

above right: 255. David Alfaro Siqueiros at work on the Chapultepec Castle murals, Mexico City, 1957.

acrylic acid) can be treated chemically to make artificial (or synthetic) binders for paint. In the 1930s these industrial paints were adopted by artists as a revolutionary act in art, under the leadership of the Mexican painter David Alfaro Siqueiros *(see-KAY-ros)* (1896–1974). Not only was he an important painter, but Siqueiros was also one of the leaders in the theory of art in this century, showing how still and movie cameras could be applied to painting, advancing the spray gun as a tool, doing the first outdoor mural paintings, as well as experimenting with new kinds of paint. Siqueiros painted the murals **[254]** in the Chapultepec Castle, a museum in Mexico City, in 1957. Notice the wall on the right, behind the scaffold, where sprayed lines suggest the larger areas of the design. The air compressor for the spray guns sits against the wall. On the table, under a tool kit, are large cans of industrial paint. On the left are the finished paintings of a strike and the dictator, scenes from the Revolution of 1910. Siqueiros applied the final coat of paint with brushes **[255]**. You can tell that the paint is thick and opaque, with an almost sculptural solidity. The synthetic resin and acrylic binders are the strongest glues known and can hold a large amount of pigment, resulting in solid, opaque paints. They also dry very fast, which means that blending colors is nearly impossible. The painter's technique has to be more like that for tempera than for oil. To blend and mix colors on the painting, the painter adds wet paint over dry with a brush to achieve scumbling or thinly sprays on the new color. Acrylic paints can be thinned with water (which makes an emulsion, not a solution) and applied as glazes, giving the appearance of watercolor or oil paint. But the powerful effects Siqueiros liked in his art depended on spraying and scumbling with the brilliant, opaque industrial colors.

"We must look to physics and chemistry to supply us with materials suitable for modern conditions." Siqueiros said.[4] Many of the industrial paints, although they are tremendously durable and tough, are mixed with solvents that are so dangerous that painters must wear protective masks. Acrylic paint is safe to use since it is thinned with water and has no dangerous fumes.

The famous "drip paintings" by Jackson Pollock (1912–1956), such as *Cathedral* [256], were a phase in Pollock's production when he took advantage of the special properties of synthetic resins. In Hans Namuth's photograph of Pollock at work [257], the artist has his large canvas on the floor and a can of synthetic lacquer in his left hand. The paint is so viscous that he can draw in the air with his brush and the syrupy paint will fly out into the air following his gesture, then fall to the canvas. Many of Pollock's heavily textured paintings were done in traditional oil paint in an alla prima technique with scumbling, but he was also one of the first to take advantage of the abstract possibilities of the new medium.

Acrylic paint is widely used both for fine art and for commercial art and design, in which its quick drying is a great advantage. Many artists are experimenting with the variety of things that can be done with this medium. Two examples of techniques and styles developed especially for acrylic are the stain-

left: 256. Jackson Pollock. *Cathedral.* 1947. Enamel and aluminum paint on canvas, 5'11½" × 2'11" (1.8 × 0.9 m). Dallas, Texas, Museum of Art (gift of Mr. and Mrs. Bernard J. Reis).

below: 257. Jackson Pollock at work, 1951. Photograph by Hans Namuth.

ing of raw canvas, as we see in *Beth Chaff* [258] by Morris Louis (1912–1962) and the colorful, brush-stroke-textured paintings of Pierre Dunoyer (*dü-nwah-YAY*) (b. 1949) [259]. Unlike oil paint, acrylic will preserve a canvas that is soaked in it, so there is no need for the glue sizing and white lead priming used on canvases for oil painting. Art conservators may have problems cleaning acrylic-canvases without removing the stain that is the art, but that, say the painters, is the conservator's problem. Dunoyer's *Blue* looks at first much like an oil painting, but two features are especially appropriate to acrylic: the thick impasto brush strokes, which dry very quickly in acrylic, and the flat, unmodulated colors. This kind of painting could be done in oil, but the thick paint would require several weeks, at least, to dry completely, and the capacity for blending and varying color tones, which was the reason oil was developed, is not needed here. Dunoyer's painting uses acrylic in ways which harmonize with the nature of the medium.

Summary for Review

The five major painting mediums all use the same colored pigments, but are different in the kind of glue **(binder)** that holds the pigment together on a **ground** (or surface), and in the **solvent** for that glue. **Fresco** is done with pigments in water applied to a wet lime plaster wall. **Watercolor** uses gum arabic as the glue and water as the solvent, and **tempera** is made by mixing pigments in egg yolk thinned with water. **Oil paint** is made with linseed oil thinned with turpentine. Oil paint differs from the others because it is slow drying, which permits colors to be carefully blended, giving a very natural appearance. Renaissance painters used an oil painting method with several steps, finishing with thin **glazes** of color over opaque thicker paint, or **impastos**. More recent oil painters have painted **alla prima**, wet into wet, or all in one coat. *Synthetic resins* and *acrylic* paints are so durable they can be used outdoors; they will hold a large amount of pigment, permitting thick paint, and they dry very quickly. This makes spraying and scumbling effective techniques for modeling colors in the painting.

7

Sculpture

Leonardo da Vinci and Michelangelo had a running argument about which was the finer art, painting or sculpture. Although that question was of great interest in their time, now it seems more a matter of taste. A century after Leonardo's death the question had changed to one that is still interesting: how do those two arts differ in their expressive potentials? Diego Velázquez's teacher Francisco Pacheco *(pah-CHEK-o)* summed up the distinction: "Sculpture has existence. Painting has appearance."[1] Modern critics still accept that statement. The special powers of sculpture are based on the fact that it exists in the same material way the people looking at it exist, as a solid thing in real space. Paintings, in contrast, exist in imaginary or illusory space, more like a dream than like the material world.

Relief and Round

Actually, sculpture spans the gradations between illusion and full material existence by different levels of massiveness, which we call low relief, high relief, and sculpture in the round. **Low relief** is characterized by forms that barely rise above the background. In **high relief** parts of the figures are free of the background, but there still is a background plane to which they are attached. *Sculpture in the round* has no background plane and can be seen from all sides. Each relief level has particular uses and settings and the gradations between them are infinite.

Doors of Death **[260]**, by Giacomo Manzù (mahn-SOO) (b. 1908), was composed of ten low-relief panels which had been modeled in clay and then cast in bronze. Viewed closely we can perceive the touch of the artist's fingers and his wooden modeling knife on the clay. The subtle highlights and shadows give an effect often called "impressionistic," a sculptural analogue of the light and color effects of Impressionist painting. Like a painting, this low relief suggests more space in the background than is really there, and more mass in the figures, which are practically flat. Illusions of this type are something we expect in painting and find in sculpture only in low relief. Manzù's panels compose into a pair of impressive bronze doors for St. Peter's in Rome. Door panels are a common use of low-relief sculpture; low reliefs may also be hung on walls like paintings.

High relief also typically has an architectural setting. The wall of the Hindu temple of Khajuraho *(KA-joor-AH-ho)* **[261]** in India acts as the background for an array of human figures (such as the woman on the left pillar), gods (such as the male figure on the right pillar), and mythical creatures and animals. The building has such a complicated shape that many of the figures at first glance seem to be sculptures in the round, but those seen in side view show how they are attached to the wall. The plumpness of the sculptural forms stresses the physical reality of everything represented—these are not gods and myths to be seen only in visions but are shown as having an earthly existence. The relief setting tells us that we are not supposed to examine them from all angles; there is one point of

185

left: 260. Giacomo Manzù. *Doors of Death*. 1964.
Cast bronze, 25'3½" × 12'¾" (7.7 × 3.6 m).
St. Peter's Basilica, Vatican, Rome.

below: 261. Lakshmana Temple at Khajuraha,
Madhya Pradesh, India. c. A.D. 950. Stone,
high relief.

view which is correct, the view from which they are best seen. Hindu sculpture is very rich in high relief. It gives an impression of tremendous, licentious exuberance, but the architectural setting and the high-relief composition provide a firm set of controls within which the sculpture operates, like a wild dance with carefully choreographed steps set to strict music.

Sculpture in the round is sometimes placed in architectural niches or against a wall, and often that fulfills the sculptor's intentions. Michelangelo's *David* [262], now set in a rotunda, was originally intended for a place before the massive walls of the Florence city hall, the Palazzo Vecchio. Although carved in the round and set where it was visible from at least three sides, it was conceived with one best view, the front view of the body, which gives a width sufficient to support visually the massive head (on left in **262**). Michelangelo's biographer tells us that he would make a small wax model of the figure he was about to carve from marble and lay it in a pan of water. Slowly lifting it from the water, he would note which parts emerged first, and then carve the marble from one side, freeing the figure from the stone just as the model had emerged from the water. A dominant view is characteristic of Michelangelo's sculptures and makes an architectural setting particularly appropriate for them.

262. Michelangelo. *David.* 1501–1504. Marble, height 13′ (4 m); height with base 18′ (5.5 m). Accademia, Florence.

263. Auguste Rodin. *The Burghers of Calais.* 1886. Bronze; height 6'10½" (2 m), length 7'11" (2.4 m), depth 6'6" (1.9 m). Cast in the Hirshhorn Museum and Sculpture Garden, Smithsonian Institution, Washington, D.C.

Auguste Rodin (*ro-DAN*) (1840–1917) admitted that not all views of his *The Burghers of Calais* [263 and 264] were equally good, but he considered six or seven views satisfactory. In a group composed of six free-standing figures there is great potential for a sculpture truly in the round, and Rodin's monument fulfills that potential exceptionally well. The sculpture was a public memorial to

264. Auguste Rodin. *The Burghers of Calais.* 1886. Bronze; height 6'10½" (2 m), length 7'11" (2.4 m), depth 6'6" (1.9 m). Cast in the Rodin Museum, Philadelphia.

six leading citizens of the city of Calais who, in 1347, gave themselves up to the enemies who had besieged their city for a year in exchange for the lifting of the siege. Dressed in sackcloth and rope halters, they are shown marching to their deaths. The monument was to be set in the square before the town hall, to be visible from all sides. The sculptor considered several ways of setting the figures, finally deciding to set them directly on the ground to increase the observer's identification with the personal tragedy of each individual. The people of Calais were offended by the openly displayed emotion and preferred to set the sculpture apart from daily life by placing it on a pedestal. The figures have a multiplicity of views, which suggests that there are also a multiplicity of meanings concerning the individual tragedy of each figure and the way each finds to face death.

Traditional Material and Technique

Carving, modeling, and casting are very ancient skills, but they will never be out of date as long as artists have ideas that need to be embodied in wood or stone, clay or metal. As we shall see a little later, another group of constructive techniques for other materials have come into use in this century, but they have added to the range of sculpture, not driven out the traditional techniques and materials.

Carving

Carving is done with chisels and hammers or mallets on wood and stone, removing material to reveal a form. In contrast to many earlier sculptors, who usually planned to remove the marks of their tools, modern sculptors usually prefer to reveal both the material and the tool marks. In José de Creeft's (1884–1982) *Cloud* [265], the heavy stone is balanced so delicately on its base that it appears light as a cloud. The contrasts of smooth, rounded forms and rough, linear shapes suggest the form of a cumulus cloud whipped by the wind. De Creeft chose a stone for its texture and color and allowed his chisel marks to show to provide contrasts of texture.

265. José de Creeft. *The Cloud*. 1939. Greenstone, height 13½" (34 cm). Whitney Museum of American Art, New York.

Sculpture _____ 189

left: 266. Constantin Brancusi. *Adam and Eve.* 1921. Chiseled chestnut and old oak, height c. 8'9″ (2.4 m). Solomon R. Guggenheim Museum, New York.

above left: 267. Mexican. Double-faced figurine from Tlatilco. 1000–500 B.C. Ceramic, height 3¼″ (8 cm). St. Louis, Missouri, Art Museum (gift of Morton D. May).

above right: 268. Mexican. Pre-Classic figurine from Tlatilco. 1150–550 B.C. Ceramic. Dallas, Texas, Museum of Art.

The artist's concern with the material and the marks of the tools is clear in Constantin Brancusi's *(brahn-KOO-see)* (1876–1957) *Adam and Eve* **[266]**. A block of limestone (for the base) and three pieces of wood were selected. The oak and chestnut show different grain and color, and the cuts by saws and the curved blade of the wood chisel, struck with a wooden mallet, can be distinguished. As we examine such a piece the nature of its materials and the processes by which it was made are among its most striking features. Then we begin to see the subject, with a feminine form above and a rugged masculine one below. The roughness or smoothness of the materials and chisel cuts contribute to the masculine or feminine idea.

Modeling

The most personal sculptural technique, since much of it is done with the fingers, is modeling of clay, wax, or plaster. Tiny clay figurines **[267** and **268]** modeled by ancient Mexicans show both the marks of their fingers and the cuts and punches of small wooden tools. They were expert at building up the bodies with fillets (narrow ribbons of clay) and balls of clay to make hair, jewelry, nipples, and clothing, and at cutting various textures into the soft surfaces. These figures fit into the palm of your hand; both their small size and expert modeling contribute to their irresistible charm.

Pottery clay is used when the final product is meant to be in clay rather than cast into another material. The sculpture must be small enough to fit into the kiln—the potter's furnace for hardening the clay into pottery. A large ceramic sculpture requires a large kiln, which requires a lot of fuel. Since clay shrinks in the heat of the kiln, the walls of sculpture must be thin enough that they shrink all at once when the heat of the kiln strikes them; thick walls and solid clay forms simply break.

The most spectacular example of ceramic sculpture is the army and administration of the emperor of China, about six thousand figures, all life-size and actually portraits of individuals [269]. These were no doubt very happy to pose, since the ceramic figures took the place of the people themselves in ancient sacrificial traditions. This emperor, who died in 210 B.C., also built the Great Wall—he was clearly not intimidated by large projects. The photograph shows archaeologists unearthing the figure of a soldier and recording its measurements. The human scale of the figures, and even horses, was a feat of modeling and firing. The kilns must have been room-size, and the amount of fuel they required must have been staggering. China was deforested in ancient times, and we can understand what happened to some of the forests when we see an imperial army made of ceramic. Life-size ceramic figures are so unusual that one must remind oneself that they are not just a technical achievement, but also artistic achievements in a very realistic style.

Casting

Sculptors sometimes want to convert a modeled form into a tougher material, often for outdoor use, so they make molds from the modeled original and cast the sculpture in metal. Although the technique has been known since ancient times, it is an expensive procedure and is usually carried out by specialized technicians in a professional foundry. For the sculptor it means planning the design so that it can be cast effectively, and then knowing how to **chase** (to clean, ornament, or sharpen detail of) the finished casting and apply the proper **patina** *(PA-tuh-nuh* or *pa-TEE-nuh)*, meaning an acid finish to color and protect the metal).

269. China, Ch'in Dynasty. Soldier of the imperial army. c. 210 B.C. Ceramic, height c. 6' (1.8 m).

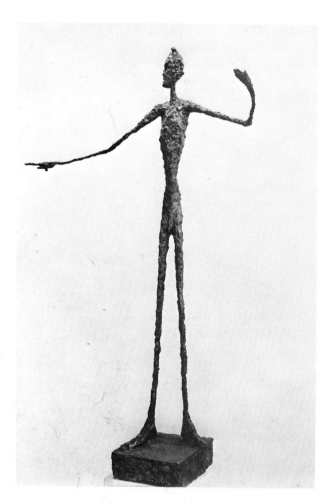

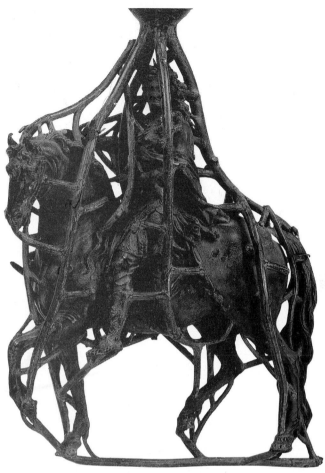

The Swiss sculptor Alberto Giacometti *(jah-ko-MET-tee)* (1901–1966) worked obsessively on his figures such as *Man Pointing* **[270]**, building up plaster around the metal rods of the armature, or framework that holds the plaster, and then cutting it away again. He described his own work:

> A large figure seemed to me false and a small one equally unbearable, and then often they became so tiny that with one touch of my knife they disappeared into dust. But head and figures seemed to me to have a bit of truth only when small. All this changed a little in 1945 through drawing. This led me to want to make larger figures [such as *Man Pointing*], but then to my surprise, they achieved a likeness only when tall and slender.[2]

Although the technique is modeling and the way in which the plaster is applied is easy to see, from the start it was intended that the plaster should be replaced by **bronze** (an alloy of copper and tin). Casting is done by making molds (of a special clay called "fireclay") in several pieces from the plaster or clay model. The molds are then usually coated with wax the thickness intended for the final metal sculpture. The molds are assembled and filled with a core of fireclay which will make the final metal sculpture hollow by acting as an interior mold. All the wax is melted out—one drop of wax in the mold will cause a terrible explosion when the molten metal is poured in. The bronze is melted and the channel between the furnace and the mold is opened and the molten bronze flows into the narrow space between the inner and outer molds. This technique is called **lost wax casting**, *cire perdu (seer-pair-DÜ)* in French, because the wax is replaced by bronze.

The cast bronze of a small equestrian figure **[271]** just as it came from the mold shows all the channels through which bronze flowed into the mold still attached, as well as vents for the escape of air, which also fill with bronze. The

In Detail: Cellini Casts the Perseus

"... With all the forces of my body and purse, ... I set to work," Benvenuto Cellini *(chuh-LEE-nee)* (1500–1571) tells us in his autobiography. Having finished the model of his statue of Perseus and its mold, he explains:

> I began to draw the wax out by means of a slow fire. This melted and issued through numerous airvents I had made. ... When I had finished drawing off the wax, I constructed a funnel-shaped furnace all round the model of my Perseus [272]. It was built of bricks, so interlaced, the one above the other, that numerous apertures were left for the fire to exhale at. Then I began to lay on wood by degrees, and kept it burning two whole days and nights. At length, when all the wax was gone, and the mold was well baked, I set to work at digging the pit in which to sink it. ... I raised the mold by windlasses and ... lowered it gently down into the very bottom of the furnace. ... [The furnace was placed in a pit mainly as a safety measure, to minimize the danger of an explosion or a break in the mold.] I next turned to my furnace, which I had filled with numerous pigs [or ingots] of copper and other bronze stuff ... resting one upon the other that the flames could play freely through them, in order that the metal might heat and liquify the sooner. At last I called out heartily to set the furnace going ... [which] worked so well I was obliged to rush from side to side to keep it going. The labor was more than I could stand; yet I forced myself to strain every nerve and muscle. To increase my anxieties, the workshop caught fire, and we were afraid lest the roof should fall on our heads. ...

Finally, exhausted and feverish, Cellini took to his bed, telling his men, "I shall not be alive tomorrow." But the copper did not melt properly and finally a workman told him, "'O Benvenuto, your statue is spoiled, and there is no hope whatever of saving it.' No sooner had I heard the shriek of that wretch than I gave a howl which might have been heard from the sphere of flame. Jumping from my bed, I seized my clothes and begin to dress. ... I went immediately to inspect the furnace and found the metal was all curdled, which we call 'being caked.'" Cellini fortified the fire with a load of hot-burning oak and threw in more metal, but still the metal did not flow smoothly.

> Accordingly I sent for all my pewter platters, porringers, and dishes, to the number of some two hundred pieces, and had a portion of them cast, one by one, into the channels, the rest into the furnace. This expedient succeeded and ... my mold was filling ... and seeing my work finished I fell upon my knees and with all my heart gave thanks to God. After all was over, I turned to a plate of salad on a bench there, ... and drank together with the whole crew.

After two days of cooling, the mold was broken open

272. Benvenuto Cellini. *Perseus with the Head of Medusa.* 1554. Bronze, height 10'6" (3.2 m). Loggia dei Lanzi, Florence. (See [491] for detail of head.)

and found to have cast perfectly except for the toes of one foot, which the artist repaired later.

Cellini's account of the casting of a bronze statue is the most famous description of that process.

From *The Autobiography of Benvenuto Cellini,* trans. J. A. Symonds (New York: Random House Modern Library, no date) 411–419.

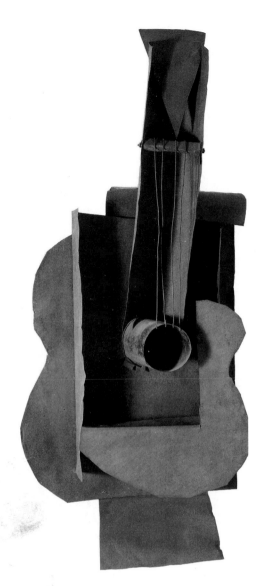

left: 273. Pablo Picasso. *Guitar*. 1912. Sheet metal, wire; 30½ × 13¾ × 7⅝″ (77 × 35 × 19 cm). Museum of Modern Art, New York (gift of the artist).

above: 274. Mambila, Cameroon. Mask. c. late 19th century. Wood, height 17½″ (44 cm). Metropolitan Museum of Art, New York (Nelson Rockefeller Collection).

sculptor's next job would be to cut all those channels off, polish the metal, chase it (cutting fine details into the cold metal with chisels), and perhaps apply an acid patina to color the bronze.

The Materials and Techniques of 20th-Century Sculpture

If you had asked Rodin what the materials of sculpture are he would have said stone (mainly marble) and bronze, with models made in clay, wax, or plaster. But in the years since Rodin's death in 1917 sculpture has been revolutionized by new materials and ways of working them. The most important factor in this shift has been the study of the art of other civilizations, especially Africa and the Pacific Islands (called Oceanic art). Artists who had been exposed to foreign styles began to see new ways to use materials such as wood and metal and to see sculptural possibilities in materials such as cloth, plastics, or the earth itself. The change in sculpture has been so rapid and so complete that few people understand what has happened, and all of us are just beginning to comprehend what the changes mean. It seems that these changes herald a large-scale shift in public attitudes and beliefs.

The changes are part of the **Modern** movement. Among its first manifestations in sculpture was Pablo Picasso's *Guitar* [273], made in 1912 of sheet metal and wire. To understand what inspired Picasso, we must look at the kind of thing he was seeing. The Mambila mask [274] from Cameroon represents an animal and is part of a dance costume. In the free geometry of its forms, Picasso saw an art liberated from the imitation of natural forms, yet still making meaningful comments on the natural world. Picasso's *Guitar* posed a challenge to modern sculptors to represent their experience of the real world without copying the forms of natural things.

Although Europeans had explored Africa and Oceania earlier, little attention was given to the peoples and their ideas until early 20th-century artists began to take a serious interest in their art. Artists began to imagine how such things could be made [275 and 276]. Most of them involved construction in some way. African and Oceanic examples freed artists for all kinds of experiments. Four new tendencies have emerged in the past fifty years and they are still full of potential: *construction in hard materials,* mainly wood, metal, or plastic; *construction in soft materials,* cloth or fiber; *site-specific* or *environmental sculpture,* in which materials are planned to fit a particular place which the observer enters; and *sculptures based on energy* rather than mass, in which color, light, or motion is the means of expression.

Construction in Hard Materials

The sculptor who accepted the challenge of Picasso's *Guitar* to represent nature without copying it was the American David Smith (1906–1965), a worker

left: 275. Malekula, New Hebrides Islands. Helmet mask. *(The Woman Ancestor of the Society Carrying Her Son).* c. late 19th–early 20th century. Wood, straw, compost, paint, tusks, glass; height 26″ (66 cm). Rockefeller Collection 65.103, New York.

below: 276. Angoram village, Sepik River, New Guinea. Mask of supernatural being. 1912. Palm fiber, length 16′ (4.9 m).

in iron and steel. His *Cubi XVIII* and *Cubi XVII* [277] are stainless steel boxes assembled on high steel pedestals which are abstract forms, yet suggest bending and leaning human figures. The surfaces have been burnished irregularly, allowing us to see the motions of the artist's hand, like brush strokes, on the shining metal, which reflects the light of the environment. Picasso's *Guitar* is a high relief, but Smith's sculptures are in the round, adding a level of complexity. Since the sculptures stand on high pedestals they are silhouetted against the sky, which makes grasping the third dimension—to see that these are massive forms receding into space—more difficult. The effort enhances the meaning, making us compare flat shapes with deep masses and encouraging us to walk around to get other views. David Smith is one of the most important of the sculptors who inherited Picasso's abstract "cubistic" attitude to form.

A more recent phase in hard constructions is represented by Alice Aycock's (b. 1946) *Collected Ghost Stories from the Workhouse* [278], a large "machine" that does no work, except in our imaginations. Aycock takes the kinds of constructions that Smith did as pure statements in abstract form and uses them to make us imagine mystical stories. Smith took mechanism seriously and glorified it as abstract form, but Aycock belongs to "The End of the Mechanical Age," the name of an exhibit of her work at the Museum of Modern Art in New York in 1968. Her sculpture make us feel nostalgic about large clanking machines, which belong more to the period of Edgar Allan Poe than to the age of the electronic robot. Aycock's work is part of a Post-Modern tendency to create representational art, in this case representations of machines, not abstract forms which are the products of machines.

Construction in Soft Materials

Construction in cloth and fiber began to play a part in modern sculpture about 1960. Although it is one of the most recent developments, it has already produced many important and original works.

277. David Smith. *Cubi XVIII* (left). 1964. Stainless steel, height 9' (2.7 m). Dallas, Texas, Museum of Art. *Cubi XVII* (right). 1963. Stainless steel, height 9'7¾" (2.9 m). Museum of Fine Arts, Boston (gift of Stephen D. Paine).

278. Alice Aycock. *Collected Ghost Stories from the Workhouse.* 1980. Cable, wire, wood, copper, steel, galvanized steel, glass piping; 30 × 75 × 120′ (9.2 × 22.9 × 36.6 m). Permanent installation at the University of South Florida at Tampa.

Among the earliest sculptures in soft materials were the Pop Art constructions by Claes *(klawss)* Oldenburg (b. 1929), such as the *Giant Soft Fan* **[279]**. The softness of the "Fan" tells us it is impotent—despite its giant size, ghostly and hanging in the air—and not to be feared. Oldenburg had been making sculptures out of every available material, and perhaps it was inevitable that he would eventually use textile fabrics, but it is hard to believe that fiber works such as

279. Claes Oldenburg. *Giant Soft Fan—Ghost Version.* 1967. Canvas, wood, foam rubber; height 8′ (2.4 m) from top of blade to bottom of base, width 4′6¼″ (1.4 m), depth 6′1″ (1.9 m). Museum of Fine Arts, Houston, Texas (gift of D. and J. de Menil).

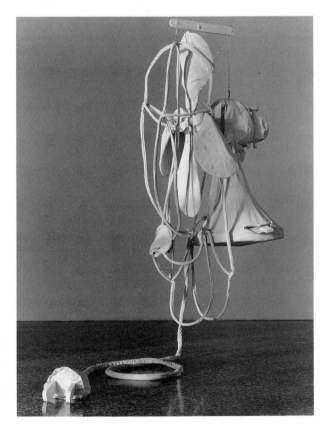

280. Magdalena Abakanowicz. *80 Backs.* 1976–1982. 80 pieces of textile impregnated with glue and molded; heights 5'1", 5'9", or 6' (1.5, 1.6, or 1.8 m). Collection of the artist.

Figure **276** were not ancestors of such soft constructions, which did not emerge from the textile craft traditions of the Western countries.

Magdalena Abakanowicz *(ah-bah-KAH-no-witz)* (b. 1930) is a Polish sculptor who works in fiber, often building her structures on a loom. But her sources lie outside the utilitarian traditions of Western textile arts and the pictorial traditions of tapestry, closer to the expressive fiber forms of Oceania or the ancient Americas. Of her sculptures such as *80 Backs* **[280]**, figure forms of burlap impregnated with glue, she has said: "My three-dimensional woven forms are about my opposition to the systematization of life and art. They grow with a leisurely rhythm like creations of nature and, like them, they are organic. Like other natural forms, they are also something to contemplate."[3]

In a drawing the sculptor Henry Moore shows us a sculpture wrapped in cloth, as if ready to be unveiled **[281]**. This was one of Moore's thoughts about the way to meet Picasso's challenge to represent nature without copying it, by wrapping a natural form so that it only hints at the contents of the package. That idea has been the basis of Christo's (b. 1935) long series of wrapped objects and veiled landscapes, which we contemplate wonderingly, very much like the audience in Moore's drawing. In *Surrounded Islands* **[282]** the "veils" are parted to reveal the small islands, which we would scarcely notice without this powerful "clothing." Christo used 6.5 million square feet (603,800 square meters) of shiny pink polypropylene cloth to outline the islands in Biscayne Bay, near Miami, Florida, for two weeks. The "skirt" of each island was sewn to follow the island's contours, was staked on the shore and supported with anchored floats at the outer edge. All this was paid for by the sale of Christo's drawings and studies for the project. In earlier work Christo wrapped a piece of the Australian coastline, put an orange curtain across a Colorado valley, and a 24-mile-long (39-kilometer-long) cloth fence across the California hills. With each project, the environmental aspect of the design has become more important, but Christo's source of inspiration lies in the possibilities of textiles for making interesting forms, with folds, bulges, colors, and textures.

Surrounded Islands made people see a group of deserted and unnoticed islets as part of a total landscape—and seeing is what art is about. Christo's sculptures originated in the older tradition of the sculpture as a form, one which can be set in various places without significantly altering the meaning of the work. His later work, such as *Surrounded Islands*, has used the cloth not to conceal, but to reveal the environment. Each of these environmental sculptures is designed for a particular place and exists for a short time. Christo's work has led a large audience to consideration of site-specific environmental art.

Site-Specific and Environmental Sculpture

There is a debate between a younger idea and an older one, the older idea maintaining that a beautiful thing is always beautiful, whatever the circumstances, the younger idea insisting that beauty depends on the circumstances, that something may be beautiful in one place and ridiculous in another. The sculptor Carl Andre, a supporter of the younger idea, summarized the history of sculpture: "The course of development: sculpture as form; sculpture as structure; sculpture as place."[4]

below: 281. Henry Moore. *Crowd Looking at a Tied-up Object.* 1942. Pen and ink, chalk, crayon, watercolor; 17 × 22" (43 × 56 cm). British Museum, London.

right: 282. Christo. *Surrounded Islands.* Biscayne Bay, Greater Miami, Florida. 1980–1983. 6,500,000 sq. ft. (603,580 sq. m) of floating pink woven polypropylene fabric.

283. Robert Smithson. *Amarillo Ramp.* 1973. Formed earth. Collection of Stanley Marsh, Amarillo, Texas.

Site-specific sculpture is designed for just one location; the place is recreated by the sculpture, which uses the environment as one of it features. The idea of site-specific sculpture grew out of the work of Robert Smithson in the 1960s and the environmental movement as it affected architecture and city planning. The younger idea, that a thing is good or beautiful only if it fits its circumstances, has been gaining ground. Currently it is an important trend in architecture and city planning, as well as in sculpture, and it brings these three fields of art together.

284. Robert Irwin. *9 Spaces, 9 Trees.* 1980. Plastic coated fencing, concrete, plum trees. Seattle, Washington.

We usually think of earth moving as something we do for utilitarian reasons, for roads or housing developments. Ancient people modeled the earth for symbolic reasons, and recently that art form has appeared again. Robert Smith-

son (1938–1973), one of the re-inventors of site-specific art, designed *Amarillo Ramp* **[283]** to rise out of an artificial lake in the Texas plains. The artist died during work on this project in the crash of the small plane he was using to view the site from the air. His work and ideas have inspired a new role for sculpture as rehabilitation of landscapes devastated by modern misuse. Although *Amarillo Ramp* is an abstract form, the curve rising from the water suggests organic growth. Smithson was also beginning to think about making sculpture that would do work in the real world. He proposed to design the terrain around a new international airport built between Dallas and Forth Worth, with the intention of rehabilitating a landscape ruined by development, and while Smithson's proposal was rejected and he did not live to have another chance, his idea has been carried on by other artists.

9 Spaces, 9 Trees **[284]** was commissioned by the city of Seattle to humanize a small rectangular plaza in front of a city office building and jail. The artist Robert Irwin (b. 1928) described the site as "a very forlorn, isolated, even hostile plaza surrounded by very grey architecture."[5] The police department garage is under the plaza, and Irwin's design was limited by the fact that the plaza is really the garage roof and would support little weight. Irwin designed a maze-like garden with a tennis-court asphalt floor, blue plastic-coated fence, concrete planters planted with sedum and reddish-leaved plum trees. They make spaces protected from the surroundings, where you might eat lunch on a nice day. Irwin considers this a new form of public monument to replace the traditional "statue-in-the-park." Irwin believes there is no standard form, such as a statue, but that each monument has to be tailored to its surroundings.

Only very recently has a representational form appeared in environmental sculpture. Michael Heizer's *(HI-zer)* (b. 1944) *Effigy Tumuli Sculpture* **[285]** covers a 200-acre (84-hectare) site beside the Illinois River which had been ruined by mining. Effigy mounds were made by American Indians as part of their belief in the sacredness of the landscape, so it is fitting that effigy mounds return as a way to restore and give meaning to land. Heizer, the son of an archaeologist, grew up visiting Indian mounds and is deeply aware of traditional Indian attitudes toward the landscape. The water strider (along with a frog, catfish, turtle,

285. Michael Heizer. *Effigy Tumuli Sculpture* (water strider). 1985. Earth mounds covering 200 acres (84 hectares). Buffalo Rock, Ottawa, Illinois.

286. Alexander Calder. *Ghost*. 1964. Metal mobile sculpture, 24 × 35′ (7.3 × 10.7 m). Solomon R. Guggenheim Museum, New York.

and snake not shown here) depicted in Heizer's mounds are all native to the Illinois River and represent the return of life to a landscape when the industrial poisons have been removed. Grass planted over the mounds will eventually merge them into the natural scene.

Site-specific sculpture has changed our thinking about how art, and all other human activities, fit into the real world. Everything is connected, in space and in time, these sculptures suggest. Architects such as Frank Gehry *(gary)* and Christopher Alexander and many contemporary city planners are carrying these ideas over into their designs.

Sculptures Based on Energy

Sculptures in which the main appeal is based on energy rather than mass seem like a new idea, but moving, or **kinetic**, sculpture was made as early as the 1st century B.C. A Hellenistic sculptor used water power as his energy source to make a group of his sculptured figures dance in a circle and turn on their bases. Beginning about the 13th century, weight-driven clockwork mechanisms drove all sorts of **automata**, most of them in clocks or theater settings, with musicians, dancing bears, sacred figures, and astronomical designs moving around. So people's fascination with sculptures in motion is nothing new, yet we have given kinetic sculpture a form of our own in the modern period.

Alexander Calder (1898–1976) is the best known of the kinetic sculptors, with his wind-driven **mobiles** representing the modern idea of sculptural movement. The name "mobile" was suggested to Calder by the artist Marcel Duchamp *(dü-SHAH)*, who liked it because in French it also suggests "motive," or idea, and Calder's sculptures ordinarily have some reference to nature; they are not just a play of forms. Calder tried out movable sculpture operated by hand crank and by electric motors, but by the mid-1930s he had turned to natural air currents as his preferred source of motion. The advantage of wind was its unpredictability; mechanical or electrical movement had to be programmed and would repeat itself eventually.

Ghost **[286]** is a delicate suspended mobile painted white, made for the great round space of the Guggenheim Museum in New York. It shimmers as it moves; it was intended to be a subtle complement to the complex architectural setting.

Sculptors working in all mediums have grown more conscious of the setting of their work in recent years, perhaps reflecting the growing influence of environmental ideas or perhaps reacting to the thoughtless placement of many earlier sculptures in locations with unfavorable light. Dan Flavin's (b. 1933) sculptures in fluorescent light tubes show this change in attitude. A single 8-foot (2.4-meter) lighted tube set at a diagonal could be set "across anybody's wall,"[6] according to Flavin in 1963. Six years later *Three Sets of Tangented Arcs in Daylight and Cool White* **[287]** were installed in the National Gallery of Canada by Flavin in a design for one specific room. For another room the design would have to be different. That is one of the basic laws of sculpture as it has emerged in recent years, and, as is the case for all laws in art, the next generation of artists will discover creative ways to violate it. But a wider focus on environment and natural conditions is important in many areas of contemporary thought and design and is sure to remain an important concern in sculpture.

Designing New Forms for the Human Body

We are all sure we know what the human body looks like—we have one of our own to look at—but the history of art provides abundant evidence that there are many different ideas about the proper way to represent people. The great subject for sculpture throughout the ages has been the human body, with animals running a poor second. There is no doubt about the reason: it is with our bodies that we express ourselves most clearly and honestly, and we all understand the language of the body. In sculptures of the body there are two basic possibilities: the body still and the body in motion. Those very general categories have been idealized and given meanings, which differ somewhat from one cul-

287. Dan Flavin. *Three Sets of Tangented Arcs in Daylight and Cool White.* 1969. Fluorescent light tubes, room dimensions 9'6" × 24'8" × 37'3" (2.9 × 7.5 × 11.4 m). National Gallery of Canada, Ottawa.

above: 288. Tiahuanaco culture, Bolivia.
Seated figure of an ancestor. c. 1st century A.D.
Stone, height c. 5′ (1.5 m).
National Museum, La Paz, Bolivia.

right: 289. Donatello, *David.* c. 1430.
Bronze, height 5′2¼″ (1.6 m). Museo Nazionale,
Florence.

ture to another. Nonetheless, stillness is always more timeless, motion more
momentary.

A large white stone seated figure **[288]** discovered on the high plateau of
Bolivia and attributed to the Tiahuanaco civilization is in a symmetrical pose, the
two sides of the body perfectly balanced. Its ribs show, its eyes stare, and it is
seated in the pose used for the burial of the dead in all periods in the South
American Andes Mountain regions. No doubt this figure represents a dead
man, someone who was very important in life. His pose is one that could be held
for eternity, and like ancient Egyptian sculpture, this one was probably meant to
exist in a timeless universe parallel to our perpetually changing time-bound one.
Such still, symmetrical poses are called *frontal* poses; the figure is said to possess
frontality. Standing or seated, its message is always the same: this figure is
eternal.

The figure in motion expresses the opposite: this figure is alive and participates with us in constant change. Its appeal is to a human audience, not to
eternal spirits. Since the body must balance even when it is in action, there is a
graceful interaction of the parts as the weight is redistributed. In the Renaissance
that counterpoise of the parts of the body was given the Italian name **contrapposto,** but it was first systematized by the ancient Greeks. They had for several
centuries represented figures in frontal poses, probably following the Egyptian

example, but about 480 b.c. sculptors suddenly began to design figures in contrapposto. It appears that the artists or their patrons and public began to believe that the audience for sculpture was a human audience, not an audience of the Greek gods, and the stone figures began to imitate the poses of the living, not the stillness of the dead. That was certainly the idea in the minds of the Renaissance artists and their audience. Donatello (1386–1466), the greatest sculptor of the generation before Michelangelo, made his bronze *David* **[289]** an appealing child as well as a victorious warrior. The pose is exactly as the Greeks had codified it: the weight is on one leg (the *engaged* leg), which pushes that hip up, and the opposite shoulder is higher to compensate. The *free* leg is balanced by the relaxed shoulder on the opposite side. The body often twists on its spine and the head is usually turned slightly.

It is interesting to compare Donatello's *David*, done about 1430, with Michelangelo's **[262]** done 70 years later. Both are in contrapposto poses, but the scale and mood changed from the lively and delicate to the superhuman. The political, social, and artistic changes during those 70 years produced a period of confidence and pride we call the High Renaissance, well represented by Michelangelo's sculpture.

The human figure is still the subject of sculpture, but the mood is quite different from that of Renaissance art. So is the method by which the figures are formed. The dominant method for representing human figures now is making casts directly from living people. The main aim of many contemporary sculptors is to make absolutely truthful statements and to persuade their audiences that these statements *are* truthful. What could be more truthful than casts from living bodies? The same intention has not always required casts from life, however— we find a tradition of extremely lifelike figures in European religious sculpture from the 12th to the 17th century. For example, Juan Martinez Montañés' *(marTEE-nes mon-tan-YASE)* (1568–1648) *Saint Francis Borgia* of 1610 **[290]** shows what can be done by simply carving the figure from wood and painting it with oil paint.

290. Juan Martinez Montañés. *Saint Francis Borgia,* detail of head. 1610. Wood painted with oil paint, life-size. University Chapel, University of Seville, Spain.

In the contemporary mode, Duane Hanson (b. 1925) makes figures [291] that also look very natural, not from wood but from fiberglass and plastic resins; the body forms are cast in parts from living models, then reassembled, carefully painted, and dressed. Hanson chooses his models from people he meets in daily life, but in the process of making a sculpture the figures are generalized to convey the artist's message about the tragic struggle of American working people in a dehumanizing world.

Relaxed poses, skin tones painted in acrylic and oil, with real eyelashes and strands of hair placed one by one and clothing, usually used, selected to identify each character make the figures eerily realistic. In this picture the artist sits between his own self-portrait and his sculpture of a woman; only the stillness of the sculptures sets them apart from living people. Yet Hanson rejects the "super-realist" label, considering himself an **Expressionist** making a strong statement about life, though he leaves it to the audience to decide exactly what he should be classified: "It is not up to the artist to say whether he is this or that," Hanson says. One member of the audience commented: "In their faces, you see a sadness and suffering, too, for the lives they've had. They weren't easy lives. They upset me in a way. People look like this, because they have to struggle to live. I don't want to see it, yet I do—every day. I know it exists. . . ."[7]

George Segal's (b. 1924) life-cast figures [292] have always been one step removed from the illusion we find in Hanson's work, set apart from life by being made entirely of the plaster in which they were cast and often retaining the white color of the plaster. The settings of Segal's figures are like the clothing of Hanson's: real doors, walls, benches, and so on, to convince us of the truthfulness of his images. The go-go dancer, in a traditional contrapposto pose, is set before a mirror which dramatizes the third dimension by reflecting the hidden side of the figure. Segal's *Go-go Dancer* belongs more to the world of art than Hanson's figures, which reject many of the traditions of figure sculpture to merge into the real world of daily life. Segal's white plaster figures are like the white marble statues of an earlier age, and the contrapposto pose also places the figure in a long sculptural tradition. By the rough textures and frankly revealed mold joints Segal emphasizes the fact that his figures are creations of an artist's hands.

This returns us to the point of departure in this chapter: that sculptures have an existence in the real world. There is surely a deep significance when the audience wishes to see in sculpture the absolute, unadorned truth about their own lives and the clothing and settings in which they live. Artists are trying to satisfy that desire by getting as close as possible to the people, materials, and locations of daily life. It is hard to find a glorification of the every day in Hanson and Segal. Perhaps that craving for realism in art reflects a widespread feeling that the everyday world is unrealistic and filled with illusions. Hanson says most of his models consider it an honor to be immortalized in art, even if the sculpture is unflattering. In Segal's sculptures we see reality raised to an ideal level, where the timeless traditions of art replace the struggles of daily life in the consciousness of the audience.

Summary for Review
The special power of sculpture is based on its existence as a solid in the real world. There are three levels of mass: **low relief**, **high relief**, and *sculpture in the round*. The traditional materials and techniques of sculpture are *carving, modeling,* and **casting** in bronze, but modern sculptors have expanded the range of materials to include *construction in hard materials* (wood, metal, plastic), *construction in soft materials* (cloth or fiber), constructing with a variety of materials in *a natural or urban setting in site-specific art,* and composing with *energy sources,* such as wind-driven mobiles and fluorescent light.

The human figure has always been the main subject of sculpture, shown in *frontal* poses to suggest a timeless pose for an eternal audience of gods or shown in an active **contrapposto** pose, as if walking, for a living audience. Some contemporary American sculptors are casting human bodies from living models to convince the audience of the truthfulness of their sculptures. These sculptures may be painted to be lifelike, or left white to recall ancient traditions in sculpture.

Part IV
Architecture
and Applied Design

What does the audience need to know about architecture and environmental design and about applied design in textiles, ceramics, or metal? These are fields that we all know something about even before we have studied them because we are surrounded by and use these designs every day. We know which ones are comfortable and efficient. Yet many of the things we continue to use—and even enjoy— are actually uncomfortable and inefficient. It seems that function, even though it plays an important part in these designs, rarely plays the dominant part. The meaning these designs express, the lifestyle they promote and glorify, is almost always the dominant part. That's why architecture and applied design are considered arts.

Some of the design applications we will examine in this section are often called **crafts**. That word suggests that the form is everything, the content nonexistent; or, to put it another way, the word implies that the work is well made but has no meaning or message. Most artists reject that idea now. The more we know about other ways of life, the more we realize that the things we take for granted as meaningless functional objects are among those that express most clearly the special quality of our own way of life.

The designer or artist often has little time to think of anything so all-encompassing as a way of life. Usefulness was the practical question all the artists discussed in this part had to consider. Here is the architect Ludwig Mies van der Rohe studying the model of a group of buildings he is designing **[293]**. Looking over his shoulder is Herbert Greenwald, the real estate developer who was the client; he had commissioned the buildings, would pay for them, and would manage the property when they were built. That sounds remarkably like the role we assigned the patron in Chapter 1. Greenwald played an important part in Mies' career, providing opportunities for the architect to build many of his best designs. Mies, who had fled Nazi Germany in 1938 and was teaching architecture in Chicago, was 60 in 1946 when he met Greenwald, then only 29. Greenwald was welleducated and ambitious to create fine buildings, the ideal client, and during the next thirteen years (until Greenwald died in an airplane crash in 1959) he and Mies worked together to perfect the design of the tall building as a box of glass and steel.

Comparison of Figure **293** with Figure **61**, both of which show a patron or client looking over the artist's shoulder, suggests that these pictures show a timeless relationship between artists and patrons. In all the applied design fields collaboration between designers and builders or manufacturers has a long history. It always depends on mutual respect between those whose specialties are in the arts and those whose specialties are in finance and administration. That such collaboration is possible is proven by the existence of the works of art and design that are discussed in the following two chapters.

No one can design and create works of art in weaving or glass without training and practice. The craft must be mastered before it can be used to create art, but that is true of sculpture, painting, or the graphic arts as well. Surely this is what the audience needs to know about architecture and applied design: that they can best be understood as arts, in which mastery of the craft is in the service of a way of life that the users believe in.

293. Ludwig Mies van der Rohe, architect, seated, and Herbert Greenwald, developer, 1955, looking at model for Lafayette Park, an urban housing project to have been built in Detroit, Michigan.

Styles and Structures in Architecture and the Environment

What makes some buildings better than others? "Durability, convenience, and beauty" were the three criteria chosen by Vitruvius, an ancient Roman writer on architecture. We usually hope to find durability and beauty in any art, but we expect convenience only in the applied arts. Convenience is surely a criterion we could agree on, meaning that the building performs its assigned functions efficiently. What is surprising, however, is that convenience, or functional efficiency, has actually played a rather small part in architecture. Serious architecture over the millennia of human building has mostly been concerned with temples and churches in which public ceremonies are almost the only functions to be served. Houses, barns, forts, and workshops, in which function was always the main criterion, have usually been considered beneath the level of architecture. We think of a Classical temple, but not a Classical barn or fort.

Functional convenience is a criterion that separates architecture from sculpture. Post-Modern sculptors, such as Alice Aycock (b. 1946), have, in fact, designed and built buildings, but these buildings cannot be made to serve any use **[294]**, except of course for their intended use as objects to look at and think about. True architecture, on the other hand, is concerned with the basic needs for convenience and efficiency, needs that bring art into contact with daily life in the real world.

294. Alice Aycock. *The House of the Stoics.* 1984. Wood, steel frame; height 32', width 11'9", depth 13'6" (9.8 × 3.6 × 4.1 m). Permanently installed in the village of Niyazaki-Mura, Japan.

295. Beauvais Cathedral, Beauvais, France. Begun c. 1225. Engraving by B. Winkles after a drawing by R. Garland.

Functionalism as a serious attitude toward art became especially important in the 20th century, although it has older roots. Two statements by American architects on function and form laid the groundwork for two different periods in 20th-century building: "Form follows function," the formula of Louis Sullivan (1856–1924), which became the creed of Modernism, contrasts with "Forms always follow forms and not function," a remark by Philip Johnson (b. 1906) that expresses the Post-Modern conviction that art traditions are more important in design than utilitarian efficiency.

Functionalism, the belief in doing a job efficiently, has a common-sense appeal. But traditionally the job of architecture was to represent the irrational and make a place where rituals could be carried out, with no concern for the demands of common sense. For example, a practical person looking at a Gothic church **[295]** might suggest that the interior could easily accommodate ten or twelve floors, instead of only one. The church could then provide space for Sunday schools, child care, meeting rooms, church offices, and many other useful services, as well as having a large—low ceilinged, of course—sanctuary on the ground floor. But anyone standing in a Gothic church realizes that the function of the church is to inspire awe and a sense of spiritual elevation, a function which the vast empty spaces crossed by beams of light successfully accomplish. It is clear that functionalism is a very useful criterion providing we define "function" broadly enough to include fulfilling our mental and emotional needs, as well as our material ones. These needs that people feel change from one period to another. Thus to understand what people were feeling during any period we must examine what they built.

Artists, like the rest of us, are stimulated by problems and puzzles. The most important puzzle facing an architect, the one which must be solved before anything else is considered, is, "How will the roof be supported?" The answer will fall into one of only a few categories, depending on the materials available for building. If the materials to be used are mainly straight beams of wood or metal, then the roof will be supported by a post-and-lintel, a cantilever, or a truss system. If blocks (stone, bricks, or mud bricks) are to be used, then the roof will be an arch, vault, or dome. If cables (of fiber or steel) are to be used, then a suspension system will be chosen. (All these terms are explained in the following pages.) It is clear that a building whose roof is a dome will be quite different in style, and hence different in meaning, from one whose roof is flat and rests on beams.

None of these structural systems is obsolete. One of the great challenges and pleasures of architecture today is the availability of the whole range of inventions made in many times and places. For example, the architects of the King Abdulaziz International Airport [296], built in Jeddah, Saudi Arabia, in 1981

296. Skidmore, Owings & Merrill. Haj Terminal, King Abdulaziz International Airport, Jeddah, Saudi Arabia. 1981.

used steel cables and fiberglass fabric, two modern materials, to form a tent similar in principle to the ancient Arabian Bedouin tents that were well adapted to their desert environment. Old forms are constantly reinterpreted and made new in this way.

In this chapter we will look at three styles that are basic in Western civilization and the structural systems on which they depend: building with beams, blocks, and cables. Educated people in every land are able to understand several different kinds of "language"; one of these is the design of buildings. Particularly in building there is a double "vocabulary" composed of the forms themselves that belong to each style and the words that refer to those forms. Western culture is especially rich in its architectural language through its inheritance from the **Classical**, the **Gothic**, and the **Modern**. With Modern architecture we will include its contemporary revision, the *Post-Modern*. At the end we will examine some contemporary ideas about architectural style.

Building with Beams

The Post-and-Lintel System

The Classical style of the Western countries uses **post-and-lintel** structure, a system these countries share with the rest of the world. Traditional ways of building in the tropical regions make use of bamboo for both *posts*, the verticals, and *lintels*, the horizontals. The house [297] under construction by Mru tribal people in Bangladesh is a sample of traditional architectural technology. Bamboo is amazingly strong and light and can be joined by lashing—there are no nails in this house. The basic structure is formed by the heaviest poles that make up the grid of posts and lintels, but bamboo is also split and intertwined to make the walls, and bamboo leaves are used for the roof thatch.

The Egyptian temple of Khonsu at Karnak [298] and the bamboo house look as different as two buildings can look, but they are both post-and-lintel structures. Though bamboo is very light and strong, stone is very heavy; it is also strong under compression (as a post), but it is weak under tension (as a

below: 297. Bamboo house under construction by Mru tribal people, Bangladesh, about 1972.

right: 298. Temple of Khonsu, Karnak, Egypt. c. 1150 B.C. (20th Dynasty, reign of Ramesses III).

299. Ludwig Mies van der Rohe. 860–880 Lake Shore Drive, Chicago. 1948–1951. Steel and glass.

lintel). The Egyptians built temples and tombs from stone because the buildings were meant to be eternal, but to assure that the stone lintels would not break they had to be very short. While the fragile-looking bamboo house can have long beams, leaving a large floor space free of posts, the Egyptian temple has most of the floor space occupied by the massive posts that support the beams (or lintels) that hold up the roof. Aside from the difference between their locations in a jungle and a desert, the criteria of durability, convenience, and beauty are entirely different for these two buildings. The jungle house needs comfortable spaces sheltered from the rain but open to the breeze for a family's activities. Its materials need to be inexpensive; if they wear out quickly they can be replaced easily. The temple, on the other hand, needs to be emotionally impressive, even awe-inspiring, and durable for eternity, at least in appearance, but it does not matter much whether it is comfortable or not.

Although the post-and-lintel system is very ancient, it is also very up to date. The twin apartment buildings built by Herbert Greenwald at 860–880 Lake Shore Drive **[299]** in Chicago were designed by Ludwig Mies van der Rohe (1886–1969) in 1948 in a style given the name **International Style.** They became models for thousands of tall buildings in the United States and around the world for the next quarter century. The building has a steel frame of 21-foot (6.4-meter) squares, repeated three times on the short side, five times on the long side, and raised to 26 stories with a flat roof. Each square is divided into four windows, which Mies had curtained in identical off-white draperies; tenants could add their own colored draperies inside, but they were not allowed to show though the windows. That dominant artistic intention extended to adding an extra steel I-beam welded onto the vertical posts and window frames to emphasize the verticality of the design. The Lake Shore Drive apartments use steel posts and beams in a way similar to the bamboo of the house in Bangladesh. Both of them are the purest expressions possible of the post-and-lintel system; for Mies van der Rohe that simplicity and revelation of structure had become an artistic ideal that went far beyond function.

Styles and Structures in Architecture and the Environment

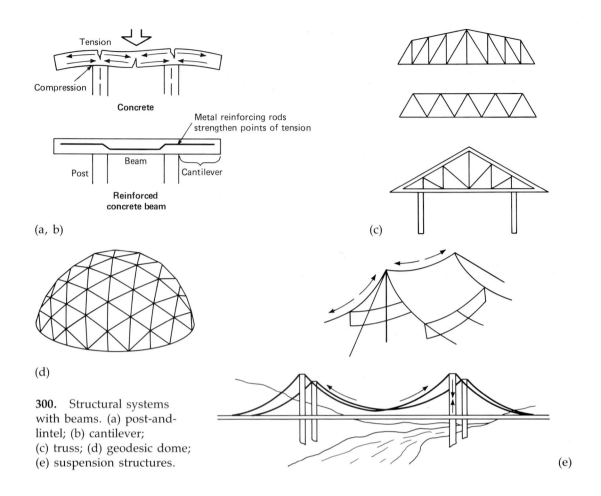

300. Structural systems with beams. (a) post-and-lintel; (b) cantilever; (c) truss; (d) geodesic dome; (e) suspension structures.

The post-and-lintel **[300a]** is the basic form of building with beams, but there are other possibilities.

The Cantilever

The **cantilever** is a horizontal beam that extends beyond its vertical supporting post **[300b]**. Cantilevers are used where a building extends over areas where supporting posts are inconvenient. The most famous cantilevered building in the United States is a house built in 1936 by Frank Lloyd Wright for Edgar Kaufmann in the Appalachian Mountains outside Pittsburgh **[301]**. The house is named "Fallingwater" since it hangs in space over the rocky bed of a stream which flows beside and under the house. The beams in the floor of the porch rest on posts which are nearly invisible in the shadows beneath it. Then the beams continue on under the massive stone walls of the house, whose weight easily balances the porch. Though we rarely see it used as conspicuously as in "Fallingwater," the cantilever is frequently employed in modern building.

The Truss

There is no question that the **truss** is one of the most useful inventions in history, nearly rivaling the wheel for both utility and simplicity. A truss is a triangle of beams. Triangles are rigid and they can be attached to each other in a variety of patterns to form larger rigid structural forms. The basic truss is made by a diagonal beam that converts a post-and-lintel into two triangles **[300c]**.

The basic truss is what we see in the roof and its supports in a medieval market hall at Mereville, France **[302]**. The tall wooden roof is divided on the inside into a series of ascending trusses by the posts and lintels of the roof

supports. Then each of the post-and-lintel systems is reinforced with a diagonal to form another truss.

The visionary engineer Buckminster Fuller (1895–1983) was especially interested in the adaptability of the truss, using it for all kinds of structural forms. The most famous of these is what he called the *geodesic dome* [300d]. Not a dome in the traditional sense described below, it is actually a series of curved trusses.

301.
Frank Lloyd Wright.
Kaufmann House,
"Fallingwater,"
Bear Run,
Pennsylvania. 1936.

302. Market hall, Mereville, France. 1511.

303.
Buckminster Fuller.
United States Pavilion,
EXPO '67, Montreal.
1967.
Steel and plexiglass
geodesic dome,
shown under
construction;
height 137' (42 m),
diameter 250' (73.3 m).

At the World's Fair in Montreal in 1967 a huge geodesic dome was built for the United States Pavilion. Figure **303** shows the pavilion under construction, with the steel pipe components stacked in the foreground. The great advantage of the geodesic system, and of trusses in general, is that they can span long distances or cover large areas with very little material. They are both lighter in weight and less expensive than a solid material would be.

Classical Architecture

The style of architecture called **Classical** was invented in Greece about 2500 years ago, and, of course, when it was new it was not called "Classical." That name signifies its continued acceptance, which is based on its deeply considered use of beams as an architectural form. The only illogical factor is that the Greeks used blocks of stone, usually marble, to build their post-and-lintel buildings. Even when Classical style is out of fashion, as it has been until recently, no one thinks it is gone forever. As you examine its basic ideas you will begin to see what the word "classic" means: that a designer can reach a simple, logical form that expresses its structure and use in every feature. Many Modern architects have been deeply impressed by Classical Greek buildings, even when they were trying to eliminate specific Classical design features from their buildings.

Although no Classical temple built of wood exists today, the design of the existing stone buildings makes it seem certain that they are descended from wooden ancestors. The system of Classical building is based on the post-and-lintel, with trusses (made of wood) forming the gable roof. Every part could have been designed originally in wood, but the design has been translated into marble in all the famous ancient buildings which have survived to our time. Two temples on the Acropolis ("upper city"), the sacred precinct of Athens, have miraculously survived to allow us to see the astonishing perfection of Greek Classical building. They are the Parthenon [304], dedicated to Athena as guardian of the city, and the smaller Erechtheum (air-ek-THEE-um) [305], which contains three small sacred shrines. First we will look at the plans of both buildings, then at their elevations.

The **plan** of a building is the shape it makes on the ground [306]. The Parthenon, whose plan is the typical one for Greek temples, is a long rectangle whose proportions were based on the number of columns which could be set along its edges; the long sides each held double the number of columns on each end, plus one. The line of columns around the edge of the platform is called the **peristyle** (peri = surrounding; style = column, as in our word stylus). The Par-

304. Iktinos and Kallikrates. The Parthenon, Athens. 448–432 B.C. White marble, 228 × 104' (69.5 × 31.7 m); height of columns 34' (10.4 m).

thenon was unusually fancy in having double rows of columns on each end. Within the peristyle is the chamber (called *naos* in Greek, *cella* in Latin) with the shrine containing the statue of the goddess. A small chamber at the other end of this building served as the city treasury.

The plan of the Erechtheum [306], however, shows that this building violates the common rule that the plan is a simple rectangle. It is a unique design because it was built to shelter three shrines to a mythical contest between Poseidon, the sea god, and Athena for the rule of Athens. They were a rock scratched by Poseidon's trident, a salt-water spring, and an olive tree, none of which could be moved. The Erechtheum (named for an Athenian hero in the story) shows that Greek Classicism could accommodate variations from its preferred regularity.

While the plan is the horizontal layout, the **elevation** is the design of the vertical structure. By comparing the elevations we discover subtle differences in these two buildings which show they were obeying different sets of rules—or we could say they follow different orders. **Order** is a key idea in Classical archi-

below: 305. Mnesikles. The Erechtheum, Athens. c. 421–409 B.C. White marble, 37 × 66' (11.3 × 20.1 m).

right: 306. Plan of the Acropolis in Athens at the end of the 5th century B.C.

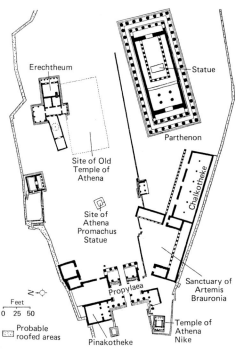

Styles and Structures in Architecture and the Environment ——— 219

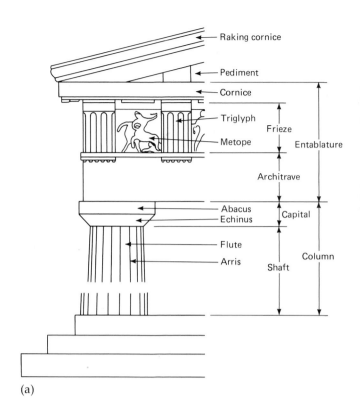

Raking cornice

Pediment

Cornice

Triglyph

Frieze

Metope

Entablature

Architrave

Abacus

Echinus

Capital

Flute

Arris

Column

Shaft

(a)

(b)

307. Doric Order. (a) The parts of the column; (b) Doric columns of the Parthenon, with the west cella (sanctuary) wall and frieze behind, c. 440 B.C.

tecture. There are two basic orders, or styles, which we see in these two buildings, expressed mainly in the way the post-and-lintel system is proportioned and ornamented. The Parthenon follows the **Doric Order [307]**, the Erechtheum the **Ionic Order [308]**. The most obvious difference is the top, or *capital*, of the column, the Doric having two distinct parts: a pillow-like *echinus (e-KY-nus)* and a square slab, or *abacus (A-buh-kus)*. The Ionic capital is adorned with scroll-like *volutes*. The volutes are not the same on all four sides, which caused problems at the corners where the Greeks preferred to see the spiral of the scroll on both outside walls. That led the Greeks to develop a third order, the **Corinthian [309]**, in which the capital is elaborately decorated like the Ionic but is the same on all four sides and thus solves the problem of the corner capital.

These were very expensive buildings—Pericles, the Athenian dictator, used the city-state's defense funds to build them—constructed with a care and precision hardly ever equaled. But the structural *system* is the simple post-and-lintel. All the weight and forces in the building are pressing straight down, and each part expresses clearly, like an abstract sculpture, the role it plays in the building. The lintel—called an *entablature (en-TAB-la-chur)*—is divided (in three parts in the Doric Order and four in the Ionic) to give a horizontal line, and it is perfectly clear that it acts as a horizontal beam pressing down on the tops of the columns. The columns dramatize their vertical position and ability to carry a load by their *flutes*. If you look at a Doric capital **[307]**, you can see that its two parts clearly reflect the transition from being a load (the abacus) to carry a load (the echinus), like a tray with a hand under it. It would not be too much to say that Classical architecture is about "building with beams." That is why it has never gone out of style for good, but keeps being revived over and over. There are other styles that also express the stable, timeless forces of structure, but none in a more satisfactory manner than the Classical style invented in Greece.

Ancient Cities

Human beings have always tried to design not only the structures they inhabit but the environment in which those structures are set. One of the oldest

Architecture and Applied Design

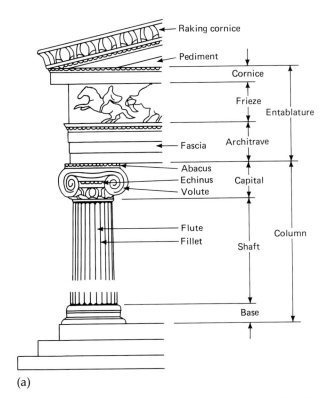

(a)

(b)

308. Ionic Order.
(a) The parts of the
column; (b) Ionic
column of the gateway
(Propylaia) of
the Acropolis,
c. 437–432 B.C.

plans for human occupation of the world is the checkerboard. It was the concept behind the Inca Empire in Peru, which the Incas called the Empire of the Four Quarters (or Tawantinsuyu). It was used for the plans of ancient cities in the Roman Empire and in Asia. Even the chess game was originally a war game for control of the world, for the black and white squares of the checkerboard symbolized the flat surface of the earth.

309. Corinthian Order. (a) The parts of the column; (b) Corinthian column of the tholos (round building) at Epidaurus, Greece, c. 360–320 B.C.

(a)

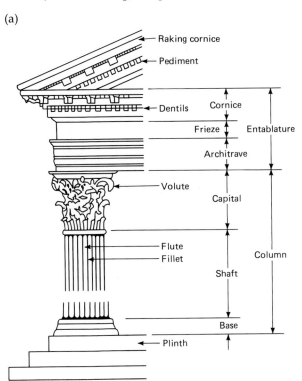

(b)

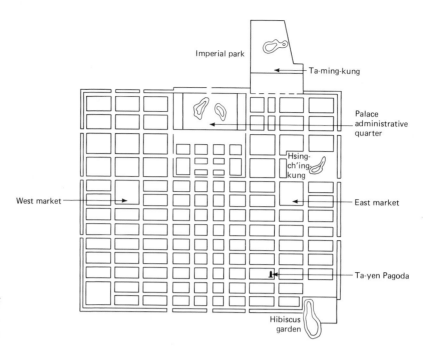

310. Plan of the city of Chang-an, China. c. A.D. 600.

Chang-an [310], the capital of China around A.D. 600, was one of the greatest cities of the world, laid out on a rectangle measuring 6 by 7 miles (9.6 by 11 kilometers) on cardinal directions. Like all traditional Chinese cities, it lay behind massive walls, pierced at intervals with gates. North being the dominant direction, the imperial palace and government buildings were located on that side, but from the outside nothing could be seen but their walls. Like the private residences of their subjects, the emperor's palaces were one-story houses

311. Courtyard of the Hall of Repose, Imperial Palace, Beijing, China.

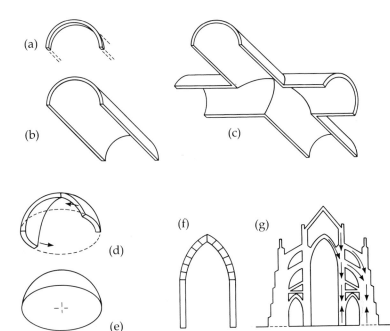

312. Structural systems with blocks. (a) arch; (b) barrel vault; (c) groin vault; (d) and (e) dome; (f) Gothic arch; (g) section of a Gothic church with flying buttresses.

around courtyards [311], and only temple pagodas rose above the first story. The city was bisected by a center street into eastern and western districts, each with its own market square. The residential districts were divided into blocks, each house ordinarily occupying one quarter of a block, the house designed around an open central courtyard. These ancient cities worked reasonably well for most of their inhabitants because they were produced by populations small enough to have plenty of land to expand into, and large margins of safety in food, water, and air. Functional buildings were the result of tried-and-true traditions of form for each function. Like cities in all times and places, Chang-an depended for food on a surrounding hinterland of farming villages.

It is easy to see that most of the towns and cities we still inhabit are based on this most ancient grid pattern of environmental planning. In the same way, we still build most of our buildings using the post-and-lintel system, the truss, and the cantilever. But just as other structural systems developed, so did other designs for the environment.

Building with Blocks

The Arch

Building with blocks is reinvented whenever people need permanent shelter in a region lacking wood. Eskimos cut blocks of snow; desert people use precious water to make mud bricks or they shape stones into blocks to make arches and vaults. Since the greatest builders of arches and vaults were the ancient Romans, we will concentrate on several of their buildings. Then, for a different style of arches and vaults, we will examine the Gothic style.

Builders refer to an **arch** as "alive," meaning that it has forces in its structure that must be balanced. An arch by itself is not a stable unit—during construction it must have "centering" (an arch-shaped wooden form) on which the blocks of the arch are laid. As soon as the last block has been fitted into the arch, the centering can be taken down, but **buttressing** is required [312a]. The basic arch form can be extended into the third dimension to form the **vault** [312b]; vaults can be joined in various ways, but most commonly they are set at right angles to make a **groin vault** [312c]. An arch can also be spun on its center to form a **dome** [312d,e]. But we must return to the basic form, the arch itself.

Styles and Structures in Architecture and the Environment _____ 223

The aqueduct [313] built by the Romans to bring water from a mountain stream to the town of Segovia, in Spain, has to cross a valley just before reaching the town. To keep the water flowing smoothly by gravity the channel had to be kept at a constant angle, so an **arcade** (a line of arches) was built under the channel. If you examine the stone masonry you will notice that no mortar was used; each stone was cut to the proper shape for its position, and the structure is supported by the pressure of stone against stone, without cement. Wooden centering had to be in place as each arch was built, but only enough wood was needed to build one arch since it could then be moved on to the next. At the end buttresses were not necessary, since each arch is supported by its two neighbors. If one stone in any arch suddenly pulverized, that arch would collapse, and then its neighbors, which had each lost one of their buttresses, would collapse, and so on until the whole line had fallen.

We see many arches in modern buildings, very few of them made with live arches. They are mostly built with curved beams or reinforced concrete cast in the shape of an arch. They belong to the structural system of post-and-lintel, even when they give the appearance of arches.

The Vault

We use the term **vault** for a strongroom because in medieval wooden buildings the arched stone foundations were the strongest and the only fireproof part of the building. But the wealth of the Roman Empire permitted huge constructions with vaulted ceilings. Vaults were an ideal solution for the Roman need to accommodate large crowds in public buildings such as markets, administration buildings, arenas, and baths. They were built of brick (the long flat brick that we still call "Roman brick") with lots of cement, using a mass of unskilled laborers. The important public buildings were then covered with marble.

There are still many Roman buildings standing in ruins which show the structural system. The ruins of the Basilica of Maxentius [314] in Rome show the large brick and concrete vaults, with "coffers" inset into the vaults to lighten and decorate them. Typical of Roman vaults, these are perfect semicircles, each vault an elongated semicircular arch called a **barrel vault**. The upper parts of the building collapsed long ago, but it is known that they were roofed with **groin vaults** composed of barrel vaults meeting at right angles.

The Dome

The word **dome** to ancient people brought to mind the shape and symbolism of the sky. Like the sky, a dome was something seen from underneath, not from outside, so the external appearance of a dome was not considered significant. A dome was appropriate in some "heavenly" context—in a temple or a tomb—and its was ordinarily decorated with pictures of the gods or astrological symbols. There is only one great ancient dome still to be seen and it is still the largest masonry (brick and cement) dome in existence: the Pantheon in Rome. It is 140 feet (43 meters) in diameter and also 140 feet from top to floor [315]. The name (pan = all; theon = gods) tells us that statues of all the heavenly gods stood in the niches around the circle, all positions being equal in importance. But the building was not merely a house for the gods; it was a model of the universe in the shape of a globe (except for its flat floor), with its axis a great shaft of sunlight entering through a 29-foot (9-meter) hole, or oculus ("eye"), at the center of the dome. This was the eye of the supreme god of the heavens, with the shaft of light, like a searchlight, moving as the hours passed. The shaft of light was also the absolute limit of existence in the universe, as we still think light to be. So physically encompassing is the interior of the Pantheon that it is impossible to photograph without serious distortion. Giovanni Pannini's (1691–1765) *Interior of the Pantheon* [316], painted about 1750, shows the building as it is in modern times, converted to a Christian church.

313. Roman aqueduct, Segovia, Spain. A.D. 10. Stone arches without mortar.

Architecture and Applied Design

left: 314. Basilica of Maxentius, Rome. A.D. 307–312.
(The Colosseum, A.D. 72–80, is in the background.)

above: 315. The Pantheon, Rome. A.D. 118–125. Brick,
concrete, stone.

316. Giovanni Pannini.
*Interior of the Pantheon,
Rome.* c. 1750. Oil on
canvas, 4'2½" × 3'3"
(1.3 × 1 m).
National Gallery of Art,
Washington, D.C.
(Samuel H. Kress
Collection).

Styles and Structures in Architecture and the Environment ———— 225

All Romans understood the live forces of the arch and they must have been fascinated by the huge dome in which every arch was incomplete, broken by the oculus. The perfect circle in the center received equal pressure all around its periphery and so was stable, like an arch laid at right angles to the curve of the dome. The surprising simplicity of the Pantheon is very satisfying, as any good engineering is likely to be, and the oculus was copied in most later domes.

From the outside the dome is nearly invisible, hidden behind a huge collar of masonry that acts as a buttress [315]. But the weight of the dome was reduced as much as possible by being made largely of brick set in concrete, which sticks together and reduces the live forces of the arch. Still, buttressing was necessary, and the walls, over 20 feet (6 meters) thick, accomplished it by extending up in the collar.

You will notice the gabled porch in Greek Classical style attached to the front of the circular domed building. By A.D. 118, when the Pantheon was built, the Classical style was traditional throughout the Mediterranean world, used by the Romans for all the decorative detail on buildings that, structurally were entirely different from the Greek Classical temples. This was the beginning of that continuing tradition of Classical ornament which we still see today on buildings employing still newer structural systems.

Gothic Architecture

It often happens that when the Classical style is popular the Gothic is unpopular, and vice versa—a fact that suggests, correctly, that these two styles are based on opposing principles.

While the Classical style is based on the post-and-lintel structure, the Gothic is based on the arch and vault. Classical buildings show a balance of the vertical posts with the horizontal lintels, but in the design of Classical buildings the horizontal lines often dominate. Not so in the Gothic, in which the vertical lines are far stronger than the few horizontals. The verticality of Gothic buildings can be seen by comparing Roman semicircular arches, with Gothic arches, which are pointed, like an upward-pointing arrow [312f and 320]. Gothic arches also gave the architect much greater freedom to vary the width and height of the arches, which are not controlled by a strict form like the semicircle. The Gothic

317. Chartres Cathedral, France. Begun 1194. View from the south.

Architecture and Applied Design

318. Amiens Cathedral,
France. 1220–1269.
West front.

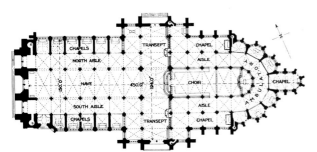

319. Plan of Amiens
Cathedral. 1220–1269.

style emphasized the principle of variety, in contrast to the unity of the Classical
style.

The Gothic style was invented in northern France **[317]** around 1150 and
quickly spread to all the neighboring countries and eventually around the world.
It was very popular in the United States about a century ago, under the name
Neo-Gothic, and was used for churches and almost every other kind of building.
Northern France has large deposits of hard, light-weight limestone—the perfect
material for building high vaults, arches, and pinnacles such as those of Amiens
Cathedral **[318]**. When you examine the plan of the church **[319]**, you see the
pattern of the ceiling groin vaults indicated by lines between the great stone

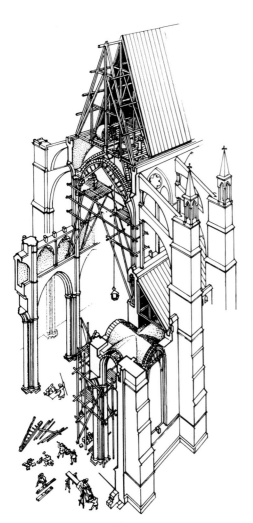

piers (a cluster of columns), showing the pattern of the reinforcing ribs of the groin vaults. The drawing **[320]** shows the building of a Gothic church, with small cut stones being raised to the scaffolds where the masons are building the ribs of the vault on wooden centering. Just below the suspended stone you see the finished vault over one section (called a **bay**) of one of the side aisles, with the centering still in place for one of the ribs. On each side of that aisle bay are the massive stone bases for the buttresses which rise to the height of the highest vaults and support arched arms leaning out against the upper walls to catch the weight of the main vaults. Since there is a space between those buttresses and the arches they support, they are called **flying buttresses** (see **312g**).

Modern architects have always found the plans **[319]** of Gothic churches fascinating because they look so modern—more like the design for a steel building than one built of stone. The wider black areas are solid stone walls and columns, and you see immediately that there are no continuous solid walls, but merely supports for the ceiling, with the line of the exterior wall to be filled with glass. The interior of Amiens Cathedral **[321]** shows the amazing result of all that architectural engineering: the vaults leap across the ceiling at 144 feet (44 meters), about the height of a fourteen-story building. At the east end of the church, behind the altar, you see the slender stone colonnettes (small or thin columns) which frame three layers of variously shaped windows. (There are actually windows at the first level, too, though they are not visible in this picture.) From the interior one gets no hint of the great cage of buttresses on the outside which are required to hold the building up. Gothic worshippers could be forgiven if they got the impression that their churches were supported by miraculous powers.

If the Classical style is about "building with beams," the Gothic is about "building with arches and vaults," with the interior spaces and windows that vaulting permits. But the Gothic is more than engineering—it is also the style most accepting of variety. In this it contrasts with the Classical, in which all the columns are alike and in which there was an accepted best form for every element. Like the "live" arch of its structure and the varying designs of columns and decorative features, Gothic form and decoration try to contain and express everything in life. There are sculptures and stained-glass windows representing God, the saints, and angels, but also human beings and even devils. The past and future, as told in the Bible, and even scenes from the present, are represented to include all history and all Creation in the decorative program.

The tolerance of Gothic design for variations is manifested most obviously in the different styles of towers on several of the greatest churches, as we see at Amiens [318] and at the famous cathedral of Chartres [317]. Although monuments to faith, they are among the most humane of buildings.

The Traditional City

Medieval and Renaissance Europe developed entirely different patterns of city building from those found at Chang-an. The Chinese city gave away none of its secrets at first glance. One glance at a European city showed a dominant structure, a castle or a church, with the houses of the citizens clustered around it, a clear demonstration of the relationships of power and duty within the city. Our modern idea of a city is deeply conditioned by old European cities which have served as models for our own cities and towns.

The old European cities have become modern cities, but pictures of them as they looked in earlier times show the ways of life that gave them their character. Giorgio Vasari (1511–1574), best known for his biographies of Renaissance artists, painted the view of Florence [322] in fresco in the city hall (Palazzo Vecchio) in 1561–1562, but he showed it during a siege by the armies of the Holy Roman Empire 30 years earlier. That explains the camps, armies, and cannons around the walls of the city. Like Chang-an, Florence was surrounded by a fortress wall. It followed no predefined geometric plan, but enclosed the built-up parts of the city on an irregular design. In the ancient rectangular city, the total plan reflected the imagined shape of the world, and human settlement was obliged to fit into the geometric pattern. The Western attitude was just the opposite: the

322. Giorgio Vasari. *View of Florence during the Siege of 1529.* 1561–1562. Fresco in Palazzo Vecchio (city hall), Florence.

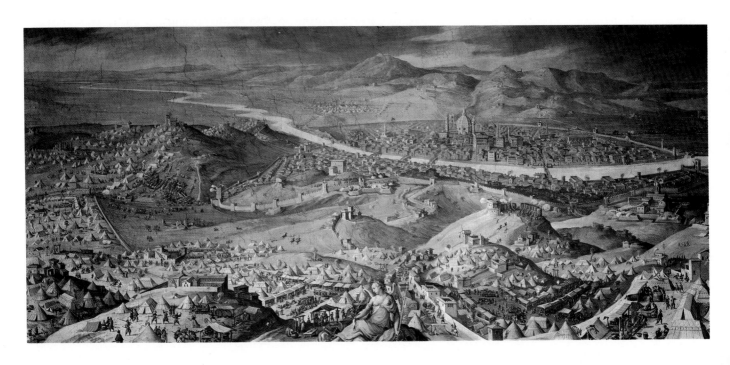

323. Giovanni Maria Butteri. *The Return from the Palio.* 17th century. Oil on canvas. National Gallery of Ireland, Dublin.

pattern of the walls had to accommodate the settlement of the people, which was dictated by the lands people owned and the ways they had used them. In ancient China land was not considered private property, and investment and speculation in land did not occur, which led to different patterns of human settlement. The power held by individuals over land can be seen in the view of Florence. The large house on the lower left, for example, is the palace of the Pitti family, an unmistakable expression of pride and power.

The focal points of Florence were, and still are, the buildings that dominate public life, the cathedral, with Brunelleschi's famous dome, clearly visible in the center of Figure **322**, and the medieval city hall, the Palazzo Vecchio, with its tall tower, just to the right of the dome. Each of these buildings faced on an open square which served as a public meeting place, and the squares were surrounded by the tall stone houses of merchant families. Streets were narrow corridors, many of them passable only by pedestrians, or perhaps by horsemen, winding between the massive outer walls of palatial houses. Florentines had good evidence that life was not perfectly safe and secure; the city walls were attacked and defended on several occasions, and within the city many houses could be turned into fortresses if the need arose, as it did from time to time.

Within and between the massive houses were an infinity of small workshops for every kind of craftsman: carpenters and furniture makers, weavers and tailors, goldsmiths and painters. In the residential areas were open squares devoted to markets, mainly for food. The streets and squares were brought to life with frequent processions and festivals on religious holidays, when leaders of the city and the church were joined by costumed and masked citizens and actors to represent sacred and mythological figures and scenes. In a Florentine street scene **[323]**, the horse, which had won in a festival race, is being led through the streets in triumph. The narrow stone-paved street is a stage for the audience observing from their windows. The streets were full of life every day, for they were practically the living rooms of the public and were only incidentally used as thoroughfares. There is no hint of green in these stony streets, but in a city the size of Florence people could escape to the country in a few minutes'

Architecture and Applied Design

walk. The city walls marked a sharp division between city and country, unlike our modern situation where city melts slowly through suburbs into country.

The features we find in Florence and the other traditional European cities provide a set of elements which we still regard as basic: a dominant center with some public structure and its square for public gatherings, residential areas with markets close by, and industrial workshops somehow connected. All these features must be joined by a system of circulation or transportation, which in Florence took up very little of the city's space. You can see that the design principles of unity, variety, emphasis, and movement are basic considerations in city planning.

The Renaissance Dome

The word "dome" brings to our modern minds a great round vault silhouetted against the sky, quite different from the dome of the Roman Pantheon, which can hardly be seen from the outside [315]. We expect a dome to be more impressive from the outside than from the inside, unlike the Pantheon. The high dome was the principal contribution of the Renaissance to architectural structure, and we find it as the point of emphasis on buildings whose decorative styles derive from the Gothic (in an Italian version) or the Classical (in a Roman version).

The first dome with this high shape, standing completely free of external buttressing and designed to be seen from the outside, was built on the Cathedral (or, in Italian, *Duomo*) of Florence in the years after 1420. The design, by Filippo Brunelleschi, became a basic part of every architect's training thereafter.

The high dome was given its standard form a few years later by Michelangelo in his design for the dome for Saint Peter's in Rome [324]. Age 72 when he designed it in 1546, Michelangelo had outgrown the styles of his own lifetime. In this superhuman design he summed up the sculptural massiveness of the an-

324. Michelangelo. Dome of Saint Peter's, Vatican, Rome. 1546.

Styles and Structures in Architecture and the Environment

The high dome was the invention of one man, Filippo Brunelleschi *(broo-nuh-LES-kee)* (1377–1446), to solve a particular problem. The Cathedral of Florence was being rebuilt in the 14th century with a very large east end where the main altar was to be set under a dome. We know this was the plan because a Florentine artist named Andrea (active c. 1350–1370) painted an imaginary view of the building, probably based on a model, when the walls below the dome were still under construction [325]. There was just one problem: given the thin, high walls and the very wide octagonal opening (131 feet, or 40 meters, across), no one knew how to build the dome. Centering on such a scale was impossible, and there was no way to place buttresses against the dome without completely encasing the new building in massive supports.

Enter Brunelleschi, who was described by his biographer Vasari as "puny in person and insignificant of feature," but endowed with "much greatness of soul."* At age 21 he came in second in an important sculpture competition in Florence, and, disgusted, set off for eight years in Rome studying architecture. He was already thinking of the problem of the dome, for the cathedral had been standing for some years with its huge opening covered with canvas and no one able to design a way to finish it. In Rome Brunelleschi made a careful study of the Pantheon and all the remains of Roman vaulted buildings. In 1407 he returned to Florence to attend an architectural congress on the problem of the Cathedral dome and offered his ideas about the design, but the commission was not finally given to him for another fifteen years. Even then he worked in a con-

325. Andrea da Firenze. *Dominican Allegory.* 1366–1368. Fresco in Spanish Chapel, Santa Maria Novella, Florence.

cient Roman buildings he had been studying and predicted the **Baroque** style of the next century. The powerful design of the drum, with its paired columns, is carried by ribs up to the lantern, where it is repeated in smaller scale. The shape of the dome is rounder than Brunelleschi's, but is still taller than a semicircle. That shape and the more massive form set the pattern for later dome-builders.

stant rain of public discussion and criticism. But the ingenuity of his plan and his machinery and scaffolding for the work eventually silenced the critics, though Brunelleschi himself did not live to see the dome completed. Even today the gallery around the base of the dome remains unfinished [326].

The problem, Brunelleschi saw, was the opposite of the Pantheon, in which the weight of the vault pressed inward on an opening at the top of the dome. In the Cathedral at Florence the main problem was that there was no convenient way to buttress the outward pressure at the base of the dome. Brunelleschi proposed to solve that problem with a chain of oak beams bolted together around the base. That chain, along with the steep angle of the dome, its octagonal shape, and hollow core walls to lighten the weight, made it possible to raise a large dome high into the air without exterior buttresses.

Now, when a Florentine is homesick, he says he is "sick for the dome." It has become the symbol of

326. Filippo Brunelleschi.
Dome of Florence Cathedral (Duomo). 1420–1436.

327. Piero della Francesca. *Madonna della Misericordia*, center panel of altarpiece. 1445. Oil on wood panel, 10'7¼" × 8'11½" (3.2 × 2.7 m). Town Hall, Borgo San Sepolcro, Italy.

the city, but even more than that, it has become a worldwide symbol for a community. Already in 1445, with the dome still unfinished, the painter Piero della Francesca *(fran-CHES-ka)* (c. 1415–1492) had painted a Madonna [327] sheltering the community beneath her dome-shaped cloak, her head copying the design for the "lantern" on top of Brunelleschi's dome. Still today, far from Florence, we think the proper design for a building symbolizing the community is the "maternal" form of a dome against the sky.

---

*Giorgio Vasari, *Lives of the Most Excellent Architects, Painters, and Sculptors*, first ed., 1550. Quotation from *Vasari's Lives of the Artists*, abridged and ed. by Betty Burroughs (New York: Simon & Schuster, 1946) 69.

The United States Capitol in Washington has always had a dome, seen by the people of the country as a symbol of the nation. The first capitol building, designed by William Thornton (1759–1828) and Benjamin Latrobe (1764–1820), was begun in 1793 when President Washington laid the cornerstone. It was burned by British troops during the War of 1812 and rebuilt with the same

328. William Thornton and Benjamin Latrobe. United States Capitol, Washington, D.C. c. 1808. Engraving by T. Sutherland, 1825. New York Public Library (I. N. Phelps Stokes Collection).

Roman-style dome the architects had envisioned **[328]**. You can see that the dome the designers had in mind was the Pantheon. By 1851 the government had outgrown the building and Thomas Walter (1804–1887) was commissioned to design a new capitol **[329]**. The new dome is modeled on Michelangelo's Saint Peter's dome, with the drum doubled to gain more height. But the new element is that this dome was built of cast iron, instead of stone or brick, a major engineering achievement at that time. The Capitol, with its high dome against the sky, has the same symbolism as its antecedent on the Cathedral in Florence, the idea of community.

329. Thomas U. Walter. United States Capitol, Washington, D.C. 1865. Cast-iron dome, height 268′ (81.7 m).

Architecture and Applied Design

Modern Architecture

In earlier centuries most buildings were designed and built by traditional artisans according to time-honored plans, but in our century almost everything we build is "architecture"—meaning it is a new invention built with art and science. Two architects, Frank Lloyd Wright and Le Corbusier, are among the great inventors of 20th-century architecture. Although there are many other important architects in many countries, those two names would appear on any list of the major innovators.

Frank Lloyd Wright

Frank Lloyd Wright (1867–1959) claimed that architecture was the "mother art," meaning that it generated the other arts and they remained dependent on it. The arts are so interdependent that to choose one as basic is just a personal point of view, but Wright's buildings and interior designs suggest that those were not empty words for him. The power of his designs rests on his conviction that architecture is the basic human expression. Wright, probably the best-known American architect, made a unique, personal, and very American contribution to modern architecture.

Earlier we looked at his cantilevered house, "Fallingwater" [301], and here we will examine two buildings that show other aspects of his work: the house built in Chicago for the Robie family in 1908–1909 and the art museum built in New York for the Solomon R. Guggenheim Collection in 1956–1959.

The Robie House [330] is one of the sources of our typical suburban "ranch house." Although it actually has three stories, the house appears to sprawl in long horizontal lines appropriate to the American plains and prairies, protected by a wide-eaved roof and centered around a fireplace and its chimney. The two pairs of main rooms—living and dining on the main floor, with the playroom

330. Frank Lloyd Wright. Robie House, Oak Park, Illinois. 1908–1909.

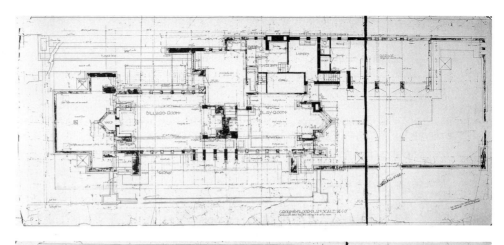

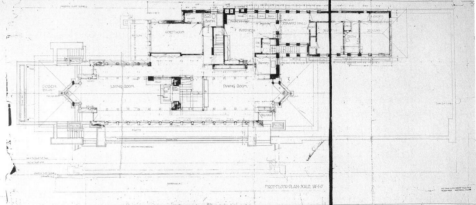

331.
Frank Lloyd Wright.
Robie House, Oak Park,
Illinois. 1908–1909.
Plans of the ground
floor (top) and first
floor (bottom).

and billiard room below on the ground floor (see plans, Figure **331**)—are separated only by the fireplace, providing the free-flowing space that the client and Wright both wanted. A view of the living room **[332]** shows the band of uncurtained windows ornamented with leaded glass which unify the interior and the outdoors. Roman brick with limestone trim, varnished wood interior details, built-in furniture, and Wright's custom-designed carpets were Wright's attempts to "eliminate the decorator," making the materials and structure of the house its decoration.

332. Frank Lloyd Wright.
Robie House, Oak Park, Illinois.
1908–1909. The living room in 1910.

333.
Frank Lloyd Wright.
Solomon R.
Guggenheim
Museum, New York.
1956–1959.

One of Wright's last buildings, the Solomon R. Guggenheim Museum in New York of 1956–1959 **[333]**, is the result of the triumph of form over function. Some critics, in fact, consider the building a sculpture because it serves its museum function poorly and, far from forming a quiet background for the art, it competes with the work exhibited. But the public has always accepted the building. The main exhibit area is a six-story spiral ramp around an open glass-domed circular court **[334]**, Wright's idea being that the visitor could take the elevator to

334. Frank Lloyd Wright.
Solomon R. Guggenheim
Museum, New York.
1956–1959. Interior.

Styles and Structures in Architecture and the Environment _____ 237

In Detail: A Client's View of Frank Lloyd Wright

In 1930 Paul and Jean Hanna read Wright's book *Modern Architecture* aloud to each other and wrote Wright a fan letter. That was the beginning of an association with Wright's architecture that lasted the rest of their lives.

In 1935 Paul Hanna joined the faculty at Stanford University, in California, and immediately the couple began planning with Wright to build a house there. He visited them in the spring of 1936 to see the lot and soon a set of plans arrived showing a complex group of hexagons [335], with a letter: "I hope the unusual shape of the rooms won't disturb you because in reality they would be more quiet than rectangular ones and you would scarcely be aware of any irregularity." Much discussion ensued between the Hannas and Wright, focusing on such things as separate bedrooms for the three children, and in January, 1937, construction began. The projected costs were originally $15,000, but by the time construction began they had reached $50,000, far beyond the Hannas' budget. But work continued, the clients angrily at one point telegraphing for completed plans. Wright responded mildly, "BEST NOT GET TOO EXCITED LONG WAY TO GO," and sent plans as they were completed. The Hannas, looking back on this period, commented: "As we reread this exchange of messages, we are amazed by both the sharp, even abrasive, language of our letters to Mr. Wright and the extraordinary tolerance with which he reacted."

Finally, in November, 1938, the Hannas moved into their new house and "began adjusting to the reality" [336]. Later they wrote: "The two floor levels were just right: an illusion of two stories without all those stairs. The variation in ceiling heights from 6 feet 7 inches to 16 feet 3 inches [2 to 5 meters] delighted us. We enjoyed the openness of the plan

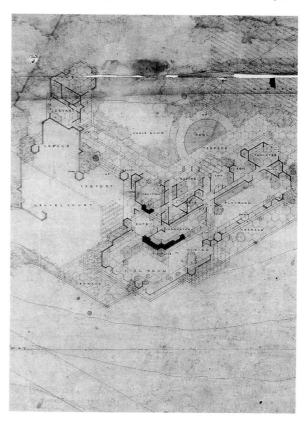

335. Frank Lloyd Wright.
Hanna House, Stanford, California. 1936–1938. Plan.

the sixth floor and effortlessly stroll down the ramp, glancing at the paintings as they flowed by. While that is certainly not the way to see art, the building itself is unquestionably a work of art. Wright saw its perfect circular form as "the quiet unbroken wave," a satisfying sculptural form.

Le Corbusier

In 1920 the Swiss-French architect Le Corbusier (*luh kor-bü-ZEEAY*, the pseudonym adopted by Charles Edouard Jeanneret, 1887–1965) published a manifesto in which he made the famous remark, "a house is a machine for living in." In other writings he compared houses to ocean liners, airplanes, cars, and motorcycles, all machines which we live in during travel and which have no room for frills. It is hard for us now to understand his remark because we take functional housing for granted. We hardly realize that most houses at the turn of the century did not have a bathroom; there was either a chamber pot under the

336. Frank Lloyd Wright. Hanna House, Stanford, California. 1936–1938. Living room.

and the free flow of space generated by the 120-degree angle." Four months after the Hannas moved into the house, Wright and 20 of his apprentices arrived for a visit. The architect had not seen the house since it had been finished; as he stood in the living room and looked around for the first time, he said "Why, it's more beautiful than I had imagined; we have created a symphony here."

From Paul R. and Jean S. Hanna, *Frank Lloyd Wright's Hanna House: The Clients' Report* (Cambridge: M.I.T. Press, 1981).

bed or a "privy" in the back yard, and bathing was done in a movable tub in the bedroom or kitchen. At that time, a house ordinarily had a certain number of rooms, each of which could be adapted to any purpose. Le Corbusier proposed to make each room serve one function, as a machine does, so that a dining room was perfect for eating but almost useless for anything else. Actually, it is the rooms that have the most machinery in them—kitchens and bathrooms—that are the most clearly functional. A machine is designed to do one job perfectly, and nothing else.

Le Corbusier was working in a period when the housing of most people was far out of date and did not begin to meet their material needs, much less their emotional needs. Reformers of his period proclaimed that housing was a social need to be solved by purely machine functionalism, but Le Corbusier always insisted that it was a problem of architectural design. Although his large apartment blocks are important contributions to the development of public housing, it is in the single-family houses that one gets the best understanding of his work. Le Corbusier's most famous house is the Villa Savoye, a Spartan but

337. Le Corbusier. Villa Savoye, Poissy-sur-Seine, France. 1929–1930.

elegant country house built near Paris in the years 1929–1930 **[337]**. The house exemplifies "the five points of a New Architecture" as Le Corbusier had defined them: (1) Leave the ground free by setting the building on stilts; (2) place a garden on the flat roof to make use of the space; (3) keep the supporting structure—which in the Villa Savoye consists of 25 steel posts—independent of the walls; (4) make the exterior and interior design completely flexible and controlled only by function and appearance; (5) use continuous strips of windows to allow natural light to penetrate the building. The ground floor is reserved for servants' quarters; the family quarters are reached by a ramp to an open terrace modeled on the deck of a ship, with an upper-deck roof garden on the highest level. The living areas **[338]** have glass on all sides, an open plan, and a monastic simplicity of form. The bathroom **[339]**, with its sunken bath and tiled reclining

sofa, may be compared to Le Corbusier's description of the ideal bathroom: "Demand a bathroom looking south, one of the largest rooms in the house. . . . One wall to be entirely glazed, opening if possible onto a balcony for sun baths; the most up-to-date fittings with a shower-bath and gymnastic appliances."[1] In 1929 that was revolutionary, but his idea of the bathroom is one of his many ideas that have been widely accepted.

As a young man Le Corbusier traveled in Greece and saw the Parthenon, which he described, rather melodramatically, as a "terrifying machine," whose design had been perfected to the point "when nothing more might be taken away, when nothing would be left but these closely-knit and violent elements sounding clear and tragic like brazen trumpets."[2] In his own buildings he hoped to achieve a stripped-down clean-lined intellectual design, a modern version of the Parthenon. The Villa Savoye fulfills Le Corbusier's idea of "a machine for living in" in various ways; it is a thoroughly rational design from which nothing might be taken away.

Later in life Le Corbusier designed another very influential building, this one a chapel to be a memorial to members of the French Resistance who had died in the Second World War [340]. The chapel, on a wooded hill near the village of Ronchamp, has been described as "the most religiously convincing building of the twentieth century," despite the fact that its designer was an atheist who commented, "The requirements of religion have had little effect on the design, the form was an answer to a psychophysiology of the feelings."[3] Le Corbusier's sources for the design go back to prehistoric French tombs

340. Le Corbusier. Notre Dame du Haut, Ronchamp, France. 1950–1955.

(a)

(b)

341. Neolithic tomb, La Roche aux Fées, Essé, France. 2500–3000 B.C. (a) exterior; (b) interior.

[341a,b], whose massive rock structures he sketched as he thought about a time-less memorial to heroism. The great rolled concrete roof, thick slanting wall pierced by small stained-glass windows [342], irregular plan, and silo-like bell towers form a rich ensemble of architectural forms. Many years earlier Le Corbusier had written the following words which he would have considered an explanation for the success of the Ronchamp chapel:

> . . . suppose that walls rise toward heaven in such a way that I am moved. I perceive your intentions. Your mood has been gentle, brutal, charming or noble. The stones you have erected tell me so. You fix me to the place and my eyes regard it. They behold something which expresses a thought. A thought which reveals itself without a word or sound, but solely by means of the shapes which stand in a certain relationship to one another.[4]

342. Le Corbusier. Notre Dame du Haut, Ronchamp, France. 1950–1955. Interior.

The Modern City

We define individuals as well balanced when they are effective and contented in a variety of different circumstances. They have a comfortable home where they enjoy life with their family and friends, they keep up with their work and are reasonably happy with it, and they enjoy some recreation (both physical and mental). Individuals who have serious problems in any of those areas of life are usually considered unfortunate or neurotic. The role of environmental planning is to help us maintain that kind of well-balanced life, with good places to live, work, and relax. Those criteria are the principles of design applied to the environment we live in. It is an educational, but often disturbing, experience to visit and analyze modern cities with those criteria in mind. Can we live well-balanced lives in unbalanced environments?

All of our cities have residential areas, commercial and industrial districts, parks, sports, and cultural institutions. The problem in 20th-century cities, and especially American cities, has been lack of unity. In practice that means these functional areas are too far apart, making movement from one to the other time- and energy-consuming. Typical American cities have about three quarters of their land area dedicated to the movement and parking of motor vehicles [343]; that land is thus removed from productive use and becomes a cost of the city to maintain, rather than producing gain through taxation. The city in the picture happens to be Los Angeles, but it could be any American city. The main freeway is about five lanes each way, with two on the entrance-exit ramps, and the cross streets are about four lanes; the left half of the picture is mostly parking lots. We are so used to this that we hardly notice it, but if you have the opportunity to look carefully at a large American city from a tall building or a traffic helicopter, you will be amazed by the amount of land taken up by our transportation system. Emphasis is clearly on the principle of movement.

Our cities have developed diseases of the circulatory system which interfere with the healthy, well-balanced lives the system was built to support. Transport has always been necessary in cities, and sometimes it has been one of the principal attractions of the city. What would be so special about Venice, for

343. Aerial view of a freeway in Los Angeles.

example, if its canals were filled and one could drive around there in a car [344]? Is there a way to solve our current problems, short of digging canals and bringing in gondoliers?

Various different proposals have been made by planners to deal with this problem, some focusing on improving the transportation systems, others on reducing the need to have such extensive systems. The starting point of current planning is that highways cannot be expanded enough to solve the problem; the city of the future will require quicker movement for more people, using less space.

One solution is the electric railroad, usually mainly subterranean; these are being constructed in many cities. The high cost of such systems is justified only by very dense concentrations of people, such as those who want to travel between downtown Chicago and O'Hare International Airport. With the subway system in place, the architect Helmut Jahn *(yahn)* (b. 1940) has designed the O'Hare Station [345] to have as pleasant an environment as possible, with curved, vari-colored, lighted glass-brick walls, to reduce the tension these noisy, crowded stations usually produce in passengers. Recent research on human biology shows that natural daylight is more healthful for people, and the nearest approach to natural daylight in a subway is mixed colors of fluorescent light, which is what Jahn provides in the O'Hare Station.

A completely different approach to the problem of circulation in cities has been proposed by a group of California architects.[5] They recommend work places scattered throughout the community, most of them self-governing groups of from five to twenty workers, with about fifteen workshops clustered around a pair of shared courtyards, and surrounded by residential areas. Different kinds of workshops should mix. Most workers could walk to work, return home for lunch if they liked, and require little transport. At first glance this proposal could be considered utopian and impractical, but economists have emphasized the economic fertility of dense concentrations of small, independent workshops. The Apollo project, which contracted with more than 30,000 independent firms to produce components of space vehicles to the moon, is an example of the kind of work situation proposed.

Probably both these alternatives—better public transport and a denser mix of functions—will be found in 21st-century cities. City planning is a community

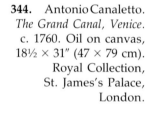

344. Antonio Canaletto. *The Grand Canal, Venice.* c. 1760. Oil on canvas, 18½ × 31″ (47 × 79 cm). Royal Collection, St. James's Palace, London.

Architecture and Applied Design

business requiring political activity by all the members of the community to control zoning for use, providing areas for noisy work and for quiet homes, for transport lines and interchanges, and for natural parks. It is important that the members of the community have the principles of design in mind as they study the problems of the environment.

345. Helmut Jahn. O'Hare Station, Chicago public transit system. 1984.

Simultaneous Perception and the Public Park

Awareness of our environment requires a kind of behavior different from concentration on a landmark or any individual work of art. It calls for unfocused attention to all our sensory experience—the quality of light; the movement and temperature of the air; the feeling of closeness of people, plants, and buildings; odors; sounds; our freedom of movement. This kind of awareness has been called "simultaneous perception,"[6] and it is only partly a visual experience. It may be satisfied by buildings, large or small, but it is an experience often associated with parks because it is an experience that is relaxing as well as stimulating, drawing us out of our focused concentration on our thoughts into a wider awareness.

Several studies of city parks show that people will use a park often—every day, or even several times a day—if it is within three blocks of their home.[7] If it is farther away, frequency of use drops rapidly. A survey of apartment-dwellers shows that they want two kinds of outdoor space: a usable private balcony and a quiet public park within a three-block walk. The best estimate for the minimum size for such a neighborhood park is 60,000 square feet (5574 square meters) or about 150 by 400 feet (46 by 122 meters), which is large enough so that a person in the middle of it can feel entirely surrounded by nature, protected from the buildings and traffic of the surrounding city. The availability of natural parkland—and the feelings of protection from the city that it brings—has been shown to be not merely relaxing but mentally stimulating—good for us both physically and mentally.

In Detail: Frederick Law Olmsted and Central Park

When Fred Olmsted was appointed superintendent of the proposed Central Park [346] in New York, at the age of 35, he had little to put on his résumé: an unprofitable experimental farm, some admired but unprofitable writing, a failed publishing business, and a varied experience of work and travel. A great city park had been long planned to be America's response to recently constructed parks in Germany and England, but when Olmsted was appointed it was still lacking a plan, although clearing the wilderness was underway.

The next year, 1858, the park commissioners opened a competition for the park's design, and Olmsted and the architect Calvert Vaux (vawks) (1824–1895) submitted the winning design, for a $2000 prize. The area set aside was large. The park is 2½ miles (4 kilometers) from north to south and ½ mile (0.8 kilometer) across—a total of 840 acres (340 hectares). One requirement was that at least four major roads crossing the park from east to west must be planned, since it was already imagined that the city, then concentrated south of the park, would grow north up Manhattan and completely surround

the park (actually, this occurred much sooner than was predicted). Olmsted and Vaux designed these roads below the ground level of the park, to interrupt as little as possible the natural scene. In the plan [347] that shows part of Central Park as it was in about 1870, you can see one of the sunken roads entering the park at 65th Street and Fifth Avenue. Although some formal walks, as near the Music Pavilion, were allowed, most of the park was carefully organized to appear natural: ponds, lakes, woods used to screen out the city and create a varied scene, with hills and valleys, rugged rocky outcrops, and, most important of all, large grassy meadows. Although it appeared natural, in actuality most of the landscape features were designed by Olmsted and constructed.

Recent photographs of the park [348]; with its plantings grown up and its grounds maintained, show a Romantic variety which would have pleased Olmsted. During his lifetime political and economic pressures seemed sure to ruin or completely destroy the park, and afterwards crime began to threaten the safety of park patrons—a problem foreseen by

346. Aerial view of part of New York City (Manhattan), looking northwest, showing Central Park.

That, of course, is not a new idea. It was perhaps best expressed by Frederick Law Olmsted (1822–1903), America's greatest park designer, in a talk he gave in Boston in 1870:

> We want a ground to which people may easily go after their day's work is done, and where they may stroll for an hour, seeing, hearing, and feeling nothing of the bustle and jar of the streets. . . . We want the greatest possible contrast with the streets and shops and the rooms of the town which will be consistent with convenience and the preservation of good order and neatness. We want, especially, the greatest possible contrast with the restraining and confining conditions of the town, those conditions which compel us to walk circumspectly, watchfully. . . . Practically, what we most want is a simple, broad, open space of clean greensward.

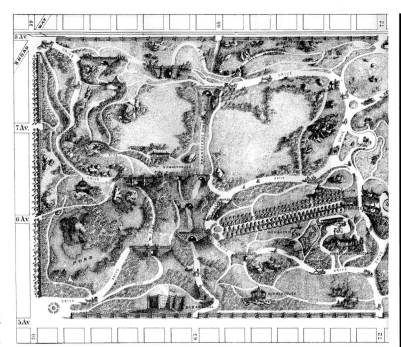

347. Frederick Law Olmsted and Calvert Vaux. Plan of Central Park, New York, as it was in about 1870, showing the southern part of the park.

Olmsted, who as superintendent hired 50 park policemen. (These policemen were to maintain good "order and propriety" and teach the rougher citizens to respect the park as "a work of art.") The crime problem gradually became more serious, but increased police protection has somewhat improved the situation in recent years. However, the park is still plagued by crime and the perceived danger of crime—which is almost as bad—especially at night and in the isolated sections. Nevertheless, the park plays a more important role than ever in the great city. Especially on weekends in good weather, it is thronged with people strolling, jogging, bicycling—and just sitting.

To Olmsted neither the country nor the city was the epitome of civilization; civilization was only perfectly embodied in the park.

Sources: Frederick Law Olmsted, Jr., and Theodora Kimball, eds., *Frederick Law Olmsted, Landscape Architect, 1822–1903* (New York: Benjamin Blom, 1970), 58–60; Laura W. Roper, *FLO: A Biography of Frederick Law Olmsted* (Baltimore: Johns Hopkins University Press, 1973).

348. View of Central Park, New York, in the 1960s.

. . . We want depth of wood enough not only for comfort in hot weather, but to completely shut out the city from our landscapes.[8]

The ecologist John Falk, who has surveyed people from many countries about their preferences in landscapes by showing them photographs, has found that even those whose familiar environments had no grasslands, showed "a deep innate preference for a grass landscape." He theorizes that the preference may be genetically transmitted, since the human species evolved on the grassy savannas of East Africa.[9]

There has been a persistent trend in American town planning toward bringing parks into city centers and planning residential areas, especially, around parks. An early and influential plan was that of Radburn, New Jersey

[349], developed in 1928, with about 300 houses occupying about 150 acres (60 hectares). It was built around several long parks, with tennis courts and swimming pools, with each house facing onto a cul-de-sac on one side and a sidewalk and yard on the other. This pattern is visible in the groups of houses in the original plan. A survey conducted in 1970 that compared the habits of Radburn residents with those of the residents of nearby unplanned communities found that Radburn residents were much more likely to shop for groceries on foot (47 percent to 8 percent), less likely to use their car for recreational trips (48 percent to 73 percent), and much more likely to use a bicycle for utilitarian trips. Radburn residents rated their community higher than residents of any other community in the survey.[10]

As we prepare to enter the 21st century, the problem of designing the environment looms as one of our greatest challenges. Obviously, the achievements of the 20th century in industry, science, and communications have produced not only solutions but also many problems. Art has its role in attempts to solve these problems. "Art is the replacing of indifference with attention,"[11] as an art historian has written. The particular contribution of art to environmental planning is to pay attention to the "whole picture" as an expression of the principles of design.

Building with Cables: Suspension Systems

As the Modern period slowly gives way to its Post-Modern successor, we cannot yet isolate one structural system that defines the Post-Modern style in the sense that vaulting defines the Gothic style. Surely the steel beam and reinforced concrete, the staples of Modern architectural structure, will remain basic. But suspension using steel cables is a structural system whose potential is just beginning to be explored [300e]. Two features are vital in any suspension system: the towers that act like tent posts and the cables suspended from them, which support the roadway of a bridge or the roof of a building. Suspension systems will make us think of tents and temporary buildings, but they have also been used for some of our largest and most permanent structures—bridges, such as the Brooklyn Bridge [350], designed by John Roebling (1806–1869) in 1867, one of

349. Clarence S. Stein and Henry Wright. Radburn, New Jersey, plan of residential districts. Begun in 1928.

350. John Roebling. Brooklyn Bridge, New York. 1867–1883. Shown under construction.

the early modern suspension bridges. In fact, for many years after its completion in 1883 its towers were the tallest structures in New York.

The Olympic swimming pool **[351]**, shown under construction for the 1972 Olympic Games in Munich, Germany, has been an influential structure. The architect, Frei Otto, considers his designs the pure expression of structure—not

351. Frei Otto. Olympic swimming pool, Munich. 1972. Suspension structure: tubular steel masts, steel wire, synthetic fabrics. Shown under construction.

symbolic or personal—and prefers to work on structures that are intended to be temporary, rather than burdening the environment with permanent monuments. Accommodating 9000 spectators for swimming events, this tent-like building still stands, along with Otto's other Olympic stadiums, and they seem to be as durable as most modern buildings.

In recent years a number of spectacular suspension buildings have been erected, some of them with floors supported by cables from a tall central tower, others with tent-like roofs. Canada Place [352], the Canadian Pavilion at EXPO '86, the Vancouver World's Fair, is modeled on a ship, the "sails," which are hollow vaults, are supported by cables between the masts. Although parts of buildings, such as the dome of the Cathedral in Florence, often become symbolic, the representational element in this Canadian building is something new. It does not seem to be just the world's fair environment that produced this slightly playful design, but a concern with history and local tradition that are increasingly important considerations in architecture. The structural technology of suspension still has a short history in our culture; it belongs to modern people, to the present moment and the future.

Post-Modern Architecture

Architecture was the first of the arts to search openly for a Post-Modern style. The break with the Modernism of Wright and Le Corbusier has been far from complete—architects now often turn to the earlier work of both of them for design ideas—but the search for new ideas is so widespread that there is general agreement that we are in a new period. At present its character is just beginning to be apparent in such things as strong and unusual color schemes (as opposed to the natural materials of Wright and the white or gray concrete of Le Corbusier), symmetry (as opposed to a common Modern preference for asymmetry), compositions of masses and spaces dictated more by sculptural excitement than by function, and acceptance of new materials and structural systems, particularly suspension and truss systems. The sculptural idea of site-specific design has become very important in current architecture.

Perhaps the greatest difference is in the attitude toward history. The earlier Modern architects expected to revolutionize building and were not much interested in the history of their art. Post-Modernism accepts history and tries to build on tradition, both ancient and modern. Currently, architects, along with all the visual artists, are trying to come to terms with history, often incorporating echoes of earlier work in their buildings and expecting the audience to understand and appreciate the historical influences.

Three Architects: Jahn, Graves, Stirling

The Post-Modern style is too young to permit us to name its greatest architects, but it is possible to select influential examples. Important buildings by Helmut Jahn, Michael Graves, and James Stirling provide a cross-section of current ideas in architecture.

The State of Illinois Center [353, 354] in Chicago was designed by Helmut Jahn, a young German-born architect working in Chicago. Finished in 1985, the Illinois Center mixes office space for the state government with businesses in a circle-and-square plan. Its circular atrium suggests a launching pad for space exploration, with the elevator shafts and the open trusses supporting the tilted glass roof (derived from a Le Corbusier design) reinforcing the focus on the sky and space. Although the building is functional in practical ways, its design and powerful color scheme make it a monument to something besides business and state government. It is "futuristic," reminding Americans of goals we have still before us and suggesting by its machine-like exposed steel that such futuristic goals are practical. The translucent blue glass walls and the exposed steel are traditional modern materials, but the building does not have the traditionally modern functional mood. It is emotionally exciting in a way we might call romantic, almost "Gothic."

below: 353. Helmut Jahn. State of Illinois Center, Chicago. 1979–1985.

right: 354. Helmut Jahn. State of Illinois Center, Chicago. 1979–1985. Interior court.

The design for the Humana Building [355] in Louisville, Kentucky, was opened for competition, and the winner was Michael Graves (b. 1934), a Princeton professor, architect, designer, and artist, whose architectural drawings are unusual for their beautiful finish. The needs of the client dictated a tall rectangular tower in the middle of an old city between well-kept low 19th-century buildings and a tall glass and steel tower. Graves' solution was to build a tall building that rejects all the qualities of the traditional American skyscraper. That means he did not try to dramatize its height, but, on the contrary, tried to make it look short. The main entrance to the building is into a seven-story section that harmonizes with the older low buildings along the neighboring streets. The vertical rise of the tall section of the building is broken into several distinct parts with different shapes, the rectangular windows were placed to make horizontal lines, and a visible arched roof was designed to send our eyes back toward the ground. Varied warm "earthy" colors also help make the building seem closer to the earthbound observer. The result is that the building compromises between the surrounding buildings, forming a focal point that unites all the opposing types around it.

Two features of Michael Graves' designs are original and distinctive: the color schemes and the revival of early 20th-century design style. For example, the balcony on the twenty-fifth floor [356] has "cubistic" shapes and proportions and simple cylindrical lamps on the wall copied from "modernistic" designs of the 1930s. Color for Graves is not just decoration, it is an essential feature of his designs. If you commission a house from Graves and then paint it a different color you have seriously altered the building. As there are historical overtones in his architectural forms, the color schemes also have an historical flavor, suggestive of the styles of the 1920s and 1930s, but even more of Roman Classical decoration, which used the same warm tans, earth reds, and violets.

We have looked at two important Modern designs for art museums—the Museum of Modern Art and the Guggenheim Museum in New York—and one of the principal examples of Post-Modern architecture is also an art museum.

left: 355. Michael Graves. Humana Building, Louisville, Kentucky. 1982–1985.

below: 356. Michael Graves. Humana Building, Louisville, Kentucky. 1982–1985. Cantilevered balcony at the twenty-fifth floor.

357. James Stirling. New State Gallery, Stuttgart, West Germany. 1977.

The English architect James Stirling (b. 1926) won an international competition in 1977 for the design of the New State Gallery in Stuttgart, in West Germany. The new building was required to harmonize with an older gallery building and adapt to a shallow lot along a busy multi-lane street. Stirling clothed the museum in a banded pattern of tan stone which matched the color of its older neighbor, but he accented the suede-colored stone with brilliant red and green metal handrails and window framing **[357]**. The regularity of the plan, which is a rectangle with an open circular court in the center **[358]**, contrasts with the

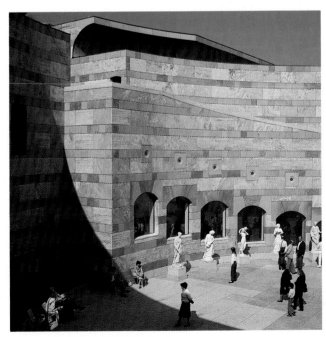

358. James Stirling. New State Gallery, Stuttgart, West Germany. 1977. Interior court.

irregular path the visitor must take into and through the museum. The entrance is off-center and the shapes and angles of walls, ramps, and roof lines are all irregular, providing an intriguing variety. Brilliant color spreads into the lobby areas of the museum, but not into the galleries, where it would compete with the works of art. All the gallery areas are pure white and lit from above by natural light to permit the true colors of the paintings to be seen.

Post-Modern architecture has a healthy variety, but its major products also share several features: concern for the surrounding natural or urban environment, an attempt to fulfill the functional needs of the clients, and a desire for historical relevance, either to a tradition or to an imagined future. The separation from Modern style is especially pronounced in the current concern for adaptation to the surroundings, which sculptors are calling "site-specific." Earlier, Le Corbusier, for example, designed a large apartment house to be built in Paris, but it was actually built in an entirely different environment in Marseilles in southern France, without changes in the design. Wright placed his Guggenheim Museum in urban surroundings which he imagined would sooner or later be replaced by the park-like environment he really wanted for his building.[12]

Post-Modern architects call into question the Modern movement's belief that logic and good design will produce buildings that will fit anywhere. The sensitivity of Graves' Humana Building and Stirling's New State Gallery to their urban surroundings, and especially the respect they accord older architecture, represent the best features of the Post-Modern movement.

Summary for Review

Durability, convenience, and beauty are the long-accepted criteria of good architecture. "Function" has been the **Modern** term for convenience. Yet since architecture has traditionally served spiritual or ritual uses, function must consider emotional needs. Building with beams, in **post-and-lintel**, **cantilever**, or **truss** systems, found early expression in ancient and medieval wooden architecture. Greek Classical temples were built in the post-and-lintel system according to sets of rules, called **orders**, of which there were three: the **Doric**, the **Ionic**, and the **Corinthian**. Roman builders continued to use Greek orders for decoration, but used **arches**, **vaults**, and **domes** for structure. The ancient city was built on the grid plan, as found in Chang-an, China. Gothic churches, composed of arches and vaults, reached awe-inspiring height. The Renaissance employed the decorative features of earlier times, especially the Classical orders, but developed the high dome as a new structure. Florence is an example of the traditional city with its dominant center and mix of functions. Frank Lloyd Wright and Le Corbusier mark the extremes of Modern architectural style, Wright emphasizing natural materials and varied designs, Le Corbusier emphasizing reinforced concrete in a geometric, or later a sculptural, style. The Modern city has increased in size and suffers from excessive space given to movement. Planning the environment centers on the principles of design to produce a balanced lifestyle. Steel, glass, and concrete dominate Modern and **Post-Modern** building, which has begun to use *suspension* structures. It departs from Modern style in using more color and placing more importance on adaptation to a specific location and in its respect for earlier styles.

9

Design Applications

Design is the application of the mind to the shaping of the world around us. One of the basic ideas of the 20th century has been that good design is at the root of a good society; to improve our people we must first improve the design of everything we use. The first brochure advertising the Bauhaus art and design school, in 1919, said: "Architects, sculptors and painters, we must all return to the crafts. . . . There is no essential difference between the artist and the craftsman. . . . Let us conceive and create the new building of the future. . . ."[1] As the century approaches its end, though most designers have lost faith in design as the cure for the world's problems—there are many problems that cannot be solved by design alone—the conviction remains that good design plays an important part in the good life. As there is no one definition of "the good life," so there is no one definition of good design; a way of life creates its style, and the style transmits the way of life, which is the meaning and message of the design style.

Many of the great figures of art and architecture have designed furniture, lamps, tableware, and cars. If you know the history of modern design, almost everything in your house or office whispers a famous name to you: Frank Lloyd Wright's chairs and table of 1899 **[359]**, Le Corbusier's idea of 1928 for an eco-

359. Frank Lloyd Wright. Dining table and eight side chairs. Designed for the Joseph M. Husser House, Chicago. c. 1899. Oak with leather-covered slip seats; each chair 4'3⅞" × 1'5¼" × 1'5¼" (1.3 × 0.4 × 0.4 m), table 2'4" × 4'6" × 5' (0.7 × 1.4 × 1.5 m). National Center for the Study of Frank Lloyd Wright, Ann Arbor, Michigan (Domino's Pizza Collection).

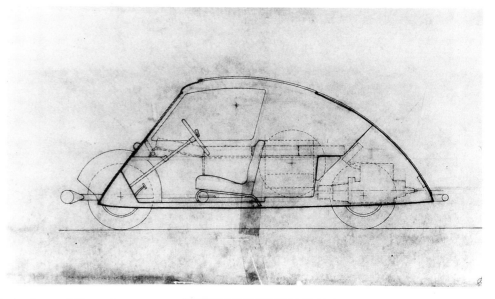

above: 360. Le Corbusier and Pierre Jeanneret. Design for a small car, "Voiture maximum." 1928. Pen and ink. Fondation Le Corbusier, Paris.

right: 361. Ludwig Mies van der Rohe. Armchair. 1926. Chrome-plated steel tubing, leather; height 32" (81 cm). Museum of Modern Art, New York (gift of Edgar Kaufmann, Jr.).

nomical car that inspired the Volkswagen "beetle" [360], or Mies van der Rohe's original 1926 cantilevered chair of steel tubing [361]. The early 20th century invented many of the forms we still consider new ideas. Despite intense competition to design commercially successful forms, new developments in applied design come slowly, and they usually depend on knowledge of what has been done before. As they search for styles suitable for our time, contemporary designers look back to two design studios, the Palace of Versailles and the Bauhaus, as strong examples of design and technique.

The Palace of Versailles and French Design

Louis XIV, king of France from 1643 to 1715, and his finance minister Jean Baptiste Colbert devised a scheme to promote French industry and international trade by building an impressive new palace and stocking it with French products, like a modern trade fair. Manufacturing in that period meant artisans working in such materials as wood, metal, fibers, ceramics, and glass. The king decided to build the new palace near Paris at Versailles (vare-SI), where he had a hunting lodge. A huge park was built around the palace, and a support city grew up outside its gates. The palace was stocked with such French luxury products as furniture, tapestries, and carpets; ornate interior design and decorative art of every kind were used. Visiting diplomats and royalty were overwhelmed by the variety and quality of French products to be seen at Versailles and went home eager to buy. Finance Minister Colbert kept all the arts and crafts under centralized control, designs and standards of quality being strictly enforced by government officials. But there was still room for individual creativity, and artists and artisans were attracted to France from all over Europe.

The interiors of the Palace of Versailles [362] were largely destroyed during the French Revolution and only in the past 20 years have they begun to be reconstructed at great expense. They show that the wealthy and powerful could employ tremendous numbers of highly skilled artists and artisans—the sheer amount of time, skill, and effort expended on furniture, textiles, light fixtures, and interior finishing of the buildings defies imagination. Artists and artisans were organized in craft guilds, with strict rules dividing up the labor. The joiners (menuisiers) did all woodwork, such as furniture, but if there was important carving a member of the sculptor's guild was called in. The joiners could attach handles and decorative metalwork, but they were not allowed to make them. Ebenistes did special veneer work in wood; tapissiers did all the upholstery.

362. Jules Hardouin-Mansart. Louis XIV's Bedroom, Palace of Versailles. 1661–1688. Tapestry: Charles Le Brun. *The Triumph of Alexander.*

363. André Charles Boulle.
Clock and pedestal. c. 1700.
Ebony, brass; height 8'6"
(2.6 m). Collection of Bernard
Baruch Steinitz, Paris.

Furniture changed during the two centuries of French cultural dominance, and it reflected changes in the way of life. In Louis XIV's day a social event meant a ceremony or a dance, so the king did not provide many chairs for his guests. A century later the rise of wealthy merchant families led to a more modest form of social life, the salon, in which conversation was the main form of entertainment, and so comfortable armchairs were essential.

The royal bureaucracy took over the long-established carpet and tapestry factories and had their designs made by artists of the Royal Academy of Fine Arts, the chosen artists of the court, in an approved style. Charles Le Brun himself, the president of the Academy and Louis XIV's art dictator, designed the tapestry *The Triumph of Alexander,* which decorated the king's bedroom [362]. Since the European nobility had no interest in the personalities of the artists who worked for them, they had no doubt that a pictorial tapestry was more valuable than a painting. In the 20th century we are interested in the personality of the artist as it is revealed by the brush stroke, but at Versailles the beauty of the texture and color of the woven fabric and the insulation it provided in drafty palaces were of much greater appeal. (The Gobelin Tapestry Factory is still producing tapestries in Paris today, often copying modern paintings and converting them into the richer textures of tapestry.)

The clock on a tall pedestal [363] was a new item in the interiors of Louis XIV's period. Its design and the *marquetry* (design of inlaid woods) on the pedestal are the work of the greatest of the royal furniture-makers, André Charles Boulle *(bool),* about 1700. The combination of skillful work in wood and metal with the exuberant, but refined, design, gives a good sense of what life was like at Versailles. Life, like this clock, was luxurious and ostentatious, but very disciplined and formal. It is the grandfather of our grandfather clocks, which have a noble background.

The Bauhaus

When compared with Versailles, the Bauhaus (*BOW-howss*) presents a surprising set of similarities and differences. Organized in 1919 in Germany as a state school of architecture and design (bau = building, haus = house, or institute), it was dedicated to training artists and designers for work in modern industry, although it also offered courses in painting, music, and drama. The school, long considered a nest of radicals, was suppressed by the Nazi government in 1933, and most of the faculty came to the United States, where they became influential teachers. The idealistic plan of the Bauhaus to improve machine-made products through better design had strong appeal in America and led American educators to use it as a model for art and design education. Like Versailles, the Bauhaus was connected with industry and commerce, but while Versailles and French design received government patronage for about two hundred years, the Bauhaus survived only 24 years and was in political turmoil much of that time. Its director, the architect Walter Gropius (1883–1969), defined its goal as "the collective work of art—the Building—in which no barriers exist between the structural and the decorative arts."[2] Students could specialize in any of seven studios: stone, wood, metal, clay, glass, color, and textiles. Architecture was not taught, although the director was an architect and the program would be considered "pre-architectural" today. Basic design emphasized the study of nature, the analysis of materials, drawing and geometry, and composition. "Building," wrote Gropius, "unites both manual and mental workers in a common task. Therefore all alike, artist as well as artisan, should have a common training. . . ."[3]

The dining room [364] Gropius designed for an exhibition in 1928 shows the lightweight, industrially produced chairs, tables, and lamp that are typical of Bauhaus design. The personality of an individual, whether artist or resident, finds little expression in these furnishings, which are designed to be inexpensive by using a minimum of material and by being almost entirely machine-made. Some of the Bauhaus designs have become classics, remaining popular year after year and copied by generations of younger designers. The springy chrome-

364. Walter Gropius. Dining room designed for the Werkbund Exhibition, Stuttgart, Germany. 1928.

plated steel chair [361] with leather seat and back designed by Ludwig Mies van der Rohe, who succeeded Gropius as director of the Bauhaus, is one of the classics of Modern design.

Post-Modern Furniture and Interiors

In recent years the Modern ideas of the Bauhaus have been rejected by a Post-Modern generation of designers who set visual image above both function and form. Italian designers have been among the leaders, calling their work of the 1980s "New Design." Some work with established manufacturers; others form studios that operate as art galleries, which, since they are largely out of contact with industry, rely on exhibits and publications to spread their ideas. Paolo Deganello designed the easy chair [365] as part of a series entitled "Torso" for a furniture manufacturer, with the appearance of an accidental mixture of supporting legs, arms, and seats, a table, and a back upholstered with a computer-designed fabric. Its subtle mixture of blue, tan, black, white, and gray enhances the low-key, casual mood of the varied shapes. Deganello's easy chair contrasts strongly with Mies van der Rohe's chair [361], which takes the basic form of the human body as its functional standard. Deganello bases his work on the history of furniture, designing something that suggests knowledge of older styles but considers all the parts movable.

A 60-year-old house in Santa Monica, California, was remodeled by the architect Brian Murphy in a mixture of its original 1920s style and Post-Modern materials and details. The breakfast alcove [366] looks out to a swimming pool through an original round window of tinted glass. The other features are Post-Modern: a skylight and industrial lamps light the room, which is furnished with a breakfast table and stools shaped like vegetables by Lisa Lombardi.

Furniture has become more than something to use—it asks us to think about it. Designers specialize in thinking about contemporary ways of life and inventing forms that express and enhance that life. Post-Modern designers have

366. Brian Murphy.
Breakfast alcove,
remodeled house,
Santa Monica,
California. c. 1983.
Furniture by
Lisa Lombardi.

not agreed on one set of forms that express our way of life, but you can draw some conclusions about their views from their work. It is certain that furniture, which we had begun to ignore, is again a serious field of art. The stone chairs [367] of Scott Burton (b. 1939) were intended as sculpture, even though it is sculpture which can be contemplated as you sit on it.

367. Scott Burton.
*Two-Part Chair,
Obtuse Angle.* 1984.
Polished pink granite,
33 × 24 × 33"
(84 × 61 × 84 cm).
Whitney Museum of
American Art, New York
(purchase with funds from
the Lemberg Foundation).

Textiles and Clothing

The use of fibers and textiles probably began with the making of cords and baskets, but when people began to adorn themselves and shelter themselves from the weather in garments made of fibers a new art came to life. Textiles have been used in many kinds of art—in tapestries [362] and in sculptures [279, 280, 281]—but it is in clothing that textiles have by far the richest history.

Ancient Greek Clothing

The Classical Greeks of the 5th and 4th centuries B.C. were very proud of their clothing style. It consisted of a rectangular piece of cloth taken straight from the loom without cutting or sewing, its size depending on how it was to be worn. Cutting and sewing were done by neighboring peoples, but Classical Greeks considered the draped costume more beautiful than the fitted. They expressed that idea over and over in their sculpture, which makes a special point of elegant drapery.

The basic garment for men was the himation (hi-ma-TEE-on), a large square of natural colored wool about 6 by 9 feet (1.8 by 2.7 meters), wrapped around the body [368]. When he went to war a Greek wore a smaller cloak (about 3 by 9 feet, or 0.9 by 2.7 meters) called a chlamys (KLAY-mis), which was pinned together at one shoulder. The first sewn garment was the chiton (KI-tun), a wool or linen tunic sewn up the sides, with or without sleeves, and long enough to be belted. It became the basic shirt, often worn under the himation.

For women the same rectangle of cloth was worn wrapped around the body under the arms and fastened over both shoulders with pins; this dress was called a peplos (PEP-lus). Greek women usually sewed up the open side and often belted it, allowing folds of cloth to fall over the belt [368]. Women also wore the chiton, often fastening it with a series of pins at the shoulders and down the arms to make a kind of ornamental sleeve.

368. Phidias. Panel from the Panathenaic frieze of the Parthenon, Athens. c. 440 B.C. White marble, height 43″ (109 cm). Louvre, Paris.

369. Moche kingdom, Peru. Scenes in a textile factory, painted on the inner rim of a ceramic flaring bowl. A.D. 100–700. Drawing by Donna McClelland. Bowl in British Museum, London.

Greek clothing has to be seen in conjunction with Greek architecture and sculpture, for they enhance each other in a remarkable way. Just as the Greeks took the simplest architectural form, the post-and-lintel, and designed natural and dramatic ways to show its parts and forces, they took the simplest rectangle of cloth and wrapped and folded it to make clothing that was natural and dramatic. The natural movement of the human body, naked or revealed by the flow of drapery over it, was the principal concern of sculptors. The studied simplicity of these arts reveals more about the Classical attitude than anything written by the Greek philosophers. It also reveals that clothing is not mere protection against the weather, but also an art designed to express ideals of truth and harmony with nature.

An Ancient Textile Industry in Peru

We usually think of applied design as belonging to the modern industrial world, but that is partly because we do not know very much about earlier practices. Ancient Peru is one place whose textile design and industry are unusually well known because the west coast of Peru is one of the driest regions on the globe and much ancient cloth has been preserved.

Scenes painted on the broad rim of a bowl show a textile factory on the coast of Peru about A.D. 600 **[369]**. Eight women are shown working on belt looms, which are strung between the wooden posts of their shelters and held in tension by a belt around their waists. By the standards of the Inca Empire, hundreds of years later, this would be a very small factory, for we know that the Incas had cloth factories employing a thousand weavers. Perhaps these painted figures are symbolic of a larger number, but they are so individualized that one wonders if they are portraits, some with neat short hair, one with messy hair, some with wrinkles, others smiling. They are all making cloth with patterns typical of well-known Peruvian styles, with their shuttles of thread at their sides and their beaters in their hands ready to comb down the weft threads (the horizontal threads woven in with the shuttles). The extremely high quality of most of the ancient Peruvian cloth is an indication that such a factory was not engaged in mass production, but considered each piece of cloth a work of art. Designs were traditional, but weavers used their own judgment and invented

A POINT IN TIME: Navajo Blankets and Rugs

A distinctive American contribution to interior design has been the Navajo (NAH-vuh-ho) rug. The Navajos, the largest Indian nation in the United States, have reservation lands in Arizona and New Mexico, where their traditional occupation has been sheep-herding. Traditional Navajo clothing includes a man's hand-woven wool blanket very much like a Greek himation, woven by his wife, the most valuable and prestigious item of clothing. When trading posts began to be established in Navajo country in the mid-19th century, the traders were eager to find ways for the Navajos to earn money so they would be able to buy trade goods. The beautiful heavy blankets worn by the men were suitable for use as rugs, the traders thought, so they encouraged the women to make extra blankets for sale. From about 1850 to the present day Navajo blankets and rugs show continuous evolution in style.

Laura Gilpin's photograph of a woman at her vertical loom [370] shows her weaving a design of bands with chevrons. In her right hand she holds a ball of hand-dyed and hand-spun wool and a comb-like beater to pack the colored wool so tightly between the white wool warp threads that only the colored design shows. Weaving is done seated on the ground, usually outdoors. Navajo rugs often show subtle slanted lines in the weave, called "lazy lines," where the weft turns back, though the color does not change. They are produced when the rug is too wide to reach across from one position and the weaver weaves higher on one side before moving to work on the other side. They reveal the process of work and are considered interesting, not a flaw.

The design of a rug made about 1880 [371] begins with a traditional pattern of black-and-white stripes called a "chief's blanket." Over the stripes five

370. Laura Gilpin, Navajo weaver. 1951.

372. Nasca culture, Peru. Three-dimensional embroidered border of mantle, representing costumed dancers. A.D. 200–600. Alpaca wool. Brooklyn Museum, New York.

371. Navajo. Third phase chief's blanket. c. 1880. Four-ply Germantown yarns with cotton warp, 4′6½″ × 5′2½″ (1.4 × 1.6 m). Millicent Rogers Museum, Taos, New Mexico.

crosses have been placed, of red, green, and blue, with lozenges in the middle of each cross. This is one of the classic Navajo rug designs.

With their strong colors and geometric shapes, Navajo rugs were a good complement to a simple

Modern interior. Since they originate as blankets they have a flat plain weave, not the knotted pile we often expect in carpets. The Navajo design style is a uniquely native American contribution to interior design.

variations. Since commercial trade was practically unknown in ancient Peru, most cloth production went into state warehouses and was distributed to people according to their rank, or used in diplomatic relations as gifts to other nations.

A large mantle or blanket to be worn somewhat like a Greek himation, from a tomb at Paracas on the coast of Peru, has a fantastic border of three-dimensional embroidery [372]. The core of the border is a strip of cotton tape on which 90 wool and cotton figures have been constructed, somewhat like the fingers of a knitted glove. Twelve colors were used to make these tiny figures, each between 2 and 3 inches (5 and 8 centimeters) high. Each figure seems to be a dancer costumed as a cat-like figure and carrying a plant—probably representing a nature spirit in an agricultural festival. The labor required to produce this border shows that no one kept track of time; the only thing that mattered was quality.

Ancient Peruvian textiles have been an inspiration to modern weavers and designers, but the modern idea is to adapt Peruvian design sense to machine production. Hand-weaving of cloth comparable to the Peruvian work is rarely considered by modern textile artists, since the individualized product of such handwork would be very expensive.

373. Jean Clouet. *François I.* c. 1525. Oil on wood panel, 38 × 29¼″ (97 × 74 cm). Louvre, Paris.

The shapes and designs of Greek and ancient Peruvian clothing were comparable, with uncut cloth off the loom being basic to both. Cloth in ancient North and South America was generally more decorated than Greek cloth, with a variety of techniques and a multitude of colors used to enrich the cloth. The ancient American ideal was not Classical simplicity, but richness of color and design.

European Clothing of the 16th to 19th Centuries

Already in ancient Greece there was important trade in cloth, and by the 16th century cloth-making was the greatest industry in Europe. As early as 1589 a machine had been invented to knit cloth, and over the next three centuries most of the cloth that was traded gradually came to be the product of machines rather than of hand-weavers. An unparalleled extravagance in European clothing followed. Industrialization was one factor in this; another was the immense wealth looted from the defeated kingdoms of Mexico and Peru.

François I [373], king of France, was painted about 1525 by his court painter Jean Clouet *(zhan kloo-AY)* (d. 1541?), wearing a matched shirt, doublet, and dogaline. The shirt has a wide horizontal neck and ruffles at the cuffs. The doublet, or tight-fitting jacket, has slashes in the sleeves and body to show the shirt. The dogaline is a long coat with very wide sleeves which were folded back and fastened to the shoulders. All these voluminous clothes appear to be of silk, with an embroidered design in gold thread. With this outfit the king would have worn bulbous breeches, hose, and low shoes. His costume is completed by a flat hat trimmed with a white feather, gloves, and an ornate sword. Conspicuous luxury clearly takes the form of extra cloth of the finest quality with extra decoration on it.

Over the next two hundred years the clothing of the wealthy changed slowly toward simpler styles with fewer layers. There was a consistent tendency to use as public wear clothing at first thought suitable only for private occasions.

374. French. Sack-back gown. c. 1730. Green silk damask, multi-colored brocade flowers. Union Française des Arts du Costume, Paris.

The sack gown or sack-back gown, derived from a nightgown or peignoir, appeared early in the 18th century and remained very popular for several decades, probably because it was comfortable. This sack gown [374] is French, of green silk with multi-colored flowers woven into the cloth (brocade technique). In the back it hangs loose from the shoulders and is open at the front over a chemise. It was worn with a small hat. Elegant as this outfit is, it is far simpler in pattern than formal dress of the upper classes had been for centuries. In that respect it led the way toward 20th-century styles.

Modern Dress

The early years of the 20th century saw an unprecedented shift in clothing styles. In 1906 the actress Sarah Bernhardt appeared in a lavish costume [375]: a

375. Street wear in the early years of the 20th century: Sarah Bernhardt in a long dress and coat, 1906.

376.
Gabrielle (Coco) Chanel.
Suit in large plaid checks.
1928. Wool jersey.
Union Française des Arts
du Costume, Paris.

floor-length dress with a slight flare and a long coat with multiple flounces on the cape-like shoulders. A large hat with bows and plumes and an umbrella completed the outfit. The sumptuous effect of such costumes was based on corsets that were flat in front and sharply curved behind, with the waist unaccented, but the skirt tight at the hips and flaring at the hem.[4] Every piece of cloth bears a pattern, pleat, flounce, or some elaboration.

By 1914, when the First World War began, the clothing of both men and women had grown simpler than that worn even a few years earlier. The catastrophe of the world war changed the lives of all Europeans, eliminating the extravagance of cloth and workmanship of traditional styles. The "liberated" hard-working life of 20th-century men and women demanded clothing that permitted free movement and little care. Among the designers who first defined the new style, Gabrielle Chanel *(shah-NEL)*, always called Coco, was most influential. Her soft suit in large plaid checks **[376]** has a skirt at mid-calf, a reaction to the much shorter "flapper" styles of the early 1920s. With very short hair, a practical small hat, low shoes, and a suit that permitted free movement, a Modern woman took on new roles in life.

Three Technologies of Fire

Three materials are worked with fire—clay, glass, and metal. Fire plays a different role in each technique: it hardens modeled clay into ceramics, but it softens glass and metal so they can then be modeled with tools and cast in molds. We take all this for granted, since our civilization is based on these fire technologies (or *pyrotechnologies*). It is hard to imagine that the earliest workers in glass considered it a stone and worked it cold by chipping and polishing.

Architecture and Applied Design

A POINT IN TIME: Coco Chanel

She had an eye to quality and proportion that was unbeatable. She had daring, freshness, authenticity, conviction. She was exceptional and she knew it. She was unfeminine in character, but totally feminine in her ability to entice, and she had great sex appeal. Chanel had qualities and talents that are very rare. She was a genius, and all her faults must be forgiven for that one reason.

These words were written by the famous photographer Cecil Beaton when Chanel died.

Coco Chanel (1883–1971) [377] dominated Paris fashions from about 1920 until her death and revolutionized women's clothing. At 30 she opened a tiny dressmaker's shop at a French beach resort and began offering her own "poor girl" creations in soft jersey fabric. Influential women, tired of uncomfortable corseted clothing, took an interest in her, and she was soon established in Paris with a variety of fashion products. In 1922 the perfume Chanel No. 5 was introduced and it remained a basic product in her line. Her enterprises at their height employed 3500 people in fashion design, a textile business, perfumes, and costume jewelry.

Women's clothing of the 20th century largely reflects Chanel's ideas: the classic "little black dress," jersey dresses and suits, bell-bottom slacks, formal dress pajamas, turtleneck sweaters, short hair, costume jewelry. Coco Chanel appears, in 1954, in her portrait wearing a cardigan with a mid-length skirt and a single piece of jewelry. A big-city business woman, single but with notorious romantic liaisons, Chanel dressed and designed for the way she lived: a busy life demanding a lot of energy, a city life with country leisure.

She said, "La mode passe, le style reste" ("Fashions change, style remains"). Her influence on women's clothing produced a modern classical style of comfortable, soft, simple clothing for an active life.

———

Quotation from Cecil Beaton, *Self-Portrait with Friends* (London: Book Club Associates, 1980) 412.

377.
Coco Chanel in her Paris apartment, 1954. Photograph by Louise Dahl-Wolfe.

In art we cannot take the technology for granted, since it is basic to the form the art takes. How the clay was formed can never be ignored, and whether the glass was molded or blown, or the metal hammered or cast, are basic to understanding the work of art. Those techniques are the framework in which the artist places symbolism and expression.

Ceramics

Ceramics (from the Greek word for potter's clay) includes all the forms of art made of fired clay, including pottery, **terra cotta** sculpture, and even brick. All of these are made by forming the wet clay into the desired form, letting it dry, and "firing" the form by placing it in a kiln (*kill* or *kiln*) where it is raised to a red- or white-hot temperature for a few hours. Right from the first, ceramics was an art associated with civilized life; since fired clay is relatively heavy and fragile, it is not of much use to nomadic or unsettled people.

Pottery-making is still a useful craft in many parts of the world. The water jars by a Guatemalan potter [378] are formed by coils built up by hand; yet the walls of the pots are smooth, round, and very thin. A potter's wheel is often used to speed this process of forming the vessel. This is the craft that lies behind all art in ceramics—the skill to dominate the clay before it can be used for symbolic expression. The Guatemalan potter has no intention of expressing symbolic meaning or making art; she intends only to make good useful water jars. For us, living in an industrial world of machine-made objects, functional hand-made pottery such as these water jars becomes art, symbolic of a life close to nature. Such pottery is background for modern ceramic art.

As the Industrial Revolution eliminated such pottery from our world during the 19th century, to replace it with mass-production pottery from factories, some people began to miss the unique hand-made pottery. In England, where "china" (as porcelain ceramics are called in testimony to their Asian ancestry) was a huge industry, the modern artist-potter first appeared. A reaction to industrialization of pottery and other traditional crafts was "The Arts and Crafts Movement" led by William Morris (1834–1896). Morris and his colleagues meant to revive handcrafts that had been put out of business by machine production. The weaving and decoration of cloth and the making of pottery were only two of the many crafts that Morris and his followers practiced, as they tried to improve the quality by having a person, instead of a machine, make the product.

Four brothers of the Martin family, the eldest of whom had learned to make pottery in one of the big china factories, set up a pottery studio to make art pottery [379]. The three brothers in the photograph are happily at work in their

Architecture and Applied Design

studio producing ceramics in styles we associate with the Victorian Period. Although most of the Martins' work is not to the taste of our time, it seems that William Morris was right: the market for ceramics is large enough for both artist-potters and factory production. Studio potters (as the artists call themselves) may make functional pots, but also works that are purely symbolic and expressive.

Bernard Leach (1887–1979) was the most influential potter to follow Morris' ideas. Hong Kong-born and trained in pottery in Japan, Leach was also an important connection between Oriental and Western pottery traditions. His studio at Saint Ives, on the English coast, was a pilgrimage center for potters from everywhere. Leach, who considered the making of pots a search for the deepest universal philosophy, wrote:

> The quality which appears to me fundamental in all pots is life in one or more of its modes: inner harmony, nobility, purity, strength, breadth and generosity, or even exquisiteness and charm. But it is one thing to make a list of virtues in man and pot and another to interpret them in the counterpoint of convex and concave, hard and soft, growth and rest, for this is the breathing of the Universal in the particular.

Leach insisted: "The pot is the man; his virtues and vices are shown therein—no disguise is possible."[5]

The New York-born potter Karen Karnes works in the tradition of Leach. The jar and lid [380] reveal in their form the interactions of the clay and the potter. Looking at the base of the jar we can imagine the lump of clay spinning on the potter's wheel, then being pressed in the center by the potter's thumbs to make a hollow center and the walls being drawn smoothly up from the base. The in and out pressure of hands and thumbs was recorded by the clay wall as it spun. At the shoulder of the jar the inward pressure of the fingers registered, and the powerful and rapid upward whirl of the neck was made. The heavy lid, its top cut to shape with a twisted wire, acts to hold down that rising line of the neck. "The pot is the woman," to rephrase Leach, and we see those personality

380. Karen Karnes.
Jar with lid. 1980.
Stoneware; height 15½" (39 cm),
diameter 11½" (29 cm).
Courtesy of the artist.

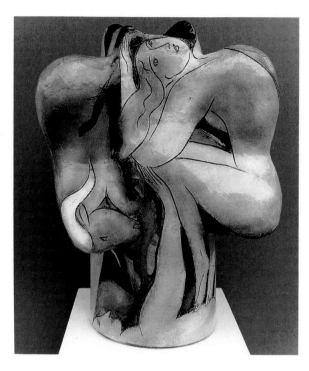

381. Rudy Autio.
Indian Summer. 1988. Stoneware;
height 35″ (89 cm), width 28″
(71 cm), depth 24″ (61 cm).
Collection of the artist.

traits of strength and generosity in the form of this vessel. Art pottery is made to manifest those human qualities, though it may also serve as containers.

One of the uses of glass is to coat pottery to make it hold liquids without seepage. Most of our pottery is **glazed** (meaning covered with glass). Not only does glazing make the pottery more useful, it also provides opportunities for decoration. Pottery can be decorated with paints made of liquified clay (called *slip*), but glazes give a wider range of colors, plus the natural shine of glass. Glazes have always tempted potters to paint pictures on their pots, as Rudy Autio does on his tall, irregular jar-like forms. *Indian Summer* **[381]** is an incised drawing on white slip put on the pot after it has been fired once (called a *bisque [bisk]* firing). The last step before the final firing is the addition of colored glazes and a clear glaze for shine.

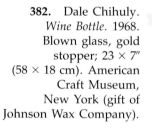

382. Dale Chihuly.
Wine Bottle. 1968.
Blown glass, gold
stopper; 23 × 7″
(58 × 18 cm). American
Craft Museum,
New York (gift of
Johnson Wax Company).

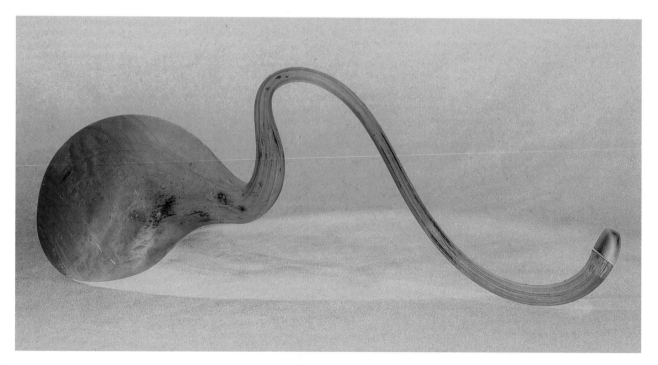

Glass

Glass has a history of about 3500 years as an independent art. Glass can be worked by many different methods and assume a great variety of appearances. It can be melted and blown into bubbles inside molds, for example, or the molten glass can be poured into molds or worked with tools into shapes. Cold glass can be cut with abrasives. Glass can be opaque or transparent, clear or colored, and has uses in fields as varied as jewelry and architecture. That array of possibilities inspires glass artists today.

The traditions of glass art come into the present day in Dale Chihuly's (b. 1941) *Wine Bottle* [382] of blown glass with a gold stopper. The crystalline transparency of the clear glass contrasted with the web of gold that mottles the surface gives an atmospheric effect which can be achieved only in glass. The expanding and contracting swirl of the blown glass reminds us that the material was worked in a molten state. Chihuly's work could hardly be called a utilitarian object, although you could serve wine from it. It functions mainly as an expressive and symbolic form, like many other contemporary works in glass.

Glass has many architectural uses. *Jungle Wall* [383], a folding screen by Patsy Norvell, is nearly 7 feet (2.1 meters) tall. Its transparency allows its use as a divider rather than as a screen for privacy, but it is more properly seen as a sculpture. The etched jungle leaves seem to float in a shining space, the foreshortening of the leaves giving an illusion of depth.

Glass is an expensive and difficult art to practice, but it is currently of great interest. Its formal qualities of color, transparency, hardness, and smoothness have special appeal to 20th-century eyes.

Metal

Metals seem to have been used for ornaments and art before they were made into tools, which means that the functional uses grew out of art. Gold and copper were the first metals to be used because both are found naturally as nuggets of pure metal which can be hammered into shapes or into thin sheets. Even after artisans learned to refine metal from ore and cast it in molds, hammering, or **repoussé** *(ruh-poo-SAY)*, continued to be a common method of work-

383. Patsy Norvell. *Jungle Wall.* 1981–1982. Etched glass, 6′10″ × 15′ (2.1 × 4.6 m)

above: 384.   Bronze Age, Hungary. Bracelet.
2000–1000 B.C. Gold, 4⅓″ (11 cm).
Naturhistorisches Museum, Vienna.

right: 385.   Middle Shang Dynasty, China.
Jia tripod wine vessel. 16th–14th centuries B.C.
Cast bronze, height 13″ (33 cm). Asian Art Museum
of San Francisco (Avery Brundage Collection).

ing metal. The 4000-year-old gold bracelet from Hungary [384] was cut from a sheet of metal and hammered over molds into its complicated shape. A pointed punch was used to make the dotted lines. Unlike copper, which requires periodic heating to reduce its brittleness, gold can be hammered without fire. This bracelet required only simple techniques, but it is far from simple in design.

When artisans learned to apply sufficient heat to melt metal and cast it in molds, its usefulness for art and tools expanded tremendously. Until the last couple of centuries, metal casting was high technology, at least as important for casting tools and weapons (such as cannons) as it was for art. The ancient Chinese grew very skillful at casting bronze (an alloy, or mixture, of copper with a little tin), which they used especially for making vessels for religious rituals. The ceremonial wine vessel [385] was made by pouring molten bronze into pottery molds. All the details of the decoration were in the original mold. The green patina, or oxidation of the surface, is the only change these vessels have suffered in more than three thousand years. Although many ancient Chinese ritual vessels survive and show a variety of forms, we have no detailed idea of the ceremonies in which they were used.

In the Western world, metal, usually bronze, was used for sculptures of the ancient gods of the Classical civilizations, but also much more commonly for small works of art which could be owned by individuals. Classical art of Greece and Rome provided the models for all kinds of small sculptures and useful objects such as lamps, inkwells, salt cellars, and the like, many of them merely cute, but some real works of art. The door knocker [386] made by Alessandro

386. Alessandro Vittoria.
Door knocker
with god of the sea and sea horses.
c. 1580. Cast bronze,
height 16″ (41 cm).
Correr Museum, Venice.

Vittoria (1525–1608) in Venice could stand by itself as a work of art and surely was considered art even by people who used it to knock on a door. The Classical god of the sea, along with two sea horses (horses with fins, not the marine species), comes back to graceful life in this late Renaissance bronze.

Modern design in metal began with the Bauhaus artists in Germany in the 1920s. Wilhelm Wagenfeld's *(VAHG-en-felt)* coffee and tea service **[387]** of Ger-

387. Wilhelm Wagenfeld. Coffee and tea service. 1924. Silver with ebony handles, height of coffee pot 8⅞″ (23 cm). Kunstsammlungen, Weimar, East Germany.

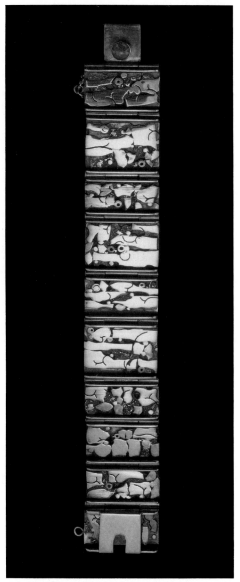

above: 388. Patricia Daunis-Dunning. Cuff bracelet. 1979–1983. Sterling silver and copper, 2 × 2″ (5 × 5 cm). Collection of the artist.

right: 389. Earl Pardon. Bracelet. 1981. 14k gold, silver, opal; fabricated, constructed, pierced; 7½ × 1″ (19 × 3 cm). Collection of the artist.

man silver (an alloy of copper, zinc, and nickel) has the simple geometric forms designed to be manufactured by machine. One of the basic considerations of Bauhaus designers was improvement in the design of objects of daily use which would be produced by machines. Only by machine production could the cost be kept low, but only by the work of the best designers could the quality be kept high. Although Wagenfeld knew that machines could produce almost any metal form, he believed that these simple forms conveyed an elegance appropriate to a new age.

Recent metal design in the United States has included two extremes in size: jewelry and architectural forms. One of the difficult techniques in metal-working is the combination of different metals, which have differing melting points and other characteristics. Such combinations have been of special interest in jewelry in recent years, in, for example, bracelets by artists. Patricia Daunis-Dunning's cuff bracelet [388] combines silver and copper in a strong design of stripes interrupted by a curve that follows the curve of the form. Earl Pardon's bracelet [389] is made of ten joined panels in which silver and gold make small abstract designs. Pardon is a painter as well as a metalsmith, and in this bracelet the color of the metal acts like paint in a modern abstract painting.

The Eagle Square Gateway in Concord, New Hampshire [390], had to be large enough for a fire truck to pass through and still harmonize with the buildings around it. Within those limits, the artist, Dimitri Gerakaris, was encouraged by the architect in charge of the project to "explode with imagination and fantasy."[6] Gerakaris designed a fantasy tree to accompany the real trees of the square, along with a horizontal band at the top to tie the flanking buildings together with an architectural form. Building the 27-foot-tall (8-meter-tall) tree in his 19-foot-high (6-meter-high) studio required breaking through the floor into the cellar. After a year of hard work, the forged steel gateway was assembled on the site in one day. The gateway represents a dramatic departure from the machine-age ideal of the Bauhaus. It even includes "a gnome, who is hammering out the last detail of the tree"[7] at the bottom where children can see it. The incorporation of naturalistic elements in design is currently very popular and opens new possibilities for young designers.

Design in Motion

A field that belongs nearly exclusively to our century is the design of such movable forms as the automobile, with designs that must change every year in response to intense market competition. Our cars must reflect our way of life. A person with four children who uses the car for short trips around town will not

390. Dimitri Gerakaris. Eagle Square Gateway, Concord, New Hampshire. 1983. Forged steel; height 27' (8.2 m), width 40' (12.2 m).

seriously consider the Alfa Romeo sports car **[391]**, although all of us like to look at it and dream a little. High-speed motion is everything in that car—the form, the function, and the visual image, too. It represents a large category of car designs since the 1920s, the early ones built for racing, the later ones incorporating the engineering and design features of the successful racing cars.

The Renault Town Car of 1910 **[392]** represents another whole category of car design in which passenger comfort and dignity are the main considerations. The design of the Renault is clearly only a small step from the carriage, although the technology is a big step away from the horse. Improvements in the engineering were the driving force for design improvements. Wind resistance hardly counted at the speeds reached by the 1910 Renault, but as speed increased, the form of the body had to be adjusted to reduce resistance and noise. We hear automobile design called "styling," which implies that it is superficial, like a haircut, but in fact it contributes to and is controlled by the function of the car.

392. Renault Town Car. 1910.

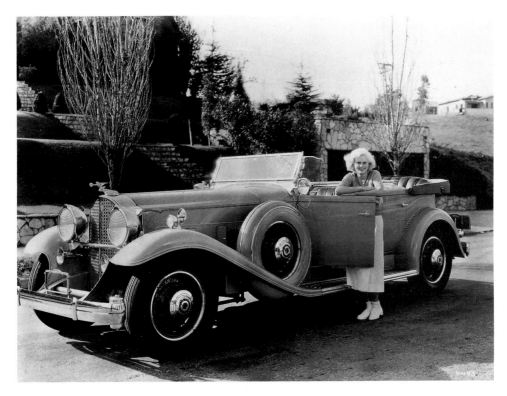

393. Packard DeLuxe
Eight phaeton. 1932.
Shown with its owner,
movie star Jean Harlow.

Those two factors, speed and passenger comfort, have controlled the development of car design. The 1932 Packard touring car **[393]** owned by movie
star Jean Harlow shows a compromise between those factors—a powerful eight-
cylinder engine combined with spacious and luxurious passenger accommoda-
tions. As the highway system expanded and roads improved, speed increased
and the distances people were willing to drive also increased. Though long-
distance travel by car began to be feasible by the 1930s, speed and comfort still
favored the train, whose diesel engines and streamlined design were ahead of
most cars. The Chrysler Airflow of 1934 **[394]** was the first car design to combine

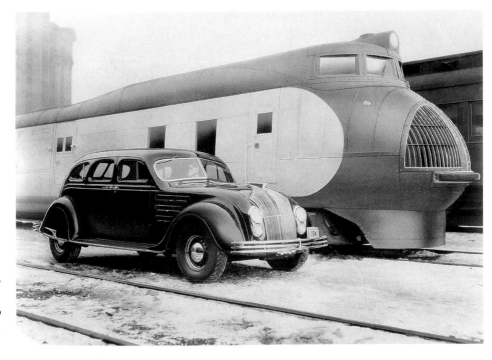

394. Chrysler Airflow
sedan. 1934.
Shown parked next to
Union Pacific Streamliner,
introduced in 1934.

395. Ford Motor Company. Probe IV. 1984.

a family-size sedan with a streamlined shape used earlier only on racing and sports models and in trains.

The factors dictating automobile development now include government regulations on safety, gasoline mileage, and pollution emissions and many other factors besides speed and comfort. Wind-tunnel studies of aerodynamics now take the place of the designer's intuitive sense of form, with the perfect teardrop form, whose mathematical coefficient of drag (C_d) is 0.07, being the ideal form.

The designers for Ford Motor Company, like all the auto designers, build "concept cars" about ten years ahead of the mass-production models. Ford's Probe series, designed with the Italian Ghia Bodyworks, is currently building the fifth model in the series, Probe V. Probe IV **[395]**, which may be a production model in the 1990s, has the lowest coefficient of drag (0.15) yet attained by a car. That was attained by removing the radiator from under the hood and rotating the four-cylinder engine downward to allow the hood to be lower and more slippery. The wheels are covered with fender skirts, and the entire body adjusts to the speed of the car by being lowered as speed increases to make it more aerodynamic. At a constant speed of 50 miles per hour the car needs only 2.5 horsepower to maintain speed, less than the power of the average lawnmower.

Engineering function currently dominates the design of the automobile, leaving behind those people who preferred the days of gracious comfort in the coach-like spaces of the early cars. But contemporary lifestyle emphasizes speed and efficiency over individual dignity.

Applied design is truly the pulse beat of a people, remaining stable when the society is stable or changing as the people change. Designers, even more clearly than other kinds of artists, are searching for a shared expression, not the expression of their own personalities. Yet when we examine the work of individual designers we find that their work has individuality and that the audience understands it as sincerity. Each period in the history of art finds its characteristic expression in its works of applied design, which makes it interesting to examine our own products as expressions of our times.

Summary for Review

Applied design creates and expresses a way of life. The Palace of Versailles was built from 1661 to 1688 to show French interior design and furnishings; it created a dominant style in its period. The Bauhaus, established in Germany in 1919, was an influential source of **Modern** design and design education. **Post-Modern** design has been emerging from Italian and American studios, inspired by historical Modernism of the 1920s, new materials and techniques, and a mood of playful fantasy. Textile arts have been mainly adapted to clothing. The clothing of the ancient Greeks expressed their artistic preference for simplicity of form. Ancient Peruvian textiles and clothing were produced in factories, each piece hand-made with brilliant color and complex design. European clothing since 1500 has changed from the extravagant use of ornamental cloth and designs to simple functional clothing of machine-made cloth. Ceramics, glass, and metal, all worked with fire, have long histories but currently show both Modern functional forms and Post-Modern representational forms. The history of automobile design is a demonstration of the interaction of technology and human desire for comfort and elegant design. The public seeks individuality in the design of its industrial products, understanding it as sincerity in the expression of a way of life.

Part V
Recognizing the Great Styles

396.
Pablo Picasso.
Woman's Head.
1908.
Oil on canvas,
28⅞ × 23¾"
(73 × 60 cm).
Private
collection.

397. Fang tribe,
Gabon. Mask.
19th century.
Painted wood,
height 19⅝"
(50 cm).
Vérité Collection,
Paris.

The story of human life on this planet is usually told as a struggle between styles. That is evident in the common use of style names—from literature, architecture, music, and the visual arts—for periods of history: Classical, Gothic, Renaissance, Baroque, and so on. Even though styles express the attitudes and ideas of groups of people at a particular time, in another sense they are timeless. As we examine several of the great styles in the chapters that follow, you will see that they offer options for the future. They are not so much like old newspapers full of out-of-date news as they are like cookbooks, full of recipes we have not made recently, but which we might like to try again.

Four great families of related styles are basic in these chapters; they are presented here in historical order. But the main idea is the expressive potential in each of those recipes (that is, styles), not the historical order. A **style** is the emphasis on particular elements of art and principles of design for an expressive effect. That expressive potential was developed by the people of a certain place and time, working together as artists, patrons, critics, and audience. To understand the style we have to understand those people, especially the audience, since their expectations—or we could call it their appetite—served as the motive for the style.

Artists especially think of these styles as recipe files. Pablo Picasso **[396]** was frank about his study of African sculpture [397]; and Fernando Botero (b. 1932) was inspired to paint a new version [398] of Peter Paul Rubens' (1577–1640) portrait (actually of his wife's sister) [399]. Neither Picasso nor Botero copied the older art exactly, but each used the design and the subject as a springboard to something new. Modern artists use earlier styles as raw material, very much as they use nature, which is similarly inexhaustible as a source of art. The fact that art based on earlier styles becomes famous and accepted by a modern audience is proof that there remains expressive potential in those styles, that they are not used up. Picasso made that point in an interview when he said: "To me there is no past or future in art. If a work of art cannot live always in the present it must not be considered at all. The art of the Greeks, of the Egyptians, of the great painters who lived in other times, is not an art of the past; perhaps it is more alive today than it ever was."* Picasso was correct that much ancient art remains "alive" in the same sense that it was alive when it was new, meaning that it has a living audience, and probably a larger audience today than ever before.

As we examine the Ancient and Classical styles, the religious arts of the Middle Ages, the optimistic, power-centered arts of the

———
* Pablo Picasso, "Picasso Speaks: A Statement by the Artist," The Arts May, 1923: 319.

398.
Fernando Botero.
Rubens' Wife.
1963.
Oil on canvas,
6′ × 5′10″
(1.8 × 1.7 m).
Solomon R.
Guggenheim
Museum,
New York.

399.
Peter Paul Rubens.
Portrait of Susanna Fourment. c. 1625.
Oil on panel,
31⅛ × 21½″
(79 × 55 cm).
National Gallery,
London.

Renaissance, and the growth of the Modern styles, we will see that styles are the way people show each other their view of life. To adopt a style is to make an agreement to experience life in ways that have something in common with other users of that style. Ancient tribes understood that very well: you had to dress, speak, and behave like the other members of the tribe or you were expelled. We see the same thing today in modern groups, in which there are always certain things that define the style of the group and determine who is in and who is out.

The notion of style is most definite when we speak of the personal style of an individual. The definition of the style must be made slightly more general when we talk about the style of a group because each individual varies somewhat. The larger the group or the longer the period, the more general the definition must be. Yet a useful picture comes to the mind of an art lover confronted with even such a general category as "Medieval art," which includes a variety of different period styles and innumerable personal styles, which nevertheless share some elements and principles. The word "style" can be compared with a word such as "message," which refers to things as personal as a slip of paper saying "Call home," and as general as a multi-volume library housing the "message of the Judeo-Christian tradition." What all uses of the word "style" share is their reference to art form; they all have something to say about the use of unity and variety, line, shape, mass, color, and so on.

For our purposes, we need only recognize the great styles when we see them. To look at a painting and be able to say "Baroque" is similar to being able to identify its medium as oil. The special look that belongs to each of these styles is the outcome of a way of life, which is one of the basic, often unconscious, messages of each of these styles.

Ancient Styles

The greatest obstacle to understanding the past is the feeling that the world came into existence when we were born. Everyone naturally feels that way. How can you make someone born in 1980 understand that life in 1970 was real? In our bones we all believe the past, before we were here, is fiction, whether it is ten years ago or ten thousand. How will you convince your own children that your life before they were born was real, with real problems and real pleasures?

The size of the numbers is another obstacle. There really is a difference between ten years and ten thousand. We know people who were alive ten years ago, and every day we see things that were in use then. But we know no one who was alive even a century ago and things used then are becoming scarce in our lives. That is one of the uses of art, which is saved from earlier times because people admire it: it provides a solid link between our time and earlier people, something we can see and touch just as they saw and touched it.

We are so time-conscious, wearing watches and watching clocks, that a century seems like a very long time. Centuries have little meaning in human life; a more realistic measure is a generation, usually calculated as 30 years. By that measure about 67 generations of children have been born since the time of Jesus and the foundation of the Roman Empire (in 27 B.C.). Recent research has pushed back the date of the earliest appearance of the modern human species, to which all living people belong, to about nine hundred centuries ago, which amounts to about three thousand generations. That is a large number, but not an unimaginable one. In this chapter we will look back at some of the things made by those earlier generations and, through those things, try to grasp the reality of their lives. Styles exist only to convey messages about people's experience. To examine a style is to try to understand the experiences of others' lives.

One of the common ancient experiences was migration into uninhabited territories. The modern *Homo sapiens* species first developed, as far as we know now, somewhere in eastern Africa or western Asia and slowly spread around the globe. As we consider ancient styles it is not so much dates we must remember as stages of cultural development. The dense populations of western Asia and its nearer neighbors developed new ways of life first, and the styles that go with them, while more isolated groups on the frontiers adopted those ways and styles much later.[1] That is why we use such terms as Stone Age instead of the dates of a period.

The Stone Age

It is a strange fact that the oldest art tradition is also one of the newest. Old Stone Age, or Paleolithic, art lay unknown for several thousand years and was discovered only in the past hundred or so years. It reappeared as part of world art at the time the Impressionist painters were working! It has had a large impact on our ideas of world history, and even on our idea of what art is. Modern artists, as we shall see, were deeply influenced by the discovery of Stone Age

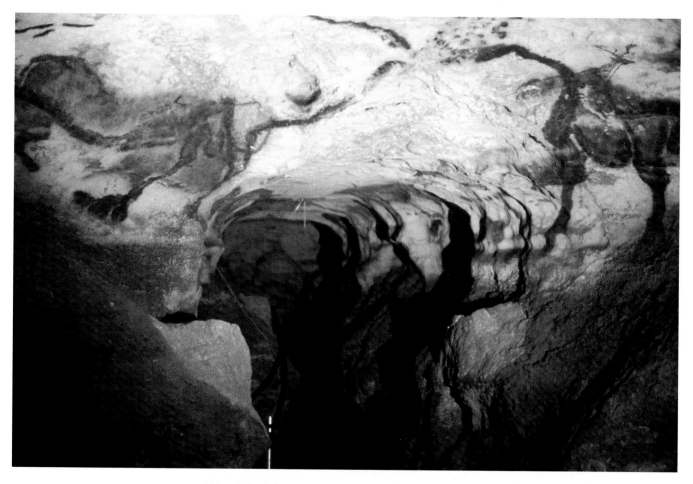

400. Paleolithic. Lascaux Cave, Dordogne, France. c. 15,000 B.C.

art. Researchers and archaeologists are constantly making new discoveries on this frontier in time.

Of the Stone Age styles, that of western Europe is by far the best known. *European Stone Age style* can be summarized as unified by its concentration on single figures of animals, or more rarely humans, without a setting. The main element is a contour line that expresses the natural action of a three-dimensional form, painted or incised on natural rock walls. Color was applied within the contours with variations that enhance the sense of mass. Figurines of people and animals, of a size to hold in the hand, were carved of stone, bone, and ivory, the masses simplified and bounded by lines.

By 12,000 B.C. people who were physically and mentally identical to modern people already had a long cultural tradition behind them. The newest modern art to them was painted in the caves of Altamira *(alta-MEE-rah)* in Spain and Lascaux *(lah-SKO)* in France **[400]**, while the oldest art, from thousands of years earlier, was stone figurines such as the *Venus of Willendorf (VIL-len-dorf)* **[401]**. Even though the little figurine was very old, people would still have understood its content, as we instinctively do today. Holding this plump little carving in the palm of your hand, it is easy to understand that it is concerned with the fertility of women. The power of human beings, and all living things, to reproduce themselves was the great mystery which dominated religion and art. The "Venus" (a name assigned later; this is not the Roman goddess Venus) suggests with her featureless face that for Stone Age people the mind, in which men and women are alike, was of less concern than their role in reproduction, in which they are different. That round figurine tells us that the female power to give a body and nourishment to babies was a sacred mystery.

Since it is obvious, looking at children, that they also inherit from their fathers, ancient people conceptualized the father's role as giving the soul. The whole universe was explained in terms of this relation of female to male, the earth being "Mother" and the sky "Father."

But animals, not humans, were the most popular subject in Stone Age art. Hunting and butchering of animals was the business of life, and everyone was expert on the appearance and anatomy of animals. The mammoth [402] carved on a reindeer antler spear-thrower shows the work of an artist who was confident of his knowledge. Artists sometimes did abstract patterns, but they were most concerned with lifelike representation. The spear-thrower was a common hunting weapon, an arm-extender (the broken trunk and tusks in 402) with a hook (the tail) which fitted into the butt of the spearshaft, used to make a longer, harder throw. The carving is decoration on a tool, but it was taken very seriously as art by the carver. We can also see the pride taken by the sculptor in his work, and the leisure time he had available to spend on art.

Very few modern people ever see animals free in nature as Stone Age people did, and everyone who has is overwhelmed with a sense of the bursting power of life. That was surely what the painters of Lascaux Cave [400] were trying to express in the herds of animals—deer, wild cattle, horses, bison—

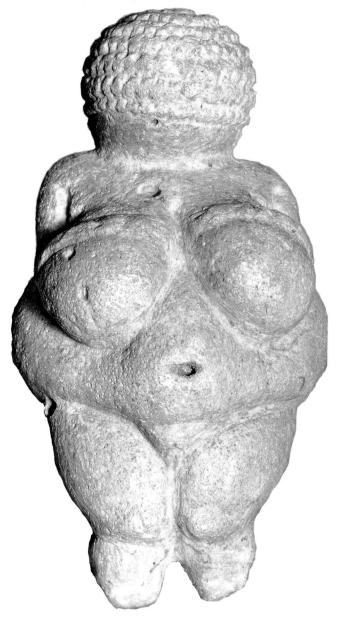

left: 401.
Paleolithic, Czechoslovakia.
Venus of Willendorf. c. 23,000 B.C.
Limestone, height 4⅓" (11 cm). Naturhistorisches Museum, Vienna.

below: 402. Mammoth carved on a reindeer antler, probably the weighted end of a spear-thrower. Paleolithic, c. 17,000–11,000 B.C., from Bruniquel, France. Length 4¾" (12 cm). British Museum, London.

A POINT IN TIME: Miró's Use of the Past

The Spanish painter Joan Miró *(hwahn mee-RO)* (1893–1984) was working in Paris as a young man when some poets, writers, and artists formed a group to practice art based on the new psychological discoveries of Sigmund Freud *(froyd)* and Carl Jung *(yoong).* They were interested in cultivating the creative powers that were believed to lie in the un-conscious parts of the mind. They called themselves **Surrealists**—we might translate that "super-realists." Miró had several friends in the group and seemed to join mostly out of friendship. No one thought of the young painter as an intellectual type. He never said much, but his art changed so much in the next few years it is clear he was listening.

403. Joan Miró.
The Birth of the World. 1925.
Oil on canvas, 8'2¾" × 6'6¾" (2.5 × 2 m). Museum of Modern Art, New York (acquired through an anonymous fund, the Mr. and Mrs. Joseph Slifka and Armand G. Erpf Funds, and by gift of the artist).

painted on the walls and ceilings. Lascaux is a small, dry cave where the ancient painters could bring their children; their footprints are still to be seen. (Other caves hundreds of yards deep have art in inaccessible chambers blocked even in ancient times by water, surely reached only by the hardiest adventurers.) Probably we should imagine those family visits as being more like going to church than like going to a museum. People naturally think first of the content of art, which in Lascaux and the other ancient caves showed images of a fertility religion.

The journalist Shana Alexander wrote of her visit to Lascaux:

Surely it is the cave of caves. Oval, arched, domed, jagged yet surprisingly symmetrical in form, it gave me an intense impression of standing inside a living body. Images of scarab or of whale came to mind—interiors of carapace or of rib cage; of

404. Paleolithic. Horses and handprints, Pêche-Merle Cave, France. c. 15,000 B.C. Natural pigments on cave wall, width 14½′ (4.4 m).

Miró came from northern Spain and was familiar with the famous and controversial discoveries of cave art, only accepted as the authentic work of ancient people during Miró's youth. "Miró's beloved Altamira caves"* were part of his own national heritage.

Prehistoric art of the caves seemed to fit into a theory of the psychological development of human beings that was popular with the Surrealists. They accepted the idea that the human personality had begun with only unconscious instincts, what Freud called the *id*, and they assumed that ancient people had never developed the conscious personalities which psychologists call the *ego* and *superego*.

———
*William Rubin, *Miró in the Collection of the Museum of Modern Art* (New York: Museum of Modern Art, 1973) 60.

Since cave art was the oldest art known at that time, it must be the product of the pure unconscious mind, they thought. In the 1920s it was hard to know what unconscious art should look like—all the people the Surrealists knew were extremely conscious, driven by their egos and their superegos, Freud would have said. Joan Miró said nothing, but in *The Birth of the World* [403] he began to treat his canvas as if it were the flat wall of a cave, rather than a window into space. He was inspired by the spots and lines as abstract marks, as we see in the horses of Pêche-Merle *(pesh-mairl)* [404], discovered and copied at just that time. Those, surely, were perfect examples of instinctive art, free of the contamination of intellect and calculation as the Surrealists believed it should be.

Art is inspired by art, but it is a surprising occurrence when the most advanced art is inspired by the oldest.

silence, darkness, waiting to be born. . . . Ancient man, who knew all caves as I know none, surely felt the perfection of this one particular cave. It was no accident that he chose in *this* rock to build his church.[2]

That sense of the cave as a living body was surely shared by ancient people, for the idea of caves as the womb of Mother Earth, from which all life—animal and human—emerges, is one of the basic ideas of early times. Lascaux Cave is the womb of earth pregnant with the herds of animals on which human life depended.

Although the most famous Stone Age art is found in western Europe, there are also important examples in the United States. Many of these are hard to date with much precision (though a guess of 18,000 B.C. was suggested by one authority[3]) and are still poorly understood, such as the moon-like face, called *The*

405. Paleo-Indian, Oklahoma.
The Frederick Head.
c. 18,000 B.C. Stone,
diameter c. 10″ (25 cm).
Great Plains Museum,
Lawton, Oklahoma.

Frederick Head, carved in stone and found in southwestern Oklahoma **[405]**. It is one of several oversize heads from the Great Plains region and, like some others, this one was found in gravel deposits more than 15 feet (4.6 meters) below the surface. The geology dates *The Frederick Head* to the Old Stone Age, but we still know nothing more about the artist than we can read from the sculpture itself. That tells us that the artist was able to grind stone into patterns of pits and grooves, a style of stone-working known worldwide and going back into pre-*Homo sapiens* remains in Europe. Only in America do the pits and grooves turn into faces, which hints that they may be relatively late Stone Age works, done by artists who invented new uses for old ways of marking stone.

Along the Pecos *(PAY-kose)* and Rio Grande rivers, in southwestern Texas, there are paintings in shallow caves—usually called "rock shelters"—which represent a later (6000–2000 B.C.) phase of art, called the Pecos Style **[406]**. They are different from the Lascaux Cave paintings because the main subjects are human—or human-like, at least. These figures are considered to be "medicine men," or *shamans (SHAH-mahnz or SHAY-mahnz)*, with antler headdresses, sometimes with wings, holding spear-throwers (the common ancient weapon worldwide). Animals appear, especially mountain lions and deer, perhaps symbolizing the hunter and his prey. You will notice that the Pecos Style is more abstract than that found at Lascaux, often with straight-lined geometric shapes and sharply defined areas of color. Those are considered features of later Stone Age (or *Neolithic*) style, of which the Pecos Style could be considered a part, though the pottery and agriculture common in Neolithic cultures are absent in the Pecos culture. But the style does suggest that the Pecos people were beginning to think in abstract symbols, not the visual images that dominate in Lascaux Cave. Abstract symbols were later to grow so important that they separated from art to become writing and numbers, leaving the pictorial parts behind to be what we still call "art." The Pecos Style shows the image and the abstract symbol still united.

Art in the Early Cities

One of the most important changes in social life was that from rural life to city life. That change followed an earlier one in which plants and animals were domesticated and people settled down in villages near their fields and pastures.

Cities developed from densely inhabited farming villages in the fertile lands on the banks of large rivers in Iraq, Egypt, Pakistan, and India and later in China, Mexico, and Peru. Despite their wide separation in time and space, all these ancient cities shared a preference for certain features of style, such as the gigantic and the miniature, story-telling art, and art produced by the use of fire, and they had systems of record-keeping that grew out of art. Stone Age art could mostly be made by one artist and would fit in the hand or on a cave wall, but in the ancient cities there was a new preference for works so large that many people had to work together to make them or, in contrast, so tiny that it is hard to imagine that a human being made them. While older art usually showed single figures or a single event, the new art of the cities preferred many figures and several events which tell a story. The technology of art also changed, with fire the main new tool, used to make pottery, metal, and glass. The audience also changed: the democratic family groups of earlier times had combined into large societies in which powerful leaders had emerged. The most elaborate and expensive forms of art were sponsored by this class of leaders, who could demand much more labor and skill than had ever been available before. These ancient cities are considered the beginning of *civilization*, a word usually signifying people who live in cities and have developed a form of writing. But the ancient cities varied dramatically, and their systems of record-keeping and communication differed.

Despite the wide differences among these cities, they all had some features in common. An idea that was shared among these ancient societies was that there were many gods who were in charge of all aspects of the natural world. The most powerful of the gods could be found on the mountaintops or in caves

406. Pecos Style. Horned and winged shaman figures, Fate Bell Shelter, Seminole Canyon, Texas. c. 4000 B.C. Pigment on natural rock wall, height of tall figures c. 7' (2.1 m).

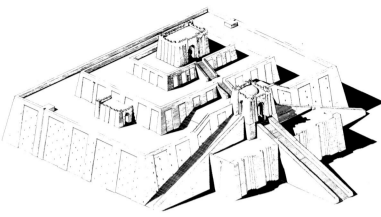

left: 407. Ziggurat at Ur, Mesopotamia (Iraq). 2250–2233 B.C. Photograph of restored building.

above: 408. Ziggurat at Ur, Mesopotamia (Iraq). 2250–2233 B.C. Reconstruction drawing (adapted from a drawing at the British Museum, London).

within the high mountains. Since there are ordinarily no mountains in the fertile river valleys where the ancient cities were located, the people worked in teams together to make their largest constructions, the artificial mountains used as temples and as tombs for their leaders. Perhaps the oldest of these are the towers in Mesopotamian temples, called **ziggurats**, a word meaning "mountaintop" [407, 408]. In almost all the early cities there is some kind of artificial mountain as part of their temple or royal tomb. The pharaohs (kings) of Egypt in early times were buried within gigantic stone pyramids, as if in a cave in the sacred mountain [409]. The Maya of Guatemala and Mexico built artificial mountains in their

409. Pyramids, Gizeh, Egypt. 2530–2460 B.C. Limestone, height of tallest originally 480' (146 m).

own style over the tombs of their kings [410]. The amount of labor which went into many of these constructions amazes modern observers. To the ancient Mesopotamians, Egyptians, and Maya the interesting fact was how large a construction human beings could build when they worked together.

The building of pyramids is a common feature of the early cities. It is one of the features, along with those enumerated above, which define the great family of ancient civilized styles. But each of these ancient civilizations had its own particular style and must be considered apart from the others.

Mesopotamia

Mesopotamia (*mes-uh-puh-TA-mya;* from the Greek for "between the rivers"; about 4000–500 B.C.) was a marshy region between the Tigris and Euphrates rivers in what is now Iraq. The oldest cities were built here about six thousand years ago. By about five thousand years ago the Sumerian people of this region had developed a system of writing with a wedge-pointed stick on clay tablets, called *cuneiform (kyu-NE-uh-form) writing.* Besides clay tablets, cuneiform inscriptions have survived on stone cylinder seals [411], which were rolled onto the clay as a signature. These tiny sculptures were at the opposite extreme from the colossal ziggurats. The small stone cylinder was cut with a pattern, sometimes abstract but often representing mythical figures. The identity of the beings in this cylinder seal is unknown, but we can guess that the idea was the conflict between the herdsman with his domestic cattle and the wild animals that preyed on them. The seal-cutters were the forerunners of the designers of coins; we are usually concerned only with the value of coins, but they are works of art in approximately the same category as the ancient seals.

Pyrotechnologies, or the technologies of fire, were the "high tech" of the ancient cities, as the artisans learned the effects of fire on different kinds of clay (which produced pottery and glass) and stone (whose ores produced metal). The

left: 410. Maya.
Temple I at Tikal, Guatemala. A.D. 600–800.

below: 411. Ur, Mesopotamia
(Iraq). Print from a cylinder seal. c. 2700 B.C.

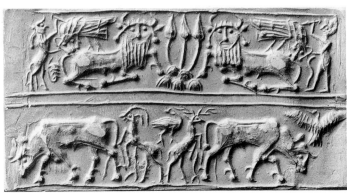

Ancient Styles _____ 293

right: 412.
Mesopotamian
region (Iraq).
King of Akkad (perhaps
Naram-Sin). c. 2300 B.C.
Bronze, height 14⅜"
(36 cm). Iraq Museum,
Baghdad.

below: 413.
Mesopotamian
region (Iraq).
Scenes of war from
The Standard of Ur.
c. 2685–2645. B.C.
Wooden box inlaid with
white shell and
deep blue lapis lazuli,
length 19" (48 cm).
British Museum,
London.

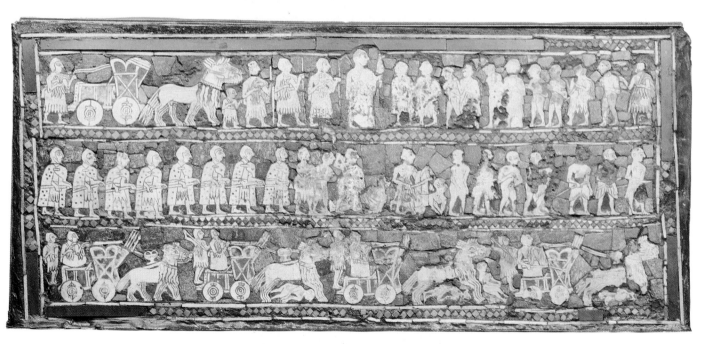

Recognizing the Great Styles

life-size bronze head of a Mesopotamian king [412] who ruled the Akkadian kingdom about 2300 B.C. is the oldest existing portrait in metal. (Its eyes were originally inlaid with precious stones, torn from their sockets by robbers long ago.) This is an idealized portrait, with every part simplified and perfected, as we see in the eyebrows. The king's hair is braided into a knot at the back of his head, and his full beard, the pride of Mesopotamian men, is shown in elaborate curls.

Mesopotamian art was especially good at telling stories. One of the oldest surviving works of art, called *The Standard of Ur* [413], is a strange wooden box inlaid with shell and deep blue lapis lazuli. The side shown here represents the Sumerian army as it enters battle; on the other side is the king's victory feast. Dividing the scene into three registers helps tell the story. The king is the larger figure in the top register, with his infantry and prisoners in the middle register, and four-wheeled chariots at the bottom. The artist had other tricks available as well: the four wild asses pulling each of the four-wheeled chariots are indicated by quadrupling the lines of their heads, legs, and tails, and you can see the story clearly as the asses in the bottom register seem to be walking slowly at the lower left, trotting in the next scene, and at full gallop at the right as they charge the enemy.

Naram-Sin, who may have been the subject of the bronze portrait head [412], had a 6½-foot (2-meter) red sandstone monument [414] set up in public to commemorate his victory over the enemy Lullubi. The king, shown larger, leads his troops up the mountain beneath the star-like symbols of the heavenly gods. The defeated enemies fall before him and beg for mercy. The artist paid close attention to the setting (note the tree) and cultural differences in the two groups, both important to the story.

The stories told in much Mesopotamian art are about the fighting, hunting, and feasting of the kings. A terrific series of low-relief panels was carved for the Assyrian king's palace at Nineveh about 650 B.C. showing the king shooting

414. Mesopotamian region (Iraq). Naram-Sin's victory over the Lullubi. c. 2389–2353 B.C. Red sandstone relief stela, height 6'6¾" (2 m). Louvre, Paris.

_____ *Recognizing the Great Styles*

415. Assyria, Mesopotamian region (Iraq). Ashurbanipal shooting lions from his chariot. c. 668–627 B.C. Stone low-relief panel, height c. 5′ (1.6 m). British Museum, London.

lions from his chariot. The lions **[415]**, previously captured, had been released from cages. The artists knew the anatomy of the lion perfectly, but they show no sympathy for the dying beasts. The actions of the king are treated as godlike, and the opinions and feelings of mere people (and lions) count for nothing before such grandeur. The power of this ancient king was so great that he and the nobles who supported him were both the patrons and the only audience that needed to be considered by the artists.

Mesopotamian artists employed a style that differed from the other styles of its stage of history in its emphasis on the texture of shapes, as you see in the hair, beards, lions' manes, and chariot. Texture gives those shapes greater mass, even though there is little setting to show a space for it. The dense packing of figures and the repetitions of lines (spears, reins) also contribute a sense of physical solidity which is much more pronounced than in Egyptian or Maya art, which looks slender and ethereal by comparison. Mesopotamian art in general, and Assyrian reliefs especially, show by their style that life in this world, with its fighting, hunting, and feasting, was the main concern.

Egypt

The pharaohs of Egypt were even more powerful and godlike than the Mesopotamian rulers, and the pharaoh's court, which was moved to a new location near his projected tomb by each new ruler, was always the most important city. The pharaoh, or king, was responsible for maintaining the principle of *ma-at (MAH-aht)*, which means order, justice, and truth. Like all Egyptian religious ideas, ma-at was personified and considered to live in a world which included all nature. Even death was merely an incident in a perpetually living world ruled by eternal gods, and in that sense Egyptian life and art are optimistic. To the Egyptians only the permanent and changeless had importance; even the changes of nature were significant only when they were part of a permanently repeating cycle.

Ancient Egyptian style, which endured for about three thousand years with only minor changes, emphasized unity by dividing its compositional field (or block of stone) into a grid pattern of vertical and horizontal lines **[416]** into which the subject was fitted, with parts reserved for writing when needed. Line was used as the boundary of shapes, which were mainly parallel to the picture plane. Masses in sculpture were likewise parallel to the planes of the rectangular block and were simplified to reduce the impression of movement. Color was flat and unaffected by light and shadow. All of these features of style expressed that sense of permanence and order.

Frontal poses were the result of that style when used for sculptures in the round; in relief sculptures the head and legs were in profile, the shoulders in front view. The original Egyptian observers of this art saw these poses as simply true—true in somewhat the same way a statement in **hieroglyphic writing** is true. This is a clear case of ideas about reality dictating an art style.

Artists did not think of their skills as something belonging to them, but as a power of the gods they worked for. When a statue was completed, a ceremony was held in which the figure's name was carved in hieroglyphic writing, to give it an identity, and "its mouth was opened," which gave it life. It is clear that Egyptian artists were not making art in the sense we use the term, for the pleasure of a living audience. Nor was the artist an individualist; on the contrary, artists were part of a professional group which had a collective identity and tradition.

The double portrait of the pharaoh Men-kau-re *(men-KOW-rah)* supported by his wife **[417]** shows the style in its massive form. Even so, you could easily make a drawing of it with lines. The lines would join to form simple shapes. The sculpture suggests a perfectly orderly eternal world where people remain for-

below: 416. Thebes, Egypt.
Working drawing with proportional grid.
c. 1400–1000 B.C.
Ink on gessoed wood panel. British Museum, London.

right: 417. Egypt. Pharaoh Men-kau-re and his queen.
2599–2571 B.C. Slate, height 4′6½″ (1.4 m).
Museum of Fine Arts, Boston (Harvard MFA Expedition).

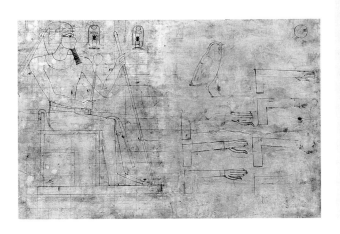

418. Thebes, Egypt. Musicians entertaining, wall painting in the tomb of Nakht. c. 1420 B.C. Tempera.

ever young. To make the sculpture truly eternal for placement in the tomb, a very hard stone was used; to make the sculpture still harder to break, it was not pierced with holes between the two figures, between their arms and bodies, or between their legs.

The lower classes were sometimes portrayed in more relaxed or active poses, as we see in the musicians **[418]** entertaining at a dinner party painted on the wall of the tomb of Nakht at Thebes. Their faces and legs are in profile and their shoulders frontal, but they play their instruments in a natural way. The girl in the center is unusual in having her head turned away from the movement of her body, giving an impression of greater action, but both her head and body are parallel to the wall surface. Egyptian artists accepted what seems to us a rigid formula for human figures and such minor departures from the ideal pattern were always rare.

A common offering in upper-class tombs was a Book of the Dead **[419]**, a papyrus manuscript of magic spells to aid and protect the spirit of the dead on its journey to the afterworld. *Weighing the Soul of the Dead* shows the dead woman, Naun, at the ceremony in which her heart (on the left side of the scale) is weighed against the small figure of the goddess Ma-at (on the right) as Naun

_____ *Recognizing the Great Styles*

419. Deir el Bahari, Egypt. *Weighing the Soul of the Dead.* From the Book of the Dead of Naun. c. 1025 B.C. Paint on papyrus. Metropolitan Museum of Art, New York (Museum excavations, 1928–1929, and Rogers Fund, 1930).

recites the list of sins she did not commit in life. Naun, who was a temple musician, is accompanied by the goddess Isis (at left) as the jackal-headed god Anubis, who is in charge of the dead, balances the scales. Thoth, the divine scribe represented as a baboon, sits on the scale and records the result. Osiris, the god of the dead, at right, proclaims "Give her her eyes and her mouth," meaning that her heart balances with order, truth, and justice and she is returned to life in the afterworld. No matter that these beliefs may seem bizarre to us; the design makes them clear and orderly.

Ancient craftspeople were so adept with their simple tools that sometimes we can hardly imagine how their works were made. The Egyptians were particularly skillful in many different materials, including ivory and glass. The glass cosmetic bottle in the shape of a fish [420], found in the Egyptian city of El-Amarna, shows the fusing of several colors of glass. The flowing of the molten glass in the designs of the body and the shapes of the fins shows that the artist was considering the characteristics of the medium in the same way a 20th-century artist would. Art in glass was first perfected in Egypt and has passed down to our day through a tradition that has been continuous in the Mesopotamian and Mediterranean regions.

420. El Amarna, Egypt. Cosmetic bottle in the shape of a fish. c. 1410–1320 B.C. Glass, length 5½" (14 cm). British Museum, London.

421. Maya. Vase. A Lord of the Underworld. A.D. 600–900. Painted ceramic; diameter 6½″ (17 cm), height 8½″ (22 cm). Art Museum, Princeton University, Princeton, New Jersey (gift of Hans and Dorothy Widenmann Foundation).

The Maya

Large towns and cities began to appear on the American continents by about 3000 B.C., but by far the best known of these ancient American civilizations is that of the Maya *(MAH-yah)*, who established city-states in the tropical forests of Guatemala, Mexico, and Belize. One of their greatest cities was Tikal *(tee-KAHL)*, which flourished 100 B.C.–A.D. 900. The central sector of the city held several tall temples covering the tombs of kings **[410]**. Maya buildings, like all ancient construction in the Americas, were built by human labor alone, there being no cattle or horses to be domesticated to haul loads of stone and earth.

Maya style was based on drawing with a brush made of flexible hair, which produced the flowing, varied line that was the main characteristic of their art. Maya line shows contours of three-dimensional forms, not flat shapes. Human figures are usually shown with their heads in profile or front view, but their bodies are frequently twisted and foreshortened in a way the Egyptian artists avoided. Color was bright and varied, but flat, with no indications of light and shadow. Sculpture was usually in low relief and still close to the drawing done on the stone. But deeper relief and occasionally real sculpture in the round were done, with deeply cut linear designs dominating the masses.

The painted vase **[421]** shows that firm flowing line drawn with a brush. The old man seated on a throne is one of the Lords of the Underworld, land of the dead, who is attended by beautiful bald young women and a rabbit scribe writing in a book bound in jaguar skin. Some color washes have been added, but they do not suggest illumination. The depth of the figures is shown in a manner seen in all the styles of the ancient cities, by overlapping body parts and doubling lines (woman's legs, rabbit's ears); notice that the faces are all in profile. The form of the vase is very simple, serving mainly as a support for the painting.

Painting on pottery is the most abundant type of Maya art, but the Maya also painted the walls of many of their public buildings with scenes of political, military and ceremonial life. The murals at Bonampak *(bo-nahm-PAHK),* painted in southern Mexico about 800, are the best known. This detail **[422]** shows prisoners brought before the ruler of the city. The victors are still in their fantastic battle gear, but the captives have been stripped and are soon to be sacrificed. Inscriptions in hieroglyphics above the figures identify the ruling family on the top of the stepped platform. Notice the poses of the captives, with the heads always in profile but the parts of the bodies foreshortened and overlapping. The colorful clothing and strange mask-headdresses of the warriors give us an idea of Maya arts of textiles and costume, but there are no examples surviving.

On stone monuments, or stelae (singular is **stela,** pronounced *STEE-luh;* plural stelae, *STEE-lee*), which the Maya leaders erected to commemorate events in the lives of the kings, a brush drawing was done first on the stone. Then the sculptor carved away the background in as many levels as needed to make the design clear, leaving low, flat planes of relief. *Stela 14* **[423]**, from the Maya city

below: 422.   Maya, Bonampak, Mexico. Mural painting. c. A.D. 800. Fresco secco, height of figures c. 24″ (61 cm). Watercolor reproduction by A. Tejeda. Peabody Museum, Harvard University. Copyright © President and Fellows of Harvard College 1972. All rights reserved.

right: 423.   Maya, Piedras Negras, Guatemala. Stela 14, the accession of a ruler. A.D. 761. Limestone, height 9′3″ (2.8 m). Museo Nacional de Antropología y Arqueología, Guatemala City.

A POINT IN TIME: The Tomb of Pacal

424. Maya, Palenque, Mexico. Cover of the sarcophagus of Pacal, ruler of Palenque. A.D. 683. Limestone, 7'3" × 12'5" (2.2 × 3.8 m).

On August 31, in the year 683, Pacal, the ruler of the Maya city of Palenque, died at the age of 81. His tomb had already been built deep inside its pyramid that was crowned by a temple. The massive limestone sarcophagus *(sar-KOFF-uh-gus*, a stone coffin) had been carved to receive his body, and the carved stone lid **[424]** measuring over 7 by 12 feet (2.2 by 3.8 meters) was ready to be rolled into place.

The relief carving on the lid shows Pacal at the moment of death falling into the Underworld, the land of the dead, which is ruled by the Earth Monster, whose mask dominates the lower part of the design on the lid. Sticking out from the lower jaw of the Earth Monster mask are two sets of curving jaws, about to draw the dead king into the Underworld. Above him rises the cross-shaped tree which represents the center of the world. A quetzal bird with its blue-green tail feathers (which are the color of the sky) sits on top, symbolizing the sky. A border of symbols for the heavenly bodies and celestial events frames the scene. On the edge of the massive limestone slab there are portraits of the king's ancestors.

The elegant carving is in low relief, which stands out sharply from the background plane. But the details on the relief areas still reveal their origin in a drawing with a pointed, flexible brush. Like the art deposited in an Egyptian tomb, this carving was not meant to be seen by living people. Its intended audience was the gods and ancestors living in eternity. It testifies to the superhuman status of the Maya king, who is shown as, in death, he takes his place in the eternal universe.

From L. Schele and M. E. Miller, *The Blood of Kings* (Forth Worth, Kimbell Art Museum, 1986), and Merle Green Robertson, *The Sculpture of Palenque* (Princeton, NJ: Princeton University Press, 1984).

---

of Piedras Negras, shows a young king newly seated on his throne, which he inherited through his mother, who stands below. Symbols of the gods that rule the universe surround the scene. The queen mother, the ladder leading to the throne, and the god symbols are all in very low relief, with the background just barely cut away from the drawn lines. The young king, however, is given much more mass by the cutting away of a deeper space around his body. The green plumes of the quetzal *(ket-SAHL)* bird, which ornamented the crowns of Maya kings, are carved in low relief on that deeper background area. Color may have been added to Maya sculptures such as this, but there are only traces of it left now.

The Classical Styles of Greece and Rome

Ancient Greece and Rome are set apart from the other ancient civilizations; these civilizations, which endured nearly a thousand years (500 B.C.–A.D. 400), are called the "Classical civilizations." They are classical in two different senses, the first referring to Greek style itself, the second to the admiration of later peoples for it. The word **classic** expresses the belief that there is one way to do something that is better than any other. The Greeks believed that there are particular forms, designs, and customs that are ideal in the sense that they really exist only in our minds as timeless truths—we might say that "they are in the mind of God," although they are very poorly reflected in the chaos of the natural world. For example, the Greeks tried to design architectural forms that would never need to be changed, that everyone would always recognize as the ideal (that is, an idea given physical form). As we have seen in Chapter 8, in architecture they came surprisingly close to success in this impossible endeavor. In sculpture and painting they experienced a short period, often called "The Golden Age," when classical idealization reigned. One authority describes Greek classicism as "the emphasis on generic life, on harmonious relation of body and soul, a belief in rational construction of artistic form, in preponderance of rhythm and proportion over naturalistic observation."[4] *Classical style* emphasized unity, which it achieved by regular repetitions of standardized motifs or elements, usually using a single material for each work. The elements of art which were emphasized were mass and line used as the contour of a mass.

But by 320 B.C. the conquering Greek king Alexander the Great had spread the Greek style from Egypt to India, and artists and their varied new audiences had begun to reject the classical ideal. In the process they invented a new style, though one still part of the Classical family. Called the **Hellenistic** style, it is unified by its single material (for example, marble) and by its use of traditional standard subjects (mainly the human figure), but greater variety appears in the use of the elements of art, especially in effects of highlight and shadow, in lines used to suggest gesture and movement, as in draperies, and in more complex compositions. This dramatic new style was inherited by the Romans of the Imperial age (27 B.C.–A.D. 410), who modified it into something a little more sober and closer to the appearance of nature.

Greece and Rome were classical civilizations in another sense for later European societies and their descendants. Long after the fall of Rome people considered the styles and languages of Greece and Rome to represent the highest standard. Although many other styles have been invented, we still use the term **Classical** (with a capital C) for the style of Greece and the Greek heritage in the Hellenistic states and in Rome, suggesting that it still has a special prestige. Classical style has been revived over and over and it would surely be a rash prophet who would predict that it would never again be taken as the model for our art. It is not so surprising that we feel close to those styles, for ancient Greece is as close to us in time as the Greeks were to Pharaoh Men-kau-re and his queen **[417]**.

Greece

Although Greek artists worked in painting, architecture, ceramics, and other arts, sculpture was the basic art. Sculpture played such an important part in architecture that to a Greek it would have seemed artificial to discuss one without the other. And painters concentrated on human figures just as they appear in sculpture, with little attention to setting. Variety found expression in Greek sculpture mainly in materials—carved marble and cast bronze were both common, and a few important works were made in gold and ivory.

In the mountains of Greece there are excellent marble quarries, and this fine stone was used for temples and their sculptural decorations. The most famous are the sculptures of the temple in Athens dedicated to the goddess who protected the city, the virgin Athena (Athena Parthenos); the temple is called the Parthenon, or "shrine of the virgin goddess" **[304]**. The most important sculpture was the image of the goddess herself which stood inside, made of thin plates of ivory (for the flesh) and gold (for the clothing). Not surprisingly, that sculpture disappeared long ago, probably when the Parthenon was converted to a Christian church in the early Middle Ages. What has survived are many of the marble sculptures which adorned the outside of the building: full round figures in the **pediments** (or gable ends); low-relief sculptures in **friezes** around the **cella** (or sanctuary chamber). The figures in the pediments told two old myths about the life of Athena: her birth from the head of the supreme god Zeus, on the east pediment, and her victory over the sea god Poseidon in a contest for the rule of Athens, on the west pediment. The main figures on both ends were destroyed when the building was blown up in warfare in the 17th century, but many of the "supporting players" in these dramatic scenes have survived in museums in Athens and London. Since they were set nearer the corners of the triangular pediments, they are seated or reclining, as the goddesses often called *Three Fates* are [425]. The identities of these figures are uncertain, but the sculptor's mastery of the human figure is not; in fact, the flow of the heavy draperies, far from concealing the forms of the bodies, enhances them. A reclining male figure from the left corner of the west pediment probably represents a river god—the flow of the drapery over the arm, as well as the flowing form of the figure itself suggest the flow of water [426]. The sculptor had carefully observed the human body to depict the twist of the torso and the pressure of the ribs into the stomach. The Greek philosopher Plato said that the mission of the artist was to hold a mirror up to nature. From the Parthenon sculptures we can see that what the sculptors meant was not what we mean by the word "nature," with its infinite variation. These human bodies are idealizations: young adults with perfect builds, not one of them too fat or too thin.

The Parthenon sculptures were all made under the supervision of the master Phidias, who probably concentrated his own work on the famous gold-and-ivory image of Athena inside the temple. Nevertheless, we can be sure that all these sculptures conformed to his style and ideas. Classic simplification extended even to the animals in Phidias' style, as we see in the head of the exhausted horse [427] drawing the chariot of the sun as it sinks beneath the horizon at sunset. The bronze bit, which was once in the mouth, pulls the horse's lips back in a very natural way, yet the whole effect is a grand simplification. It is truly an idea given form.

It could also be said of Egyptian art, that it gave form to ideas, but the Greeks revolutionized art so thoroughly that as one authority has put it, "to say

425. Phidias. *Three Goddesses* or *Three Fates*, east pediment of the Parthenon, Athens. 437–432 B.C. Marble, height 4' (1.2 m). British Museum, London.

Recognizing the Great Styles

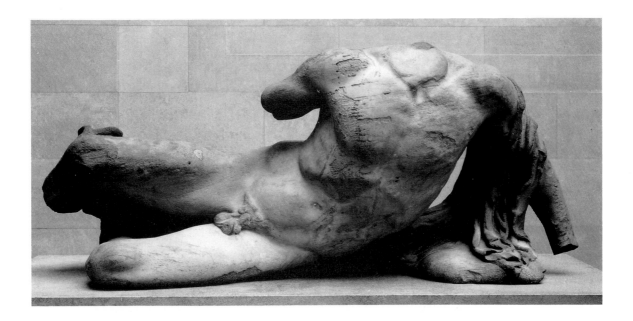

that the Greeks invented art . . . is a mere sober statement of fact."[5] That statement is perhaps clarified if we amend it to say that the Greeks invented the role
of the artist as an *imaginative* creator. The Egyptians and the Mesopotamians
never granted their artists the liberty to try out new patterns for common subjects; their styles remained classical in the sense of an accepted pattern more
than the Greek style ever was. What was new in Greek art, which makes it the
foundation of our own, was the idea that the artist should invent a world in the
imagination, and that each artist should create a new vision. This was a shocking
new idea to many people of the time, the philosopher Plato among them. In his
description of the perfect civilization he banned all artists since, in his opinion,
they were all professional tricksters, showing mere illusions.

If we look at two vase paintings done about a hundred years apart, it is
clear that artists were working seriously to develop their inventive powers, despite the objections of Plato and other conservatives, who would have preferred
to settle on one pattern and never change it. In the earlier painting of about
520 B.C. five men compete in a sprint, their bodies painted black on the brick red

426. Phidias.
River god, west
pediment
of the Parthenon,
Athens c. 430 B.C.
Marble.
British Museum,
London.

427. Phidias.
Chariot horse of the sun,
east pediment of the
Parthenon, Athens.
c. 430 B.C. Marble.
British Museum, London.

428. Greek. Runners in the Panathenaic games, from an amphora. c. 530 B.C. Black-figured pottery. Metropolitan Museum of Art, New York (Rogers Fund, 1912).

ground of the clay [428]. You will notice that their heads and legs are in profile, their eyes and chests in front view, similar to the Egyptian stylization. The later painting, from about 420 B.C., shows boys practicing athletics, their bodies left red with the black background painted around them [429]. That change from black figures to red, which occurred about 480 B.C., gave the bodies more mass by giving them the warm color, rather than the black, which had the flattening effect of a silhouette. But beyond the color change, the boys are in a variety of poses seen from a front or back angle. Starting with an accepted pattern for the male figure, the artists have begun to observe people and make additions to the traditional patterns, arriving at new and more natural patterns. One right way no longer existed, and from this point on, art was open to a constant process of invention—a process that still upsets people today.

The active poses that Greek sculptors began using for their figures early in the 5th century B.C. (see Chapter 7 for a discussion of the contrast between **frontal** and **contrapposto** figures) opened the way for an infinity of poses. The figures Phidias designed for the Parthenon are in a tremendous variety of poses, and it is hard to believe that little more than fifty years had passed since the first

429. Polion. Boxers and runners practicing, from a volute krater (mixing bowl) from Attica. c. 420 B.C. Red-figured pottery. Metropolitan Museum of Art, New York (Fletcher Fund, 1927).

_____ *Recognizing the Great Styles*

contrapposto figures had been carved. In later centuries the contrapposto figure became the new standard pose in Greek and Roman art, used almost as universally for the single figure as the frontal figure had been in Egyptian art. The gentle movement of the contrapposto pose always carried a double meaning: that the figure represents a mortal, who lives in time, and is posing beautifully for a living audience. For that reason, Greek art is the first which was art in our sense, made to appeal to the aesthetic taste of living people. That is why the first true art collectors were people of the Greek world who cherished art not because it served some useful purpose such as decorating their houses or sheltering their souls after death, but just because they liked it.

The name of the sculptor Praxiteles is associated with such figures in relaxed walking poses, with idealized faces. The *Marathon Boy* **[430]**, a bronze sculpture rescued from the sea off Marathon, in Greece, is probably about as close as we can get to Praxiteles' style, since no original by him is known. The graceful gesture, probably one of pouring wine, is an extreme version of the **contrapposto** pose.

Hellenistic Art, 330–30 B.C.

Greek art of the earlier periods especially appealed to early-20th-century people because they shared its concern for abstract forms and geometric compo-

430. Greek. *Marathon Boy*, in the style of Praxiteles. c. 350 B.C. Bronze, height 4'3" (1.3 m). National Museum, Athens.

431. Hellenistic, Thrace. Coin showing Alexander the Great with ram's horn of Zeus Ammon and diadem. c. 286–281 B.C. Silver tetradrachm, diameter 1¼″ (3 cm). Museum of Fine Arts, Boston (Theodora Wilbour Fund in Memory of Zoe Wilbour).

sitions. For example, the work of such early-20th-century sculptors as Constantin Brancusi and Aristide Maillol is the result of a modern style sharing features with an old style because both sculptors were searching for ideal forms. Later Greek art of the Hellenistic period especially appeals to the late 20th century because we share its interests in dramatic subjects and the psychology of the figures.

"Hellenistic" refers to the Greek (or Hellenic) style carried by the conquests of Alexander the Great to non-Greek lands—Persia, Mesopotamia, Phoenicia, and Egypt. Alexander, who succeeded to the throne of the Greek state of Macedon at the age of 20 and died of malaria in the Mesopotamian city of Babylon at age 33 (in 323 B.C.), was the focus of the whole period. On his death his generals divided up their conquests into kingdoms and one of them put a portrait of Alexander on his silver coins [431]. The face is idealized, but the inspired look in the deep-set eyes is found in all Alexander's portraits; the ram's horns on his head are the sign of the Egyptian god Ammon and remind us that the conqueror, after being crowned pharaoh, made a strange pilgrimage to that god's desert shrine where Ammon claimed him as a son, it was said. In this union of Greek and Egyptian we have a key to the Hellenistic world: it had the first "world culture," when trade, travel, and all kinds of contacts brought people together. Greeks settled in new cities, such as Alexandria, in Egypt, bringing traditional Greek style with them. Non-Greek peoples in Egypt and western Asia adopted many of the basic elements of Greek classicism. The absorption by Rome three hundred years later of large parts of Alexander's empire spread

432. Roman copy from Pompeii of Hellenistic sculpture. *Dancing Satyr.* c. 200 B.C. (original). Bronze, height 28″ (71 cm). Museo Nazionale, Naples.

433. Roman copy from Herculaneum of lost Hellenistic painting at Pergamon. *Hercules Discovering His Son Telephos.* c. 150–133 B.C. (original; copy c. 70 B.C.). Fresco, height 7′2″ (2.2 m). Museo Nazionale, Naples.

Greek culture to western Europe and North Africa and made it the foundation for western European culture.

The restrained poses and expressions that were typical of earlier Greek art gave way in Hellenistic art to unabashed exuberance. *Dancing Satyr (SAY-ter or SAT-er)* **[432]** was cast in bronze, probably at the city of Pergamon on the Turkish coast about 200 B.C., but, like much Hellenistic art, it is known to us in a Roman copy found in the ruins of Pompeii, where it decorated a courtyard. Half goat and half human, satyrs could not control their love of wine, women, and dancing; this one seems to burst with animal high spirits, dancing and snapping his fingers. The horns on his head differ from Alexander's godly horns; here they go with his tail to show his goat nature.

Another Hellenistic work from Pergamon which was copied by the Romans is the fresco painting of *Hercules Discovering His Son Telephos* **[433]**. The kings of Pergamon claimed that their dynasty was founded by Telephos, shown as a baby being suckled by a doe after he was abandoned in the wilderness by his mother. His father, Hercules (son of the god Zeus, represented by the eagle), has finally found his son and looks on approvingly, with the nymph who is the spirit of the mountain where the child was left. The great goddess Arcadia, who rules that abundant land, is seated at the left, accompanied by a young satyr. The land and ancestry of the kings of Pergamon are thus represented by human and animal figures—we could almost call them actors since they are more expressive in pose and more individual in face and body type than personifications in earlier Greek art—many of them standing for places (such as a mountain) or a quality (such as fertility).

Ancient Styles ———— 309

434. Hellenistic Greek. *Winged Victory of Samothrace.* 180–160 B.C. Marble, height 8' (2.4 m). Louvre, Paris.

One of the most popular sculptures of all time, even though the head and arms are missing, is the *Winged Victory of Samothrace* **[434]**, which was set up at the city of Samothrace to commemorate a victory in a naval battle. Modern audiences have forgotten its original symbolism, but it has a new meaning for us as the triumphant human spirit. In her original setting she seemed as if alighting on the prow of a ship coming into port and holding out a wreath of victory in her right hand. Below the gray marble base shaped like a ship prow were two large pools of water, one with a rippled floor to produce waves, the lower one holding some great boulders, symbolizing the harbor. "Victory" seems to stride against the wind, her body dramatized by the drapery and lifted by the broad wings. Such picturesque and sensational art was a Hellenistic invention. The theatrical

Recognizing the Great Styles

quality of Hellenistic sculpture was enhanced by the elaborate settings they were given; actually, their style shares something with popular 20th-century films more than with our more intellectual fine arts.

It is interesting to compare a 5th-century Greek depiction of the goddess of victory with the *Victory of Samothrace* of about 300 years later. A different kind of energy is expressed in the tiny gold earring representing the goddess of victory (whose name was Nike [NI-key]) driving her two-horse chariot [435]. Only 2 inches (5 cm) high including the hook and the enameled palmette which covered the earlobe, the hollow gold figure and horses are shown in microscopic detail. Each feather of the goddess' wings is shown. The drapery of her costume is blowing, and she wears bracelets and even earrings of her own. This may have been the jewelry of a gold and ivory statue. The Hellenistic Age could hardly improve on the art it inherited, but it added a grandeur and theatricality all its own.

Hellenistic artists were the first to make pictorial **mosaics**, using small *tesserae* (singular is *tessera*), that is, squares of colored stone, or later of colored glass, set in cement or plaster. *View of the Nile Valley* [436] was a large pictorial floor mosaic done in Italy, about 75 B.C., the work of a Hellenistic Greek artist patronized by the Roman dictator Sulla. Egypt at that time was still ruled by Hellenistic Greeks (of whom Cleopatra was the last). The annual flooding of the Nile River was a phenomenon that fascinated the civilized world. The artist gives us a bird's-eye view over the flooded delta, showing boatmen poling their small reed canoes and larger pleasure boats, with many native animals (crocodiles and hippopotami in the lower left, for example). The artist was acquainted with Egypt, for he shows typical Egyptian tower houses, with classical temples and farm buildings mixed among them. The whole mosaic measures 16 by 20 feet (4.9 by 6.1 meters)—the illustration is a detail—but it was intended to be examined up close by people walking over it, so the artist wrote in the names of many of the animals that were strange to Roman eyes.

The Romans took over the Hellenistic kingdoms piece by piece, ending up with Egypt, incorporated into Roman territory in 31 B.C. by Augustus in the

left: 435. Northern Greek. Earring: Nike driving a chariot. c. Late 4th century B.C. Gold, height 2″ (5 cm). Museum of Fine Arts, Boston (H. L. Pierce Fund).

below: 436. Hellenistic Greek artist for a Roman patron. *View of the Nile Valley*, detail. c. 75 B.C. Floor mosaic, entire floor 16 × 20′ (4.9 × 6.1 m). Archaeological Museum, Palestrina, Italy.

above: **437.** Dioscorides. c. A.D. 10. Cameo portrait of the Emperor Augustus. Engraved sardonyx, height 5″ (13 cm). British Museum, London.

above right: **438.** Roman. Pompey the Great. c. A.D. 30. Marble, life-size. Ny Carlsberg Glyptotek, Copenhagen.

process of founding the Empire. The Romans had native Italian art traditions of their own, but by that time they had developed a passion for Hellenistic Greek art, which they purchased, patronized, copied, or stole at every opportunity. Yet there are features of the art of Rome that belong to it alone.

The Roman Empire

When Julius Caesar was assassinated in 44 B.C., Rome was plunged into civil war for thirteen years. Caesar's nephew Octavius emerged the victor and became the first emperor of the Roman Empire, adopting the name Augustus. "Augustus was remarkably handsome and of very graceful gait even as an old man," wrote an early biographer, "but negligent of his personal appearance." He lived very simply, considering that he was the most powerful individual in the world. It is interesting to compare a description of this man of simple tastes with his portrait carved in sardonyx by the gem-engraver Dioscorides [437]. "Augustus' eyes were clear and bright, and he liked to believe they shone with a sort of divine radiance . . . his hair [was] yellowish and rather curly, his eyebrows met above the nose; he had ears of normal size, a Roman nose, and a complexion intermediate between dark and fair."[6] This cameo 5 inches (13 centimeters) high appears to be a good likeness, but an amazingly luxurious object. It is only one of a group of cameo portraits of the imperial family done by that artist.

Sculptured portraits were popular among the Romans in much the same way photographic portraits are popular with us, as a way to remember the appearance of our loved ones. The white marble usually used was painted to bring it to life, but quite a number of Roman portraits are grim faces based on casts made from the features after death. The best of the portraits, such as that of the general and statesman Pompey (*PAHM-pe*) [438], give us a wonderful sense of personality. Far from the idealized faces of Greek Classical and Hellenistic sculptures, Pompey's face is unique, with its curling locks of hair over a broad brow, his small eyes under their raised eyebrows, and his tight-lipped mouth. It is a face that suggests a politician more than a military leader.

The military life was an inescapable part of leadership for men of the Roman upper class as they tried to regulate and expand a vast empire of peoples with little in common. The Emperor Trajan, who was a soldier by preference, spent most of his life on campaign and recorded the conquest of Dacia (now Romania) on a famous monument in Rome [439]. The Column of Trajan carries on the tradition of victory monuments that the Mesopotamian leaders erected, but the Roman monument is more factual and less mythological, despite the presence of some mythological figures such as the river god below the pontoon bridge (bottom row). The column and its base are 123 feet (38 meters) tall, the shaft carved with a spiral scroll-like design which tells the history of the war in much the way a movie would, with as much accurate detail as possible. The attention to engineering shown by the emphasis on the pontoon bridge (bottom row) and the erection of the fortified camp (next two rows) is surely a clue to the success of Roman armies. Trajan appears over and over, as the star of this "movie."

It might seem impossible to see a design wound around such a tall column, but the monument was set among buildings (including two famous library buildings, one for Greek, the other for Latin, books) from which it may have been more easily seen. All these structures were part of a vast **forum,** or public mall, built by the emperor for his city [440]. It included, besides a temple dedicated to the emperor as a god, a concert hall, market buildings, and administrative offices. Large architectural complexes were the specialty of the Romans and perhaps their greatest art.

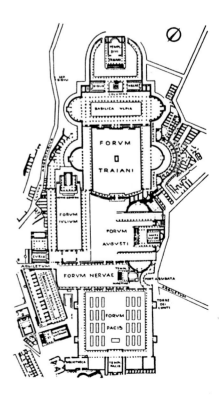

left: 439. Roman. The Column of Trajan, Rome. A.D. 113. Marble relief; height 123' (37.5 m), width of bands c. 36" (91 cm).

below: 440. Roman. Plan of the Forum of Trajan, Rome, with neighboring areas. C. A.D. 100.

The best known of all their great buildings is the Colosseum **[441]**, an oval amphitheater that accommodated about 45,000 people. Its name does not come from its size, however, but from a huge statue of the Emperor Nero that once stood near it. When it was opened the show lasted for one hundred days, with animal shows, gladiatorial battles, and even a sea battle staged in the flooded arena. Later peoples admired many Roman achievements, but probably none more than the architectural skills to build such a practical and efficient structure. We may not approve of the gory shows put on there, but from the architectural viewpoint it provided easy access and good visibility for large crowds. The Colosseum would serve as a definition for the Roman version of Classical architectural style: where the Greek was rectangular in plan and structure (using the post and lintel), the Roman added curving and circular plans and structures (arches, vaults). Where Greek public buildings were often mainly to be seen from the outside and rarely had large interior spaces, Roman public buildings were designed to hold large crowds and permit all sorts of events (bathing, combats) to be carried out inside. Even the Colosseum, which had no permanent roof, could be covered with a tremendous canvas sunshade suspended from the upper parts of the walls.

We know only a little about the relationships between Roman artists and their audience from literature, which was more concerned with other topics. Art critics then were not specialists, but works of art were often the subject of short, witty poems or descriptive essays, and artists were sometimes the subjects of biographies. Most of the ancient writings on art were used by the Roman scholar Pliny (*PLIN-ee;* he died at Pompeii in the eruption of Vesuvius in A.D. 79) as sources for his encyclopedia, called *Natural History.* Pliny himself was not much interested in art, but he knew there was a large audience with a passionate interest in art and artists. His writings on art brought together a storehouse of Classical art history and criticism and were passed down to later ages as models.

Relations between the artists and their patrons were conditioned by their somewhat contradictory desires: the artists to follow the traditional Hellenistic style while making some fashionable innovations and the patrons to have something uniquely their own. Thus the anonymous painters of a room in the country house of P. Fannius Sinistor at Boscoreale, near Pompeii, painted between 65 and 30 B.C., used a traditional set of architectural and landscape subjects, but

441. Roman.
The Colosseum, Rome.
A.D. 72–80.
Long axis 620' (189.1 m),
short axis 513' (156.5 m),
height 160' (48.8 m).

442. Roman. Mural in the Villa Boscoreale, near Pompeii. 65–30 B.C. Fresco on lime plaster, average height 8′ (2.4 m). Metropolitan Museum of Art (Rogers Fund, 1903).

they also seem to show the patron's own house, somewhat idealized and improved, but individualized and not merely traditional[7] **[442]**. Both artists and patrons worked within firm traditions which indicated appropriate subjects for particular places.

By the end of the Classical civilizations, all the elements of the art world (as we conceive it in our time) were in place: the artist as imaginative creator, the patron, the critic and writer on art, and the audience.

Summary for Review

The ancient styles endured thirty thousand years and show the gradual accumulation of skills (stone carving, metal casting, building construction) and ideas (idealization, personification, art criticism) which are basic to our idea of art. Stone Age art was carved of stone or painted on stone walls and emphasized subjects of human and animal fertility. Later Stone Age art, such as that found in the Americas, changed toward more abstract designs, implying interest among artists and their audience in the developing ideas of numbers and writing, which were to branch off from art. Early city-dwellers were fascinated by the gigantic (such as pyramids) and the miniature (seals), liked to tell complex stories in their art, and developed techniques using fire with pottery, glass, and metal. Not only did the style and technique change, but also the audience changed to one dominated by a small class of rulers and priests who could command the labor necessary for large or expensive art production. The Classical civilizations of Greece, the Hellenistic kingdoms, and Rome emphasized sculpture (of human figures to personify places, things, and ideas) and architecture (public buildings), seeking ideal forms, which would never need to be changed. The later period of Classical style grew more interested in natural figures and portraits and in the functional efficiency of buildings.

Styles of the Middle Ages, 400–1400

Between the fall of Rome to Germanic armies (in 410) and the Renaissance, beginning about 1400, lie the Middle Ages, a period of about a thousand years. Three great world religions spread their own special art styles around the globe during the Middle Ages: Christianity, centered in Europe; Islam, which had its main centers in western Asia and North Africa; and Buddhism, which dominated eastern Asia. All three of those religions were in competition with older traditions. The Vikings in northern Europe converted to Christianity only in the year 1000; Islam had to contend with ancient traditions in Africa; Buddhist missionaries in China never succeeded in eliminating Daoism *(DOW-izm)* and Confucianism. You can easily imagine that art quickly became a weapon and a tool to win converts, teach the faithful, and glorify the special virtues of each of these different religions. In those days it was hard for a Buddhist to be tolerant of Daoist art or a Moslem to admire Christian art. Educated followers of all these faiths have learned that it is possible to study art styles of other religions without damaging one's own, but in those days religion was a public matter—when the king changed religions, so did all his people. For that reason *medieval* (which means "of the Middle Ages") art was concerned with public matters at least as much as it was with personal beliefs, often playing roles we assign to newspapers, magazines, and television.

Christian Styles of Europe

The big story in Europe was the migration of hordes of people out of the plains of western Asia into Europe, their settling down, and their creation of a new civilization based on the Christian religion. The patrons of art were the less than 5 percent of the population who led the Church and the secular state. The church was ruled by the Pope, just as the state was ruled by the emperor, heirs at least theoretically of the rulers of the ancient Roman Empire. Under the Pope there were cardinals, bishops, abbots of monasteries, and the clergy and members of religious orders. The secular state was divided into many political units, large and small, but in theory the Roman Empire still survived, and powerful central European rulers kept the title of emperor. Under the emperor were kings, dukes, counts and earls, barons and knights. The secular state depended on the Church for leadership in religious, intellectual, and artistic matters, and the Church depended on the state for military leadership, but the two realms were very closely linked.

Byzantine Art

Europe was divided another way too, between the Byzantine Empire, with its capital at Byzantium *(biz-ZAN-tee-um;* now Istanbul, Turkey), and the Holy

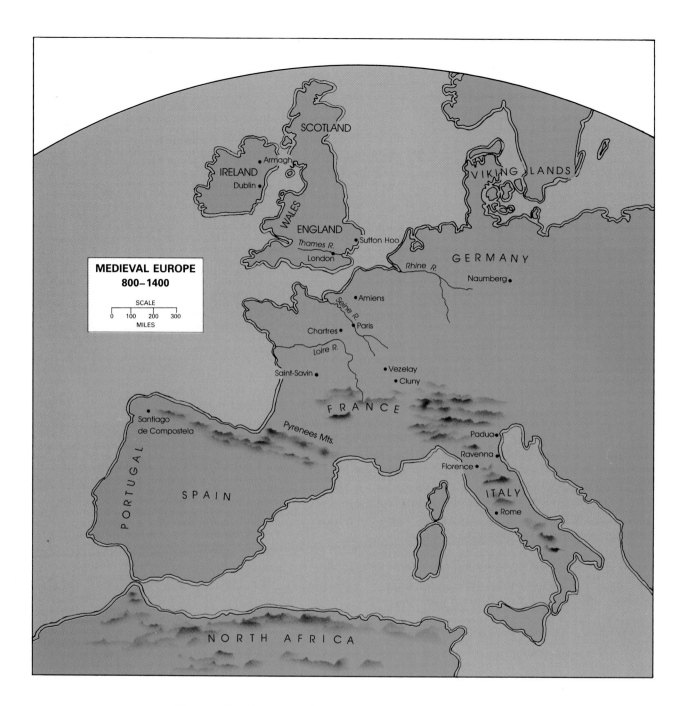

Roman Empire and other independent nations in central and western Europe. The Byzantine emperor did not recognize the authority of the Pope, but ruled as head of the church as well as the state. That explains the halo around the head of the Byzantine Emperor Justinian in a mosaic **[443]** on the wall of a church in Ravenna, a Byzantine outpost in Italy. Justinian is accompanied by his body-guards and by leaders of the church led by Bishop Maximianus, whose name appears above his head. But you will notice that it is the emperor who has the halo, an idea carried on from ancient Roman times indicating that the ruler himself was a god. The scene is not as natural as ancient Roman artists would have made it, partly because the gold background takes the place of a landscape or interior of a building, suggesting that the scene is surrounded by a heavenly light. The disregard of spatial illusions might have suggested to an earlier Roman artist that the figures were stepping on each others' toes. But the Byzantine people who saw the mosaic understood the spiritual reality it was meant to

443. Byzantine. Emperor Justinian with his attendants. C. A.D. 547. Mosaic. Church of San Vitale, Ravenna, Italy.

show, the eye contact of every figure in the picture with the observer enhancing the sense of spiritual communication.

Mosaic was an important technique in the Byzantine Empire, despite its expense. Unlike Roman mosaic made of stone, each bit of color was fired enamel or gold leaf on glass set into cement so the gold or color was sandwiched between a glass surface and the cement on the wall. Durable and brilliant, mosaic favored decorative abstract patterns more than natural illusions, and that unworldly appearance was just what Byzantine artists and their audience were looking for.

Justinian had one of the world's great churches built in his capital in 532, called the Church of Holy Wisdom—or, in Greek, Hagia Sophia *(HAG-ya so-FEE-uh)*—with the interior almost entirely covered with mosaic **[444]**. It also had the second largest dome in the world (after the Pantheon in Rome): 108 feet (33 meters) in diameter and 180 feet (55 meters) above the floor. The 40 small windows all around the base of the dome and the gold mosaic background which reflected their light made the dome seem to float in air. A writer of Justinian's period said it seemed "not to rest upon a solid foundation, but to cover the space as though it were suspended by a golden chain from heaven."[1]

Western European Art

The Byzantine Empire was the direct descendant of the Roman Empire, but in Northern and Western Europe some people had either never been part of the Roman Empire or had preserved traditions of their own throughout the centuries of Roman rule. Medieval art in Western Europe is varied in style and falls into several major periods: Celtic art in Ireland (600–850); Carolingian *(ca-rol-IN-jee-un),* named for the Frankish emperor Charlemagne (meaning Charles the Great, *Carolus Magnus* in Latin, 800–900); Ottonian (named for German emperors named Otto, 900–1002); Romanesque from 1000 to 1150; Gothic, beginning about 1150 and remaining popular as late as the early 1500s.

The Celtic and Carolingian Periods. Two separate styles, the abstract art of the Northern peoples and the representational art of the Romans, were competing and merging during the Celtic and Carolingian periods. Celtic and other Northern artists specialized in jewelry, weapons, horse gear, and ship

444. Byzantine. Church of Holy Wisdom (Hagia Sophia), Byzantium (now Istanbul). A.D. 532–537. Height of dome 180' (55 m), diameter of dome 108' (33 m).

prows, such as the graceful prow of the Oseberg Viking ship from Norway **[445]**. Ornamental richness was always the aim of the Northern artists, as opposed to the naturalistic pictures and story-telling of Roman art. This struggle between Northern abstraction and Mediterranean naturalism was more than an artistic competition. The Christian church in Ireland, with its headquarters at Armagh *(ar-MAH)*, was busy founding monasteries in Switzerland and even in Italy, monasteries where the Celtic decorative style was used and political allegiance was to Armagh, not to Rome. The conversion of England to Roman Christian allegiance (about 600) and the coronation of the Frankish king Charlemagne *(SHAR-luh-main)* as Holy Roman Emperor on Christmas Day in 800 marked Rome and its pictorial style as the eventual winners of this competition.

The northern people who worshiped the ancient pagan god Wotan had a tradition of burying their kings in ships accompanied by their treasure. Such a buried treasure ship was discovered in a long earth mound in eastern England at a place called Sutton Hoo. It was a memorial to a king, probably one named Redwald who died about A.D. 630, just at the time the British Isles were turning to Christianity. An ornamental helmet with a protective face mask, a sword and shield, silver bowls and dishes, a drinking horn, and a purse containing 37 gold coins minted in France are among the buried treasures. One of the items of personal jewelry is a gold buckle [446], more than 5 inches (13 centimeters) long and nearly a pound (414 grams) in weight, ornamented with bosses and an interlace design. The interlace was the favorite design of all the northern peoples, one they continued to use after their conversion to Christianity.

As a general rule, the farther from Rome, the weaker the Roman classical elements in the new Christian art, and the more it looks like the Oseberg ship [445]. A wonderful example of the meeting of Roman representational art and Northern abstraction is found in Saint Mark's lion in the *Gospels of Saint Wil-*

below left: 445.   Viking. Prow of the Oseberg ship.
c. A.D. 800. University Museum of National Antiquities, Oslo, Norway.

below right: 446.   Anglo-Saxon England. Buckle from Sutton Hoo ship burial.
c. A.D. 625. Gold and enamel; length 5¼" (13 cm), weight 14⅝ oz. (414 g).
British Museum, London

447. Celtic, Ireland. Lion of Saint Mark, from the *Gospels of Saint Willibrord*. C. A.D. 690. Manuscript illumination. Bibliothèque Nationale, Paris.

librord **[447]**, which was painted in Ireland about 690. The artist sprang from a long tradition of artists in metal, such as those who made the Sutton Hoo treasure, but he must have had a naturalistic picture of a lion to copy, a picture imported from the lands around the Mediterranean. But if you compare the lion's coat with the Oseberg ship **[445]** or the Sutton Hoo belt buckle **[446]**, the inspiration for that curly pattern is clear. The frame is not merely a window; it is as important as the lion, with an intriguing mirror symmetry. To an artist living in the vast and undisciplined world of the end of the 7th century, that frame design must have suggested a heavenly order and dependability.

Charlemagne was a king of the Franks who conquered most of Western Europe to create a new empire in lands which had been part of the Roman Empire four and five hundred years earlier. In 800, when he was crowned Roman Emperor by the Pope in Rome, his ambition was actually to revive the Roman Empire, with the stability, security, grandeur, and cultural achievements that went with that name. A revival of education and literacy was a basic necessity. Monasteries were established which functioned like modern universities in their educational and cultural roles, and they became centers for the copying and illustration of books. Since all books were hand-written, hand-copying was the only way to obtain another copy, and hand-painted ornament became an indispensable part of a book. The story-telling power of Mediterranean pictorial art had an obvious appeal to Charlemagne and his advisers. Pictures could serve an educational and propaganda function which Celtic abstraction, beautiful and spiritual as it was, could not. Thus Charlemagne's sponsorship went to the copying of books with Roman-style illustrations.

In Roman books a portrait of the author was customary, shown with his muse, the messenger from God who told him what to write, and that became a Christian tradition. Bibles and prayer books were the most beautiful books produced by Charlemagne's scribes; they included portraits of Matthew, Mark, Luke, and John, who wrote the Gospels, the four chapters (or "books") of the Bible which recount the life of Christ. In the *Gospels of Saint Medard of Soisson* [448], Mark is shown as a young man who turns to look up at a winged lion, God's messenger and the usual symbol to identify Mark. (Each of the four "evangelists," or Gospel authors, had a standard symbol; the others are a winged ox for Luke, an eagle for John, and an angel for Matthew. They are very common subjects in medieval art.) Mark is listening to the lion, who reads to him the word of God which Mark will transcribe. In a similar way, the scribe, who did the lettering, and the artist, who painted the illustrations, were also copying from earlier books.

The *Gospels of Saint Medard of Soisson* was copied at Charlemagne's court about 800, probably for the emperor himself. The artist was surely copying from an older book in a more Roman or Hellenistic style. The actual book he was

448. Carolingian. Saint Mark, from the *Gospels of Saint Medard of Soisson*. c. A.D. 800. Manuscript illumination. Bibliothèque Nationale, Paris.

copying no longer exists, but we can imagine its style as similar to Roman and Hellenistic wall painting [442]. Traces of that Mediterranean style are still found in the little "cameos" in the frame and the arch, as well as in the angel and saint in landscapes in the upper corners. Despite his patronage and the book given him to copy, this artist was more interested in the abstract patterns he could make. The draperies become a set of angular lines, the capitals of the columns become flower-like shapes. The bench and desk he put into a reverse perspective so they seem to grow larger as they recede in space, a system of representation not used by Roman artists. The result is a new style that is more abstract than its classical ancestors, but still much more naturalistic than traditional Celtic and Viking art.

Romanesque Style. Many Christians expected the end of the world and the Last Judgment to occur during the year 1000, but when it became clear that the world would continue they began to build more ambitious and durable churches and to ornament them with art in the **Romanesque** style: massive religious buildings using Roman-like round arches, ornamented with relief sculptures and mural painting in a dynamic linear style.

After 1000, with the vast migrations of earlier times a thing of the past and the Vikings, pagan raiders for centuries, turning to more settled and Christian ways, life in Western Europe was much more peaceful and orderly, and large building and artistic projects could be organized. The great project of the period, however, was the Crusades, which were religious-military missions to try to reconquer Jerusalem from the Muslims, efforts that took people out of their provincial villages into the great world. Pilgrimages to religious shrines, a peaceful form of travel, were even more popular. After Jerusalem, the second most popular pilgrimage was to the tomb of the apostle Saint James (in Spanish, Santiago) at Compostela in northwestern Spain, but there were shorter pilgrimages to many famous shrines. In other words, religion was the unifying factor in medieval life and art.

The Romanesque church at Vézelay *(vay-zuh-LAY)* in eastern France was an especially fine building of that time. Vézelay was a pilgrimage shrine dedicated to Mary Magdalene and a starting place for the pilgrimages to Santiago in Spain. Perhaps most importantly, it was the starting point for the Second and Third Crusades, whose members confidently set out to save the souls of strange foreign peoples, the same mission that Christ gave to his apostles as he sent them out into the world. The sculpture of the main portal [449] shows Christ above the door in the area called the **tympanum** *(TIM-pah-num)*, with rays of light bursting from his hands, giving their mission to the apostles. The peoples of those unknown lands are shown below and in frames around the main scene as humans with gigantic ears, pig snouts, and dog heads, all dressed as pilgrims to the shrine of Vézelay. Healing, one of the missionary's duties, is shown around the arch above, and the zodiac, representing God's control of time, appears in the outer border.

The sculptor was able to represent clouds behind Christ, a subject you might not expect in carved stone. Incised lines and shapes with sharp edges in the clouds, but also in the clothing and other subjects, show a sculptural style based on drawing. Originally these sculptures were painted (the paint has long since worn off), which must have made them look even more like drawings or paintings. You can see that Romanesque sculptors learned their art in large measure from decorated books. The shallow space of the relief and the restless lines give the composition terrific nervous energy—enough to send you off on a crusade or a pilgrimage.

Medieval churches used a standardized floor plan [450] in the shape of a cross, the vertical post of the cross symbolized by the main area of the church, called the **nave**, and the crossbar of the cross symbolized by two wings on the

449. French Romanesque. Portal, Abbey Church of La Madeleine, Vézelay, France, 1125–1135.

building, called the north and south **transepts**. The transepts always faced north and south because the church always had its main doors toward the west, and the congregation inside always faced east, toward the altar and the hopeful symbol of the sunrise, which symbolized rebirth. After the year 1000, as church buildings began to be more elaborate, stone vaults replaced wooden ceilings to make the churches more fireproof and to improve the sound of the musical services held in them. At Vézelay the vaulted ceiling is dramatized by alternating

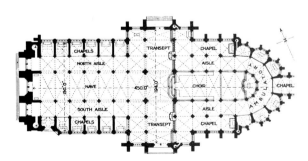

450. Plan of Amiens Cathedral, France.

451. French Romanesque.
Interior, Abbey Church of La Madeleine, Vézelay, France. 1125–1135.

light and dark stone in the main ribs of the vault **[451]**. The builders were proud of the vaults, which were expensive and hard to build, and they wanted to be sure they were noticed.

    While the imperial churches of Byzantium were decorated with mosaic, the modest churches of western Europe had painted walls and ceilings, a much less expensive form of decoration. The monastery church at Saint-Savin in western France has some of the best-preserved paintings of this period in its stone vaulted ceilings. Painted in a few earth colors in a slashing linear style, they tell stories from the Old Testament with the energy of news photographs. At the building of the Tower of Babel God suddenly appears to the toiling masons

Recognizing the Great Styles

One of the greatest of all medieval Christian monasteries was the Benedictine Abbey of Cluny, in eastern France, the mother church of about 1450 monastery churches spread far and wide in western Europe between about 1000 and 1100, one of which was the church at Vézelay.

A plan [452] of the monastery of Cluny shows the huge church like a double-armed cross (today only one "arm," or transept, still stands). To the right of the church are the cloister and the refectory (dining hall), the chapter house for meetings, the infirmary, and the priory, where the monks had rooms. At the main entrance through the monastery walls was the abbot's palace. Mixed among these buildings were stables, laundry, bakery, granary, and gardens. About three hundred monks lived here in 1100, which was an unusually large number for a monastery.

Religious services were the main duty of the monks, who were called by the bell to services every three or four hours, beginning with Matins at midnight. In winter and in Lent they ate only one meal; in summer, when food was more plentiful and more farm work was required, a noon meal and a supper were served. Meat was forbidden, but fish, fowl, and eggs were eaten, and even meat was allowed in the infirmary. No talk was permitted—speech and song were reserved for the religious services—and at meals a monk read aloud from a religious book. In the smaller monasteries there was much work to be done: growing food, cooking, cleaning, weaving cloth, and so on. At wealthy Cluny hired servants and specialists did much of the hard work, leaving the monks free to develop elaborate rituals and church music.

Monastic life is hard for us to imagine, but secular life of that period is equally foreign to us. Even great nobles lived in one or two main rooms, with no privacy and almost no furniture, while peasants had one-room hovels. Joan Evans wrote of "the fantastic ecstasy and the ascetic ferocity of medieval religion," and of the churches of the Cluny monks as "irradiated by an entirely human love of beauty, dignity and splendour." The beauties of ritual, music, architecture, and art were rare in medieval times but abundant in the life of Cluny's monks.

Quotations from Joan Evans, *The Romanesque Architecture of the Order of Cluny* (Cambridge: Cambridge University Press, 1938) 152. See also Christopher Brooke, *The Monastic World, 1000–1300* (New York: Random House, 1974) esp. 59–74.

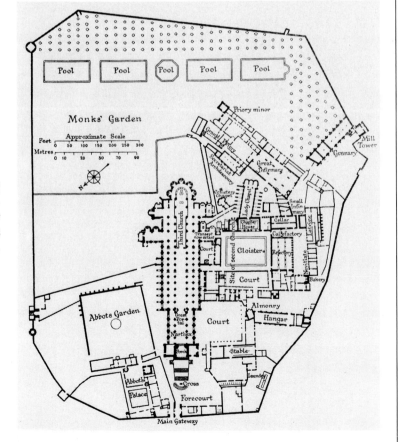

452. French Romanesque. Plan of the monastery of Cluny, Saône-et-Loire, France, showing the Abbey Church and monastic buildings as they were in the 17th century.

453. French Romanesque. The building of the Tower of Babel, Church of Saint-Savin-sur-Gartempe, France. c. 1125. Ceiling fresco in the vault.

hauling stones on their shoulders [453]. The dynamism of God is manifest in his whirling pose and flying robes, both expressed by strong open lines. Judging by its art, the religion of the Romanesque period would seem to have been active and energetic, not much given to quiet meditation.

Gothic Style. The **Gothic** style was the final statement of the Middle Ages, and its greatest achievements are in church architecture. The aim was to make buildings as tall and open to light as possible, with pointed arches reach-

454. French Gothic. West front, Chartres Cathedral, France. Façade c. 1194–1260, south tower (right) c. 1180, north tower (left) 1507–1513; width 157′ (47.6 m), height of south tower 344′ (104.9 m), height of north tower 377′ (114.9 m).

ing heavenward, sunlight streaming through the stained-glass windows that told Bible stories, and the stone columns and walls ornamented with sculptures of sacred history. Gothic stone masons are among the few builders in history who used their material at the very limit of its strength, finally achieving church towers in lacy stonework taller than a 50-story building. In the hundred years from 1140 to 1240 about twenty gigantic churches were begun in northern France, which was the creative center of the Gothic style. The prosperous cities of that region wanted to be proud of their churches; thus they supported one of the most ambitious bursts of creative energy ever seen. All the neighboring countries—especially England, the Low Countries, Germany, and Spain—also participated in the Gothic style.

The Cathedral of Chartres (SHAR-truh) was one of the earlier churches built in this style. Many of the younger masons and sculptors who learned their trades as apprentices at Chartres later worked on other well-known churches, carrying its style to their new jobs. The church is famous for its two different towers [454], the older (built about 1180, on the right) in the simple early Gothic style, the newer (1507–1513) in the later Flamboyant Gothic style. The oldest part of the church is its main portals [455], along with the south tower the only parts of the church to survive a disastrous fire in 1194. Their style represents the transition from Romanesque to Gothic, with the linear patterns and shapes of drapery and ornament dominant over the mass of the figures and forms, recalling the earlier source of medieval style in drawing. Each figure is unique, but in the early Gothic sculpture not much attention is paid to individual personality.

455. French Gothic. Main (west) portals, Chartres Cathedral, France. c. 1145–1155.

As the Gothic style developed over its four-hundred-year span, sculptural figures grew more massive, less linear, and more individualized.

Christ at the Last Judgment appears over the center door, with the elongated figures of biblical kings and queens on the columns flanking the doors. If you compare these columns with those of ancient Greek buildings, which are all alike, the variety of Gothic building is overwhelming: the figures are all different, as are the decorative patterns on the shafts, and the sculptured stories in the capitals.

When you go inside the church [456], at first glance all the columns holding up the vaults look similar, but they too are varied: large round columns with small octagonal colonnettes alternating with large octagonal columns with small round colonnettes. Thus the two different towers on the front, built about three hundred years apart in different styles, are not simply strange, but are part of the general variety of the style.

Later Gothic sculptors began to portray specific individuals, in contrast to the earlier depiction of people as types. Ekkehard and Uta [457] on Naumburg Cathedral in East Germany look so much like portraits from life that it is hard to believe that the artist never could have met them; that noble couple lived about two hundred years before their portraits were carved. Ekkehard is something more than the typical rugged warrior, and Uta expresses a pride and sensitivity that go beyond good looks. In facial features, body build, clothing, gesture, and expression of personality they are portrayed as specific individuals.

Illustrated books continued to be an important place for Gothic paintings, but there was not much opportunity for mural painting because Gothic churches had such large windows that there was little wall space. The solution

left: 456. French Gothic. Interior, Chartres Cathedral, France. 1194–1260.

below: 457. German Gothic. Ekkehard and Uta, Naumburg Cathedral, East Germany. 1250–1260. Stone.

Recognizing the Great Styles

A POINT IN TIME: Villard de Honnecourt's Sketchbook

Villard de Honnecourt salutes you, and implores all who will work with the aid of this book to pray for his soul, and remember him. For in this book one may find good advice for the great art of masonary, and the construction of carpentry; and you will find therein the art of drawing, the elements being such as the discipline of geometry requires and teaches.

With those words the French master mason Villard introduced his book of drawings, covering architectural plans and elevations, building-machine designs, human figures and sacred scenes, animals, and even a fly and a grasshopper. The drawings in the book were collected over Villard's whole lifetime, between about 1230 and 1280, beginning as sketches done for himself and finally left as a manual for his successors. It is now in the National Library in Paris.

"Leo" [458] was inscribed by Villard: "Here is a lion seen from the front. Please remember that he was drawn from life." Although to our eyes the drawing may not look very natural, it is important that Villard drew from the living animal in a traveling menagerie, not from his imagination. Perhaps he mentioned that to impress us with his courage, for the lion looks fierce. We often think of Gothic art as devoted solely to religious subjects, but Villard reminds us that Gothic artists were also fascinated by nature. Even so, it was hard to overcome the training in geometry that was especially important for a mason and architect. The head of the lion still shows traces of the perfect circle Villard drew as a basis for the top of the head down to the nose.

Villard also drew pictures of the training of a lion, commenting:

I will tell you of the training of the lion. He who trains the lion has two dogs. When he wants to make the lion do anything, he commands him to do it. If the lion growls, the man beats the dogs. When the lion sees how the dogs are beaten he becomes afraid. His courage disappears and he does what he is commanded. I will not speak of when he is in a rage, for then he would not obey anyone's wish either good or bad.

Villard's understanding of the psychology of the lion reflects the ideas of his time in the same way his drawing reflects the style of his time, with its regular pattern of curls in the mane and its flat shapes for the head and body.

All quotations are from H. R. Hahnloser, *Villard de Honnecourt* (Vienna, 1935).

458. Villard de Honnecourt. *Leo*, from the *Sketchbook* of Villard de Honnecourt. c. 1240. Lead or silverpoint on parchment drawn over in brown ink (probably bistre), c. 10½ × 6¼" (27 × 16 cm). Bibliothèque Nationale, Paris.

to that problem was to fill the windows with stained glass. At Chartres Cathedral there are 394 stained-glass windows, originally valued for their power to tell stories to the illiterate, but now among the priceless treasures of world art. "Stained glass" gives the wrong impression since the glass was colored all the way through, cut into solid-color shapes, and fitted together in lead frames (called "cames") to form designs. "Mosaic glass" would be a more accurate name. The only color painted onto the glass was a brownish-black enamel used for details. A window in the south aisle of Chartres shows the creation of Adam,

above: 459. French Gothic. The creation of Adam and Eve and the temptation, Chartres Cathedral (third window of south aisle of nave). 1200–1225. Stained-glass window.

right: 460. Giotto. *The Kiss of Judas*. 1305–1306. Fresco, 7′7″ × 7′9″ (2.3 × 2.4 m). Scrovegni Chapel, Padua, Italy.

Adam in the Garden of Eden, the creation of Eve, and the temptation [459]. The illustration is just a small part of a large window put together with innumerable small pieces of colored glass which make the figures and the background patterns. The heaviest black lines are iron bars that frame the window in sections. The smaller black lines are lead cames that hold each piece of glass in place. That technology led to the simplified forms and landscape elements. Light makes the frames less noticeable and brings out the jewel-like brilliance of the colors: a powerful ruby red, a deep celestial blue. Gothic windows are one of the first great light shows.

In Italy, where the sun is stronger, there was less desire to replace the walls with glass. Mural painters, of whom the most famous was Giotto (JAH-to) (1266?–1337) of Florence, had many commissions, one of the most important of them the whole interior of the Arena Chapel in Padua. About 1305 Giotto painted the life of Christ, of which *The Kiss of Judas* [460] is a part. For an audience long accustomed to the style we see in the Saint Savin murals [453], Giotto's style was amazingly natural, but it was in harmony with the main trend in Gothic style toward expressions of mass and psychology, as we see in *Ekkehard and Uta*. Giotto shaded the figures in light and shadow as had not been done in many centuries, and in scale and action they appear lifelike. In the center Judas kisses Christ to identify him to the soldiers who have come to arrest him. Peter, at left, as he tries to protect Christ, cuts off the ear of the high priest's servant. Earlier painters were often effective story-tellers, but Giotto's lifelike figures expressed the drama of the story by the naturalness of their facial expressions and the movement of their bodies. That naturalness was the part of Gothic art that later Renaissance painters wanted to keep and improve. Long after Giotto's death the ruler of Florence had an inscription put up on his tomb: "Lo, I am he by whom dead painting was restored to life, to whose right hand all was possible, by whom art became one with nature. . . ." After Giotto's time, it was not until the 20th century that artists and the public again grew interested in the kind of abstract art found in the early medieval illustrated manuscripts.

Art of Islam

When Islam (which means "commitment") burst upon the world scene in 622, the year Mohammed founded the new religion in Arabia, its followers rapidly conquered a vast territory. In 639 Islamic armies invaded Egypt (then part of the Christian empire of Byzantium) and in forty years they conquered all of North Africa. The Great Mosque of Kairouan [461], in Tunisia, founded in 675,

461. Islamic.
Great Mosque, Kairouan, Tunisia.
c. A.D. 675. Aerial view.

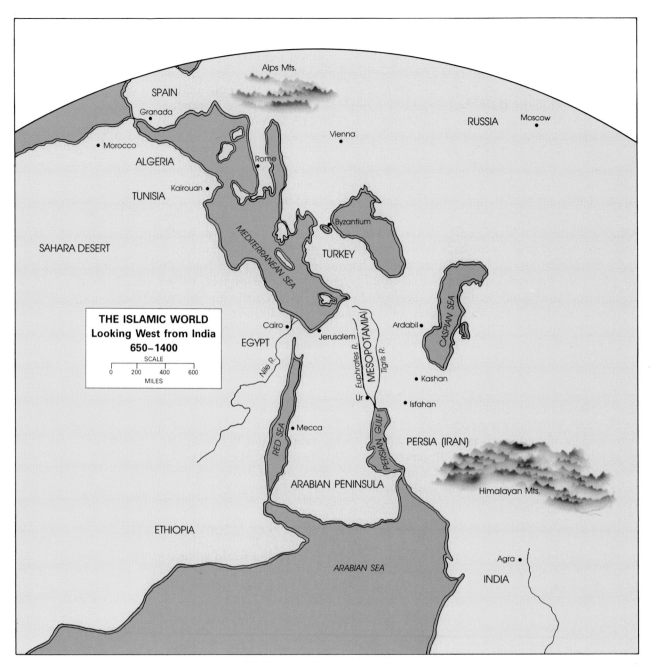

THE ISLAMIC WORLD
Looking West from India
650–1400

SCALE
0   200   400   600
MILES

shows the large flat-roofed assemby hall, open courtyard, and tower *(minaret)* built by the Islamic conquerors. Eventually all the desert regions of northern Africa were converted to Islam, but the forest and agricultural lands of central Africa continued to follow their own traditions in religion and art, to be discussed later.

Although Islam inherited many varied art traditions—among them Mesopotamian, Roman, and Christian—it molded them together into one of the most integrated styles in the world. Besides the laws and lore of the religion and the use of the Arabic language in its observance, Muslims (the followers of Islam) were unified by a sense of the contrast between the earthly and the infinite. Unlike Christianity, Islam provided no religious patronage for representational art (which might encourage idolatry), so we find no statues or paintings in religious buildings or books. Instead representational art is found only in the regions that already had a picture-making tradition, where it was limited to secular subjects. The religion was expressed by abstraction and writing or by any design that conveyed the perfection of the eternal or the infinite.

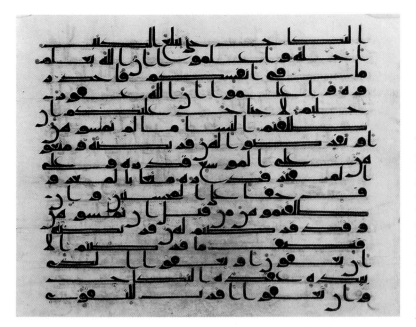

462. Islamic, North Africa. Page from the Koran in Kufic script. c. A.D. 1000. Ink and opaque watercolor on vellum, 12⅝ × 15⅝" (32 × 40 cm). Los Angeles County, California, Museum of Art (Nesli M. Heeramaneck Collection, gift of Joan Palevsky).

A page [462] from the Koran, the Islamic holy book, shows the most admired kind of early Islamic art: the holy word turned into a pattern, unmarred by any image of a mortal thing. **Calligraphy**, the art of writing, is the supreme art of Islam; it serves as the basic ornament on buildings, pottery, and metalwork and to a great extent takes the place of painting. There are many different writing styles, each with its own expressive character; this example is in Kufic script of about A.D. 1000 from North Africa.

Written inscriptions from the Koran naturally were common decorations on religious assembly halls, or **mosques.** In a mosque the direction of Mecca, the center of Islam, is indicated by an empty niche which is especially decorated. In the Friday Mosque [463] in Isfahan, Iran, the niche (called a *mihrab*), has bands of

463. Islamic, Iran. Mihrab of Oljaytu, Friday Mosque, Isfahan, Iran 14th century.

464. Islamic, Iran. Portal, Royal Mosque, Isfahan, Iran. 17th century.

writing forming the decoration around both the pointed arches, in their rectangular frames, and even worked into the vine pattern filling the larger arch.

But any idea that suggests infinity conveys the religious idea. The great courtyard of the Royal Mosque in Isfahan has gigantic arched niches **[464]** in the center of each side, each large arch containing a half-dome filled with small half-domes, all covered with blue patterned tiles. This beautiful effect was called "honeycomb" or "stalactite" vaulting (*muqarnas* in Arabic) and was popular in Islamic art.

The Islamic rulers of southern Spain built a famous palace in Granada called the Alhambra (*al-AHM-brah*) which has renowned "stalactite" ceilings

465. Islamic, Spain. Ceiling, Hall of the Two Sisters, Alhambra Palace, Granada, Spain. 1350–1400. "Stalactite" vaulting.

466. Islamic, India. Mughal Empire. The Taj Mahal, Agra, India.
c. 1635. White marble; 186' (56.7 m) square, height of dome 187' (57 m).

[465]. Made of wood and plaster in an uncountable number of tiny dome segments, these are very light in weight. Since the one shown has sixteen windows around the base of the upper dome, it almost appears to float in the air, weightless and filled with light.

The dome has a long, rich history in the Islamic world. One of the most beautiful domed buildings ever built is the tomb of the Mughal Empress Mumtaz Mahal in Agra, India, called the Taj Mahal **[466]**. The design is symmetrical, with the bulbous dome seeming to float like a huge balloon above the pointed arches whose shape it repeats. The Emperor, Shah Jahan, is supposed to have planned a black marble tomb for himself, facing the Taj Mahal's white marble, but it was never built.

The Mughal Empire in northern India, of which Shah Jahan was the third emperor (reigned 1627–1659), attracted painters from Iran (or Persia) where pictorial painting had long been popular (see Figure **93**). Works of European art were also purchased by the court, and it became a center for representational art

467.   Bichitr. *A Mughal
Prince in a Garden*.
Mughal Empire, India.
c. 1620. Tempera.
15¼ × 10½″
(39 × 27 cm).
Chester Beatty Library,
Dublin.

such as *A Mughal Prince in a Garden* [467], painted by Bichitr (*BICH-it-er*) for
Emperor Jahangir (reigned 1605–1627). Bichitr, a Hindu artist from India, was
mainly a portrait painter, and his ability to make convincing likenesses is displayed in this painting. It has a wonderful mood of serenity, with refreshments
being served, a singer entertaining, and in the background a flower garden and
a beautiful sunset. The subject is not religious, but secular, and cosmopolitan in
its sources. Persian manuscript painting stands behind the flat decorative colors
and patterns. European Renaissance art suggested the natural, three-dimensional poses of the figures, but these sources are merged in an original style.

Two arts, ceramics and textiles, are especially associated with the Islamic
countries of western Asia, from which they spread through North Africa and
Spain to Europe. A bowl signed by the artist Abu Zayd and dated 1187 has a
painting of a mounted prince with his retinue [468]. This is an early example of
pottery decorated with colored **enamels** on a glazed soft **porcelain** (or frit-ware),

which quickly became very popular. Abu Zayd lived in the Iranian city of Kashan, an early center of polychrome (that is, multicolored) pottery. Potters made not only bowls and dishes, but also colored tiles, which became a popular veneer for fine buildings inside and out, as in the Royal Mosque [464].

Central and western Asia was a great center for textile arts from the earliest times. The oldest pile carpet known in the world, made about 500 B.C., was found in a central Asian tomb and "Persian" rugs (many of them made in other countries) have been treasured for more than two thousand years. Used to cover floors, tables, or walls, they are a basic element of interior design in that region, but they have also been a very valuable export to other regions. The Ardabil rug [469] is one of a pair woven in wool pile cloth in northwestern Iran in 1539–1540. It has what is called a yellow "medallion" in the center and a deep blue background with a complicated pattern of plants and flowers. This famous pair of rugs was made for an important mosque in Ardabil; their design was meant to suggest a perfect flower garden, which was a symbol of heaven.

Compare this carpet with the dome in the Alhambra, which is similar in pattern. If you think the Islamic builders and artists were trying to design a paradise on earth, you are not far from the truth.

below: 468. Abu Zayud of Kashan, Iran. A mounted prince and his retinue. A.D. 1187. Glazed ceramic bowl; diameter 8½" (22 cm), height 3¾" (10 cm). Metropolitan Museum of Art, New York (Fletcher Fund, 1964).

right: 469. Maksud of Kashan. Ardabil rug, detail, Tabriz, Iran. 1539–1540. Silk warp and weft, wool pile; 36'6" × 17'6" (11.1 × 5.3 m). Victoria and Albert Museum, London.

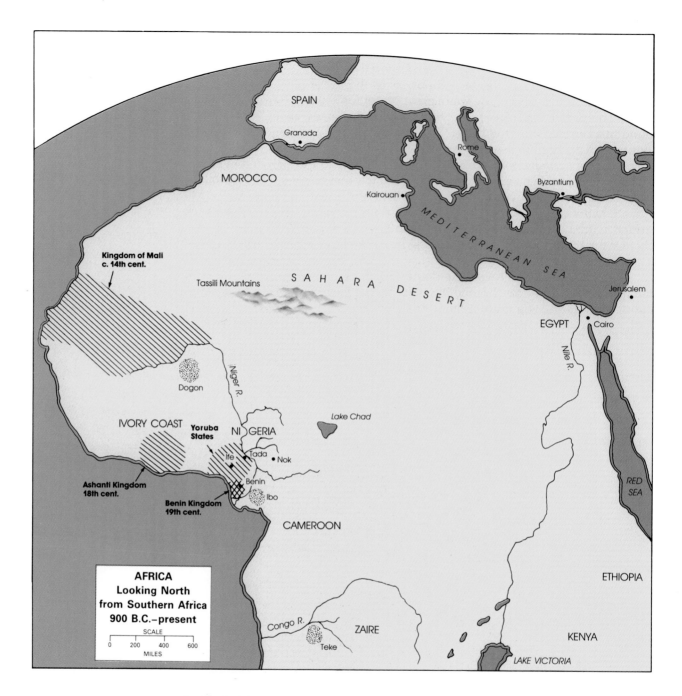

AFRICA
Looking North
from Southern Africa
900 B.C.–present

SCALE

0   200   400   600
MILES

Art of Africa

It is interesting to look at African and Islamic art together because they complement each other so well. Architecture and its decoration were the principal arts in Islam, with sculpture practically unknown, but sculpture is the greatest of the African arts.

African arts divides into two parts: royal art and commoners' art; the difference is based on process. Metal and ceramic, both worked with fire, were the main materials of royal art. Commoners did not have free access to metal techniques, particularly because the royal courts controlled the forging and casting of metal into weapons and tools, as well as art, and treated the craft as a kind of religious ritual. The spiritual symbolism of fire is based on its power to transform and refine materials that pass through it, as ore and clay are transformed. Ivory was also a royal material, but only because it was rare and valuable. In more recent times arts and crafts using fire have spread beyond the traditional courts, but even today art used for popular ceremonies is usually carved of wood or is made of unfired clay or mud. It is easy to see why almost all the most ancient African art is royal art: ceramics and metal are much more durable than wood and unfired clay or mud.

The little ceramic head from Nok *(nahk)* [470], in Nigeria, is so old—maybe as early as 900 B.C.—that we do not know much about the people who made it, except that they were using fire to work iron as well as pottery clay. Some of their ceramic figures are as large as 4 feet (1.2 meters) tall, and all of them have a simplified or stylized naturalism that we see in this head. It has a childlike look, with its bulbous head and big eyes, but the beard and moustache tell us it is a grown man. From the strange hairdo as well as the ceramic material, we might guess that it represents someone associated with a royal court.

470. Nok culture. Head of a man. 900 B.C.–A.D. 200. Ceramic, height 5½" (14 cm). Jos Museum, Nigeria.

The head from Nok also tells us some important things about the African style. Although it has sometimes been thought that African art lacks a long history, the Nok figure shows us there is a tradition of art going back nearly three thousand years in the core region, the African coast from the Ivory Coast to Cameroon, where the style of sub-Saharan Africa was first established. The *African style* is defined by its concern for simplified sculptural masses, as we see in the forms of the Nok head, with references to nature but with abstraction dominant. Lines, shapes, textures, and colors may be applied to the large masses, but the unity of the design always depends on the main masses. In two-dimensional arts, such as painting and textiles, shape replaces mass as the element that unifies designs.

From about 800 to 1400 is the finest period of African royal art in the lands of the Ibo and Yoruba peoples of Nigeria. A seated man [471] is represented a little under life-size in a bronze sculpture from the town of Tada. It has been

471. Ife culture. Seated man, Tada, Nigeria. c. 10th century. Bronze, height 21" (53 cm). Ife Museum, Ife, Nigeria.

472. Ife culture. A queen of Ife. c. 1200. Ceramic, height 9¼" (25 cm). Ife Museum, Ife, Nigeria.

damaged by a thousand years of ritual washing and polishing. This plump man is surely no hardworking farmer, but probably a king, as his proud and serious face seems to tell us. Although the figure is smooth and made to look perfect it is not abstract. The artist's intention to make the figure true to nature is evident if you look at the ear or the foot.

Several noble portraits of ancient kings and queens of Ife (*EE-fay;* now a city in Nigeria) have been found in excavations there, most of them just heads **[472]**. They seem to have been attached to clothed wooden bodies for the funeral and for preservation in a memorial shrine. We do not know the name of that thoughtful young woman of eight hundred years ago, but her crown tells us she was a ruler. She probably died of old age, but she was portrayed as youthful and beautiful. African sculptors, like the classical Greeks, idealized the subjects of their portraits. That, along with the artist's skill, led Europeans to imagine, when these sculptures were first discovered, that a Greek artist must have made them, or at least taught the Ife sculptors. But these portraits are entirely African in style and technology: they were made of the royal materials—metal or ceramic—in a sculptural style using large abstract masses to represent natural forms, with lines, patterns, and textures for contrast with smooth masses.

Although metal, ceramic, and ivory were traditionally worked only in the royal courts, wood-carving was a democratic art and could be done by anyone without restriction. But the African audience has always had very definite ideas about quality, and a master wood sculptor is well known and admired. Although their work can be bought by commoners, they are also patronized by royalty. Olowe of Ise, for example, who died in 1938, was commissioned to carve wooden doors for the royal palaces of several Yoruba kings ruling the old city states which have been incorporated into modern Nigeria. About 1910 he carved doors [473] for the ruler called the Ogoga of Ikere, who is shown seated on his throne on the left door, surrounded by his courtiers. On the other door is shown the district commissioner of the British Empire sitting in a litter carried by two porters, with all his expedition. These doors are about 6 feet (1.8 meters) high, and the figures are carved in high relief. You can tell by the broken figure (lower right) that they stand nearly free of the background.

Wood sculpture is certainly a very ancient art, but since wood rots, ancient wood sculptures are very rare. Fortunately, there is a living tradition of wood sculpture. Mashudi, a modern sculptor from the city of Meko, carved the mask [474] used in the annual Gelede (*guh-luh-DAY*) ceremony in honor of the feminine powers of the universe. A dancer wore this mask, which represents snakes eating a monkey. Not only is it a complicated design, it was also painted and in motion it must have made a striking display. The Gelede ceremony is meant to be entertaining, and many of the masks, like this one, have no religious symbolism, but illustrate popular sayings or current topics.

The other material used in popular religious art is mud, a material that has deep meaning as the flesh of the earth spirit. Mud sculptures are made to honor

below left: 473. Olowe of Ise. Doors, Palace of the Ogoga, Ikere, Nigeria. c. 1910. Wood, height c. 6' (1.8 m). Museum of Mankind, London.

below: 474. Yoruba, Republic of Benin. Gelede mask. Early 20th century. Wood, paint; height 14½" (37 cm). Walt Disney Imagineering, Glendale, California.

left: 475. Ibo of Nigeria. The traditional god of thunder in modern dress, with his wife, Owerri, Nigeria. 1966. Mud, wood, string, earth pigments, iron; height 4'6" (1.4 m).

above: 476. Teke culture, Zaire. Kidumu mask. 19th or early 20th century. Wood, fiber; height 14" (36 cm), width 12¼" (31 cm). Walt Disney Imagineering, Glendale, California.

the gods, especially Ala, the earth goddess, and Amadioha, the sky god [475]. A framework of wood and string supports the dried mud, which is painted, but mud sculptures are not meant to last more than a few days. When the ceremony is over the sculptures are allowed to return to the earth from which they came. For that reason we have only recent examples, despite the fact that this kind of art has a long tradition. The careful work lavished on such ephemeral art, made to last no more than a day, points up another feature of much popular art in Africa: the process of making it and the occasion of showing it are important, but keeping it later as a treasure is of no concern.

European and American artists and their public suddenly became very much interested in African art at the beginning of this century. African sculpture provided models for an art entirely different from the late Renaissance styles which at that time seemed exhausted. Although everyone admitted the Ife sculptures were fine, it was the more abstract styles that inspired modern artists on other continents. The colorful low-relief disk of the Kidumu mask [476] made by the Teke people of Zaire barely suggests a face, with its tiny eyes and nose. The symmetrical design is roughly cut in geometric designs and colored red and white. Hanks of fiber were laced through the holes at the edge to hide the dancer who wore the mask. The inventiveness and power of the design, which seems to copy nothing in nature, but is just pure art, appealed to people who knew nothing about its use or symbolism in Africa. Kidumu masks may originally have been used in rituals of political power, but the meaning of the design remains unknown despite the fact that such masks are still made. The power of the design, with its simple geometric shapes in a symmetrical order, each shape bordered by a line and a relief frame and given a flat white paint, satisfies a human desire for order that appears here in a purely African style. Artists and audiences in other countries felt no need to understand the original African subject and content; they simply adopted African wood sculpture as a part of Modern art, giving it new meanings of naturalness, purity, and spontaneity.

Art in China

The thousand years from about A.D. 400 to 1400 were the greatest period in Chinese history. For nearly three centuries (618–907, the Tang Dynasty) the Chinese Empire stretched across most of eastern Asia, from the Caspian Sea to Korea and Vietnam. Just as Christianity dominated European cultural life, Buddhism spread from India into China and the other Asian countries and inspired most of the art of this period. But China in her greatness was tolerant of other religions and progressive in her government. Still, it is a miracle that any art survives from this period, since wars and revolutions destroyed so much art at the imperial courts, and religious persecutions had the same effect on the great temples and monasteries. Fortunately, making copies and new versions of older masterworks was a respected artistic practice, so there are often good copies of famous works whose originals were long ago destroyed.

The pre-Buddhist Daoist religion inspired the strange figure of a humanized ox [477], which represents one of the constellations of the zodiac, like our Taurus. This painting is an ancient copy of a lost original by Zhang Sengyou *(seng-yo)* (c. 470–550), who was a general and court official. Like many educated people, he was also a serious painter. His audience was made up of people like himself, educated officials of the imperial administration. The strange figure in its graceful flowing robes was painted with watercolor on silk and delicately tinted, the technique most characteristic of Chinese art through the ages. A mound of churning sea water is the only setting. Background settings were

477. Style of Zhang Sengyou. *The Ox Constellation* from *Deities of the Constellations.* c. A.D. 500–550. Ink and color on silk, height 10¾" (27 cm). Municipal Museum, Osaka, Japan.

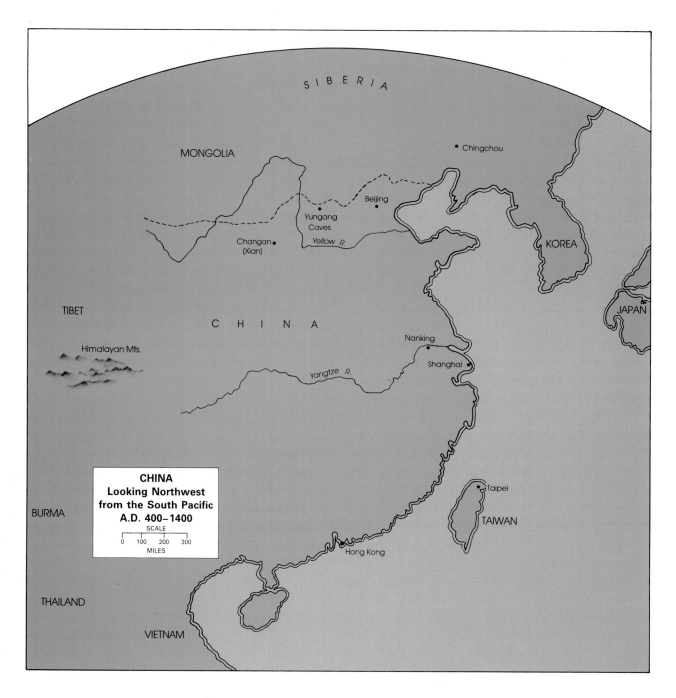

CHINA
Looking Northwest
from the South Pacific
A.D. 400–1400

SCALE

0   100   200   300

MILES

usually ignored in paintings of people and animals in this period, but, in any case, it is hard to imagine what could serve as an appropriate setting for this figure. To our eyes the subject is pure fantasy, but its original audience took it more seriously as a symbol for a season of the year as defined by the stars. Part of the emperor's duties, in which he was assisted by the court, was to carry out rituals to keep the stars and seasons working properly.

The Ox Constellation **[477]** serves as a first step toward defining a Chinese style. The use of the writing brush as the basic tool led to a style dominated by lines, with the flowing gestural quality produced by the brush. Lines make the contours of masses or the edges of shapes; subtly shaded tones of color suggest rounded forms, but do not show shadows and highlights. A setting or landscape is absent or minimal in this work and in much early Chinese art.

But a wonderful style of landscape painting had been invented by 600, called "the blue and green manner." It was supposedly invented by General Li of the Imperial Guards, but no paintings by that famous artist have survived. We can see his style in *Emperor Ming-huang's Journey to Shu* [478], copied by an unknown artist. The finger-like rocks are blue and green, the trees a deeper green, and the sky the tan of the ancient silk, making the scene a fantasy from a story book. The emperor's caravan enters at right with its horses, mules and camels, stops to rest in the center—notice the horse rolling on its back—and disappears into a deep canyon on the left. This style of landscape may have old roots in Buddhist versions of paradise, and it is still a popular style with humble artisans who are content with old traditions. Note the similarities and differences between the *Ox* and the *Journey:* the linear organization of the forms and the modeling of colors are similar, but the landscape introduces a complex composition with foreground, middle, and vast misty background areas, with richer color.

It is not an accident that the *Ox* and the *Journey* were both painted by officers of the imperial army. The subjects of both paintings refer to the whole expanse of the world and the universe, which was the way the Chinese rulers saw their duty, as a universal mandate from heaven to bring order to the world. In a similar way, modern media convey to an audience the sense of mission and the framework of ideas held by modern governments.

"With one small brush I can draw the vast universe," wrote the poet Wang Wei.[2] He is credited with the invention of a poet's style of landscape painting using the writing brush and black ink, sometimes with a little soft color. Al-

478. Tang Dynasty, China. *Emperor Ming-huang's Journey to Shu.* 8th century. Watercolor on silk, 22 × 32″ (56 × 81 cm). National Palace Museum, Taipei, Taiwan.

479. Li Cheng.
*A Solitary Temple amid
Clearing Peaks.*
c. 940–967.
Ink and slight color on
silk; hanging scroll,
height 44″ (112 cm),
width 22″ (56 cm).
Nelson-Atkins Museum
of Art, Kansas City,
Missouri (Nelson Fund).

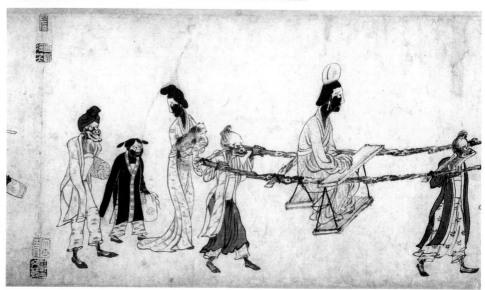

_____ *Recognizing the Great Styles*

though none of Wang Wei's own paintings survive, the style is easy to find among his many successors. This style is considered especially close to writing—the Chinese, like the Muslims, hold **calligraphy** to be the noblest art of all—but it is a development from earlier Chinese pictorial conventions.

A Solitary Temple amid Clearing Peaks [479] was painted by one of the most famous of those successors, Li Cheng, about 950. Li Cheng was a well-educated man of the upper class who painted as a hobby. The Chinese have especially admired that kind of artist, who paints as a form of spiritual meditation, never selling his work but perhaps giving the paintings as gifts to friends. In the country inn in the foreground we see people at their meal. Beyond the temple spreads an immeasurable world of misty mountains animated by long water-falls, not much different in conception from Emperor Ming-huang's Journey to Shu. Li Cheng's style blends lines and tones more subtly, achieving a more natural expression of masses and spaces by the gradations of gray tones. However, light and shadow still play no part.

There is still another side of Chinese fantasy to be found in Jung Kuei, the Demon-Queller, on His Travels [480], painted by Gung Kai in the 1200s. Jung Kuei was a scholar's ghost who was appointed Great Spiritual Demon-Chaser of the Whole Empire by the emperor, who met him in a dream. The Demon-Queller, accompanied by his sister, casts a suspicious look back over his retinue of sub-dued demons. Here the poet's black ink is used as a modern cartoonist might to express weird and funny characters in the simplest possible style. It is hard to believe that seven hundred years separate the ox-headed figure by Zhang Sen-gyou and this painting, they are so similar in technique and style. That style, which was formulated during the Middle Ages, has remained basic in Chinese art down to the present day.

By the Middle Ages sculpture already had a long tradition in China, espe-cially in bronze and ceramic, but the Buddhist religion introduced new subjects and new settings. The 45-foot (13.7-meter)-tall Buddha carved into a cave at Yungang [481] was cut into the living rock of the cliff. It gives an idea of the missionary fervor of the early Buddhists. The front of the cave has collapsed, revealing the sculpture in daylight, but originally it was set in semi-darkness within a deeper cave. Exposure has also resulted in the original paint washing off. The sculptor's idea was a meditating figure in colossal scale, its rich colors seen by lamplight in the cave.

480. Gung Kai. *Jung Kuei, the Demon-Queller, on His Travels.* Southern Song Dynasty. 13th century. Ink on paper, 1'1" × 5'6¾" (0.3 × 1.7 m). Freer Gallery, Smithsonian Institution, Washington, D.C.

above: **481.** China. Colossal Buddha, Cave XX, Yungang, Shansi, China. A.D. 450–500. Stone, height 45' (13.7 m).

above right: **482.** China. Temple model (stupa). Tang Dynasty. Early 8th century. Stone, 27¼ × 24½" (69 × 62 cm). Nelson-Atkins Museum of Art, Kansas City, Missouri.

You can get an idea of what the entrance to such a cave temple looked like from a 2-foot (61-centimeter)-square sculptured temple model **[482]** that once had inside its door a miniature meditating Buddha similar in design to the one at Yungang. This small shrine was protected by fierce guardians—dragons and lions carved on the outer wall—and an energetic dancer is poised above the door. Buddhist sculptors, who did not hesitate to carve caves into cliffs with 45-foot-tall Buddhas inside, seem to have considered stone as soft as butter. They attacked it with confidence, making all the figures on this small shrine twist and whirl in the space imagined within the stone. Looking at that stone surface, it is hard to see it as solid; the fluid lines, curving shapes and masses,

483. China. The god Guanyin. Southern Song Dynasty. c. 1200. Painted wood, height 7'11" (2.4 m). Nelson-Atkins Museum of Art, Kansas City, Missouri.

and varied levels in the relief tend to break down the solidity of the wall and give us a sensation of space. Those are common features of Chinese sculptural style.

That feeling of self-confidence is wonderfully expressed by a Buddhist deity called Guanyin [483], shown relaxing on a rock in his South Sea Island paradise. It is hard to tell that the figure is painted wood, with its complicated draperies, knots, and buckles. The sculptors who carved this, about six hundred years later than the colossal Buddha at Yungang, were trying to create a more human and kindly image than the cool, dignified, and overpowering figure in the cave temple. Yet both these sculptures share certain features of style: masses tend to be submerged in shapes and lines that look as if they could be drawn with a brush. Zhang Sengyou, who drew the *Ox* [477], would have considered it possible to represent Guanyin using his style of lines and tones painted with the brush on silk.

The Middle Ages were a great period for Chinese ceramics, the new element being the introduction of colored glazes, which were used on both sculptures and pots and dishes. The useful vessels reached a perfection rare in history. About the same time the Guanyin was being carved, a potter made the flower pot stand [484] in a pottery type called Jun ware for the use of the imperial court. The form was thrown on the potter's wheel, but then carefully modeled to give it a scalloped rim. Subtle glazes of purplish blue and liver red were fired onto the inside and outside.

When you think of China you probably think of pagodas, the traditional Buddhist towers that originally marked the tombs of saints. Wooden pagodas were once common in China, but the only surviving old pagodas are of brick and stone, plus three mast-like pagodas of cast iron built around 1100. The White Pagoda [485] at Qingzhou *(ching-sho)* in northeastern China shows what the pagoda style was like around 1200: seven octagonal stories with a pointed-dome top. The ornaments on this stone tower are based on traditional ways of building roofs on wooden brackets, but converted into pure decoration on these stone walls.

The imperial palaces of the Middle Ages have long since perished in wars, but the "Forbidden City" district, which was the old imperial palace, in Beijing preserves the old styles pretty much as they were. Beijing still has an ancient city

below left: **484.** China. Jun ware flower pot stand. Yuan-Ming Dynasty. 13th–15th century. Ceramic stoneware, diameter 9¼" (23 cm). Cleveland, Ohio, Museum of Art (John L. Severance Fund, 57.33)

below: **485.** China. White Pagoda. Quingzhou, Jehol, China. 11th or early 12th century. Brick.

plan described by Marco Polo as built to resemble a chessboard, with straight streets running between city gates and each family allotted one square of land (see Chapter 8). The Grand Ancestral Shrine, or Tai Miao [486], now renamed the Working People's Palace of Culture, was built about 1400 following very old plans. It is perfectly symmetrical, raised on a stepped platform and crowned with a massive curving tile roof, and for a wooden structure it is large in scale. The great curving roofs with their deep overhanging eaves were new features of Chinese buildings in the Middle Ages.

The interiors of these palaces were basically **post-and-lintel** constructions in wood decorated with sculpture and painting. A wooden ceiling [487] from a 15th-century Buddhist temple in Beijing shows the kind of elaborate design that could result: the beams form an octagonal cupola with a small dragon in each segment and a super-dragon in the center, all symbolizing the mystic powers of the sky. Like most Chinese sculpture, this cupola was painted. Temple and palace interiors were also ornamented in strong colors, including a powerful red, giving a sumptuous effect that is distinctly Chinese.

Summary for Review

The styles of the Middle Ages were dominated by religion, which directed artists in their choice of which elements and principles to emphasize. Christian artists chose line, color, space, and variety to express the Christian idea of God as creative, energetic, and more concerned with the spirit than the body. Islamic religious art concentrated on calligraphic inscriptions from the Koran, used in decorating mosques, where arches, domes, and tile veneer are typical. Rhythmically repeated designs without central emphasis, which could be extended to infinity, are common. The idea of paradise as an enclosed garden inspired building plans and rugs. African artists considered the materials and techniques: wood and clay belonged to the people, while materials (metal, ceramics) worked by transforming fire belonged to royalty. Sculptural mass and unity were emphasized in idealized natural figures or abstract figures. China's imperial tradition, along with ancient Daoist nature worship, inspired landscape painting in which misty space predominated or demons and dragons appeared. Buddhist art brought sculptures stressing flowing lines that suggested serenity more than action. Artists were often government officials who painted as a hobby for an audience of highly educated scholars and officials, usually using the same brush and ink used for writing. During the Middle Ages art everywhere played a major role in disseminating religion and the beliefs of the ruling class, with the style— emphasizing line or color, mass or space—counting for more than the subject in conveying the ideals of the religion.

Styles of the Columbian Age: 15th–18th Centuries

The five hundredth anniversary of Christopher Columbus' discovery of the Americas has focused attention on the changes produced by that voyage and by the many other explorations of the Columbian Age. The growth of powerful European styles which were carried by explorers to every other continent, the struggle for survival by native traditions, such as that of the Japanese, against the encroaching European styles—those are major themes in the history of world art during that period.

Beginning about 1400, the Renaissance (*REN-nuh-sahns*, from the French for "rebirth," a wide-ranging cultural movement) laid the foundations for the modern world. The many small principalities of the Middle Ages began to consolidate into the modern nation-states, using the modern languages. The growing populations began to concentrate in towns and cities, and trade expanded widely. Though pilgrimages and crusades had accounted for most of the European contacts with other regions in the Middle Ages, by 1400 European commercial interests were leading toward exploration of the whole planet. We often think of modern art as being essentially one style all over the globe, despite many local variations. That tendency toward a global style began with Renaissance (1400–1600) and, especially, Baroque (*buh-ROKE;* 1600–1750) art, which were carried around the world by explorers and colonizers.

The American continents were discovered at least twice by the Europeans, and the different outcomes of those two discoveries are illuminating. Leif Ericsson landed in eastern North America about A.D. 1000, which led to a short-lived colony, but in that period Europe had too few people and too little commerce to take advantage of the new lands. Archaeologists have searched in vain for artifacts or art brought to America by the Vikings. Five hundred years later, with Columbus' discovery, the Europeans were eager to seize the opportunities for the exploitation of capital, raw materials, labor, and markets which the new lands offered. European expansion after 1488 (when the Portuguese first rounded the southern cape of Africa) was responsible for the global unification we see in our own time. The Portuguese reached Japan in 1543, the first contact between the Western countries and that Far Eastern nation—contacts that are still increasing today. Baroque art flourished in such distant regions as Peru and the Philippine Islands, and archaeologists and art historians can scarcely catalogue the abundant remains.

In this chapter we will begin with the art of Italy, Flanders (modern Belgium), and Japan, three countries that made especially distinctive contributions to art during the period after 1400. Each has a style that you will find easy to recognize, yet they share some fundamental attitudes about art and about how societies should manage and use their art. After 1600 Spain, France, Holland,

and Germany were all making important contributions to Baroque and Rococo (*ro-KO-ko*) art, the latter a fanciful and refined style which brought the Renaissance period to a close.

The Renaissance and Baroque styles are close enough to the taste of our own day that many people still think of them as the way "real art" should look. When people speak of the "Old Masters" they mean artists working in the Renaissance and Baroque styles. The Renaissance was a major revolution in art, one that required nearly a century to accomplish, but a revolution, nevertheless: different groups in society began to play the roles in art, different kinds of materials came into use, and different subjects became popular. The Baroque style represents the secure establishment of the new order in art, one which in many respects lasted right up to the beginning of our century. Many people still accept ideas about art that are the inventions of the Renaissance and Baroque critics and audience. As you read about these periods and look at their art, ask yourself whether those attitudes and styles still have contemporary validity for you.

The Renaissance in Italy

Italian people of the 15th century called their own period modern times, just as we do ours, but in the 19th century historians began to call it the "Renaissance'" since the rebirth of interest in Greek and Roman Classical styles in art and literature was an important feature of the period. Behind that change, and many others, was one that is often neglected: the emergence of bankers and business people as a new class of art patrons. Their interests played a large part in shaping the new style.

Artists and Patrons

Now we take it for granted that wealthy individuals patronize the arts, but we inherited that assumption directly from the Renaissance. The patrons of art in earlier periods were the nobility and the church. In the 15th century a new class of business people attained wealth and rank by their own efforts and intelligence, unlike the nobility, who had inherited rank and property, or the leaders of the church, whose positions depended on the institution. The children of successful business people were often happy to accept a noble title or a position in the church; the younger members of the Medici (*MED-ih-chee*) family, most important of the Florentine bankers, became dukes and even popes. But it was their banker grandparents who were the greatest patrons of art.

These new patrons were first of all interested in immortalizing themselves. Lorenzo de' Medici, nicknamed "the Magnificent" [488], was the third generation of a long line of his family to rule the city of Florence. His portrait, modeled by Verrocchio (*vuh-ROCK-ee-o;* another nickname, meaning "True Eye") (c. 1435–1488), shows Lorenzo as tough, humorous, and clever, dressed in the simple clothing of the middle class, not what we would expect from his nickname. An older generation must have wondered why Lorenzo's portrait should be made at all, for he had no title or public position, though in fact he ruled his city-state from behind the scenes. His claim to a place in our memories, and our museums, rests on his personal abilities and achievements, one of which was the patronage of great art.

With the emergence of a new class of patrons, a new class of artists also developed. Gradually freeing themselves from the courts of the nobility and the monasteries of the religious orders, they became independent business people, with studios full of apprentices and assistants, capable of producing almost any kind of art or craft, from a decorated plate to a chapel.

Patrons were expected to take an active part in the planning and design of the works they commissioned. The Renaissance was different from our times,

left: 488. Andrea del Verrocchio. *Lorenzo de' Medici*. 1480. Painted ceramic, height 26″ (66 cm). National Gallery of Art, Washington, D.C. (Samuel H. Kress Collection).

above: 489. Titian. *Isabella d'Este*. 1534. Oil on canvas, 40½ × 25⅜″ (103 × 64 cm). Kunsthistorisches Museum, Vienna.

when most of our consumer goods are factory-made and the buyer chooses from among finished products. A Renaissance merchant and his wife wore tailor-made clothing, lived in an architect-designed house, sat on furniture designed and made especially for them and, naturally, enjoyed paintings made especially to their requirements. The ideas of the artists are recorded mostly in their art, but we know a great deal about the ideas of the patrons from their letters.

Isabella d'Este, who became Marchesa of Mantua upon her marriage, was an outstanding patron. Her portrait was painted by the Venetian painter Titian [489] and drawn by Leonardo da Vinci, to whom she offered several other commissions. Isabella delighted in inventing elaborate subjects for paintings, which created difficulties for the painters. She asked Leonardo for a painting of a youthful Christ, "about twelve years old," as she wrote in her letter to Leonardo, but the painter declined the commission.[1]

The wealthy merchant Giovanni Rucellai explained his heavy expenditures on art and architecture by mentioning that these things gave him "the greatest contentment and the greatest pleasure because they serve the glory of God, the honor of the city [of Florence], and the commemoration of myself," and added that "buying such things is an outlet for the pleasure and virtue of spending money well."[2] Patronizing art was one of the marks of the gentleman. The author of *On Noble Behavior*, a how-to book for gentlemen of 1404, remarks: "The beauty and grace of objects, both natural ones and those made by man's art, are things it is proper for men of distinction to be able to discuss with each other and appreciate."[3]

The Artists

The inclusion of art, along with nature, among objects of beauty and grace tells us something about the style these Renaissance patrons admired. When we look at Fra Angelico's (c. 1400–1455) *Saint Lawrence Distributing Alms to the Poor* **[490]**, we see the skillful drawing, the illusions of space and mass produced by an understanding of the geometry of form and of linear perspective, the use of **chiaroscuro** to make a convincing effect of light and shade, and a narrative subject which can be discussed by an educated person. The Classical architecture is not only beautiful but proves the artist was well educated in the ancient style. The figures are natural, and each one represents a misfortune or disability— the blind, the aged, the poor, the legless man in the foreground, each has a story to be told. Yet each one makes a graceful gesture. These are the basic hallmarks

490.
Fra Angelico.
Saint Lawrence Distributing Alms to the Poor.
c. 1450.
Fresco, 9' × 6'6"
(2.7 × 2 m).
Vatican, Rome.

491. Benvenuto Cellini. *Perseus with the Head of Medusa,* detail of Medusa head. 1553. Bronze, height of entire statue and pedestal 18′ (5.5 m). Loggia dei Lanzi, Florence. See Figure **272** (p. 193) for whole statue.

of the Renaissance style. If "beauty and grace" are present, they mostly take forms familiar to us from nature: beautiful people and buildings, graceful gestures.

Working for patrons who were concerned most about life in this world, artists achieved an ability to represent this world with an accuracy rarely imagined before even in Hellenistic and Roman times. It was for these highly developed skills that the masters such as Fra Angelico were paid far more than their less skillful helpers. In 1447, while he painted one work, Fra Angelico was paid 200 florins plus his living expenses. His best assistant was paid only 84, and their two helpers were paid 12 florins each. Since artistic skill was rewarded, it had to be clearly visible in skillful drawing of natural forms and in demonstration of a thorough knowledge of basic mathematics and geometry in the design. Boys were sent to school in Florence to learn mathematics and geometry and they were taught how to draw in perspective and to represent volumes in space—and to criticize art in those terms. (Girls in those days gained what education they could at home.) Paper was becoming common in Europe for the first time and with it drawing became a common and much collected art. Besides being able to draw, an artist was expected to be at the forefront of technology in his field, in metal casting if he was a sculptor or the chemistry of paint if he was a painter.

The Audience and the Critics

As he examined Benvenuto Cellini's *(chel-LEE-nee)* bronze *Perseus with the Head of Medusa* **[491]** the Duke of Florence commented: "Although this statue seems in our eyes a very fine piece, still it has yet to win the favor of the people." "The people" who formed the serious audience for art were a fairly small proportion of the whole population: educated business and professional people, members of the church and the nobility. Later, when Cellini reluctantly exposed the not quite finished statue to public view, "a shout of boundless enthusiasm went up in commendation of my work," he wrote in his *Memoirs.* Then the

critics went to work. "The folk kept on attaching sonnets to the posts of the door. . . . More than twenty were nailed up, all of them overflowing with the highest panegyrics [praise]."[4] The audience was far from passive, and not all works were so enthusiastically received by the public. It was just as common to find a sarcastic poem posted alongside a work of art as one of praise. Since the poems were signed, the poet revealed not only his opinion but also his critical ability.

Subjects

The name of the period—the Renaissance, or Rebirth—refers more to the subject matter of art and literature than it does to style. There were two principal categories of subject matter in Italian art of this period: Christian subjects and Greek and Roman Classical mythology [492 and 494]. The difference between them would have been described as the Christian subjects being true, the pagan ones being entirely fictional. Only in Christian subjects, they thought, could anything really serious be expressed. Classical mythology was a kind of alternative reality, full of stories and characters which were known mainly to educated people. But Renaissance people were especially intrigued by the history and style of the pagan Greeks and Romans, whom they began to see as their own ancestors. Botticelli's *(bah-tih-CHEL-lee)* *The Adoration of the Magi* [492] is a good example of a Christian subject, but it is set in the ruins of a Classical temple. Christianity is modern, he shows us, in contrast to the religion and architecture of ancient times.

Those characteristics of the Renaissance style mentioned earlier all add up to the power to produce illusions, to take a raw material and make it seem to be something else. It is hard to tell what the portrait of Lorenzo de' Medici is made of—it might be wood, or bronze, but actually it is fired clay, or **terra cotta [488]**. Verrocchio so completely dominated his clay that we cannot see it at all. We see only Lorenzo de' Medici.

The power to dominate and transform was the great preoccupation of the Italian Renaissance. A typical political book of the period was Machiavelli's *The Prince*, a manual on how to gain and retain political power or, you might say,

A POINT IN TIME: Michelangelo's Youth

During the summer of 1489, when Michelangelo was a boy of fourteen, he was selected as one of about six to form the first sculpture class in the Medici Gardens under the supervision of the aged sculptor Bertoldo. The ruler of Florence, Lorenzo de' Medici, "the Magnificent," had set up the school to assure a supply of sculptors to adorn his beloved city. Michelangelo was delighted at the opportunity to work freely, carving stone, after three years of unhappy schooling and a year of apprenticeship to a painter.

Michelangelo's frail mother (who died when he was six) had been unable to nurse him when he was born, and the baby was given to the wife of a quarry worker in the town of Settignano, where Michelangelo remained until he was ten. In later years Michelangelo said, "I also sucked in with my nurse's milk the chisels and hammer with which I make my figures." Although he received many commissions to make paintings, he always considered himself a sculptor, and especially a carver of marble.

The first few carvings the boy made after he entered the Medici Gardens were so impressive that Lorenzo the Magnificent called in Michelangelo's father, Ludovico Buonarroti, to arrange for the boy to be taken into the ruler's own household. Ludovico objected to his son becoming "a stonecutter," a mere laborer with his hands. Michelangelo had to struggle all his life against that prejudice as he tried to gain the respect he thought artists deserved. The ruler's will prevailed, and the boy became virtually the foster son of the Medici family. His father was rewarded with a position as customs official.

Three years later, in 1492, the young sculptor carved a marble relief, *Battle of the Centaurs* [493], taking a Greek myth as his subject. For a seventeen-year-old, it is a remarkable achievement, and Michelangelo kept it for himself all his life. Its churning action and powerful muscular bodies forecast the direction of his work for the rest of his long life (he died at age 88 in 1564). The sculpture was never completely finished. You can see the marks of the pointed chisel at the top, used to rough out the basic forms, and the marks of the toothed chisel in various places between the figures, used to refine the forms. Those two kinds of chisels were Michelangelo's favorite tools all his life. More than any other sculptor in history, Michelangelo was a direct carver in stone, visualizing the figure within the block and cutting away the meaningless masses of stone that hide it. It is amazing to see forecast in this youthful work the direction of a whole lifetime.

Quotation from Giorgio Vasari, *The Great Masters*, trans. Gaston Duc de Vere; ed. M. Sonino (New York: Hugh Lauter Levin Assoc., 1986) 208.

493. Michelangelo. *Battle of the Centaurs.* c. 1492. Marble, 33¼ × 35⅝″ (84 × 90 cm). Casa Buonarroti, Florence.

494. Titian. *Bacchus and Ariadne.* 1520. Oil on canvas, 5'8" × 6'7⅞" (1.7 × 1.8 m). National Gallery, London.

how to mold people to your will. Another kind of book was invented by Renaissance writers, the novel, in which words gained the power, never so fully realized before, to transport us into an experience so completely that we cannot remember having read the words. Similarly, Renaissance painting draws us into the experience, making us forget the paint and canvas.

In Titian's *Bacchus and Ariadne* [494], Bacchus, the god of wine, leaps from his leopard-drawn chariot, transfixed by the power of love at first sight. You can imagine the artist's pleasure in his craftsmanship, which makes us see flesh and hair, cloth and leopard pelt, distant mountains and open sky. To Renaissance eyes the skill is admirable precisely because it has become invisible, like an actor who is so convincing we forget he is acting. For the Renaissance and Baroque audience, an artist was admirable to the degree he could dominate the imagination of the viewer by his illusions. Educated Italians of Titian's period were all well acquainted with the ancient story of Ariadne, abandoned by her lover on the lonely island of Naxos, where she met and married Bacchus. Titian's problem was not to tell the familiar story, but to reveal it in a convincing setting. Venice, where Titian worked, preferred sumptuous color to the more intellectual linear style popular in Florence. That explains the greater emphasis on aerial perspective in the deep blue background, instead of the linear perspective of the ruined stable which makes a setting for Botticelli's *Adoration of the Magi* [492], in good Florentine style.

That admiration for skill which we see reflected in contracts gave special prestige to the best artists. The new class of patrons understood that greatness was achieved by effort and intelligence, and a few artists in each generation were picked out as especially distinguished. That was only possible because the audience was exceptionally cultivated and had produced many patrons, critics, and historians, such as Giorgio Vasari, painter and author of *Lives of the Artists.*

The people of that period immortalized themselves by the richness of their cultural life, which keeps them still fresh in our memories.

Three Phases of Renaissance Style

We can divide the style of the Renaissance in Italy into three phases: Early Renaissance (1400–1500), High Renaissance (1500–1520), and Mannerism (1520–1600). Those phases are particularly applicable to Florence and Rome. Venice, as we shall see, developed on a pattern of its own, prolonging the High Renaissance style and skipping the Mannerist.

Early Renaissance. The artists of the first phase laid the groundwork for reviving Roman Classical types of architecture and human figure, they invented linear perspective, and they developed a painting style that emphasized the illumination of masses. All these achievements have been discussed in other chapters, but we might stop to consider Masaccio (*ma-ZAH-cho*), who died at the age of 27 but whose work "became a school for the most celebrated sculptors and painters," as Vasari wrote.[5] Masaccio's fresco, *The Tribute Money* **[495]**, showing Christ instructing his disciples to "give unto Caesar that which is Caesar's," helps us understand why it was that both painters *and sculptors* studied his work. The most important new element in art of this time was the third dimension in space and mass, and Masaccio's figures, painted in very simple large areas of color, are given solidity by their illumination, or, as the Italians said, by **chiaroscuro**, or light and shade.

The middle of the 1400s saw Florence still the dominant city culturally, but artists in other cities began to achieve fame that even the Florentines recognized. The mathematician and painter Piero della Francesca, in central Italy, and Giovanni Bellini and Andrea Mantegna in northern Italy, are among the great names that show the spread of Renaissance style. Florence retained its importance with three distinctive masters: the painter Botticelli **[492]**, the sculptor Verrocchio **[488]**, and his pupil, the painter, draftsman, scientist, and inventor, Leonardo da Vinci.

495. Masaccio. *The Tribute Money.* c. 1427.
Fresco, 8'4" × 19'8" (2.5 × 6 m). Church of Santa Maria del Carmine, Florence.

It is impossible to sum up the achievements of this important period in a few words, but the distinctive new elements are fully expressed in Leonardo's *Madonna of the Rocks* **[496]**, a painting so much admired that he painted it twice for different patrons. One of the first oil paintings by a Florentine painter, it has the rich, dark sheen of that medium. Leonardo had learned Masaccio's lesson so well that we take for granted the golden light streaming into the scene from the upper left. Leonardo's study of nature turns the rocks and plants into geological and botanical specimens, but most impressive of all is the personality revealed in the face and gesture of each of the figures. The stable pyramidal composition—you can trace it out by following the imaginary lines that run from the top of Mary's head through her hands to form a large triangle—is also characteristic of this period, which preferred a calm, dignified design and expression. In all these respects Leonardo led the way into the next period, the High Renaissance.

496. Leonardo da Vinci. *Madonna of the Rocks.* 1483–1485. Oil on panel, transferred to canvas; 6'6½" × 4' (2 × 1.2 m). Louvre, Paris.

In Detail: Leonardo, Artist-Scientist

These days we speak of a "Renaissance man" as one who is interested in many things. Leonardo da Vinci (1452–1519) is the model Renaissance man—we can see the evidence in the *Madonna of the Rocks.*

The wild rocky caverns and peaks in the background [497] were a common symbol of wilderness, but Leonardo was not content with symbols of rocks. He took pains to show the texture and stratification; we can imagine him setting up small rocks to use as models. We know that in later years Leonardo made trips into the Alps to study geology and botany. He was particularly interested in fossils of sea life which he found high in the mountains and which he theorized must have been left when the sea once covered the mountains, an idea unheard of in his time.

The drawing of rocks on the bank of a pond [498] was done four or five years before the *Madonna of the Rocks,* when the painter was about 26. You can see the kinds of natural rocks which were the source of the background in the painting and how carefully Leonardo considered them. All sorts of vertical and horizontal stratification and erosion are examined in detail. Leonardo is admired as an early scientist, but his greatest weakness as a scientist, which was his inability to generalize, was his strength as an artist. Art and truth for Leonardo came only from "experience, mother of all certainty, first-hand experience," as he wrote. "If you despise painting, which is the sole means of reproducing all the known works of nature, you despise an invention which with subtle and philosophic speculation considers all qualities of forms: seas, plants, animals, grasses, flowers, all of which are encircled in light and shadow."

———

Quotations from Leonardo's *Trattado,* chaps. 8, 29, in Kenneth Clark, *Leonardo da Vinci* (London and Baltimore: Penguin, 1958) 75, 135.

above: 497. Leonardo da Vinci.
Madonna of the Rocks, detail of background.

right: 498. Leonardo da Vinci.
Ravine with Water Birds. c. 1478–1480.
Pen and ink on pinkish paper, 8¾ × 6¼"
(22 × 16 cm). Royal Library, Windsor Castle, England.

High Renaissance.   The High Renaissance was a short period during the first twenty years of the 1500s when the popes were building and decorating Saint Peter's and the Vatican Palace in Rome. Both in size and in quality, the projects carried out in that short time have been considered among the supreme achievements of Western civilization. The massive forms of Masaccio and Leonardo led to a style in both painting and sculpture in which balanced, large

499. Raphael. *The School of Athens*. 1501–1511.
Fresco, 18 × 26′ (5.5 × 7.9 m). Stanza della Signatura, Vatican Palace, Rome.

massive forms were dominant, movement appeared to be rational and con-
trolled, and unity was the dominant principle. Primary colors played a major
role, suggesting optimism and openness. Michelangelo's sculptured *Moses*, his
Sistine Chapel ceiling, and his architectural designs for Saint Peter's, along with
Raphael's paintings, are considered high points. You may wish to look back to
Chapter 6 to review Michelangelo's Sistine Chapel ceiling, but here we will take
Raphael's *The School of Athens* as our example.

Raphael *(RAF-ay-el)* (1483–1520) painted *The School of Athens* **[499]** in fresco
on a wall in the Vatican Palace. The setting, in which Plato (left center) and
Aristotle stand among ancient scholars and poets, is modeled on the new Saint
Peter's church, which was under construction next door. No Athenian of Plato's
day ever stood in such a building, of course, since the architecture shown in the
painting is in a later Roman style, but it makes a powerful and impressive perspective centering behind the heads of the two great philosophers. The painting
was much admired as an illustration of ancient learning, each figure being identifiable and shown in a characteristic pose. The symmetry adds great dignity to
the figures, who stand erect or move in calm, geometrically ordered, postures.

A century earlier such a subject and design would have been impossible to
paint. The perspective system was still barely a hundred years old, the ancient
Greek philosophers and poets had become well known only during more recent
years, and the exact knowledge of Roman architecture in the background shown
by Raphael was an even more recent achievement. *The School of Athens* was at the
forefront of knowledge in several fields when it was painted.

Mannerism. Raphael died young (at age 37) in 1520, and that is usually taken as the end of the High Renaissance despite the fact that Michelangelo lived another 44 years. But the mood had changed from confidence to pessimism, expressed in art by exaggeration: figures became elongated or massive, contrasts of scale were extreme, colors were dominated by subtle mixtures that blend from hue to hue and tint to shade. The later work of Michelangelo dominated and inspired the period called *Mannerism* (1520–1600), in which doubt and introspection ruled in art, at least in Rome and Florence.

Michelangelo's fresco *The Last Judgment* [500], on the front wall of the Sistine Chapel, is the greatest work of the period, but a tragic and frightening scene. The calm geometry of the earlier compositions has given way to a churning mass of figures. Without the straight lines provided by an architectural framework, the crowds of saved or damned souls seem to whirl in space. A powerful figure of Christ implacably condemns the sinners as the trumpets sound in the heavens. Viewed from Rome, the world was in unprecedented danger of damnation, for Protestantism had risen in northern Europe to challenge the rule of the pope. It was not until 1600 that Catholicism recovered its self-confidence and found a new form of expression in the Baroque style.

500. Michelangelo. *The Last Judgment.* 1536–1541. Fresco, 48 × 44' (14.6 × 13.4 m). Sistine Chapel, Vatican, Rome.

Venice in the 1500s

Venice had no such crisis of confidence and it was unrivaled as an art center throughout that century. The mantle of the older master Giovanni Bellini (c. 1430–1516) fell to two great disciples, Giorgione (1478–1511), who died young, and the very long-lived Titian (1477–1576) **[489 and 494]**. Since Venice was built on islands and pilings in a shallow sea, the walls of its buildings were mostly considered too damp to be suitable for fresco, so mural decoration began to be done in oil on canvas which hung free of the wall. Venice was one of the first places in Italy to adopt oil painting, which was invented in northern Europe early in the 1400s.

Tintoretto (1518–1594) marks the transition from the Renaissance to the Baroque, as we can see in his *Adoration of the Shepherds* **[501]**, an oil mural from the vast set of decorations for the School of San Rocco, a religious fraternity. The complicated scene, in which the Holy Family is set back in a loft lit by shafts of light through the ruined roof, anticipates the theatrical space and light in the art of the next century. It is not the serene dignity of the early Renaissance style, but an energetic and emotional style. The contrasts of light and dark are extreme, the gestures are muscular (notice especially the men in the lower left corner), and the spaces are organized in surprising ways—this may be the only Nativity scene in which the Mother and Child are shown in a loft. Tintoretto gives us a solid barn built of strong beams to act as the framework and perspective for this scene, but removes the roof to let in a divine radiance.

The Renaissance in Northern Europe

Flanders, then an independent county (ruled by a count) and now part of Belgium, was the center of art development in northern Europe during this period. It was also a center of trade. The city of Bruges, for example, was a busy port town with canals leading to the brick warehouses of the Hanseatic League, a vast trading association of northern cities. English wool, Russian furs, almonds from Spain, and spices from the East passed through her markets. Throughout Flanders, industry and labor were organized in guilds similar to modern unions and trade associations.

There were also trade and art connections between Flanders and Italy. Jan van Eyck's *Arnolfini Wedding Portrait* **[502]** provides clues to these connections and also shows some of the differences between the two regions. The groom, Giovanni Arnolfini, was an Italian who managed the Medici bank in Bruges. He and his Paris-born Italian bride, Jeanne Cenami, patronized the leading Flemish painter, Jan van Eyck (1370?–1440?) to record their marriage vows. Flemish painting was admired in Italy; fifteen years after his death Van Eyck was described by an Italian critic as the foremost painter of the age. The Arnolfinis seem at home in their Flemish bedroom with its Gothic decoration, and they are both shown with the delicate proportions of the Gothic tradition in figure art, quite different from the Classical athletes who had again become the models for the human figure in Italy.

You can learn to recognize the style of the Flemish painters just by a careful examination of this painting. First of all, notice the dimensions: 33 by 22½ inches (84 by 57 centimeters). You might compare that with the painting by Fra Angelico, *Saint Lawrence Distributing Alms to the Poor* **[490]**, which measures about 9 by 6½ feet (2.7 by 2 meters). Some very large paintings were made in northern Europe, but on average Italian paintings were larger for one good reason: they were more often painted in fresco directly on the walls of buildings, as was the Saint Lawrence painting. The Arnolfini wedding portrait is painted on a wooden

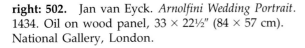
above: **501.** Tintoretto. *Adoration of the Shepherds.*
1576–1581. Oil on canvas, 17'9" × 14'5" (5.4 × 4.4 m).
School of San Rocco, Venice.

right: **502.** Jan van Eyck. *Arnolfini Wedding Portrait.*
1434. Oil on wood panel, 33 × 22½" (84 × 57 cm).
National Gallery, London.

panel in a mixture which included oil paint, of which Jan van Eyck was one of
the inventors.

Saint Lawrence is shown in a large public building, presumably a church,
despite its Classical columns; the Arnolfinis are in a small bedroom of their own
home ornamented with Gothic carving on the bed and chair. To a northern
European that room looks cozy, and the Italian church looks cold and drafty. It
seems contradictory that the Arnolfinis' home is decorated in the Gothic style,
which we think of as a church style, not the Classical style (which was pagan in
origin) of Fra Angelico's church; notice the carving on the bed and the arm of the
chair, as well as the ornate brass chandelier. The cool northern climate, of
course, accounts for the warmer clothing the Arnolfinis wear, but it does not
explain the difference in their body proportions from people in Italian paintings.
The question always arises whether Jeanne was pregnant on her wedding day.
Kenneth Clark, in his book *The Nude*, describes what he calls the Gothic ideal of
the feminine figure: ''Her pelvis is wider, her chest narrower, her waist higher;
above all, there is the prominence given to her stomach.''[6] This Italian couple is
portrayed in a Gothic figure style that remained popular in the North into the
1400s, and Jeanne's prominent stomach only tells us about art and clothing style,
not about her behavior.

The Northern style was also strongly affected by its use of oil paint, which
came into Italian art about two generations later. Oil permits very fine gradations of color blending, such as we see on the back wall, and fantastic illusions of
natural textures, such as we see in the fur trim of Arnolfini's robe, the shine of

above left: 503. Robert Campin. *Portrait of a Woman of Tournai.* 1425–1430.
Oil on wood panel, 16½ × 11½" (42 × 29 cm). National Gallery, London.

above right: 504. Leonardo da Vinci. *Mona Lisa.* c. 1503–1505. Oil on wood panel,
30½ × 21" (77 × 53 cm). Louvre, Paris.

the chandelier, and the texture of the bride's dress. All these features of the
Flemish style were so impressive that the Italian painters were worried by the
competition and began to experiment with linseed oil and turpentine to mix and
thin their colors.

The setting in a middle-class house was also typical of the North. The
northern cities were important commercial centers, with a middle class whose
power rested on industry and trade. The merchant class of Bruges, to which the
Arnolfinis belonged, grew wealthy and began to adopt the pleasures and privileges of the nobility, including the patronage of artists. Perhaps in reaction, the
nobility cultivated a fairy-tale kind of elegance, emphasizing chivalry and
knightly virtues after they had become obsolete in warfare. Wherever there was
wealth, among the merchants or the nobility, the patronage of art was a supreme pleasure of the time.

Jan van Eyck, like many of the leading artists of his day, was a courtier and
diplomat, employed often by the powerful Duke of Burgundy. Court artists such
as Van Eyck were expected to design floats, costumes, and mechanical appara-
tus for festivals, decorate manuscripts, design furniture and paint it, organize
and mount state ceremonies, as well as paint state portraits which were supposed to be perfect likenesses. They might be asked to design a tomb, decorate a
ship, or paint an altarpiece, with the help of their students and apprentices.

Realism and Spirituality in Northern Art

Realism based on careful looking at nature is an important feature of Northern art. About the time Jan van Eyck was painting the Arnolfinis, Robert Campin (c. 1375–1444) painted the portrait of an unknown woman of Tournai [503] in that city. It was painted about 75 years before Leonardo da Vinci painted the *Mona Lisa* [504], but they make an interesting comparison. Both women were members of the middle class—Mona Lisa was the wife of a banker in Florence— each fashionably dressed for her time and place. Campin concentrated on the face, but in the *Mona Lisa* there is a balance between the head and the body which the revived Classical ideas required. Leonardo also gives us a generalized, superhuman character whose face is designed by abstract geometry to fit the mouth and veil on a perfect circle. That kind of dehumanized abstraction was the opposite of Northern realism, which took nature, not an abstract ideal, as the model.

Saint Luke Drawing the Virgin [505] may be a self-portrait of the painter Rogier van der Weyden (1399–1464) in the guise of the writer of the Gospel. Saint Luke, who was supposed to have been an artist, seems frozen in a genuflection before the stiff but cheerful Child and his gentle mother. Luke is making a silverpoint drawing, which would be a study for a painting. Rogier made designs in which lines and shapes played a strong part—notice the elaborate folds of the garments and the strong pattern of light and dark. Line and shape gave special elegance and spirituality to his style, which was extremely popular with the audience of his time. Those two trends, realism and spirituality, were both strong in Northern art.

Subjects

Ancient Greece and Rome, which seemed to the Italians like their own heritage, meant far less to these northerners, whose ancestors had been conquered by Rome and who knew of Greek Classicism only from books. Having no

505. Rogier van der Weyden. *Saint Luke Drawing the Virgin.* 1435–1437. Oil and tempera on wood panel, 4′6⅛″ × 3′7⅝″ (1.4 × 1.1 m). Museum of Fine Arts, Boston (gift of Mr. and Mrs. Henry Lee Higginson).

506. Albrecht Altdorfer. *The Battle of Alexander and Darius.* 1529.
Oil on wood panel, 5′2″ × 3′11″ (1.6 × 1.2 m). Alte Pinakothek, Munich.

Greek and little Roman art around to study, they made no attempt to revive the ancient styles, but they used the newly fashionable stories and characters in their art. *The Battle of Alexander and Darius* [506] was painted by Albrecht Altdorfer (1480–1538) for the Duke of Bavaria, who saw no inconsistency in the medieval armor and castles, nor in the vast Alpine setting, which made Alexander seem part of medieval German history instead of ancient Greek.

Another character from ancient literature, Penelope, the faithful wife of Odysseus in the *Odyssey*, the Greek epic of Homer, was portrayed in a Flemish tapestry [507]. The art of tapestry was brought to great heights in Flanders, and the subject was surely chosen as a perfect one for a woven art. Hoping her long-absent husband was not dead, Penelope promised her suitors that she would wed again only when her weaving was done. She is shown at her loom, where each night she unwove the work of that day. She is dressed as a noble lady and sits in a northern palace whose columns are Gothic, not Greek.

Flamboyant Gothic in Secular Buildings

The Gothic architectural style remained popular a century longer in the North, where it was native, than it did in Italy. But instead of churches, it was used for city halls, market buildings, and fine houses, all things required by the new merchant class in their developing cities. The tall, steepled city hall of Louvain [508] could be mistaken for a church, with its pointed arches and its hundreds of statues. The Late Gothic buildings are of a richness unparalleled in earlier times. One glance will tell you why this style is called Flamboyant Gothic.

left: 507. Flemish. *Penelope at Her Loom.* 1480–1483. Tapestry fragment, wool; 5'1" × 3'⅜" (1.5 × 0.9 m). Museum of Fine Arts, Boston (Maria Antoinette Evans Fund).

below: 508. City Hall, Louvain, Belgium. 1448–1463.

left: 509. House of Jacques Coeur, Bourges, France. 1443. Detail of street front.

above: 510. Richard Morris Hunt. Vanderbilt Mansion, "Biltmore," near Asheville, North Carolina. 1895.

The house that Jacques Coeur *(kur)*, the first great French entrepreneur, built for himself in his hometown of Bourges **[509]** is one of the early examples of the Gothic style used for a house rather than a church. It is very grand, but it incorporated Coeur's business offices as well as his home. It was the model for a long string of noble houses called castles (*chateau*, plural *chateaux*, both pronounced *sha-TOE*) though they were not fortified that were built by French courtiers; much later Coeur's house served as a model for the palaces of American merchant princes **[510]**.

Bosch, Grünewald, Bruegel

Although the supreme individual artist of this period, Albrecht Dürer (1471–1528), was more important as a printmaker than as a painter (see Chapter 5), three great painters sum up the achievements of a hundred years of Northern art from about 1470 to 1570—Jerome (or Hieronymus) Bosch (1453–1516); Mathis Gothart Neithardt, called Grünewald *(GRU-nuh-valt)* (c. 1470–1528), and Pieter Bruegel *(BROO-gul* or *BROY-gul)* (c. 1525–1569). In both Italy and Northern Europe, Renaissance art drew on two contrary sources, one of them an objective study of the natural world, the other an imaginative world carried down in the traditions of each region. In Italy, Greek and Roman Classicism provided that imaginative world, but in the North it was the ancient pagan religion which survived on the margins of Christianity in the form of fantastic folktales. These three painters made especially potent use of the fantastic.

Philip II, king of Spain and a religious fanatic, had ten paintings by Jerome Bosch. Among Philip's purchases was *The Hay Wain Triptych* **[511]**, which is still in Philip's palace near Madrid. The critics at Philip's court considered it an illustration of Isaiah 11:6–8 ("the lion will eat straw like the ox"), but modern historians have suggested that Bosch was thinking of a Flemish proverb that says the world is a pile of hay from which each seeks to grab what he can. In the left wing, as God creates Eve in Paradise, the rebel angels are expelled from heaven like a swarm of insects. In the center Christ looks down from the clouds as everyone on earth fights for material goods, even those supposedly committed to the spiritual life. The great hay wagon rolls toward Hell, drawn by weird demons. In the right panel is the fiery landscape of Hell. Bosch's visions suited a pessimistic period of religious war and persecution, but behind their fantasy is a cool, rational design of incredible complexity and richness. Notice the wide landscapes, with aerial perspective, that provide a stage for fantastic events.

Grünewald's greatest work is another altarpiece, the *Isenheim Altarpiece*, which is a polytych (a painting composed of many panels, in this case ten). The

multiple-panel painting, with folding wings painted on both front and back, was the Northern answer to the problem of major public art. It might be compared to an Italian chapel frescoed on all four walls, or to a medieval manuscript with paintings on every page. Patrons and the public found it a satisfactory way to tell elaborate stories, and the triptych and polyptych became the standard format for the Northern masterpiece until 1600.

The *Isenheim Altarpiece* has a set of wood sculptures at the center, by another artist, which are overshadowed by Grünewald's powerful paintings. *The Crucifixion* [512], 9 feet 9½ inches (2.9 meters) high, at the center of the outside of

511. Jerome Bosch.
The Hay Wain Triptych.
1490–1495.
Oil on wood panels;
center 4'7⅛" × 3'3⅜"
(1.4 × 1 m), each wing
4'9⅞" × 2'2"
(1.5 × 0.7 m).
El Escorial, near Madrid.

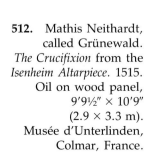

512. Mathis Neithardt, called Grünewald.
The Crucifixion from the
Isenheim Altarpiece. 1515.
Oil on wood panel,
9'9½" × 10'9"
(2.9 × 3.3 m).
Musée d'Unterlinden,
Colmar, France.

the altarpiece, has the Christ, fearfully wounded, larger than the other figures, unnatural in scale but true in a spiritual sense. On the left Mary swoons in the arms of John the Evangelist, as Mary Magdalen gives expression to an agony of grief. John the Baptist, who had died before the Crucifixion, is placed on our right, with the inscription "He must increase, but I must decrease." Perhaps it is the color which conveys the expression even more than the tortured shapes and the extremes of light and dark. The strong contrast of Mary's white robes with John's red and the green shading of the body of Christ shine like jewels in the darkness of the scene.

Dated 1515, the *Isenheim Altarpiece* was painted at almost the same time as Michelangelo's Sistine Chapel ceiling. When we speak of beauty being a cultural value, not an objective absolute, these two complex works are good examples. Michelangelo's sculptural figures seem serene compared with the passion and color of Grünewald's. The difference between fresco and oil paint is also a factor, for oil provided a much greater color range as well as a shiny surface, which gives the shadows greater depth.

Pieter Bruegel was described as "Bosch reborn" by a contemporary because his first works were engravings of Flemish proverbs ("The Big Fish Eat the Little Fish") elaborated with Bosch-like fantasies. Bruegel brought this Northern tradition to a close, for during his time the Italian style had begun to be copied by Flemish painters. In his mature work Bruegel turned away from fantasy toward realistic portrayal of the daily life of common people. His patrons were middle- and upper-class collectors, including the German Emperor Rudolf II, who enjoyed Bruegel's paintings of peasant life. His original audience saw vulgar humor in Bruegel's work, but that is largely lost to modern eyes.

Hunters in the Snow [513], which belonged to Rudolf II, is one of the best of Bruegel's later paintings. Bruegel never painted a portrait, but sought to portray humanity as a type, not an individual. A master of body language, he makes every pose and gesture tell. Examine the legs of the hunters, the bent bodies of the fire-tenders, or the movements of the skaters—what more could their faces tell us? From a hill we scan a vast craggy landscape in which people live a rough, but evidently harmonious, life in nature.

When Pieter Bruegel painted *Hunters in the Snow* about 1565, the first Europeans had reached Japan, on the far side of the globe, only 22 years before. *Hunters in the Snow* was one of a set of four paintings on the seasons of the year, a favorite subject in Japanese art and one they would have understood immediately, despite the great difference in style. Compared with the varied textures and colors in Bruegel's painting, and the mountains with their definite horizon, Japanese paintings (such as **517**) look abstract and ethereal. Yet in their attitude toward nature they have something in common.

The Wave and the Rock: Art in Japan, 1500–1700

When Columbus set off on his voyages of discovery, it was not America he hoped to reach (since its existence was unknown to him), but Zipangu, described by Marco Polo as islands of incredible wealth off the coast of China. Zipangu—or, as we would say, Japan—was reached 50 years later, in 1543, by Portuguese explorers who were busy establishing trading colonies throughout the Far East. They were followed by Saint Francis Xavier, founder of the Jesuit order of monks, who succeeded in converting many Japanese to Christianity. A century of close contact ended in 1638, when the Portuguese were expelled and Japan turned inward, cutting off almost all foreign contacts until 1854, when the American Commodore Perry forced a trade treaty on a reluctant Japan. The East and the West, so different from each other in some respects, had enough in

513. Pieter Bruegel the Elder. *Hunters in the Snow.* 1560–1565. Oil on wood panel, 3'10⅛" × 5'3⅜" (1.2 × 1.6 m). Kunsthistorisches Museum, Vienna.

common that both sides were enriched, not by the gold that the early explorers hoped to find, but by the stimulus of contact with a different culture.

The Japanese were most interested in the technical devices of the Namban ("southern barbarians"), as they called the Europeans: large sailing ships, guns, eyeglasses, and clocks. Western art had little perceptible influence in Japan before the 19th century. The Japanese arts described by the Portuguese Christian missionaries between 1543 and 1638 comprised two distinct traditions, one native Japanese, the other introduced from China and naturalized with a Japanese form.

The Cult of Shinto and the Yamato Style

During the period when the Europeans were in Japan, the greatest painter was Tawaraya Sotatsu *(SO-tahts)* (1576–1643), a free-lance artist in the old capital and temple city of Kyoto. None of the Europeans seem to have met him, and his art shows no awareness of European art. But a Jesuit missionary describes paintings much like those of Sotatsu:

> I was taken to see one of their country houses, which was adorned with *byobu* [screens], or pictures about the height of a man. Each one of them was made up of four panels which folded into one when they were closed up. They were made of wood and covered with paper, on which the pictures were painted; and when these *byobu* were erected and set up, they covered the walls. . . . They were painted so realistically that the spectator seemed to be looking at the actual thing. . . .[7]

514. Tawaraya Sotatsu. *God of Wind.* c. 1630. Watercolor and gold foil on paper screen, 5'2" × 5'8" (1.6 × 1.7 m). Kenninji, Kyoto, Japan.

Sotatsu painted the *God of Wind* **[514]** on such a screen, which made a pair with a *God of Thunder*. The green demon charges through smoke-like clouds, his long hair flying. Nature divinities were traditional subjects, but the large size (just over 5 feet high; 1.5 meters) and free style were new. In the subdued light of a Japanese house, the gold-foil background would have given the painting a rich radiance. A Japanese critic writes of "the sense of vitality and vehement movement"[8] in these paintings, which catch the adventurous spirit of the age.

Sotatsu was patronized by a well-to-do merchant class in Kyoto, not too different from the emerging merchant class in Europe. Their preferences were for subjects from history or nature, rather than from religion. The subjects of the *Thunder God* and *Wind God* screens come from the native Japanese religious tradition called Shinto. It is assumed that Sotatsu chose the subjects himself, which would show him to have been very original.

The cult of Shinto formalized ancient ideas about the origin and form of the universe which were the basis of Japanese ideas about proper behavior and cultural value. Every natural thing, place, or process had its spirit, was in a sense living, and must be treated with the respect due a powerful being. Such a belief

515. Hon-Ami Koetsu. Tea bowl. Japanese, Edo Period, 1558–1637. Raku ware, 3⁷/₁₆ × 14¹⁵/₁₆" (8.7 × 12.5 cm). Freer Gallery of Art, Smithsonian Institution, Washington, D.C.

does not lend itself to art. After all, if the stone is entirely inhabited by a spirit, it is hard to chisel off parts to give the stone more meaning. Thus, it is mostly in attitudes toward nature and materials that we see the effect of Shinto, rather than in works of representational art. João Rodrigues, one of the Portuguese Jesuit missionaries, tells us: "There are many rules regarding the way of putting flowers into the vase and private people learn them by reading books and practising under teachers, always making it their best endeavor to imitate nature and its lack of artificiality." Another Jesuit missionary wrote that "the king of Bungo [actually a local nobleman, and a Christian convert] once showed me a small earthenware tea bowl for which in all truth we would have no other use than to put it in a bird's cage as a drinking trough; nevertheless, he had paid 9,000 silver *taels* for it, although I would certainly not have given two farthings for it."[9] The tea bowl [515] was made by Honami Koetsu *(Ko-ETS)* (1558–1637), friend and patron of Sotatsu and an artist as well as a powerful court figure. Tea bowls that appeared to be crude natural objects, flowers arranged as if by nature, gardens carefully arranged to hide the fact that they had been constructed by humans— those were the purest expressions of the Japanese tradition.

As a young painter, Sotatsu had the unusual opportunity to restore some 400-year-old scrolls in a native Japanese style, from which he learned at first-hand to paint in that style. Those old scrolls must have been similar to *The Burning of the Sanjo Palace* [516]. That scroll, painted in the 13th century, tells the

516. Japan, Kamakura period. *The Burning of the Sanjo Palace.* 13th century. Ink and colors on horizontal paper handscroll, 1'4¼" × 22'10" (0.4 × 7 m). Museum of Fine Arts, Boston (Fenollosa-Weld Collection).

story of a battle that started a civil war in 1159, a battle in which the imperial palace was burned. Like the warrior kings in Europe at the same time, the military leaders who ruled Japan enjoyed seeing the exploits of war raised to the level of mythology. Small figures race across the scene and horses gallop and prance as flames boil from the palace. Defenders who survived the slaughter were cast down the well. "Alas," reads the text, "the lowermost are drowned in water, those in between are crushed to death, while those on top are engulfed in flames."

From an examination of *The Burning of the Sanjo Palace, God of Wind,* and the tea bowl, we can define the *native Japanese style,* what the Japanese call the *Yamato style:* natural materials and processes are respected, in line with Shinto beliefs, and in painting, line, shape, and color dominate, expressing dynamic action by curvilinear shapes. Designs are usually asymmetrically balanced between figure and ground, with empty ground often being the larger area and implying space.

Zen Buddhism

Another style was also in use in Japan during this period, one whose source was China. Buddhism, which had come into Japan in the 6th century from India and China, had long existed harmoniously with the native Shinto beliefs, and one Buddhist sect, called Zen, was particularly identified with a painting style with Chinese roots. Zen Buddhism taught that salvation is achieved by a mystical experience that comes like a lightning bolt in the midst of everyday life. Zen lifestyle, which emphasized simplicity and the renunciation of luxury, fitted harmoniously with the native ideas of Shinto, but its painting style was quite different from that of Sotatsu. The *Zen style* is brush painting with black ink, very freely drawn, with each stroke symbolizing some natural

517. Sesshu. *Bridge of Heaven.* c. 1503. Ink on paper
with faint watercolor, 2'11" × 5'8" (0.9 × 1.7 m). National Museum, Kyoto, Japan.

518. Flying-Cloud Pavilion (Hiunkaku), Kyoto, Japan. 1594.

feature. Tones or washes of ink were supplementary to line. Landscape was the principal subject.

Most of the great painters in the Zen style were monks. The greatest of all was Sesshu (1420–1506), and it was paintings in his style that the Portuguese missionary João Rodrigues saw and described: "In keeping with their melancholy temperament they are usually inclined towards paintings of lonely and poignant scenes, such as those portraying the four seasons of the year."[10]

Bridge of Heaven [517] was painted about 1503 when Sesshu was 83 years old. This is not an imaginary place, but a famous spot considered one of the three most beautiful places in Japan. You will recognize the painting style as a development from the style of Wang Wei and Li Cheng (see Chapter 11) in China. Sesshu traveled in China in middle age to study religion and art, but found no painters there who were his equal. On his return home he established a studio which he named The Heaven-Created Painting Pavilion, where he received more commissions than he could fulfill. Before painting he would look from his window over the landscape of mountains and seashore, drink a cup of sake wine, and play a melody on his flute. Having gotten in the right mood, he would paint with brush and ink scenes of the precipitous mountains he had seen in China. Though the basic style is Chinese, Sesshu's combination of soft gray tones and powerful slashes and stabs of the brush is unique and was a model for many other Japanese painters. Sesshu's paintings were surely known to Sotatsu, but Sotatsu turned to a more purely Japanese painting tradition. Those two painters represent the opposite poles of Japanese painting during this period.

In 1594 the ruler, or shogun, Hideyoshi built the Flying-Cloud Pavilion [518] in Kyoto as one of his palaces. To the Europeans it must have seemed hardly grander than a country inn, with its irregular plan, unfinished wood, and thatched roof. Hideyoshi, a peasant boy who had risen by courage and diplomacy to be dictator of his country, could have had anything he wanted; why did he choose this?

The Flying-Cloud Pavilion is actually unusually grand for a Japanese house, rising in Chinese style to three stories in the center. Japanese critics describe this palace with the term *sukiya*, "artless," as if a product of nature rather than of human skill. Several basic principles of Japanese aesthetics—irregularity, simplicity, and perishability—all find expression in this building, which appears to have grown like a plant in its natural-appearing garden. The interior shares that *sukiya* simplicity—elegance achieved by severe understatement.[11]

Hideyoshi was devoted to the tea ceremony and kept at his court one of the famous "tea masters" who specialized in that ceremony in which naturalness and simplicity were raised to rituals. With roots in Shinto ideals and in Zen Buddhism, it appealed especially to powerful people who craved relief from extravagant luxury. It was held in a tiny, primitive-looking tea house with a door so low you had to bend over to creep in. The utensils were carefully chosen to be as rough and natural as possible. Every move of dipping tea and pouring was ritualized; in fact, the tea ceremony is like 20th-century "performance art" in which the whole activity is symbolic. The cup **[515]**—really a bowl with no handle—was also simple and rough, as if made by nature instead of human hands. The tea ceremony was a composite work of art in which the setting and every object and motion was part of the design.

In contrast to the simplicity of the tea ceremony, clothing developed to an amazing richness. Hideyoshi's wife, for example, wore the gorgeous robe with a cloud pattern **[519]** over a yellow-green and purple honeycomb design. The *kimono*, a robe tied with a sash, was a simplification of older costumes worn at

519. Japan, Momoyama period. *Uchikake* overrobe worn by wife of Hideyoshi. Late 16th century. Silk brocade imprinted with silver leaf, length 47¼" (120 cm). Kodaiji, Kyoto, Japan.

Recognizing the Great Styles

520. Japan. *Kosode* robe. 17th century. Silk satin brocade with embroidery, ink painting, gold leaf. National Museum of Japanese History, Sakura, Japan (Nomura Collection).

the imperial court, and, worn by both men and women in slightly different ways, it became an important way to display personal style. The designs were woven into the cloth in a brocade technique.

Another beautiful robe of white satin **[520]** from the 1600s has a design of a golden waterfall that plunges from black rocks, at the neck and shoulders, to a black-footed flower-arranging tray, near the hem. Varicolored flowers and splashing golden foam make an irregular design that recalls the compositions of Sotatsu. Although it represents natural subjects, the design is disciplined like a Zen ritual. The audience for these great painters had cultivated a sensitivity to design, color, and craft that integrated daily life and art. These people of the audience decorated their walls with screens and carefully designed their houses

A POINT IN TIME: Ernest Fenollosa
Synthesizes East and West

"Japan! What romantic thoughts and memories arise at the name!" Writing those words, Ernest Fenollosa was recalling his arrival as a 25-year-old philosophy professor at Tokyo University. Japan had opened to foreigners only a quarter-century before, and there was still suspicion of outsiders, but Ernest's enthusiasm for Japanese culture and art overwhelmed all obstacles. He learned Japanese and adopted the Buddhist religion. Rapidly westernizing, many Japanese were ready to discard their past, but Ernest preached loyalty to tradition. Old works of art were being cast aside, and he took the opportunity to build a great collection, later purchased for the Boston Museum of Fine Arts by Dr. G. C. Weld.

Ernest discovered the visual arts only after graduation from Harvard. He took his first drawing and painting classes at the new Art School of the Boston Museum. Recruited for Tokyo University, he soon began to concentrate on art, first as national chief of art education, later as founder and director of the national art museum. Children were being taught to write and draw with a pencil, Western style, but Ernest directed the revival of traditional brush drawing. He brought American organizational skills to the task of fostering Japanese culture.

In 1890 Ernest returned to Boston as first curator of oriental art at the Boston Museum and soon became friends with the painter Arthur Dow, recently

521. Sesshu. *Monkeys and Birds in Trees.* 1491. Ink, watercolor on 6-fold screen; height 5'3¼" (1.6 m), width 24" (0.61 m). Museum of Fine Arts, Boston (Fenollosa-Weld Collection).

to express the *sukiya* spirit, so it is not surprising that a Japanese lover might be discouraged if "a disillusioning glimpse of her sleeve . . . suggested the lady lacked a perfect sensitivity to color harmonies. . . ."[12]

By the time Ogata Korin (1658–1716) painted the screen *Waves at Matsushima* **[522]** in the tradition of Sotatsu in about 1700, Japan had expelled the Europeans (in 1638) and closed its borders to foreign contact for what would be two hundred years. The painting epitomizes the place of Japan in the age of Columbus: rocky islands in a turbulent sea, fortress-like against the wave of European exploration and colonization, cultivating its own ancient traditions of naturalness, beauty, and skill.

opposite: 522. Ogata Korin. *Waves at Matsushima.* c. 1700. Watercolor on paper screen, 5'1" × 12'1½" (1.5 × 3.7 m). Museum of Fine Arts, Boston (Fenollosa-Weld Collection).

Recognizing the Great Styles

returned from studies in Paris. Kindred spirits, Ernest and Arthur embarked on the invention of a method of art instruction that would synthesize East and West. Ernest had a vision of an emerging world culture which the system of art instruction would help create. Arthur became his assistant curator and began studying Japanese woodcuts, even making his own woodcuts following examples in the Boston Museum collection [523]. Ernest and Arthur became a team, teaching drawing, design, and art history at Pratt Institute in Brooklyn; later Dow moved to Columbia University where he became an influential teacher of methods of art instruction.

The American art world, bored with copying Renaissance styles, was ripe for the new system, which concentrated on expression through abstract lines, shapes, values, and compositions. The Japanese word *Notan,* meaning dark against light, was a key idea, along with "spacing," Ernest's term for composition. Georgia O'Keeffe and many of her contemporaries were frank about their debt to the Fenollosa-Dow system. Nearly a century later, this book still uses concepts of the elements of art and the principles of design given their first formulation by Ernest and Arthur. American art has become the synthesis of East and West that caught Arthur Dow's imagination when Ernest described it to him in the fall of 1893.

Based on E. F. Fenollosa, *Epochs of Chinese and Japanese Art* (New York: Dover reprint, 1963) and Frederick C. Moffat, *Arthur Wesley Dow, 1857–1922* (Washington, D.C.: Smithsonian, 1977).

right: 523. Toshusai Sharaku.
The Actor Otani Hiroj III as the manservant Tosa no Matahei. 1794–1795.
Woodblock print. Museum of Fine Arts, Boston (Bigelow Collection).

PRIMO INTERMEDIO DELLA VEGLIA DELLA LIBERATIONE DI TIRRENO FATTA NELLA SALA DELLE COM·
DIE DEL SER.ᵐᵒ GRAN DVCA DI TOSCANA IL CARNOVALE DEL 1616. DOVE SI RAP.ᵛᵃ IL MONTE D'ISCHIA· CON IL GIGANTE
TIFEO·SOTTO·

524. Jacques Callot.
First Interlude:
The Giant Typhon on Mount
Ischia. 1617. Etching,
11⅞ × 9⅜" (30 × 24 cm).
Art Museum,
Princeton University,
Princeton, New Jersey
(bequest of
Junius S. Morgan).

European Art from 1600 to 1750

Baroque Style

We still look back to the time of the **Baroque** style as a period when art reached unsurpassed heights. The seriousness of the artists, their great ambitions, and the prestige accorded them by their audience combined to produce a period of exceptional achievement.

By 1600 Europeans knew they were living in a new period of history. The last of the great Renaissance artists had died, and people were ready for new styles and ideas. The division of Europe and her colonies into Catholic and Protestant nations, which began when Martin Luther nailed his "95 theses" to a church door in 1517, was recognized as irreversible by 1600 and both sides began to take positive approaches to their own religious interpretations. Italy, Spain, and Belgium became great centers of Catholic Counter-Reformation art, while the Netherlands and northern Germany became strongholds of Protestant art. Music and drama were the most inventive arts of the period, taking especially significant form in combination as opera. These new performing arts, whose main centers of development were in Italy, were so impressive that visual artists couldn't help but adopt theatrical poses and settings in their own work. You can recognize Baroque art by these theatrical qualities.

An etching by Jacques Callot *(kah-LO)* (1592–1635) shows an opera-ballet performance at the court of the Grand Duke of Tuscany in Florence in 1616 **[524]**. The large stage, with elaborate scenery of forest and mountain, expands down curving stairways to permit performers on the main floor, like an arena. The breadth of the scene was a challenge to the artist; notice the clever changes in perspective from the nearer figures back to the stage. He also exaggerated, but only a little, the fantastic costumes and animated poses of the audience to make the scene more theatrical. Baroque period audiences enjoyed distortion of perspective, of pose and costume—of anything that made the effect more dramatic.

There were great differences between the Catholic and Protestant countries, but also much in common. Protestant England, for example, produced far less visual art than Catholic Italy; England's greatest Baroque artist was Shakespeare, who set many of his plays in Italy because that was the center of theatrical art. In the Protestant countries, art, including religious subjects, was usually done for private patrons, not for the churches, and many Protestants opposed art as promoting idolatry. The Protestants rightly considered that abundant use of art would make their churches look like Catholic churches, for the Catholic Church had adopted art as one of its main educational and missionary tools.

The Society of Jesus, often called the Jesuit order, was one of the typical Catholic organizations of the period. Its mother church, Il Gesú in Rome, was decorated in the Baroque style, with a ceiling fresco by Giovanni Battista Gaulli (1639–1709) representing *The Triumph of the Name of Jesus* **[525]**. Although Ba-

525. Giovanni Battista Gaulli. *The Triumph of the Name of Jesus*, ceiling of the nave, Gesú Church, Rome. 1674–1679. Fresco.

526. Gianlorenzo Bernini. *Apollo and Daphne*. 1622–1624. Marble, life-size. Borghese Gallery, Rome.

roque artists were not the first to paint ceilings, it was typical of Baroque art to try to envelop the audience in an illusionistic world. Sections of the painting cross the frame into the real space of the church, to confuse the observer about what is real and what imaginary. The boundary between the reality of your own body and its space and the fresco and its illusion of heaven is so hard to define that you begin to accept the idea that the ceiling really has opened up to show crowds of angels adoring the radiant name of Jesus.

Gianlorenzo Bernini. Gianlorenzo Bernini (1598–1680) was not only the greatest sculptor of the Italian Baroque, but typical in his mixture of theater and religion. He was deeply devout and attended Mass every morning. He numbered among his friends and patrons eight popes, various cardinals, and the head of the Jesuit order. He was also fascinated by the theater—an art that gave scope to his versatility. John Evelyn wrote in his diary of having attended a performance in Rome at which Bernini gave a "Publique Opera . . . where in he painted the seanes, cut the Statues, invented the Engines, composed the Musique, writ the Comedy, and built the Theater all himselfe."[13]

In *Apollo and Daphne* [526] the young Bernini (he was between 24 and 26) turned the immobile block of white marble into agitated movement. The god Apollo, in love with Daphne, has pursued her and is about to seize her when he is amazed to see her turn into a laurel tree, the answer to her prayer to the earth goddess for help. Dramatic expressions and gestures are basic to this sculpture in which marble takes on the shapes and textures of flesh, hair, cloth, bark, and leaves.

Among stones white marble is a good actor whose neutral color and texture permit it to play many parts. That is one reason Baroque sculptors favored it, the other reason being its use by Greek and Roman sculptors. When the ancient sculptures were new they were finished with paint and wax, but when they were dug up after a thousand years all the paint had worn off. That established a new taste for unpainted stone, which first affected Renaissance sculp-

Recognizing the Great Styles

tors. Bernini was conscious of the problem of expressing color in a colorless material and tried to overcome it by subtle hollows and bulges, making a play of light and shadow that substitutes for color.

Compared to Renaissance sculptures such as Michelangelo's *David* [262], Bernini's *Apollo and Daphne* helps us define the Baroque style: the Renaissance figure is shown in a moment of stillness, poised for action, but Bernini's figures are shown at the climax of action. The Baroque also chose the climactic moment, when a personality or story is fully revealed and the audience attains insight into the meaning of the subject. Renaissance artists sought balance and unity, but Bernini and the other Baroque artists considered variety and movement among the most important principles. That led to contrasts of light and shadow, of texture, and of color in painting, much stronger—more dramatic, you might say—than are found in Renaissance art. The patrons of the Baroque were popes and kings, such as Louis XIV of France (who patronized Bernini but finally decided his style was too agitated to conform to the royal dignity).

Peter Paul Rubens.   Peter Paul Rubens (1577–1640) exemplifies the Baroque style in painting, as Bernini did in sculpture. Both men were extroverts, as you can tell just by looking at their art, prolific workers, and the favorites of powerful rulers. Rubens, a Belgian, absorbed the Italian style at its source when he was a court painter in Italy from age 23 to 31. His painting *The Horrors of War* [527] was in the collection of the Grand Duke of Tuscany, a descendant of the Medici family, whose opera-ballet was drawn by Callot [524].

In a letter to a friend, Rubens described *The Horrors of War* mainly in terms of the subject of the picture:

> The principal figure is Mars [god of war], who rushes forth with shield and blood-stained sword, threatening the people with disaster. He pays little heed to Venus,

527.   Peter Paul Rubens. *The Horrors of War.* 1637. Oil on canvas, 6'9" × 11'3" (2.1 × 3.4 m). Palatine Gallery, Florence.

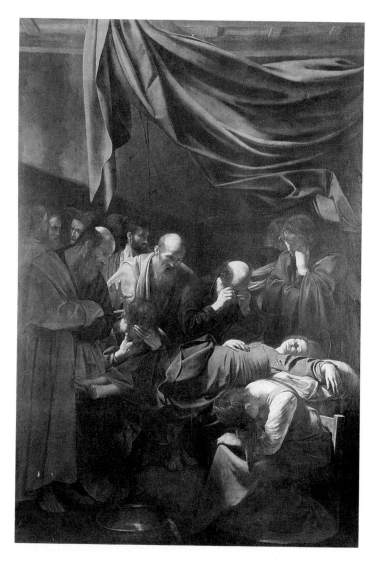

528. Caravaggio. *The Death of the Virgin.* 1605. Oil on canvas, 12 × 8′ (3.7 × 2.4 m). Louvre, Paris.

his mistress, who . . . strives with caresses and embraces to hold him. From the other side, Mars is dragged forward by the Fury Alekto, with a torch in her hand. Nearby are monsters personifying Pestilence and Famine, those inseparable partners of War. . . . That grief-stricken woman clothed in black, with torn veil, robbed of all her jewels and other ornaments, is the unfortunate Europe who, for so many years now, has suffered plunder, outrage, and misery. . . .[14]

The painting is only secondarily about physical solids, but mainly is a field for the interaction of forces. Notice Rubens' use of verbs in his description: rushes, strives, dragged. Venus, for example, performs a spiral movement beloved by Baroque artists: her feet are planted toward the left, showing that she had been facing toward the figure symbolizing Europe, and her shoulders turn to the right as she clutches at her warlike lover. Notice that war and peace, Europe and fury, are all personified as they would be in a play, and everything is acted out—over-acted, we might say, since a different acting style is in use today. We sometimes think of Baroque art as worldly and voluptuous, but it was also deeply concerned with moral and spiritual matters. Rubens' painting, which seems sensual and unserious to people now, to the artist and his audience was a serious statement about tragic conditions.

Caravaggio. The theatrical appearance so common in Baroque art gave rise, as you might expect, to its opposite, though it may be hard for us today to see the opposition which was so clear to people at the beginning of the 17th

Recognizing the Great Styles

century. Michelangelo Merisi (1565–1609), called Caravaggio after his hometown, aimed to represent nothing but the visible truth, eliminating the imaginary and conventional. *The Death of the Virgin* [528], begun by Caravaggio in 1605 for an altar in a Roman church, was not accepted by the patrons because the painter rejected the customary idealized figures acting out traditional stories. Caravaggio's figures were painted from models chosen from the streets of Rome; they pose in his dark studio illuminated only by a shaft of light from a single window; they are shown as objectively as possible, without idealization. Still more shocking to the Roman audience, Mary is shown as simply dead, though the ancient traditional way to show Mary's death was to include the ascent of her spirit to heaven to be welcomed by Christ. The ascent of the spirit was invisible to Caravaggio, who insisted that accurate representation of the visible was the whole job of the artist.

To our eyes the shaft of light and the deep red curtain in the upper right still seem theatrical; Caravaggio's innovations were more superficial, but more significant to his audience since they showed that the sacred stories had a foundation of material truth in this world. Although conservative members of the audience objected to this worldly idea, artists were impressed. Rubens was in Rome buying paintings for the collection of the Duke of Mantua when *The Death of the Virgin* was rejected and immediately arranged to have it purchased. Before the painting could leave Rome an exhibit was arranged at which great crowds came to see the notorious work.

Two aspects of Caravaggio's style reverberated through the art world: the dramatic spotlighting of significant features in a deeply shadowed space, called *tenebrism* ("shadow-ism"), and his expression of the idea that spiritual realities are believable only when they affect common people. Both those features of Caravaggio's style were learned by the young Velázquez, but it was Rembrandt, especially, who brought them to the highest development.

Rembrandt.   Movement and emotion—those are key words for the Baroque. Emotion is expressed in gesture and facial expression and we find artists studying those. Several artists left portraits of themselves making faces in the mirror to study different kinds of expressions. Rembrandt did several small etchings like the one here [529] of himself frowning, smiling, or snarling. These expressions do not appear to show real moods; they are dramatizations, typical of their period.

529. Rembrandt. *Self-portrait in a cap, open-mouthed.* 1630. Etching, 2 × 1¾" (5 × 4 cm). Rijksmuseum, Amsterdam.

A POINT IN TIME: Rembrandt's Bankruptcy

In 1656, the year he turned 50, Rembrandt declared bankruptcy. Yet after his bankruptcy Rembrandt continued to receive many commissions. Historians have been trying for years to understand the relationship between Rembrandt's art, his audience, and his finances.

Rembrandt's most famous painting, *The Sortie of the Civic Guard,* usually called *The Night Watch* [531], painted fourteen years earlier, in 1642, has been considered one of the clues to this puzzle. One of Rembrandt's pupils later described *The Night Watch* as the basis of Rembrandt's fame, but it also marks the high point of his patronage and the beginning of his descent into poverty. Was this painting somehow flawed in the eyes of his patrons?

The subject of the painting, according to art historian Gary Schwartz, is the marching out of a company of musketeers to welcome the queen of France on her visit to Amsterdam in 1638. The painting was one of six large group portraits to be hung in the musketeers' clubhouse at their shooting range. Membership in a civic guard company was a social and political advantage and the officers were all wealthy and powerful. Frans Banning Cocq, in black, is shown as captain, with Willem van Ruytenburgh, in white, as lieutenant, with the musketeers loading their weapons and preparing to march. Sixteen members of the troop contributed to the cost of the painting and were included as portraits. Originally the painting was a little larger on all sides; it was cut down to fit a later location.

Earlier historians suggested that the patrons were dissatisfied with the painting because many of the faces were not clearly portrayed, but that was not the case. The painting was accepted and admired; its story-telling style of group portrait was adopted by other painters. Even the contrast of brilliant light and deep shadow, which was a distinctive feature of Rembrandt's style, was acceptable.

But it is true that Rembrandt's personal fortunes began to decline the year the painting was finished. In June of that year his wife Saskia died, leaving Rembrandt with a baby son, Titus, and Saskia's will in which all the joint property was willed to baby Titus. Never again could Rembrandt claim personal ownership of any property he owned at the time of her death, when he was 36. In addition, Saskia's death deprived Rembrandt of the social connections she had brought him, which were indispensable for patronage in Amsterdam. Patronage by the state administrators also declined about this time. Rembrandt's problems with money, family, patrons, and political connections each made the others worse. In later years the painter was rumored to have had an excessive love of money, but that fault is easy to understand under the circumstances. Rembrandt's art always attracted patrons and admirers, but important patronage of the sort that resulted in *The Night Watch* depended on social and political connections which Rembrandt lost when Saskia died.

Gary Schwartz, *Rembrandt: His Life, His Paintings* (New York: Viking, 1985).

opposite: 531. Rembrandt. *The Night Watch.* 1642. Oil on canvas, 11′10″ × 14′4″ (3.6 × 4.4 m). Rijksmuseum, Amsterdam.

530. Rembrandt. *Christ Preaching the Forgiveness of Sins.* c. 1650–1658. Etching, 6 × 8¼″ (15 × 21 cm). Rijksmuseum, Amsterdam.

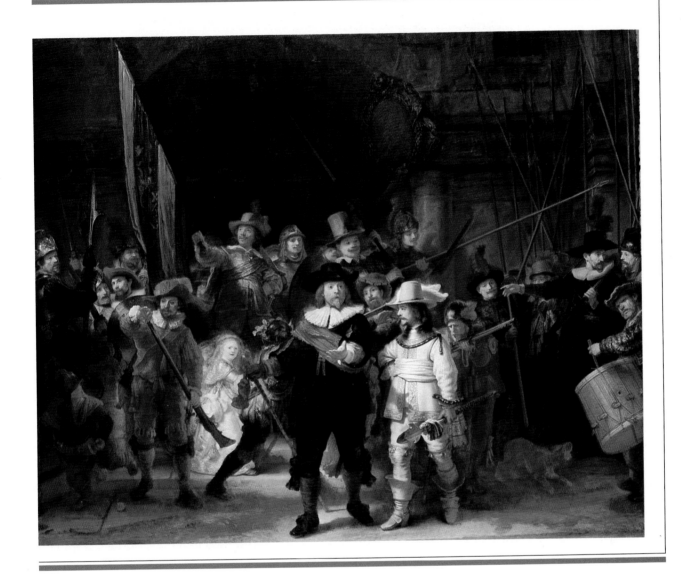

Rembrandt (1606–1669), who worked in Amsterdam, was the greatest artist of the Protestant Christian North. Amsterdam had a large Jewish population whose members were often portrayed by the artist, especially in scenes from the Bible. Study of the Bible was encouraged in the Protestant countries, and Rembrandt knew it thoroughly, to the point that he sometimes illustrated events that probably happened but are not exactly described. *Christ Preaching the Forgiveness of Sins* is one of those **[530]**. The humble crowd gathers around, each one an individual with a unique personality. In the foreground a child is absorbed in his drawing in the dust. Every pose and face has been observed in the real world, yet the result is a spiritual statement. Both features of Caravaggio's style are found here, but completely absorbed by Rembrandt. Although some of the figures, such as the turbaned men on the left, were not to be found on the streets of Amsterdam, there are no idealized types. Even Christ is not idealized nor given any mark of his superhuman status, so that it comes as a surprise to find an unobtrusive halo over his head. Yet Christ is clearly the focus of the light in the picture, his lighted figure with its contrasting dark hair standing out against the deeply shadowed background areas. In his paintings Rembrandt increased this effect of spotlighting for very dramatic effects.

532. Jan Vermeer. *The Art of Painting.* c. 1665–1670. Oil on canvas, 4'3¼" × 3'7¼" (1.3 × 1.1 m). Kunsthistorisches Museum, Vienna.

The Optical Record in Baroque Painting. Two important Baroque artists, Jan Vermeer and Diego Velázquez, were mainly concerned with the creation of a perfect record of vision. Their cool, scientific objectivity sets them apart from the main trend of the Baroque, but it has contributed to their continued popularity throughout many changes of artistic fashion; they have seemed "modern" to generations of art lovers.

The Dutch artist Jan Vermeer *(vur-MERE)* (1632–1675) painted *The Art of Painting* **[532]** for himself, for it was still in his possession at his death, yet it is one of his larger and more ambitious works, and collectors could never get enough of his work. It is not a self-portrait, but shows an artist in fine clothes of the previous century, his studio wall decorated with a map of the Low Countries in that earlier time, before Belgium and Holland separated. The model is costumed as the Muse of History, and on the table is a plaster cast of an ancient sculpture. Painting, Vermeer seems to say, is a record of history; its practitioners devote themselves to the spirit of history and are rewarded by fame—the book and the trumpet carried by the muse. Vermeer himself painted quiet scenes from middle-class life, never historical events, but he evidently saw this painting as especially relevant to his own life and work. The scene is imaginary but probably based in some measure on a set-up of furniture and a model which could be painted from life. The dark curtain has been drawn back to reveal a room lit only by a hidden window on the left, and it is that light which unites the design, reveals the masses, and sets each thing in its place in space. Vermeer appeals mainly to our eyes, whose sensitivity is primarily to light; he ignores the muscular (or kinesthetic) and the dramatic emotions which are basic elements of Baroque style. Fame came to Vermeer on his own terms, which stressed the optical in place of the theatrical.

Recognizing the Great Styles

The optical style of Baroque painting transcended political and religious borders, for its other great practitioner was the painter of the Spanish court, Diego Velázquez (1599–1660). In the *Surrender of Breda* [533], he shows the surrender in 1625 of a Dutch town to Spanish forces after a long siege. The Dutch general offers his sword to the Spanish leader, who generously refuses it. This large painting hung in the palace in Madrid and was testimony to the gallantry of the Spanish general and the power of Spanish arms. Although the surrender is a satisfying dramatic incident, it is a minor part of the appeal of the painting, which rests mainly on the visual contrast between the figures ranged across the foreground and the vast misty landscape of the battlefield. That contrast is enhanced by the view of landscape through the fence-like ranks of Spanish lances on the right. Like Vermeer, Velázquez preferred to paint from things he could see. Although he did not witness this historical event, he could set up soldiers and horses as models, but the main unifying features—light and color—had to be imagined.

Vermeer and Velázquez were on opposite sides of the great religious and political questions of their period, but they agreed on the question of style. Painting for them was a record of vision in which light and color were the main actors.

A World of Baroque Architecture.   Looking at *The Surrender of Breda* we remember that at that time Spain was consolidating a vast empire in the Americas and the Pacific, bringing back immense riches and giving in return European

533.   Diego Velázquez. *The Surrender of Breda*. 1634. Oil on canvas, 10′ × 12′2″ (3 × 3.7 m). Prado, Madrid.

above left: 534.
Baldassare Longhena.
Santa Maria della
Salute, Venice. 1631.

above right: 535.
Baldassare Longhena.
Interior, Santa Maria
della Salute, Venice.
1631. View toward the
high altar.

culture, including the Baroque style. The Baroque style in architecture was used for Christian churches everywhere European culture penetrated, adapted to the materials and building traditions of a thousand different regions.

The most sophisticated version of the style can be found in the church of Santa Maria della Salute [534] in Venice, a landmark in a great European city by an architect, Baldassare Longhena *(lawn-GAY-nuh)* (1604–1682), who won a design competition against the most highly trained architects of his day. The structure and decoration of the church are integrated in a two-story octagon supporting a dome. Scroll-like volutes accent the eight sides, each topped by the statue of a prophet. The volutes are not mere decoration, but serve as buttresses for the dome. The interior [535] duplicates the column-and-arch design of the exterior, with the altar set in a stage-like chapel. Longhena carefully controlled the light and space for theatrical effects, thinking in the same terms as Bernini, Rubens, or Vermeer. Like all Baroque architecture, this Venetian church was designed to inspire emotion, whether awe, gloom, fear, or, in Longhena's church, delight.

At Tepotzotlán in Mexico, on the frontier of the European culture, the Jesuits built a school for priests with its church in a Mexican version of the Baroque style [536]. Its massive walls are pierced by an arched door and a heavily framed rose window and are decorated with niches flanked by columns. Looking at Santa Maria della Salute [534, 535], it is hard to see the structure and the decoration as separate, but in the Mexican church the front is basically a flat wall pierced by an arched doorway with elaborate decoration added, like frosting on a cake. That the structure and decoration can be considered separately is the result of the designer being a priest, educated but not really an architect. The straight, solid walls were ornamented with patterns taken out of design books brought from Europe. Even with its simpler structure, the Mexican church at Tepotzotlán is still Baroque in its use of abundant ornament to overwhelm the senses and inspire a heavenly emotion.

Rococo Style

The **Rococo** style (1700–1750) developed from the Baroque and carried on most features of its style, but turned away from the heroic and the melodramatic toward more modest, good-humored art. The patrons of the Baroque were popes and kings, such as Louis XIV of France. When Louis XIV died in 1715, the Baroque style died with him, but France became the center of the new Rococo style. To followers of the Rococo style the grandeur of the super-colossal began to look old-fashioned; something on a human scale had more appeal. Patrons of the new style were members of the upper middle class, who preferred its charm and its escapist mood, for most of them were working hard for a living. Park-like landscapes and scenes from the theater and from comfortable daily life were preferred, in subtle light and color. If the Baroque was masculine and heroic in tone, the Rococo is feminine, reflecting a period when women began to play more active roles in public life.

Watteau. A young painter in Paris, Antoine Watteau (1684–1721), who was a great admirer of the paintings of Rubens, created a new image for the new period, one that sums up the Rococo style. In his painting *Venetian Festival* [**537**], Watteau brought together many of the threads that formed the style of his time. The gods and goddesses of Baroque art have turned into statues in the background, with slim young people in beautiful clothes dancing and making music in the foreground. Watteau showed himself as the bagpiper in this scene. A picnic with music, conversation, and flirtation appears to be the ideal of Rococo life. In his own time such scenes were considered entirely cheerful, but later times have found a subtle undercurrent of melancholy, for pleasure always ends, as in this case the Rococo ended in the French Revolution of 1789.

The theater, which in the 17th century belonged to the nobility, in the 18th century began to belong to the people, becoming so much a part of life that life

below left: 536.
Church of
San Francisco Xavier,
College of the Jesuits,
Tepotzotlán, Mexico.
18th century.

below: 537.
Antoine Watteau.
Venetian Festival. 1717.
Oil on canvas, 22 × 18″
(56 × 46 cm).
National Galleries of
Scotland, Edinburgh.

538.
Antoine Watteau.
Gilles. 1717–1719.
Oil on canvas,
6′½″ × 4′11″
(1.8 × 1.5 m).
Louvre, Paris.

itself was often seen as a comedy. Watteau did a fine portrait of his friend Gilles **[538]**, who had retired from the stage to open a restaurant. Like all Watteau's patrons, he was a private citizen, not a king or a noble. Gilles is shown playing the part of Pierrot, one of the stock characters in comedy, a lover who is clever, sentimental, and poetic. The high seriousness of the Baroque has given way to subtle personal attitudes and moods.

Meissen Porcelain. The Rococo provided the style for the newly invented porcelain ceramics. Porcelain had been known in China for about three thousand years and was a valuable export industry. Ever since Marco Polo described its use in China in his account of his travels, the Europeans had been trying to break the secret of its manufacture. Finally, after a six-year crash program comparable to the invention of the atomic bomb, a team led by an alchemist (a practitioner of the pseudo-scientific ancestor of chemistry) solved the problem in 1708. Its patron, the ruler of Saxony in Germany, set up a factory at Meissen *(MY-sen)*, which is still in operation. Despite efforts to keep the process secret, it rapidly spread to other European centers.

Temple of Love [539] was made by the most successful sculptor associated with the Meissen factory, Johann Joachim Kändler. It stands nearly 4 feet (1.2 meters) tall and is made of 114 separate pieces. This served as a centerpiece and you must imagine the porcelain place settings that were to surround it. That was not a setting for a disorderly revel; good table manners were one element in the refinement that the Rococo brought to European life.

France as the Center of Culture. This was the period when educated people everywhere spoke French and adopted French manners and styles. Paris, which had become a great cultural center in the Baroque period, consolidated that position in the Rococo and retained it until 1940. It was the reasonableness, charm, and good manners that shine out of the art of Watteau and his contemporaries which attracted people all over the world to the Rococo culture of France. That style is recognizable mainly by its modest scale, its good humor, the charm of individual personalities, and very often its glorification of women and feminine qualities, all in strong contrast to the masculine virility of the Baroque that preceded it.

Houdon. A glimpse into the personalities of many of the real people who lived at that time is offered to us by the portraits of Jean Antoine Houdon (*oo-DAWN*) (1741–1828). We are lucky enough to have portraits of Washington, Jefferson, Franklin, and several other notable Americans from the hand of this French artist.

Houdon modeled the head of his daughter Sabine [540] just for himself, unrestrained by a patron's demands, and we see his sensitivity to personality at its best. The deeply cut pupils give an especially lifelike expression to the eyes, but if you cover them you will see how much expression there is in the mouth and the eyebrows.

This sensitivity to personality runs through the whole of Baroque and Rococo art, and the gradual rise to economic power of the middle class during these

below left: 539.
Johann Joachim Kändler. *Temple of Love.* c. 1750. Meissen porcelain table centerpiece, 114 separate pieces; height 45⅝″ (116 cm). Museum für Kunsthandwerk, Frankfurt-am-Main, West Germany.

below: 540.
Jean Antoine Houdon. *Sabine Houdon,* detail. 1791. Plaster, life-size. Louvre, Paris.

Styles of the Columbian Age: 15th–18th Centuries _____ 397

periods allowed them to become both the patrons and the subjects of art. Those periods laid the foundations on which we have erected the art and culture of our times.

Summary for Review

By 1400 Italy was leading the European countries into a new period, now called the Renaissance ("rebirth"). The rise of commerce in Europe and Japan brought a new class of patrons who considered understanding art a mark of prestige. Skillful illusions of nature were preferred in Italy, requiring knowledge of perspective and anatomy. Portraits, religious subjects, and revived interest in ancient Greek and Roman mythology provided the subjects. Northern Europe (especially Flanders) retained Gothic elements in its style, while Italy studied ancient Roman and Greek styles. Fresco and tempera dominated painting in Italy in the 1400s, but Flemish painters introduced oil painting, with detailed illusions, and by 1500 oil paint was in use throughout Europe. Japan continued to use watercolor, tempera, and ink for traditional screens and scrolls, with a native Japanese (Yamato) style competing with a Chinese (Zen) ink style. European missionaries settled in Japan for a century, followed by two centuries of exclusion of all foreign influences during which Japan cultivated its native "artless" aesthetic principles. About 1600 Europe adopted the optimistic, theatrical **Baroque** style, used mainly for Catholic subjects in southern Europe and for varied subjects (portraits, landscape, religious subjects) in Protestant northern Europe. Artists sought to express the climax of action in Baroque compositions, often with heroic themes. European expansion carried Baroque style to Mexico, the Philippine Islands, and further. By 1715 the **Rococo** style had become popular, with upper-middle-class patrons seeking good-humored escapist subjects from the theater, mythology, and middle-class life. France began to replace Italy as the center of artistic culture.

13

From Neo-Classicism to Post-Impressionism, 1750–1900

In earlier sections we have seen the European nations exploring the globe and discovering other peoples with different ways of life. The first reaction of the European explorers was to conquer and exploit whatever wealth was easily available, then to convert the conquered nations to Christianity and make them as much like the Europeans as possible. (The Japanese were among the few who successfully resisted this wave of European expansion.) But by the middle of the 18th century there were already signs that the European nations and their Western culture were being deeply changed in turn by their contacts with other peoples and by their explorations of history and nature. In this chapter we will examine what happened to the Europeans—and their descendants in the new nations such as the United States, Canada, and Mexico—as shown by changes in their art.

Few periods in the history of the world have been so rich in change. People were fascinated by new discoveries and often overwhelmed by political turmoil. Looking back at the beautiful art of that period, we often believe it was made to be simply beautiful. Strangely, it seems that in every period both the artists and their audience considered the art of the previous period beautiful but believed that their own art must sacrifice beauty for the higher goal of truth. The truth looked different to every generation and in the 18th and 19th centuries we begin to see the rapid give-and-take of ideas and styles which is so characteristic of our own century. The great styles of the period—Neo-Classicism, Romanticism, Realism, Impressionism, and finally Post-Impressionism—were associated with social and political ideas whose truth was a matter of public debate. It is hard for the 20th-century audience to take a deep interest in 19th-century politics, but we need to remember that 19th-century art was often considered by its original audience to be ugly but important because it reflected political issues.

Each of these styles had particular strengths and weaknesses. For example, Neo-Classicism, like any classical style, was based on the principle that there is one best answer to any problem. This produced a high general level of art, since the best answer could be learned by anyone willing to make the effort, but it eliminated the genius who refused to follow the rules. Romanticism, on the other hand, believed that there are no absolutely right answers, but only answers that are right for the individual. That resulted in a breakdown of the standards of quality, since no one could say that a work was bad; the work only needed to find an audience that liked it. As we shall see, the career of Francisco Goya dramatizes this conflict.

Despite the fact that these arguments are now a century or two old, they are by no means settled. The art world today struggles with the same questions. We are still asking ourselves questions such as, "Are there no standards? How can anyone tell whether the work is good? Why don't artists paint about real life?"

Neo-Classicism:
The Art of Reason

The discovery of other cultures based on entirely different ways of life stimulated Europeans to reconsider their own beliefs and ways. The increasing pace of scientific discoveries and new inventions and their application in the Industrial Revolution contributed to the feeling that by using the mind people could build a better world. The Scottish philosopher John Locke (1632–1704) had proposed that there were rights which humans were born with, which did not depend on the goodness of a king, and the French writer Jean Jacques Rousseau (1712–1778) believed there were more natural ways of life than were lived in Europe, and that they produced better people. Voltaire (1694–1778) noted that the world was full of devout and moral people who had never heard of Christianity. These ideas were in large part the result of contacts with Asian, African, and American nations, whose very existence called into question everything the Europeans had always believed. An early result was a burst of scientific experimentation produced by the new mood of looking at the world and asking "why?"

Art and Science

Joseph Wright of Derby (1734–1797) in England may have produced the first depiction of the "mad scientist," now a stock character, in his thrilling and mysterious *An Experiment on a Bird in an Air-Pump* **[541]**. The scientist looks out at us, inviting us to witness the experiment, illuminated only by a hidden candle on the table. One girl hides her eyes as the dove flutters in the increasing vacuum of the bell jar. The deep seriousness of this varied group of people gathered around the table on a moonlit night helps us understand the excitement of the new age. Already, in 1768, the image appears of the scientist playing with life and death in his resolute search for truth. This English painter is usually classified among the Neo-Classic artists, those who believed a firmly drawn line was the basis of style (as opposed to those who preferred color as the most important element), but this painting is more important in the history of science and general culture than for any stylistic innovation.

Neo-Classic style looks so familiar to us now that it is surprising to realize it was the first of many styles to be developed in Western culture as a result of exploration; in this case the explorations founded the field we call archaeology. Two explorations were especially influential. One was the discovery of the ruins of the Roman cities of Pompeii and Herculaneum beneath the volcanic dust and lava that had covered them since A.D. 79, revealing for the first time an intimate glimpse of ancient Roman life. The other was the first exploration of Greece, then a province of the hostile Turkish Empire. The historians and critics joined in promoting the importance of Greek and Roman art. *Thoughts on the Imitation of Greek Works* by Johann Winckelmann was published in 1755. Greek art, Winckelmann thought, "marked for us the outermost limits of human and divine beauty." The Parthenon sculptures, which were purchased by the British ambassador to the Turkish court and brought back to London, had such an impact on the European public that everything Greek was suddenly fashionable.

The 23-year-old Parisian socialite Madame Récamier had her portrait painted by Jacques Louis David *(dah-VEED)* (1748–1825) wearing a Classical Greek-style gown, her hair done in the style of Athenian women of the 5th century B.C., and reclining barefoot on a Neo-Classical couch beneath a Neo-Classical lamp (both made especially to be painted in this picture) **[542]**. The somber color and stark setting suggested the seriousness and high ethical tone

which were attributed to the Classical civilizations. Neo-Classic style symbolized political and moral reform to the audience; from King Louis XVI's point of view it was dangerously revolutionary, and by the time Madame Récamier's portrait was painted (in 1800) the king had been replaced by a republican government. As Napoleon gained control of the French nation David emerged as the official state painter, his cold, precise style the official style of the new regime.

Neo-Classic style was modeled on Greek and Roman art, which was known mainly in sculpture and vase painting, and it retained the linearity and simple color with light and shadow that it learned from those sources. Its subjects were also taken from Classical sources or, if modern subjects were shown, it was with the seriousness attributed to the Classical cultures. Scientific objectivity was the admired approach.

541. Joseph Wright of Derby. *An Experiment on a Bird in an Air-Pump.* 1768. Oil on canvas, 6 × 8′ (1.8 × 2.4 m). National Gallery, London.

542. Jacques Louis David. *Madame Récamier.* 1800. Oil on canvas, 5′8½″ × 8′ (1.7 × 2.4 m). Louvre, Paris.

A POINT IN TIME: Marie Guillemine Benoist, Portrait of a Woman

Portrait of a Woman **[543]** (catalogued in the Louvre as "Portrait d'une négresse") is the best-known work by Marie Guillemine Benoist *(ma-REE ghee-yuh-MEEN ben-WAH)* (1768–1826), whose life spanned the French Revolution, the dictatorship of Napoleon, and the restoration of a constitutional monarchy. The name of the woman portrayed is unknown, but her appearance in this dignified portrait reminds us of several kinds of liberation that were occurring during Benoist's lifetime. The portrait, shown for the first time in 1800, "had the character of a manifesto both of feminism and of black emancipation."* In 1794 France abolished slavery, just about the time the portrait was painted. It made Benoist's reputation when it was shown at the national Salon exhibition; it was surely seen as a celebration of black liberation.

Benoist studied art with two of the best-known artists of her day, Élisabeth Vigée-Lebrun *(vee-ZHAY luh-BRUNH)* (1755–1842) and Jacques Louis David. As a pupil of David, Benoist had access to the patronage of Napoleon's government, and she was successful enough that she was commissioned to paint several portraits of Napoleon himself. But the portrait of the unknown woman remained her most admired work, described by one critic as "comparable to the best portraits of David."† Benoist received an annual stipend from the government and was awarded a gold medal in 1804.

Women, as well as blacks, achieved liberation from many restrictions during this period, as the careers of Vigée-Lebrun and Benoist show. But with the restoration of the monarchy in 1815 Benoist's husband was appointed to a position in the new government and he asked her to stop exhibiting her work in public. Lawrence Gowing tells us that "her heartbroken letter to him ended, 'let's not talk about it again or the wound will open up once more.'"‡

---

*Lawrence Gowing, *Paintings in the Louvre* (New York: Stewart, Tabori & Chang, 1987) 562.

† Emmanuel Bénézit, *Dictionnaire critique et documentaire des peintres, sculpteurs, et graveurs . . .* (Paris: E. Gründ, 1924).

‡ Gowing 562.

543. Marie Guillemine Benoist. *Portrait of a Woman.* c. 1795. Oil on canvas, 32 × 25⅝" (81 × 65 cm). Louvre, Paris.

In the 18th century artists discovered a new specialty, the painting of ruins, brought to great popularity by Pannini (see his *Interior of the Pantheon* [316]) and Giovanni Battista Piranesi (1720–1778). *Temple of Saturn* [544] is one of a series of etchings of views of Rome by Piranesi which established in the public mind the grandeur of the Classical ruins. Architects had been using a more or less Classical style since the early Renaissance, but archaeological studies gave them a new understanding of Greek and Roman buildings. For example, Thomas Jefferson, who besides being president of the United States was also an archaeologist and an architect, designed the capitol building for the state of Virginia [545] in a style based on the Erechtheum in Athens [305].

Greek and Roman art, reinforced by philosophy and literature, had an especially strong appeal to European people, who naturally regarded those ancient cultures as their own remote ancestors, but it was not long before other ancient and exotic cultures were discovered. When Napoleon invaded Egypt in 1798 he took along with his army a company of scientists and artists to study the ruins of ancient Egypt. The pyramids and the Sphinx, painted reliefs and hieroglyphic writing amazed the public. Similar explorations were going on in Central America, where Frederick Catherwood portrayed the ruins of Maya temples using a **camera obscura**. It was only a short step to the use of photographic film, which permitted still more accurate and objective views of distant foreign places.

Ingres and the Later Neo-Classic

Jean Auguste Dominique Ingres, who died at 87 in 1867, dominated French painting throughout the first half of the 19th century. He painted subjects from Classical mythology and portraits, but in the long run it seems to be paintings such as his *Odalisque with Slave* [546] (an odalisque is a Turkish harem woman)

above left: 544.
Giovanni Battista
Piranesi.
Temple of Saturn,
from *Views of Rome.*
c. 1774. Etching.
Metropolitan Museum
of Art, New York
(Rogers Fund, 1941).

above: 545.
Thomas Jefferson.
Virginia State Capitol,
Richmond.
Designed 1785–1789.

546.
Jean Auguste Dominique Ingres.
Odalisque with Slave. 1840.
Oil on canvas mounted on panel,
28⅜ × 39⅜″ (72 × 100 cm).
Fogg Art Museum, Harvard University
(bequest of Grenville L. Winthrop).

that remain popular and influential. Ingres depended on travelers' accounts for the setting, and the precision of his style and the calculation of the design take it out of real experience into a world of fantasy. Yet the Islamic countries were no mere fantasy for the French public at the time this was painted, for France was fighting for an empire in the Islamic regions of North Africa, and many men had been there in military service. Ingres, who was a good draftsman, considered himself among the Neo-Classic artists and defended the style of sharply defined lines and shapes, but in subjects he shared a Romantic taste for the exotic.

Romanticism: Emotion Revalued

"To say the word Romanticism is to say modern art—that is, intimacy, spirituality, color, aspiration toward the infinite, expressed by every means available to the art."[1] Charles Baudelaire, the French poet-critic, wrote that definition in 1846, and it marks a late period in the Romantic movement. The Englishman Edmund Burke laid the groundwork 90 years earlier in an essay entitled *The Sublime and the Beautiful,* in which he described beautiful things as small, smooth, delicate, and tending to arouse love. Sublime things were vast, difficult, magnificent, dark, and rugged, and "fill the mind with that sort of delightful horror." Romanticism aimed at the sublime rather than the beautiful. It was especially at home in England, Germany, and Spain. It was also a style of music, represented by Beethoven and Chopin, among others, which aimed at the sublime. If rationalism was a powerful movement, one which we associate especially with the 18th century, it was followed by a reaction in the Romantic movement, no less powerful and widespread, which reached its climax in the first half of the 19th century.

The *Romantic* style emphasized color applied freely, allowing the individual brushstrokes to show, and strong light and shadow and chose subjects from modern life or any place except ancient Greece and Rome. Personal style was cultivated and subjects were expressed emotionally, emphasizing such things as the height of mountains and the power of storms.

A procession of monks makes its way through the snowy graveyard of the ruined monastery, carrying a coffin, in Caspar David Friedrich's (1774–1840) painting **[547]**. The irregularity of Gothic architecture appealed to Romantic taste, seeming closer to nature than the more symmetrical Classical style: the ruined church fits with the gnarled and broken oaks. Spirituality, aspiration toward the infinite, were Friedrich's subjects, and he found them mainly in

547. Caspar David Friedrich. *Monastery Graveyard in Snow.* 1819. Oil on canvas, c. 3'11" × 5'10" (1.2 × 1.8 m). Formerly National Gallery, Berlin (now destroyed).

548.
Joseph M. W. Turner.
Calais Pier.
1803. Oil on canvas,
5′7¾″ × 7′10½″
(1.7 × 2.4 m). National
Gallery, London.

nature—the sea, hills, and forests, often at dusk or night. Nature exceeds the powers of the mind and we can only marvel at it, not understand it, the Romantics believed.

Joseph M. W. Turner's (1775–1851) view of nature was dominated by the sky, whose atmosphere and light slowly took over his paintings. *Calais Pier* **[548]**, an early work painted when Turner was 27, still shows us the solids—pier and boats—but the surge of the waves and especially of the clouds forecasts his future work. Turner's paintings are often compared with the poems of Wordsworth, but we can find the Romantic approach closer to home. The naturalist William Bartram, in an account of his travels in Georgia, wrote:

> It was now after noon; I approached a charming vale, amidst sublimely high forests, awful shades! darkness gathers around, far distant thunder rolls over the trembling hills; . . . threatening all the destruction of a thunder storm; . . . the mighty cloud now expands its sable wings, . . . and is driven irresistibly on by the tumultuous winds, spreading its livid wings around the gloomy concave, armed with the terrors of thunder and fiery shafts of lightning; now the lofty forests bend low beneath its fury, their limbs and wavy boughs are tossed about and catch hold of each other; the mountains tremble and seem to reel about, the ancient hills to be shaken to their foundations.[2]

The appreciation of nature and awe at its powers were a fundamental part of the audience's outlook. People such as William Bartram had the concepts and vocabulary to deal with Turner's and Friedrich's paintings and found satisfaction in the recognition of a kindred spirit in the artist.

Romantic painting in the United States was connected with the exploration of the vast country, which made landscape paintings doubly popular. Albert Bierstadt (1830–1902) learned an illusionistic style in a German academy before joining a party exploring a wagon route over the Rocky Mountains to California. He made sketches of everything he saw, later developed into large oil paintings such as *The Rocky Mountains* **[549]**, which established our idea of the appearance of that region. Beyond a foreground full of incidents and Indian life rise the awe-inspiring snowy peaks, their drama subtly enhanced but not so much as to seem exaggerated to down-to-earth Americans.

Delacroix

The French stand apart in their preoccupation with modern life in the city—in Paris, to be precise. Eugène Delacroix (*del-la-KRWAH*) (1799–1863), the greatest of the French Romantic painters and the artist Baudelaire had in mind when he defined Romanticism, was set up by the audience as the opposition to Ingres. Anyone could easily see the difference between their work: in that of Ingres

_____ *Recognizing the Great Styles*

[546] you could not see the brush strokes, but in Delacroix's paintings [550] each stroke was identifiable; in Ingres's each area of color had a definite edge that could be seen or imagined as a line, but in Delacroix's the color belonged to the brush stroke and flickered in and out of the shapes. Although both Ingres and Delacroix painted scenes of Turkish or Algerian life, Delacroix avoided Greek and Roman history and mythology. In what is surely Delacroix's most famous painting, *Liberty Leading the People* [550], he created instead a kind of modern mythology, with the heroic figure of Liberty—or, more properly, the personification of the nation—leading the people. The painting was inspired by an uprising of the people of Paris during July, 1830, when the government began systematically withdrawing the right to vote and other democratic privileges from the citizens. Delacroix witnessed the street fighting, but apparently did not participate in it. Among the thousands of scenes of revolutionary fighting that have been produced in the last two hundred years, Delacroix's is one of the few to have retained an audience beyond its own period, even beyond its own country. Although the details of the clothing and setting, with Notre Dame in the distance, are specific to Paris in 1830, the inclusion of the superhuman figure of Liberty, a Classical goddess given new life by her modern setting, makes the scene timeless and universal. This is as close as Delacroix came to a Neo-Classic subject, and the Classical goddess lent her prestige and dignity to the modern political movement.

Goya and the Irrational

Francisco Goya (1746–1828) lived through the period when the Neo-Classic style was replaced by the Romantic, and he contributed powerfully to the change. The Neo-Classic standards taught in art academies of Goya's day emphasized "one right way" of linear drawing, with sculpturesque shading which was accepted as the rational, intelligent way to make art. That style was never natural to Goya, but he learned to use it well enough that he became director of the Royal Academy in Madrid, where he began to introduce the Romantic style. Once established as a successful artist, Goya found it easier to give his imagination free rein.

During his own lifetime Goya was better known to a wide public for prints such as *The Dream of Reason Produces Monsters* [551]. Dreams, and especially

opposite above: 549. Albert Bierstadt. *The Rocky Mountains.* 1863. Oil on canvas, 6'1¼" × 10'¾" (1.9 × 3.1 m). Metropolitan Museum of Art, New York (Rogers Fund).

opposite below: 550. Eugène Delacroix. *Liberty Leading the People.* 1830. Oil on canvas, 8'6" × 10'8" (2.6 × 3.3 m). Louvre, Paris.

right: 551. Francisco Goya. *The Dream of Reason Produces Monsters,* from *Los Caprichos.* 1796–1798. Etching, aquatint; 8½ × 6" (22 × 15 cm). Metropolitan Museum of Art, New York (gift of M. Knoedler & Company, 1918).

nightmares, were an obsession of the Romantics, and Goya used the subject for an attack on rationalism. He issued four sets of etchings, the first and most popular under the title *Los Caprichos*, fantastic or imaginative subjects which made the name Goya a byword for imagination.

In Goya's abundant production it is hard to pick out the most important works, but *The Burial of the Sardine* [552] is typical. The title refers to a celebration during Carnival season in Madrid when masked celebrants took to the streets. Goya often painted crowds in which the irrational dominates and people are in a waking state not far from that of a dream or nightmare. Anything but a tourist scene of folklore, *The Burial of the Sardine* is a commentary on the general madness of mankind. In style, Goya is the bridge from the great 17th-century painters such as Velázquez, whose work he studied, to the Impressionists, who learned from him. His quick, sketchy brushwork has been taken as a model of expert painting by generations of painters.

Realism: Nothing but the Truth

The early Realist painters claimed to paint just what they saw. This sounds quite sensible to us now, but when Gustave Courbet said the artist must represent "the ideas and things of the period in which he lives," many members of the audience disagreed with him, maintaining that the whole tradition of art was the depiction of the imaginative. "Show me an angel and I'll paint one," was Courbet's famous retort. But the artists who accepted the name of Realists were part of a larger movement in literature and politics that was determined to show the grim reality of life for the great majority of people. This was a controversial idea only because the audience for art was restricted to the affluent upper classes

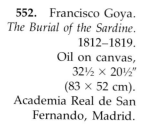

552. Francisco Goya. *The Burial of the Sardine.* 1812–1819. Oil on canvas, 32½ × 20½" (83 × 52 cm). Academia Real de San Fernando, Madrid.

who were doing well in the new industrial and commercial world and did not appreciate art that reminded them of others' misfortunes.

Courbet and Millet

Gustave Courbet *(koor-BAY)* (1819–1877) and Jean François Millet *(mee-LAY)* (1814–1875) both exhibited paintings in the Paris Salon of 1850–1851, the important exhibition when Realist art was first shown. *The Stonebreakers* **[553]** shows the lifelong hard work and poverty of unskilled laborers building the roads; Courbet made no effort to glamorize the scene—it is intentionally crude and graceless in design to emphasize its meaning. A flamboyant personality, Courbet reveled in political and artistic battles in Paris. Millet, like Courbet, came from a well-to-do farming family and was also well acquainted with both the pleasures and pains of rural life. Of a more retiring personality, Millet settled in the village of Barbizon to escape the turmoil of the city. *Laundresses* **[554]** shows two country women by the river where they have been washing clothing. Like Courbet, Millet shows no faces, but concentrates on the silhouettes that reveal the action.

Such country people made up three-quarters of the population of France when this was painted, but the audience for art was almost entirely drawn from the upper classes of city-dwellers. For this audience Millet's work could have only one of two possible interpretations: the sentimental, imagining a simpler world of rustic innocence, or the political, arguing that the life of poverty and grinding labor of the poor should be improved by some kind of political action. Millet himself seems to have rejected both those interpretations as shallow and felt that his main theme was the close relationship of humans to the earth. That is probably closer to the way we see Millet's art, now that the political and social situation has changed.

Millet was able to sell his work consistently, mostly, it appears, to upper-class city-dwellers who gave it a political interpretation. Millet was among the first generation of artists to work on contract with a dealer, who paid him a salary to deliver 25 paintings a year.

An International Movement

Realism was an international movement that attracted important artists in many countries. Artists were divided, just as Courbet and Millet were, by the question of what their work meant: was it a simple statement of the facts, or even a celebration of a way of life, or was it a call to reform? The answer, of course, always rests with the audience, which changes its mind as conditions change. In the Russian painter Ilya Repin's *(RyEP-in)* (1844–1930) *The Unexpected*

above left: 553.
Gustave Courbet.
The Stonebreakers. 1849.
Oil on canvas,
5′3″ × 8′6″ (1.6 × 2.6 m).
Formerly
Gemäldegalerie,
Dresden, East Germany
(now destroyed).

above: 554.
Jean François Millet.
Laundresses. 1853–1855.
Oil on canvas,
17⅛ × 21⅛″
(43 × 54 cm).
Museum of Fine Arts,
Boston (bequest of
Mrs. Martin Brimmer,
1906).

[555], the drama of the young man suddenly returned from exile in Siberia appeals to audiences who may have forgotten Czarist injustices. The expressions on the faces of his wife and children, slow to recognize him, and the shock of his mother, seen from the back, along with the cool northern light and casual-seeming composition, draw us into the reality of the scene.

On the other side of the world, Thomas Eakins (1844–1916), in Philadelphia, employed a Realist style with the seemingly simple aim of telling the truth. He would have approved of Courbet's insistence that art should be about the visible world around us. *The Gross Clinic* [556] shows the famous surgeon Dr. Samuel David Gross performing an operation on a young man's leg and lecturing to the assembled students and observers, including the patient's mother, whose presence as a witness was required in charity cases.

Eakins frequently had difficulty with his audience and critics, who considered his paintings too harshly realistic. The blood on the surgeon's hand bothered them. Not a criticism or a call to reform, it celebrates the achievements of modern medicine. Dr. Gross is shown brilliantly lighted by the surgical lights, deeply serious and thoughtful, practicing a profession calling for heroic work against illness and disease. Although surgical garb has changed, the interpretation of Eakins' painting has changed little in a century.

Impressionism

Impressionist painting has become the most beloved art of the 20th century; yet it was the most maligned of the late 19th century. For a few years a chasm of misunderstanding opened between many artists and a large part of their audience. The principal factor in that unusual situation was a great broadening of the audience for art. Cities everywhere were growing, with people hungry for a better life, which included all the things that the old noble classes had enjoyed, especially education, leisure, and the arts. The members of this large new audience had little experience of art and were not confident of their ability to tell good art from bad, but they knew by experience that hard work and a skilled hand were valuable. The people in that audience admired the careful drawing and the highly finished paint surface, with brushstrokes invisible, of the late Neo-Classic style; therefore it took many years for this general audience to grow accustomed to the unblended colors and visible brushstrokes of Impressionism.

555. Ilya Repin. *The Unexpected.* 1884. Oil on canvas, 5'3¼" × 5'5¾" (1.6 × 1.7 m). Tretyakov Gallery, Moscow.

556. Thomas Eakins. *The Gross Clinic.* 1875. Oil on canvas, 8′ × 6′6″ (2.4 × 2 m).
Jefferson Medical College, Philadelphia.

A POINT IN TIME: James Whistler,
The Artist in His Studio

557. James Abbott McNeill Whistler. *The Artist in His Studio.* c. 1867–1868. Oil on paper mounted on panel, 24¾ × 18¾" (63 × 48 cm). Art Institute of Chicago (Friends of American Art Collection).

Born in Massachusetts, raised in Russia, educated in art in Paris, resident of London, James Abbott McNeill Whistler (Jimmie to his friends) (1834–1903) seemed to belong everywhere and nowhere. Yet there is hardly an aspect of 19th-century art in which he did not take some part.

The Artist in His Studio [557] is an oil study for a proposed large painting (which was never executed) showing the artist at his easel in his London studio. Whistler appears to be left-handed, but he was painting what he saw in a mirror. His model and mistress Jo Heffernan is seated in a white dress on the white chaise longue and a model nicknamed "La Japonaise" wears a peach-colored robe and holds a Japanese fan. On shelves at the left are Whistler's many pieces of Chinese blue-and-white porcelain, of which he was an early collector.

The mirror on the wall was also a studio accessory. Cicely Alexander, who posed for her portrait when she was nine (it is now in the Tate Gallery, London), later described the experience: "He used to stand a good way from his canvas, and then dart at it and then dart back, and he often turned around to look in a looking-glass that hung over the mantelpiece at his back—I suppose to see the reflection of his painting." (The mirror view helps the artist see compositional weaknesses.)

The subtle tonalities and large background field, as well as the model, make clear Whistler's fascination with Oriental art. His "art-for-art's sake" ideal, a common reaction against politically inspired Realism, took an Oriental form in his painting. On the other hand, Courbet, the most political of the Realists, was a friend and painting companion. The subject of this painting was partly inspired by a painting by Courbet, done a dozen years before, of himself in his studio surrounded by his friends and all humanity in symbolic figures. Whistler also planned to include his painter friends in his final version. The sketchy modesty, delicate color, and truth to life make Whistler's painting just as appealing in its own way.

Sources: Tom Prideaux, *The World of Whistler, 1834–1903* (New York: Time-Life Books, 1970) 94, 102. Denys Sutton, *Nocturne: The Art of James McNeill Whistler* (Philadelphia: Lippincott, 1964).

After about 1860, artists began to think that a spontaneous record of the scene before their eyes was the most satisfactory work of art. Impressionist painting—the name, given by the critics, originally in derision, came from the title of a painting by Monet, *Impresssion, Sunrise,* of 1872—allowed the brushwork to show, a frank record of the process by which the picture was made. The name, both of the painting and of the style, was no accident, for the word "impression" referred to the imprint on a human mind made by an event in real life. Critics distinguished between art that was a "photographic" record of appearance and Impressionism, which they considered poetic and which had "soul." The **Impressionist** style was part of a new idea of experience theorizing that our eyes can tell us nothing about the solidity of objects, that our eyes receive information only from the colored light that strikes them. The critic Jules

Castagnary wrote in 1874: "They are *impressionists* in the sense that they render not the landscape, but the sensation produced by the landscape."[3]

A painting, the Impressionists said, to be true to nature and itself must be the record of an impression of colored light. To give color its greatest intensity, they relied on the eye to mix primary colors laid as spots on the canvas. A red spot next to a blue spot, seen from a certain distance, gives the visual sensation of purple, and so on. From a certain distance the paintings looked very natural, but up close they looked rough and unfinished, especially to members of the audience whose visual education was just beginning. Even granting the subjectivity of the impression, the new style set itself apart from earlier styles as much in its insistence on vision as the source of knowledge about reality as in its color and brushstroke. The Baroque style, for example, had assumed tactile and kinesthetic (muscular) knowledge of reality, in which **chiaroscuro** and illusions of mass and motion are expressed. Impressionism represented only light, not darkness (which is invisibility), and only the light from surfaces, not their mass.

Impressionism found some audience right from the start, but the first large exhibit of the new style, in 1874, in which Monet, Renoir, Degas, and 27 other artists exhibited, was rewarded with hostile criticism of the unfinished appearance of the paintings and their "tasteless" modern subject matter.

Monet

Claude Monet *(mo-NAY)* (1840–1926) was one of the leading Impressionists and the one most faithful to its basic intentions. In 1877 he exhibited eight views of *Saint-Lazare Station* **[558]**, one of the Paris railroad stations. This was the first of many sets of paintings of the same subject—a cathedral, haystacks, a lily pond—in which the natural change of light and color was the real subject. Monet made a point of painting only what his eyes could see, which might have made him a Realist, except that his eyes focused on the total scene, not on the human figures, and he did not make any comment on the lives of the people in his paintings. Paul Cézanne joked about Monet: "He is only an eye, but what an eye."[4] Monet might have considered that praise, if the eye is imagined as having "soul."

Monet was not a camera; his subjects were carefully chosen and composed, and he often touched up the work in his studio, though the basic idea was to paint exactly what he saw on the spot. Monet preferred to call the style *plein-airisme (play-nair-eezm,* meaning "outdoor-ism"), to make it clear that he painted from vision, not imagination.

When Monet painted the station the railroads were new, the latest in modern transport. The powerful engines with their smoke and steam and the cast-iron structure of the station were dramatic evidence that this was an art about modern life. In his later work Monet grew more abstract, creating color harmo-

558. Claude Monet. *Saint-Lazare Station.* 1877. Oil on canvas, 32¾ × 40" (83 × 102 cm). Fogg Art Museum, Harvard University (bequest of Maurice Wertheim, Class of 1906).

nies based on landscapes reflected in water, such as *Water Lilies* [559], based on the scene in his own beloved garden in Giverny in the suburbs of Paris. But even in this work Monet takes as his point of departure what his eyes could see rather than what his mind could invent.

Renoir

Monet and his friend Pierre Auguste Renoir *(ruh-NWAHR)* (1841–1919) painted the same scenes together at times in the early 1870s, but Renoir's basic interest was the human figure, especially women and girls, who have never been more lovingly depicted. *Dancing at the Moulin de la Galette* [560] shows the crowd at a popular outdoor Paris café. All the main characters are Renoir's friends, many of them artists and models. We have learned to see through Renoir's eyes and see nature as he did. But the softly flicking strokes of color were surprising to the first audience, even though Renoir had learned much of his technique by studying 17th- and 18th-century paintings in the Louvre museum. Far from the grim reporting of the Realists, this tells a delightful truth about the pleasures of middle-class life in the city. This painting was a carefully concocted studio painting, although based on studies made from the living scene at the café. In spite of Monet's idea that the new painting style could be done only outdoors in the original setting, few of the Impressionists attempted many paintings outdoors. It was simply too inconvenient. Instead they relied on their sketchbooks, painting from sketches made on the spot to keep their work true to nature.

Degas

You can practically relive Parisian life of a century ago by looking at Impressionist paintings. Edgar Degas *(duh-GAH)* (1834–1917) shows people in the streets, playing music, at the horse races; he painted portraits of the well-to-do, studies of laundresses at their work, prostitutes, and ballet dancers, all created thoughtfully in the studio from sketches. Although Degas exhibited with the Impressionists and is ordinarily classified with them, he did not paint outdoors ("Painting is not a sport,"[5] he said), and his use of color is controlled by the composition, not the visual experience of nature.

Degas's compositions were unusual. A friend, Edmond Duranty, wrote a book on the new painting which must reflect what he saw in Degas's work and learned from conversations with the artist. He wrote that "views of people and things have a thousand ways of being unexpected in reality" and mentions that in Degas's paintings a figure "is never in the center of the canvas, or of the setting . . . not always seen as a whole, and sometimes appears cut off at midleg, half-length, or longitudinally." The compositions described by Duranty show Degas consciously adopting poses and compositions from photography to increase the impression of objective reality in his paintings. Photographic plates (the ancestors of our film) were invented during the 1830s and Degas, fascinated

559. Claude Monet. *Water Lilies.* 1920–1921. Oil on canvas, 6′6″ × 19′7″ (2 × 6 m). Museum of Art, Carnegie Mellon University, Pittsburgh, Pennsylvania (bequest of Mrs. Alan M. Scaife, 1962).

Recognizing the Great Styles

with the record of the unposed and the momentary, was one of the earliest
artists to incorporate features of photographic recording into his compositions.

    The Dance Class [561] of Opera ballet dancers is one of several versions of
this subject. It shows the ballet master, Jules Perrot, leaning on his stick sur-

560.
Pierre Auguste Renoir.
*Dancing at the
Moulin de la Galette.*
1876. Oil on canvas,
4′3½″ × 5′9″
(1.3 × 1.6 m).
Louvre, Paris.

561. Edgar Degas.
The Dance Class. c. 1874.
Oil on canvas, 32⅝ × 29⅞″
(83 × 76 cm). Metropolitan
Museum of Art, New York
(bequest of Mrs. Harry
Payne Bingham, 1986).

rounded by a crowd of young dancers. A dancer is cut off at the left margin and the next group overlaps, hiding the faces of two of them, just as Duranty describes. The scene recedes in perspective, the dancers becoming smaller, to the far wall where their mothers wait. The blankness of the left wall is opened up by the mirror reflecting the windows, out of sight on the right. The subtle color—black and white, pale greens and tans, and a few accents of red and pink—is typical of Degas.

Cassatt

In 1874 Degas was introduced to a young American woman whose work he had admired, and who, in turn, had advised her wealthy friends to buy Degas paintings. This was Mary Cassatt *(kuh-SAHT)* (1845–1926), one of the best Impressionist painters born in America. Like almost all American artists of the period, she had felt that only in Paris was it possible to be an artist. Daughter of a Philadelphia banker, she had money to devote herself to art without having to consider public taste. Almost all her work represents her family and friends, most often in scenes including the children, shown naturally without cuteness. The typical comment on paintings such as *Mother and Child* **[562]** was that Cassatt's women were not pretty, but the educated audience saw the unusual combination of a deep sympathy for her subjects and wonderful control of the brush and the color. Cassatt settled in France to be at the center of the art world of her time, but she maintained close connections with American collectors.

Manet and the End of Impressionism

The critics and the audience had a definition of Impressionist style in mind, but, as we have seen in the case of Degas, many of the recognized Impressionist

left: 562.   Mary Cassatt. *Mother and Child.*
c. 1890. Oil on canvas, 35⅜ × 25⅜″ (90 × 64 cm).
Wichita, Kansas, Art Museum (Roland P. Murdoch Collection).

below: 563.   Édouard Manet. *Le Déjeuner sur l'Herbe (Luncheon on the Grass).* 1863. Oil on canvas, 7′ × 8′10″ (2.1 × 2.7 m). Musée d'Orsay, Paris.

A POINT IN TIME: Mary Cassatt's "Japanese" Prints

From April 25 to May 22, 1890, a large exhibition of Japanese woodcut prints was shown in Paris, and its effects were both instantaneous and long-lasting. The painters Berthe Morisot *(mor-ee-SO)* (1841–1895) and Mary Cassatt visited the show together, and Cassatt bought a number of prints. Japanese prints had been known in Europe for many years, their influence slowly spreading through the community of artists. Cassatt returned from the exhibit inspired to make a series of a dozen prints based on Japanese woodcuts. But instead of woodcut she chose the very difficult method of color etching, using **aquatint** for the color areas and **drypoint** for the lines. "It amused me very much to do them although it was hard work," she wrote in a letter.

In the Omnibus [564] was shown with the other prints in the series at Durand-Ruel's gallery in April, 1891, in Cassatt's first Paris show. Camille Pissarro wrote his artist son about Cassatt's prints: "It is absolutely necessary, while what I saw yesterday at Miss Cassatt's is still fresh in mind, to tell you about the colored etchings she is to show . . . rare and exquisite works. . . . the result is admirable, as beautiful as Japanese work."

The Japanese look is produced by the contrast of flat areas of very subtle color with lines which are independent of the colors. The delicate, varied lines are quite different from the heavier Japanese woodcut lines, being cut into the copper plate with acid and a steel etcher's needle. Though these prints were some of Cassatt's most original and influential work, for years they found no buyers either in Paris or New York. But artists had seen them. They established Cassatt's reputation in Paris as a serious artist and they made a strong contribution to print and illustration style of the next 30 years.

564. Mary Cassatt. *In the Omnibus*. 1891. Etching, drypoint, soft-ground, aquatint; 14 × 10¼" (36 × 26 cm). National Gallery of Art, Washington, D.C. (Rosenwald Collection).

Quotations from Nancy Hale, *Mary Cassatt* (New York: Doubleday, 1975).

---

masters conformed to that definition only in part. Édouard Manet *(mah-NAY)* (1832–1883) adopted the Impressionist style in mid-career and rarely painted outdoors. He did not intend to be revolutionary, but rather to work in the great tradition of European art. Manet told his friend Antonin Proust, as they watched some women swimming in the river, "I copied a picture of some women by Giorgione, the women with the musicians [*Fête Champêtre*, Figure **46**, now attributed to Titian]. . . . I want to re-do that and to re-paint it in a transparent atmosphere with people like those you see over there. I know it's going to be attacked but they can say what they like."[6] The painting which resulted, known as *Le Déjeuner sur l'Herbe* [563], or *Luncheon on the Grass*, was not only inspired by Titian, but Manet modeled the three main figures on designs by Raphael, all brought up to date in style and costume. Many of his paintings have compositions or details taken from earlier masterpieces, and he always believed natural appearance had to be balanced by the requirements of composition.

565. Édouard Manet. *The Bar at the Folies-Bergère.* 1881–1882. Oil on canvas, 3'1½" × 4'3" (0.9 × 1.3 m). Courtauld Institute Galleries, London.

Yet Manet revolutionized painting in spite of himself and is a forerunner of 20th-century art. His last great painting, *The Bar at the Folies-Bergère* **[565]**, is a good example, for critics have been trying to explain its space relationships ever since it was first shown. Exactly in the center—her buttons bisect the canvas—is the grand figure of the barmaid, modeled by a young woman named Suzon who really was a barmaid at the Folies-Bergère, a popular vaudeville theater in Paris. Her vacant expression suggests that she is exhausted, despite the lively surroundings. Behind her a mirror reflects the bar, her back, and her customer, who faces the barmaid and must thus be the observer of the painting. The reflected figures imply that the mirror is at an angle, but that is belied by the angle of the reflected bar—the reflections are inconsistent. The scene reflected in the mirror—a balcony with seated figures, chandeliers, and, in the upper left corner, the feet of an aerialist on a trapeze—belongs inside the theater, not in the lobby with the bar. Although the painting is *about* the Folies-Bergère, it is not really an *impression*, in the Impressionist sense, of a view there. Manet departed from the aim to paint pure vision. Instead Manet used an Impressionist technique to construct images which could exist only in the mind or memory, made up of various views.

Manet and his contemporaries were great admirers of the Spanish painters Goya and Velázquez. You can see the influence of Goya's crowds **[552]** in the crowd in Manet's painting. Manet's work is a good example of the truth that originality is often based on a careful study of what went before.

Rodin and Impressionism in Sculpture

Despite the importance of painting during this period, the most famous artist of the later part of the 19th century was a sculptor, Auguste Rodin *(ro-DAN)* (1840–1917). Not only was his work a sculptural declaration of independence from Greek and Roman work, from Michelangelo and Bernini—it simply created a period of its own. Rodin worked in marble and in plaster to be cast in bronze. He was a popular portrait artist, but he also received important commissions for public monuments, practically none of them satisfactory to the commissioners. The public monument, by its nature a statement about history, seems to demand a traditional style. The new, original, or personal are slow to find acceptance by public committees, who usually compromise on the most conservative opinion.

A good example is the case of the monument to the writer Honoré de Balzac that was commissioned by a literary society in 1891. Balzac, who had died in 1850, was short and fat, with a powerful head and a well-developed ego. Rodin obtained Balzac's measurements from his old tailor, only to conclude that a figure in modern dress would not do. He made some nude studies that have a wonderful vigor, very appropriate to this vigorous writer, and a rough surface that appears truly Impressionist **[566]**. In the end Rodin decided to clothe the figure in a long dressing gown thrown over his shoulders, which Balzac is supposed to have worn when he wrote at night **[567]**. The originality of the design and the roughness of the surface, whose many irregularities can be compared to the color spots of Impressionist painting, annoyed the commissioners, and the society refused to accept the statue. Rodin wrote, "Without doubt the decision of the Société is a material disaster for me, but my work as an artist remains my supreme satisfaction. . . . I sought in 'Balzac' to render in sculpture what was not photographic. . . . My principle is to imitate not only form but also life."[7]

Photography could not be ignored by artists of this period, whether they adopted its effects or rejected them, as Rodin said he did. The visual impressions Monet received outdoors Rodin found drawing from the model in the studio. Thousands of quick pencil and watercolor sketches from models as they posed or moved around the studio provided the record of "life" which Rodin contrasted with the photographic record of mere "form."

Balzac gives the effect of such a spontaneous sketch, full of life but irregular in form. It is still astonishing, not the kind of monument you walk by without noticing. Private patrons wanted to buy casts of Balzac, and though none were made during Rodin's lifetime, several have been erected as monuments since then.

below left: 566.
Auguste Rodin.
Balzac. 1893–1895.
Bronze study, height
4'2¼" (1.3 m).
Collection of Mr. and
Mrs. Alan Wurtzburger,
Pikesville, Maryland.

below: 567.
Auguste Rodin.
Monument to Balzac.
1898. Bronze, height
9'10" (3 m).
Hirshhorn Museum and
Sculpture Garden,
Smithsonian Institution,
Washington, D.C.

Post-Impressionism

Impressionism was based on the idea that painting was the record of a visual sensation received by a subjective individual, not the scientific recording of light before the eyes. But by the 1880s even the theory of an art based mainly on vision was beginning to be unacceptable to the most advanced artists.

Four painters made major contributions to a new art, each quite different from the others, but all derived in some way from Impressionism: Georges Seurat, Paul Cézanne, Vincent van Gogh, and Paul Gauguin. For Seurat and Cézanne it was an intellectual order—a geometry—that was lacking in Impressionism; for Van Gogh and Gauguin it was the expression of emotion and deeper invisible spiritual meanings. These four artists represent the main line of development in art as it has been envisioned by 20th-century artists and art historians.

Seurat and Pointillism

Georges Seurat *(suh-RAH)* (1859–1891), who died at the age of 31, nevertheless left ten years of work, including several large and influential paintings. *Sunday Afternoon on the Island of La Grande Jatte* [568] is nearly 7 feet (2.1 meters) high and more than 10 feet (3 meters) wide. Although the scene shows people at leisure in a city park, it "ticks like a Swiss watch," as one critic has written. The rough brushwork of the Impressionists has been disciplined so that each stroke is a similar dot or point of pure color—a technique called "divisionism" or **pointillism**. The same discipline has been imposed on the shapes, as firm and smooth as if carved of stone. Seurat's style has been called Neo-Impressionism, but if Impressionism gives a sense of the spontaneity of life, Seurat's work seems to be about some imaginary ideal world of perfect order. Color printing in the 20th century adopted Seurat's method of combining colors by printing dots of pure color side by side. (Look at a section of a color reproduction in a newspaper

568. Georges Seurat. *Sunday Afternoon on the Island of La Grande Jatte.* 1884–1886. Oil on canvas, 6′9″ × 10′6″ (2.0 × 3.2 m). Art Institute of Chicago (Helen Birch Bartlett Memorial Collection).

569. Paul Cézanne. *The Bay of Marseilles, Seen from L'Estaque.* 1886–1890. Oil on canvas, 31⅝ × 39⅝" (80 × 101 cm). Art Institute of Chicago (Mr. and Mrs. Martin A. Ryerson Collection, 1933).

through a magnifying glass.) It is no wonder his paintings look mechanistic to us, for his method was one ideally adapted to the discipline of the machine.

Cézanne

Paul Cézanne *(say-ZAHN)* (1839–1906) said his intention was "to make out of Impressionism something enduring and solid like the art of the museums."[8] From Impressionism Cézanne accepted brushwork of pure colors mixed in the eye of the viewer, but the strokes of color were used for a new goal, to represent—"construct" might be a better word—a world of solid forms in space. That, of course, had been the aim of painting from the Renaissance up to the Realists, but Cézanne followed the Impressionists in rejecting the use of Renaissance chiaroscuro, and he went one step farther and also rejected Renaissance perspective. Of the methods used by earlier painters to represent solid forms in space Cézanne kept nothing, and so he had to invent an entirely new method. Alone at his family estate at Aix-en-Provence, in southern France, the intense and introspective artist succeeded at this gigantic task. It was not until 1895, when he was 56, that Cézanne had his first solo show in Paris and other artists began to appreciate his achievement.

The Bay of Marseilles, Seen from L'Estaque **[569]** is a good demonstration of his method. The composition, with an arm of the Mediterranean Sea separating two shores, would offer some difficulties in a linear perspective view since there are no buildings or roads on the water, but it is ideal for Cézanne, who relies on color to locate objects in space. Using aerial perspective as the sole system of construction for the first time, he keeps the entire foreground in warm colors—yellows, oranges, browns, with green as the coolest color. Note that the roofs and walls do not obey the rules of linear perspective, although objects are shown smaller in the distance. On the farther shore all the colors are cool—blue, blue-gray, with touches of very grayed reds, yellows, and browns so you will know it is earth. This system of indicating closer parts with warm colors and farther parts with cool colors, which we call aerial perspective, had a history going back at least to the 17th century, but it had never been used exclusively and systematically before. Other artists recognized this representational world built of color as a basic invention.

Landscape and still life were the subjects most easily adapted to Cézanne's slow methods of work, but he also painted human figures, some from his imagination but some from life. *Boy in a Red Vest* [570], like many of those painted from life, is less fully finished than the still lifes because the model was less patient than a bowl of fruit. The black lines that sketch in the boy still show clearly, but the basic color problem—how to dress a figure in red and blue, a warm color and a cool color—was solved by putting the red vest over the blue at his neck and waist and cooling the red with purple and gray tones. By the mid-1890s, when this was painted, Cézanne was confident enough of his new method that he could take it for granted. It is the slender young man, relaxed and dreaming in his shadowy space, that comes across to the audience, not the method by which he came into existence.

No one looks at the work of Cézanne and Seurat for purely intellectual stimulation; it is the emotional satisfaction of finding a world that is orderly and logical. Both those men also lived normally orderly lives, different from the spectacularly disorderly lives of Van Gogh and Gauguin (it is Van Gogh and Gauguin who have been the subjects of movie biographies, not Cézanne and Seurat). Van Gogh and Gauguin were friends and housemates for a short period, but the tensions and emotions that powered their art also made them unusually difficult companions. Although both had learned to paint in a purely Impressionist style, both sought an art that showed more truth than could be seen by the eyes.

Van Gogh and Expressionism

The Dutchman Vincent van Gogh *(van GO)* (1853–1890), son of a Protestant minister, first dedicated himself to caring for the poor and exploited, serving as a lay preacher among the Belgian coal miners—men, women, and children working under conditions we can scarcely imagine. But he had always been interested in art and finally, in 1880, he decided to devote himself to it as a way of bringing the plight of the poor to public attention. His early work is powerful but crude. It was not until he went to Paris in 1886 to educate himself in the new styles that his mature style appeared. Much of his best work was done in the sun-drenched landscape of Arles, in southern France. During the last four years of his life he produced several hundred paintings, only one of which was sold before he ended his life at the age of 37. Van Gogh is often taken as the example of a great artist neglected by an indifferent public, but the public had merely had insufficient time to get acquainted with his work. A few months before his death he was invited to exhibit in an important show in Brussels, and he was the subject of an article in a well-known Paris magazine. In the 1890s the professional audience was already aware of his work, and it reached a vast audience in later years.

Road with Cypresses [571] was done in May, 1890, and he wrote about it in a letter to Gauguin:

> I still have a cypress with a star from down there [in southern France], a last attempt—a night sky with a moon without brilliance, the slender crescent barely emerging from the opaque shadow cast by the earth—a star with an exaggerated radiance, if you like, a soft brilliance of pink and green in the ultramarine sky, where some clouds are hurrying. Below, a road bordered with tall yellow canes, behind these the blue Lower Alps, an old inn with orange lighted windows, and a very tall cypress, very straight, very somber.[9]

This down-to-earth description hardly prepares you for the intensity of the experience, in which not only the trees and sky, but even the building and the road writhe with uncontrollable emotional tensions. A careful examination of Van Gogh's brushwork shows the discipline of his craftsmanship, even when it was in the service of his emotions. Painters copying or faking Van Gogh's style sometimes think a wild, uncontrolled brush is called for, but Van Gogh painted very much as he wrote in his numerous letters, carefully and with conscious intellectual control. Describing his style in a letter to his brother, Van Gogh wrote:

"instead of trying to reproduce exactly what I have before my eyes, I use color more arbitrarily, in order to express myself forcibly."[10] The search for expression through intensification of color and exaggeration of shape became in the early 20th century the defining features of the style called **Expressionism**. Van Gogh was seen as the precursor of that movement.

Gauguin and Synthetism

Like the other Post-Impressionist painters, Paul Gauguin (*go-GAN*) (1848–1903) learned to paint in an Impressionist style, but, also like them, he sought a style that gave more personal expression. Synthetism, as Gauguin called his style, did not come easily to him, but was slowly worked out between 1883 and 1889. He had begun painting as a hobby while working as a stockbroker, then began taking lessons from the Impressionist Pissarro. Finally, in 1883, he gave up his job, left his wife and family, and dedicated himself to art, ultimately sailing away to Polynesia. That he was not an average drop-out is shown by his productivity in all kinds of art—painting, printmaking (see Chapter 5 on woodcuts), and sculpture.

The title Gauguin gave *The Spirit of the Dead Watching* **[572]** was "Manao Tupapau," which, Gauguin wrote, "has two meanings, either 'she thinks of the spirit of the dead,' or 'the spirit of the dead remembers her.'" Painted in Tahiti, it shows a Tahitian girl lying face down with an anxious expression and tense hands; "these people are very much afraid of the spirit of the dead," Gauguin continued. "There are some flowers in the background, but being imagined, they must not be real. I made them resemble sparks. The Maoris [i.e., Tahitians] believe that the phosphorescences of the light are the spirits of the dead. Finally, I made the ghost look very simply like a small, harmless woman, because the girl cannot help but imagine dead people when she thinks of the spirit of the dead."[11]

This mixture of the natural and the supernatural is as carefully composed as a Cézanne or a Seurat, but its shapes are organic-looking and the colors are somber—"sounding to the eye like a death knell: violet, dark blue, and orange yellow,"[12] wrote Gauguin. An Impressionist such as Monet surely must have wondered what it means to say "sounding to the eye," since it suggests that the

below left: 570.
Paul Cézanne.
Boy in a Red Vest.
1893–1895. Oil on canvas, 35¼ × 28½" (90 × 72 cm). Collection of Mr. and Mrs. Paul Mellon.

below: 571.
Vincent van Gogh.
Road with Cypresses.
1890. Oil on canvas, 35¾ × 28" (91 × 71 cm). Kröller-Müller State Museum, Otterlo, The Netherlands.

572. Paul Gauguin. *The Spirit of the Dead Watching.* 1892. Oil on canvas, 36¼ × 38¾" (92 × 98 cm). Albright-Knox Art Gallery, Buffalo, New York (A. Conger Goodyear Collection, 1965).

eye has powers that go beyond seeing. To Gauguin the whole intention of art was to go beyond seeing into imagining—imagining decorative patterns, colors that affect our emotions the way music does, and subjects that have a reality in our minds and emotions, but not necessarily in the visible world. That defines the *Synthetist style,* which was Gauguin's personal style, but a style that was so fully developed that it was adopted by other artists and was influential in the evolution of 20th-century painting.

The Battleground of 19th-Century Art

Art was one of the great public battlegrounds during the 19th century as the ever-growing audience argued with the artists. The public, which was deeply worried about the frightening changes in their way of life, in both technology and society, longed for the security of traditional depictions of beauty and good taste. But many of the artists and their patrons, and a considerable group of critics, did not want art to be an escape from the real world, but wanted to find new ways to show reality. As the public began to understand the new styles, the artists, supported by a body of patrons and critics, marched on ahead to make art that was still harder to understand and to like. So much has this situation characterized the art world of the last one hundred and fifty years that many people have begun to think it is the natural and inevitable relationship between new art and the public. But looked at as a part of the long history of art, this period of disagreement between artists and the general public is very unusual and tells us much about the instability of the period.

Summary for Review

Five important styles of European art dominate this 150-year period: Neo-Classicism, with its linear, sculpturesque style; Romanticism's search for the sublime and the awe-inspiring, with color and individuality; Realism, showing objective views of rural and urban workers and daily life; Impressionism, seeking to record the subjective vision of light on natural scenes; Post-Impressionism, introducing a variety of personal styles to enhance individual expression. New influences on art from archaeology, psychology, and the natural sciences, photography, contacts with other regions (especially Japan and Polynesia), and the rising political power of working people are all reflected in the subjects and styles of this period.

Styles of
the 20th Century

Behind the bewildering variety of styles and movements in the 20th century there is a general pattern, a set of major ideas that set the direction for many artists and large segments of the audience. Those ideas may be summarized as follows:

1. At the beginning of the century many believed that artists and their audience must reject everything that had been done in art during the past five hundred years and start over from scratch. There was a widespread feeling that Western culture had become over-developed, too civilized, and needed to return to basics.

2. Another powerful set of ideas developed in psychology, especially from the writings on psychoanalysis of Sigmund Freud and Carl Jung, which proposed that the mental sources of creativity were in the unconscious parts of the mind and could be reached most easily in dreams, daydreams, slips of the tongue, and other moments when the unconscious makes its appearance. Those two ideas led to another:

3. The models for a new art had to come from outside the European Renaissance tradition, especially from arts which seemed to Europeans and Americans to be closer to the unconscious sources of art and less technically developed in terms of illusions of the third dimension, light and shadow, and natural textures.

Every one of the 20th-century styles has been greeted with controversy—something unheard of before the end of the 19th century. It is strange to discover the passions aroused by something as seemingly harmless as a painting, particularly one made up of nothing but abstract shapes and colors, which you might think could hardly offend anyone. But everyone involved enjoyed the situation—the artists were happy to shock if it made people look at their work, the audience mocked them with glee or defended them passionately, the critics unleashed their most sarcastic attacks and most high-toned defenses, and—most important of all—the patrons bought their work. Despite much lamenting of the plight of the artists, they have been more successful, influential, and admired by a much larger audience in this century than at any other period in history.

While the more conservative members of the audience have charged **Modern** artists with playing tricks on the public, the motivation for all the Modern styles was to be as truthful as possible. The popular words were "authentic," "primitive," "original," and "sincere." An artist who could be described by those words was surely truthful and must be avoiding technical tricks that fool the eye with illusions. It was a virtual requirement for art to be, or appear to be, technically primitive to be accepted as authentic and original. A primitive technology was a guarantee that the artist was rejecting the Renaissance tradition

573. Pablo Picasso. *Family of Saltimbanques.* 1905. Oil on canvas, 6'9¾" × 7'6⅜" (2.1 × 2.3 m). National Gallery of Art, Washington, D.C. (Chester Dale Collection).

and starting over and that the art was an authentic expression of the unconscious mind, not a product of the calculating conscious mind.

The great importance of the unconscious mind in Modern art theory was that it was considered the part of the mind where most of the basic human experiences are stored, such as hunger, sex drive, loves and hates, fears and needs. The conscious mind was considered the home of all the concerns that make us individuals and separate us, making communication more difficult. While this theory can be very persuasive and is basic to the understanding of Modern art, it has not been accepted by most **Post-Modern** artists and their audience after 1970, as we shall see.

Art in Paris, 1900–1940

Paris remained the center of world art through the first four decades of the century and was home to two of the major art movements of the period— Cubism and Surrealism—and a major center of Expressionism and Abstraction. After 1940, New York emerged as a great art center, and in recent years both art creation and sales have spread to many cities.

Cubism

The art of this century has been defined by painting, and of all the painters Pablo Picasso (1881–1973) played the leading role. Picasso, a Spaniard who settled in Paris when he was nineteen, made basic contributions to Cubism, Expressionism, and Surrealism. In his twenties he painted nostalgic scenes of circus performers, such as *Family of Saltimbanques* **[573]**, a painting which sums up the work of his early years and seems to bid farewell to Romantic art and its late-19th-century descendants.

The **Cubist** style was the product of a few years of work toward a more geometric and non-representational style. Between 1907 and 1920, Cubist painting developed from depicting simple sculptural human figures in simple backgrounds to a very abstract style emphasizing shape, pattern, and texture. In the earlier paintings there are geometric shapes in tones of brown and gray, textured with brushstrokes to give an architectural or sculptural effect; in later years there is more color, often in flat areas, which reduce the sense of space and mass, but with clearer representation of a subject. Although Cubist art at first looks unemotional, the artists all considered it a means for expressing ideas and emotions. "We have kept our eyes open to our surroundings, and also our brains,"[1] as Picasso said.

Picasso. Picasso took the first step toward Cubism in his famous 8-foot (2.4-meter)-high painting later named *Les Demoiselles d'Avignon* ("Girls of Avignon"), **[574]** in 1907, which shows the young artist considering ancient Spanish and African sculpture as sources of new geometric faces. The composition began as a moralistic picture of a sailor surrounded by nude women, food, and flowers, with an intruder carrying a skull entering from the left. Months of work on the painting, during which Picasso's friends expected to find the artist had hanged himself behind the canvas, transformed it into a figure study with no story at all. Though it was abandoned unfinished, it is important as evidence of the struggle to form a new style. Each figure is an angular shape divided into smaller angular shapes by geometric lines. The African-looking masks of the faces on the right seem to be a declaration of independence from the European tradition and the adoption of a more abstract design.

Picasso made sculpture throughout his life, but among his most influential are those in the Cubist style, such as *Mandolin* **[575]**, a small relief designed to hang on the wall. This construction was a result of about two years of inventive work in drawing and **collage** (cut and pasted paper) (see Figure 82), which was flat but suggested the third dimension. As carpentry *Mandolin* is not to be taken seriously, but it set an entirely new path for 20th-century painting and sculpture, one still being explored creatively in the late 20th century. The flat planes of rough wood, with a little color added, are a simplified version of the painted

below: 574. Pablo Picasso. *Les Demoiselles d'Avignon.* 1907.
Oil on canvas, 8′ × 7′8″ (2.4 × 2.3 m). Museum of Modern Art,
New York (acquired through the Lillie P. Bliss bequest).

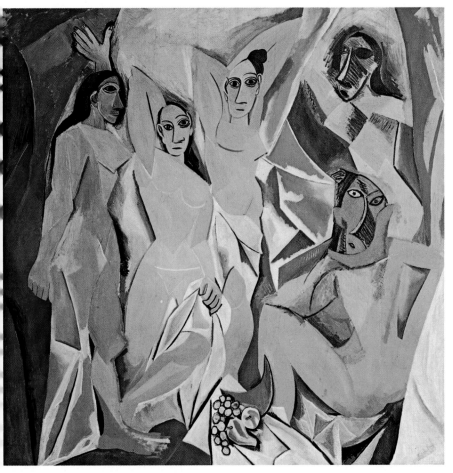

above: 575. Pablo Picasso. *Mandolin.*
1914. Wood construction, height
23⅝″ (60 cm). Musée Picasso, Paris.

left: 576. Georges Braque. *The Portuguese.*
1911. Oil on canvas, 46 × 32″ (117 × 82 cm).
Kunstmuseum, Basel, Switzerland.

above: 577. Fernand Léger. *Soldiers Playing at Cards.*
1917. Oil on canvas, 4′2¾″ × 6′3¾″ (1.3 × 1.9 m).
Kröller-Müller State Museum, Otterloo, The Netherlands.

compositions Picasso and Georges Braque [576] had been making. *Mandolin* took Cubism to its logical conclusion, and revealed a whole new range of possibilities in the style. "When we invented cubism," Picasso said later, "we had no intention whatever of inventing cubism. We wanted simply to express what was in us."[2]

Braque. Only a real expert can tell the work of Picasso from that of Georges Braque *(brock)* (1882–1963) during those years. Braque's *The Portuguese* [576] was based on a man playing a guitar in a bar; people playing stringed instruments were a favorite subject of both artists, mainly because the instruments had a cubistic set of curves and straight lines that established a design vocabulary for the painting. Braque introduces letters and numbers as if they were stenciled on, like signs and posters, but suggesting as well that the figure is also a sign, simplified to become part of a language of forms, shapes, and colors. With these ideas the Cubist style set the ground rules for a large part of art for the following fifty years.

Léger. Fernand Léger *(lay-ZHAY)* (1881–1955), who was the same age as Picasso, developed a Cubism of his own that was not inspired by sculpture and musical instruments, but by machines. Léger, more than any other artist, took an optimistic view of the machine age. Even service in the artillery, in which he was wounded, did not discourage him; he said, "I was dazzled by the breech of a 75-millimeter gun which was standing uncovered in the sunlight: the magic of light on white metal."[3] *Soldiers Playing at Cards* [577], painted in 1917 after his discharge from the army, was inspired by a tradition of paintings on that subject, including a famous one by Cézanne. But Léger's version is composed of robot-like gray figures in a machine environment. Shades of primary colors brighten the scene. No negative idea about a mechanical world was intended, just the smooth, shiny, functional beauty of machines. Léger used a Cubist style throughout his career as a way of expressing the classical perfection of a machine-like world.

Expressionism

The broadest current in Modern art is **Expressionism**, which means just what it says: the artist aims to express a subjective reaction to experience. That is true of a great many styles, but artists working independently in the anonymity of modern cities, without the demands of a patron to consider, have been much freer to consider their own feelings than artists in earlier times. Although Expressionist style is varied, common features are strong color chosen for its emotional effect and representational subjects drawn with distortions that express emotion. We often think of Expressionist art as anguished, but the early-20th-century movements in France and Germany tended to concentrate on a joyous mood.

Matisse and Derain.   Henri Matisse *(mah-TEECE)* (1869–1954) was the leader of the first group of Expressionist painters in Paris about 1905, producing colorful paintings that earned the painters the joking name "wild beasts," or *Fauves (fove)* in French. Matisse and his friend André Derain *(duh-RAN)* (1880–1954) spent the summer of 1905 at the Mediterranean beach resort of Collioure. Derain wrote a friend: "Light here is very strong, shadows very luminous," and described the new style they were working on in which light and shadow were expressed by pure color, without mixing black and white or even complements. These artists were far from being "wild beasts" in person; Derain invited Matisse to meet his parents to show that artists were respectable types. But Matisse's *Girl Reading* [578] shows an unrestrained use of color that was something new. Its

578. Henri Matisse. *Girl Reading (La Lecture).* 1905–1906. Oil on canvas, 28½ × 23⅜" (72 × 59 cm). Museum of Modern Art, New York (promised gift of Mr. and Mrs. David Rockefeller).

A POINT IN TIME: Georgia O'Keeffe and New Mexico

Georgia O'Keeffe learned her Cubist style in New York before 1920, producing non-objective paintings with large, simple shapes and colors. O'Keeffe was sensitive to landscape, and her paintings usually express a lyrical mood in her surroundings or in natural forms.

She first saw New Mexico in the summer of 1917. Santa Fe and Taos were already well-known artists' colonies, despite their remoteness. "I loved it immediately. From then on I was always on my way back," she said later. The starkness of the New Mexico desert and its traditional ways of life remained inspiring to her for the rest of her long life. She wrote:

> I have always wanted to paint the desert and I haven't known how. I always think that I cannot stay with it long enough. So I brought home the bleached bones as my symbols of the desert. To me they are as beautiful as anything I know. To me they are strangely more living than the animals walking around—hair, eyes and all with their tails switching. The bones seem to cut sharply to the center of something that is keenly alive on the desert even though it is vast and empty and untouchable—and knows no kindness with all its beauty.

From the Faraway Nearby [579], an oil painting done in 1937, brings together as almost a religious icon the elements of New Mexico that especially fascinated her: the red desert hills, the sky with its summer clouds, wild flowers, and the skull of an antlered deer.

O'Keeffe, who was born in Wisconsin in 1887, grew up at a time when it was hard for anyone to make a career in art, but she was determined. She turned away from several romances that were interfering with her concentration on art, but she finally married Alfred Stieglitz, photographer and gallery owner, because he shared the most important thing in her life, her work. O'Keeffe was apt to be curt with reporters and fans, but Stieglitz, a powerful promoter of modern art, acted as her dealer and agent. In 1924 he sold a set of six of her flower paintings to a French collector for $25,000, an amazing amount in those days. He told a reporter that European collectors were coming to buy American art, while American collectors still neglected it. O'Keeffe, overwhelmed by the publicity, fled New York to the cold, rainy coast of Maine.

In those days it was even harder for a young woman to become an artist than for men because there were no famous women artists to emulate. Georgia O'Keeffe became the famous woman artist for American women to model their careers on in the 1920s and 1930s. In more recent years artists and public do not seem to consider that the differences between men and women come out very strongly in art, but during much of O'Keeffe's life she was thought to exhibit a special feminine awareness that set her apart from the men.

In 1945, after years of migrating between New York and New Mexico, O'Keeffe bought a ruined adobe house and three acres at the tiny village of Abiquiu. There was a grand view of red desert hills— "red hills of apparently the same sort of earth that you mix with oil to make paint," O'Keeffe said. "A red hill doesn't touch everyone's heart as it touches

580. André Derain. *The Turning Road.* 1906. Oil on canvas, 4'2½" × 6'4⅝" (1.3 × 1.9 m). Museum of Fine Arts, Houston, Texas (John A. and Audrey Jones Beck Collection).

430 _____ *Recognizing the Great Styles*

579. Georgia O'Keeffe. *From the Faraway Nearby.* 1937. Oil on canvas, 36 × 40⅛" (91 × 102 cm) square. Metropolitan Museum of Art (Alfred Stieglitz Collection, 1959).

mine." The house was rebuilt with big windows, fireplaces, and adobe benches in place of furniture, and finally was given a coat of mud plaster mixed by the local workmen and, following tradition, smeared on the walls by their wives. "Every inch has been smoothed by a woman's hand," O'Keeffe said of her house. She died there in 1986.

Source: Lloyd Goodrich and D. Bry, *Georgia O'Keeffe* (New York: Whitney Museum; Praeger, 1970).

ancestors were the paintings of Vincent van Gogh and Paul Gauguin, but Matisse allowed his work to retain a "quick sketch" appearance unlike the more finished appearance of the earlier work. You can see by the lively style why Matisse gave the title "The Happiness of Life" to one of his paintings.

In *The Turning Road* **[580]** Derain uses more outline on the color shapes, but all the lines are red or blue. The result is a more controlled composition than Matisse's, and a less exuberant expression. Derain was one of many young artists to use the Expressionist style for a few years, but he later turned to a less colorful, more sculptural style. **Fauvism** was not simply an explosion of emotion. It had an idea about how nature could be represented using color without black and white. Personal expression was limited by that system, but the results were a richness of color that had never been seen before. Fauve painting, and especially the work of Matisse, has sometimes been considered purely decorative—without expression or meaning—by those who think of Expressionism as anguished and tragic. Pleasure, serenity, and generosity are the expressions that dominate in Fauvism and Matisse's work.

Kirchner and German Expressionism. Matisse and his friends were not the only ones who studied Van Gogh and Gauguin. Artists all over Europe were fascinated with their work, and Expressionist styles sprang up in many cities. The German Expressionist movement is the best known, first organized by a group of young architecture students in Dresden in 1905 who called their group The Bridge Artists' Group (usually shortened to "Die Brücke"). Ernst Ludwig Kirchner *(KIRK-ner)* (1880–1938) was one of the leaders. *Girl under Japanese Umbrella* **[581]** shows Kirchner's version of Expressionism: brilliant color, with colored lines and color used to indicate light and shade (in place of black and white or complements), a very free, spontaneous brushwork, and a subject suggesting romance, pleasure, and the exotic. Kirchner and his friends were especially interested in African and Oceanic arts, which they saw in the local museum and which they tried to duplicate for their own living and studio areas, hanging draperies printed with New Guinea and African designs. They were also exhibiting prints, both woodcuts (which became some of their most famous works) and etchings.

Expressionism was a popular and widespread style in Germany and throughout northern Europe. It was both decorative and exciting. Those two aspects were in Kirchner's mind when he painted the design of active figures across the background, like a hanging. The feeling of a freer, more primitive life is the main message of this painting. We have to remember that it was painted at a time and place in which the harsh discipline of industrial labor in factories dominated every aspect of life. The appeal of Expressionist art for people surrounded by an industrial revolution is easy to see.

Chagall. While many artists passed through periods of Expressionist style, for others it formed the basis of their life work. The Russian Marc Chagall *(shuh-GAHL)* (1887–1985) tried out some Cubist compositions, but a more emotional style suited him better. *Peasant Life* **[582]** was painted in France, which became his home after 1924, but it is about memories of his youth in Vitebsk, in Russia. At the time this painting was done, Chagall had been offered membership in the Surrealist group in Paris, but had refused. We can only imagine his reasons by comparing his work with that of Ernst or Dalí [585, 587]. Perhaps it was a feeling that the psychological probing that fascinated the Surrealists was inappropriate to his style, in which color—the most emotional and decorative element—had always been most important. Memories were Chagall's main subject, but he never psychoanalyzed them.

Chagall did important illustrations for books, most important of all for the Bible, as well as stained-glass windows and murals. Expressionism has been the vehicle for important religious art, a subject we sometimes overlook when we think of our own century. Chagall, with his Jewish heritage, emphasized Old Testament subjects, while Rouault, a Christian, concentrated on the New Testament in both prints and paintings.

Rouault.   *Head of Christ* by Georges Rouault *(roo-OH)* (1871–1958) **[583]** is over life-size, very thickly painted in oil, with heavy black lines and encrusted areas of color. It looks like medieval stained glass, which is no accident, since Rouault had worked as a young man in a stained-glass studio. Christ has huge dark eyes which look a little to the left of the observer, full of sadness and suffering, but not accusing. Rouault's art is more concerned with moral and spiritual subjects than Chagall's, which was more varied in subject. The work Rouault has left us pays little attention to problems of artistic form; he was an exceptional master, but not an experimenter. He was entirely involved in the subject and its meaning, which is exactly what one would expect of an Expressionist.

Expressionism is the broadest of the Modern styles, with representational and abstract wings and political and religious specialists; just about every kind of art had some connection with it. That fact can be explained by the definition we commonly give art, as "self-expression." As we have seen earlier (Chapters 1 and 2), artists are never trying to express only themselves, but always—even when they deny it—seeking something in themselves with which others can identify. That art is the artist's self-expression has not been a common idea in other periods, when credit for the creation of a work of art was given to the community or the patron that sponsored it, with little interest in the personality or ideas of the person who actually did the work. In this sense, Expressionism, with its emphasis on the feelings, ideas, and brushmark of the artist, is an especially 20th-century style.

583.   Georges Rouault.
Head of Christ. 1938. Oil on
canvas, 41¼ × 29½" (105 × 75 cm).
Cleveland, Ohio, Museum of Art
(gift of Hanna Fund).

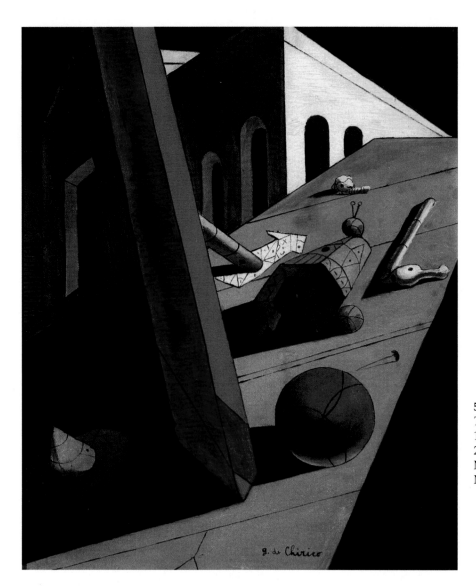

584. Giorgio de Chirico. *The Evil Genius of a King.* 1914–1915. Oil on canvas, 24 × 19¾″ (61 × 50 cm). Museum of Modern Art, New York (purchase).

Surrealism

Surrealism means "super-realism," in the sense of "more than" or "higher realism," and suggests that there is a reality we all experience in our minds which is more real than the material world around us. That idea is one of the basic principles of psychology, a field of study that was just becoming widely known in the early part of this century. Experiences such as those of André Breton, who worked with "shell-shocked" psychological cases during the First World War, made vivid the powers and vulnerability of the mind. In Paris in 1924, after the war, Breton, a writer and critic, founded the **Surrealist** group, incorporating anti-war activists from the **Dada** movement along with other advanced thinkers in the arts. But dream-like psychological art, which we now call Surrealist, already had a good start and always remained a widespread style. Late Romantic moodiness, psychoanalysis, and the horrors of modern war were the main stimuli for Surrealist art. We will look at works by four of the artists now usually grouped under the Surrealist label: Giorgio de Chirico, Max Ernst, Marcel Duchamp, and Salvador Dalí.

De Chirico.   The Italian Giorgio de Chirico *(KEE-ree-ko)* (1888–1978) arrived in Paris the summer of 1911, when he was 23, to spend four years painting in the atmosphere of tremendous creative excitement that was Paris before the

First World War. (In 1915 he returned to Italy to enlist in the army.) In *The Evil Genius of a King* [584] a late afternoon light illuminates a scene that could exist only in the mind: a building obscured by a slanting plaza on which some strange geometric forms rest. Although the things depicted could exist in the natural world, the total composition could not. That became a basic theme of Surrealist art, as it is of our dreams: objects from the real world in an unnatural setting. As the critic Guillaume Apollinaire wrote: "Monsieur de Chirico has just bought a pink rubber glove, one of the most impressive articles that are for sale. Copied by the artist, it is destined to render his future works even more moving and frightening than his previous paintings. And if you ask him about the terror that this glove might arouse, he will immediately tell you of toothbrushes still more frightening. . . . "[4]

Duchamp. Marcel Duchamp (*du-SHAWN*) (1887–1968), like De Chirico, was most productive in his early years, working in Cubist and Surrealist-related styles. *The Bride* [585], in brown tonalities that allow a dream-like space to be represented in which strange plumbing or a chemical laboratory is set up, is the type of painting in which Duchamp was most influential. A serious-looking painting, it is still making fun of romantic love, hinting that a bride is no more than a bizarre collection of tubes and containers. Duchamp, a rational, intellectual type, was also an influential spokesperson for the irrational and inspired in art.

Ernst. "On the first of August 1914 M.E. died. He was resurrected on the eleventh of November 1918 as a young man who aspired to find the myths of his time."[5] Thus Max Ernst (1891–1976) described his four years of war and his postwar dedication to art. Well educated and articulate, Ernst became the leading artist, among writers and poets, in the Surrealist group in Paris. *Elephant of the Celebes* [586], painted before the group was organized, was bought by a Sur-

below left: 585.
Marcel Duchamp.
The Bride. 1912.
Oil on canvas,
35¼ × 21¾"
(90 × 55 cm).
Philadelphia Museum of
Art (Louise and Walter
Arensberg Collection).

below: 586.
Max Ernst. *Elephant
of the Celebes.* 1921.
Oil on canvas,
4'1¼" × 3'6⅛"
(1.3 × 1 m).
Tate Gallery, London
(Roland Penrose
Collection).

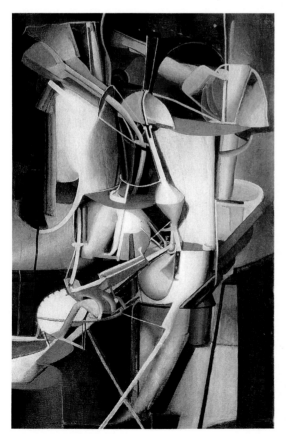

realist poet. The mechanical vat with a bull's head is huge, but powerless, and everything is in the wrong place: fish in the sky, a broken statue in the foreground of a vast plain. Ernst was not looking for any traditional myths, but was searching for the "collective unconscious" in which psychoanalysis taught there were shared dreams and visions. Anything that could be explained by the conscious mind was automatically rejected by the Surrealists, in favor of the unpredictable, the inexplicable.

Ernst made a series of collages, including two complete books, using old engraved illustrations as the basic elements. He made just enough changes to convert them into psychologically disturbing dream images. In *Une semaine de bonté* ("kindness week") **[587]** you can recognize the eagle, seashell, knife-wielding man, and nude woman that originated in different pictures. Together, they record a weird dream which we feel we might have had. That is what Surrealist art is about and, strange as it is, hardly anyone says they don't understand it.

Dalí.   The youngest of the artists associated with Parisian Surrealism was Salvador Dalí (1904–1989), an internationalized Spaniard. He said, "To tell the truth, I am nothing but an automaton recording, without judging and as exactly as possible, the dictates of my subconscious." Another remark: "The only difference between me and a madman is that I am not mad."[6] Dalí's conservative training and his interest in Renaissance painting led him to a very detailed illusionistic style which set him apart from the mainstream of the Modern movement, but it made his visions very convincing. *Soft Construction with Boiled Beans (Premonition of the Spanish Civil War)* **[588]** was painted in 1936 and suggests a nation tearing itself apart, as Spain was then about to do. Dalí's reaction to Spain's troubles took the form of a nightmare; Picasso's *Guernica* **[172]**, painted a year later, dealt with the same subject in a style derived from Synthetic Cubism.

Dalí has been criticized as calculating rather than in the grip of his dreams, but that reflects a misunderstanding of psychological art. The *sources* of the subjects and compositions of De Chirico, Duchamp, Ernst, and Dalí are in the imagination, in the unconscious and dreams, but the pictures they made are conscious products, the fruit of learning and controlled work.

below: 587.
Max Ernst.
Plate from *Une semaine de bonté,* or *Les Sept Éléments Capitaux.*
1934. Reproduction of collage of cut-up wood engravings from popular magazines of the late 19th century.
11⅛ × 9″ (28 × 23 cm).
Museum of Modern Art, New York (Louis E. Stern Collection).

below right: 588.
Salvador Dalí.
Soft Construction with Boiled Beans (Premonition of the Spanish Civil War).
1936. Oil on canvas, 39½ × 33″ (100 × 84 cm).
Philadelphia Museum of Art (Walter and Louise Arensberg Collection).

589.
Wassily Kandinsky.
Improvisation 30
(on a Warlike Theme).
Oil on canvas, 3′7¼″
(1 m) square.
Art Institute of
Chicago (Arthur
Jerome Eddy Memorial
Collection).

Non-Objective Art

Non-objective art is a general term for art that *is* an object, but does not *depict* any object. Artists of the 20th century have divided non-objective, or non-representational, art into two opposite categories: **abstract** and **concrete**. Abstract art symbolizes abstract qualities (heroism) and things that have no visible form (song). Concrete art is intended by the artist to exist as an object and to have no symbolism; that violates the accepted idea of art as a symbolic or communicative form. Although the idea of a concrete art has been proposed a number of times, and we shall examine examples later, the dominant tendency has been to consider non-objective art abstract—having reference to things outside the work itself, usually to spiritual or mental states which could not be adequately represented by visible things.

Non-objective art has appeared in two styles, Expressionist and Cubist-related, and they have acted as important connecting links between European and American art. Wassily Kandinsky and Piet Mondrian were among the most important European artists to adopt non-objective styles, both of them with the idea that their work had references to the real world.

Kandinsky.   In 1912 Wassily Kandinsky (1866–1944) wrote a book entitled *Concerning the Spiritual in Art*, which emphasized the need for an emotional commitment by the artist to the spiritual meaning of his work, a meaning that must be transferred to the observer through the form of the art. His *Improvisation 30* [589], painted in 1913, shows his Expressionist style. Kandinsky was one of the first to paint non-objective improvisations with the idea that they revealed his subconscious mind. That idea became a basic doctrine of Surrealism in the 1920s, usually in a less spontaneous style than Kandinsky's. But Kandinsky changed in later years to a geometric style derived from Cubism in which a predetermined spiritual message could be expressed. *Soft Pressure* [590] is an image of the spiritual which can be interpreted according to Kandinsky's published principles: "As a picture painted in yellow always radiates spiritual warmth . . . green represents the passive principle." The light circle at the top center is textured to suggest movement and potentiality, and the horizontal rectangle in the upper right extends an arm to the right, the direction Kandinsky described as "away from the spectator (spiritual)." By studying his writings and his paintings one can learn to interpret Kandinsky's art, which reveals only part of its meaning to the untutored observer. Kandinsky believed that the audience would develop its powers to understand art; then "the artist will be able to dispense with natural forms and colors and to use purely artistic means,"[7] he wrote.

Mondrian. The Dutch artist Piet Mondrian (1872–1944) worked in Paris during much of his mature career. But in Paris non-objective art was never dominant; the Cubist, Surrealist, and Expressionist styles used there always retained a subject from nature. It was among the northern Europeans that abstraction and non-objective art had most appeal: Kandinsky was Russian and Mondrian Dutch.

Mondrian was the purest of the non-objective painters. In Chapter 4 we looked at *Composition Gray-Red* [159], a white rectangle with solid black lines and some color fields. That is "classic Mondrian," the mature style he reached in his late forties and used until near the end of his life. But there is a "before" and "after" in Mondrian's art which help us see the potential for self-expression in what seems, at first, like an expressionless style. When he painted *Composition No. 7 (1914): Facade* [591], Mondrian had already eliminated almost the last trace of pictorial representation from his painting, though *Facade* still hints at depiction of the front of a church which appeared in earlier work. Black lines, pale tints of red, yellow, blue, and gray forecast his later work, but a few curves and diagonals remain. Mondrian's was an art of elimination: curves, diagonals, colors other than primaries; even the artificial flower in a vase in his room had its leaf painted white since Mondrian claimed he could not stand green.

Mondrian was searching for a universal language of art, which could be achieved only by simplification, by eliminating the purely personal, and specific examples from nature. "Art has to follow not nature's Appearance but its Laws," Mondrian wrote. "In order to approach the spiritual in art, one employs

590. Wassily Kandinsky. *Soft Pressure.* 1931. Oil on plywood, 39½" (100 cm) square. Museum of Modern Art, New York (Riklis Collection of McCrory Corporation; fractional gift).

591. Piet Mondrian. *Composition No. 7: Façade.* 1914. Oil on canvas, 3'11½" × 3'3⅜" (3 × 2.5 m). Kimbell Art Museum, Fort Worth, Texas.

reality as little as possible. . . . Art must transcend reality. . . . "[8] Neo-Plasticism was the name Mondrian and his Dutch colleagues gave the style.

In 1940, when he was 68, Mondrian left Europe to escape the Second World War and settled in New York, assisted by a young American painter friend, Harry Holtzman. Mondrian lived the last three years of his life in New York and discovered, unlike many European emigrés of that period, that he felt at home there. Holtzman introduced him to American jazz and Mondrian became a great fan of boogie-woogie. *Broadway Boogie Woogie* [592], painted in New York, shows a new development of the style, with colored lines and many small color spots. Mondrian's late work exhibits an exuberance and youth quite different from the severe black-lined paintings of earlier years, but it was the fruit of a single year of

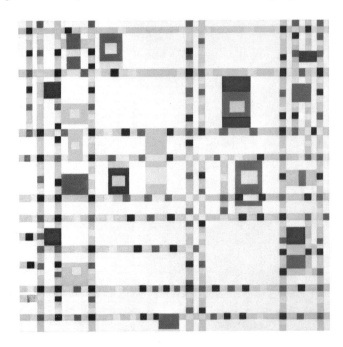

592. Piet Mondrian. *Broadway Boogie Woogie.* 1942–1943. Oil on canvas, 4'2" (1.3 m) square. Museum of Modern Art, New York (anonymous gift).

A POINT IN TIME: Art as Performance: Yves Klein

New York was the center of Happenings and Performance Art in the 1950s and 1960s, but if you were not there at the time you will find it difficult to capture the feeling of those occasions. They were fun, crazy, inventive, and when they were over there was almost nothing left as a record. By 1960 the idea of art as an event had spread to Paris, where it inspired Yves *(eve)* Klein, a young (32) judo instructor

593. Yves Klein directing his performance event at Galerie Internationale d'Art Contemporain, Paris, March 9, 1960.

work. Pneumonia killed the painter before this late development of the style could appear in more than a few paintings.

Art in the United States, 1940–1990s

American artists have been among the major participants in five important styles during the past fifty years: Abstract Expressionism, Hard-Edge Abstraction, Conceptual and Minimal Art, Pop Art, and Post-Modern Figuration. Every member of the art world during this half-century will tell you this is an oversimplification, which is true, but it is true of all historical summaries. Art has been of passionate interest to a vast audience in the United States during these years, and everyone involved has personal favorites and a personal viewpoint. That means only that art is alive and well.

Abstract Expressionism

Art critics have always played a part in the art world, but they have been especially important in the development of art centered in the United States, perhaps because the audience today is widely dispersed and depends more than and avant garde artist. Klein's events were dominated by the artist, and a record survives showing them to have been elegant, beautiful, and funny—a rare combination.

On March 9, 1960, Klein staged a "great action-spectacle" at the Contemporary Arts Circle in Paris before one hundred invited guests in formal dress. An orchestra of 20 played Klein's composition of 20 minutes of sound followed by 20 minutes of silence. Klein, in a dinner jacket, directed three nude models who coated their bodies with blue paint and smeared and printed themselves on white paper spread on the floor [593]. The event received international coverage in the press. The body prints were both works of art and records of an artistic performance by Klein (the models acted merely as his "brushes" to apply the paint); they captured the imagination of a large audience. Klein produced other body prints in the studio, some by direct printing, others by spraying around the model. Although they were considered innovative, they recall the most ancient art form of printing a hand, or spraying around it, as found in Paleolithic cave art [404]. Klein's comments were characteristically obscure, but imply that symbolism was not intended: "Only the body lives, omnipotent, and does not think," he said.

Performance art in the United States also had a tendency to turn into body art, often of a masochistic sort. Klein, too, played with violence in his performance art, but it was faked rather than truly performed. *Leap into the Void* [594] was published in two different versions (the man on a bicycle is missing in the other), which reveals that the photograph has been "doctored," which is to say turned into a

594. Yves Klein. *Leap into the Void.* Fontenay-aux-Roses, near Paris. 1960. Photograph.

work of art, rather than a record of a suicide. Klein died of a heart attack at the age of 34.

Source: Pierre Restany, *Yves Klein* (New York: Abrams, 1982).

ever before on publications to keep track of new art. In 1952 the critic Harold Rosenberg described Abstract Expressionism as it had evolved in the previous ten years:

> At a certain moment the canvas began to appear to one American painter after another as an arena in which to act—rather than as a space in which to reproduce, re-design, analyze, or "express" an object, actual or imagined. What was to go on the canvas was not a picture but an event.
>
> The painter no longer approached his easel with an image in mind; he went up to it with material in hand to do something to that other piece of material in front of him. The image would be the result of this encounter.[9]

That article gave a name, Action Painting, and a description of a technique of painting, which many artists and their public accepted at that time, although the style is remembered now under the name Abstract Expressionism. It also launched an idea of art as an *activity* rather than an *object,* which led to various dramatic events such as Happenings and Performance Art in which no object resulted, but a more or less spontaneous activity took place. The **Abstract Expressionist** style was expressionist in its use of color and gesture as expressions of emotion or mood. It was abstract in its rejection of the depiction of natural subjects, although not all artists in the group followed this tendency (De Koon-

595. Jackson Pollock. *Male and Female.* 1942. Oil on canvas, 6'1" × 4'1" (1.9 × 1.2 m). Philadelphia Museum of Art (gift of Mr. and Mrs. H. Gates Lloyd).

ing most notably). Paintings were large, usually 5 or 6 feet (1.5 or 1.8 meters) high, and the brushmarks are similarly large, suggesting sweeps with a housepainter's brush, to emphasize the mark of the artist's hand.

Pollock. The paintings by Jackson Pollock (1912–1956) and filmed records of him at work were mainly responsible for the idea that performance was the essence of art, that the action was more important than the product. That idea had a wide popularity, but it was not shared by Pollock.

Jackson Pollock grew up in California and Arizona but was studying art in New York before he was 20. By 1942, when he was 30, Pollock was able to paint *Male and Female* **[595]**, which summarized all the things he had been studying— Cubism, Surrealism, and Expressionism all contribute to it—but it also has a free-swinging vitality of its own. The two tall rectangular human figures stand against a blue sky full of fireworks made of colored slashes, drips, and spatters. During the next five years subjects slowly disappeared as his method changed to "drip painting," which became his most famous style. *Number 1, 1948* **[596]**, more than 5 by 8 feet (1.5 by 2.4 meters), was painted by pouring the paint on the canvas as it lay on the floor. "In the arena" was where Pollock said he was as he painted, in action with the painting. "When I am *in* my painting, I'm not

596. Jackson Pollock. *Number 1, 1948*. 1948. Oil on canvas, 5'8" × 8'8" (1.7 × 2.6 m). Museum of Modern Art, New York.

aware of what I'm doing," he wrote later. "It is only after a sort of 'get acquainted' period that I see what I have been about."[10] But Pollock always denied that accidents were responsible, or that chaos resulted. The large swinging rhythms of line, shape, and color in *Number 1A, 1948*, reminded the audience not only of the artist's actions, but of galaxies, atomic reactions, microbiology, and all the complex interactions that were on people's minds.

De Kooning.   The other dominant figure in the Abstract Expressionist style was Willem de Kooning (b. 1904), the painter other artists most admired. Cubism was the main point of departure for De Kooning, but the controlled straight lines and curves of Picasso and Braque increased to mural size and the brush was swung from the shoulder instead of the wrist. If you compare Braque's *The Portuguese* [576] with De Kooning's *Woman I*, [597], you notice that the canvas has increased in size (from 46 to 76 inches, or 117 to 193 centimeters, high), but, more important, the brush stroke has increased in size. The geometric shapes in light and shade dominate Braque's painting, but the slashing stroke of color dominates in De Kooning's paintings. De Kooning has never completely eliminated representation from his paintings, often returning to female figures—usually rather ferocious women, as in *Woman I*—but other paintings, such as

597. Willem de Kooning. *Woman I*. 1950–1952. Oil on canvas, 6'3⅞" × 4'10" (1.9 × 1.5 m). Museum of Modern Art, New York (purchase).

598. Willem de Kooning. *Easter Monday*. 1955–1956.
Oil, newspaper transfer on canvas; 8′ × 6′2″ (2.4 × 1.8 m).
Metropolitan Museum of Art, New York (Rogers Fund, 1956).

Easter Monday [598], often have a landscape or cityscape quality. Whatever the subject, or lack of it, De Kooning's color scheme is distinctive: white, pink, pale yellow, pale green or blue, and gray, with black lines. His colors, which are easy to identify, have contributed to post-Modern color preferences.

Hard-Edge Abstraction and Minimalism

Non-objective art has been a powerful current since the 1940s, taking a slightly different form—and name—with each generation of artists. The first generation, of the 1940s and 1950s, were the "color-field" painters, followed by Hard-Edge of the 1960s and **Minimal** and conceptual art of the 1970s. The artistic problem was defined differently by each generation, but they share the ideal of Kandinsky and Mondrian that meaning in art rests in the form—especially in color, shape, and size—not in the subject.

Newman. Barnett Newman (1905–1970), the founder of color-field painting, began a new kind of painting in 1948 when he tried out a red-brown canvas with a strip of tape down the center, which he painted orange. It dawned on him that he had something new: a powerful color divided symmetrically by a narrow stripe. Taped edges had been done before (by Mondrian, for example, who composed his paintings with strips of tape), but Newman used his tapes as breaks in a color field; he called them "zips" since he zipped off the tape after the color field was painted, exposing an undercoat. He raised his paintings to very large size—*Vir Heroicus Sublimis* [599] is 18 feet (5.5 meters) wide—so the stripes become divisions of a color environment, always with a numerical relation of area to area, usually with symmetry a factor. Newman composed his pictures not with drawings, but with a series of numbers. There is a mystical content in Newman's work that Mondrian would have appreciated it, but it is often hard to express in words. A spiritual meaning is most explicit in his late series of black-and-white paintings which he gave the title *Stations of the Cross*, yet even they are non-objective and we must interpret such formal traits as lack of color, proportion and shape, to arrive at a thought.

Stella. By the 1960s the audience for art was used to Abstract Expressionism and, despite the fact that it was a very popular style, artists were bored with emotional expression. The influential critic Clement Greenberg explained the change: "The look of the accidental had become an academic, conventional look."[11] Greenberg had argued for "purity" in the arts, by which he meant that painting should have no qualities that might belong to sculpture or any other

599. Barnett Newman. *Vir Heroicus Sublimis.* 1950–1951. Oil on canvas, 7'11⅜" × 17'9¼" (2.4 × 5.4 m). Museum of Modern Art, New York (gift of Mr. and Mrs. Ben Heller).

art. Painting, he thought, could reach purity only by eliminating representations of nature, illusions, and subject matter. Greenberg thought, as Kandinsky had, that art would inevitably develop in that direction.

Although Greenberg was not impressed by the early paintings of Frank Stella (b. 1936), they were taken by the art world as fulfillment of Greenberg's prophecy and his demand for purity. Stella's *Jill* **[600]** was one of the young Stella's "black paintings" which were accepted by many artists and critics, especially those of his own age group, as defining a new direction. It was a direction mainly defined by negatives: no color (just white lines on black), no brush strokes (just flat enamel and carefully smoothed lines), no subject, no illusions of space and form (just a regular symmetrical pattern). They were described as "poker-faced," cool, secretive works, just the opposite of the dramatic, colorful, emotional, personally revealing paintings of Pollock and De Kooning. Stella shared a non-objective style with Newman and the other color-field painters, but led into the "hard-edge" style in which geometric areas of flat color had sharp "hard" edges and the canvas was more evenly divided between two or more colors.

600. Frank Stella. *Jill.* 1959. Enamel on canvas, 7'6¾" × 6'6¾" (2.3 × 2 m). Albright-Knox Art Gallery, Buffalo, New York (gift of Seymour H. Knox, 1962).

Recognizing the Great Styles

601. Donald Judd. Untitled. 1966–1968. Stainless steel, plexiglass; 6 cubes, each 36″ (91 cm) on each side, at 8″ (20-cm) intervals. Milwaukee, Wisconsin, Art Museum (Layton Collection).

The emotionally cool was fashionable in the 1960s and 1970s in music and manners, as well as art. Artists took two contrasting approaches: Minimalist artists chose to make non-objective art that was intended to have no spiritual or emotional meaning; Conceptual artists chose to write words on paper explaining actions they had done or would do, but which remained concepts for the audience in the sense that no form was available to be seen. The concepts were usually Minimalist, such as a line between two points or a mirror set at a certain place. Frank Stella was one of the earlier artists who preferred to think of their work as concrete, not abstract, having no reference to the real world, but existing in the real world as an object. As part of that aim, the canvases Stella used for his paintings were stretched over a framework (called stretchers) made of especially thick wooden bars to make the paintings more massive, more thing-like.[12]

Judd. The Minimalist sculptor Donald Judd (b. 1928) wrote: "Things that exist exist, and everything is on their side. They're here, which is pretty puzzling. Nothing can be said of things that don't exist."[13] Judd's sculpture exists **[601]**, but emotions and ideas are not claimed for it: "I didn't want work that was general or universal in the usual sense. I didn't want it to claim too much. . . . A shape, a volume, a color, a surface is something itself."[14] This statement is the definition of concrete art, rejecting the spiritual ideals that Kandinsky and Mondrian considered to be embodied in their abstract art. The machine finish of Judd's sculpture was designed to eliminate any trace of the artist's handwork and achieve absolute impersonality. In many cases the artist did not make the work of art, but simply drew the plans and had it built in a machine shop or carpenter's shop. That was another reaction against the overpowering personalism of Abstract Expressionism.

Pop Art

The name **Pop Art** was based on "popular art," meaning "art of the people," and referring to advertising, commercial art, and industrial design—all the things that surround us in a consumer society. But there was more to it than making pictures of pots and pans, chairs, cars, and television sets. It was partly a response to the great abstract styles that had dominated the art world for about fifteen years. Many of its major names and works have appeared in earlier chapters: Andy Warhol, Robert Rauschenberg, Jasper Johns, and Claes Oldenberg. When Pop Art first appeared in the art galleries in the late 1950s it seemed to be a funny, cool response to an art world that was taking itself very seriously, but

602. James Rosenquist. *Silver Skies.* 1962. Oil on canvas, 6'6" × 16'6" (2 × 5 m). Chrysler Museum, Norfolk, Virginia (gift of Walter P. Chrysler, Jr.).

as time passed and the artists developed, it began to merge into other representational styles. James Rosenquist's *Silver Skies* [602] not only belongs exactly to its own Pop Art movement, but also forecasts painting styles of the next three decades.

Rosenquist. *Silver Skies* is large—16½ feet (5 meters) wide—and was seen as an arty billboard. The style of large, strongly shaded simple shapes with shiny highlights and including subjects associated with advertising (a girl, a car, tires, and a bottle) belonged to American commercial and street life. Actually, James Rosenquist (b. 1933) learned to paint at nineteen by painting billboards, which he later did to support himself while he studied art in New York. There he began to realize the difference between commercial art and fine art.

> When I met the top artists of the time, like Franz Kline and De Kooning, I realized I was in for a different experience than I had expected. They weren't bums, but they weren't successful like businessmen, and their paintings weren't selling well. But they had tremendous reputations for being very good. I felt I might never be an artist, that it might be a long journey and I might never achieve anything in my lifetime.[15]

But at 27 he quit his job as a billboard artist, got married, rented a studio, and began trying to make serious paintings. "Abstract Expressionism had become this corny-looking habit. The drip had become a cliché. . . . but I didn't want to do hard-edge paintings either," he said later. Jasper Johns' show in 1958 (see Chapter 6) inspired him. "I decided to make pictures of fragments. . . . I wanted to find images that were in a 'nether-nether-land,' things that were a little out of style, but hadn't reached the point of nostalgia."[16] In 1962, when *Silver Skies* was painted, with its pale reds, blue, and grays and its geometric slices from a commercial reality, it was precisely in tune with the evolution of New York art. The critic Thomas Hess wrote: "The whole [Pop Art] movement evolves with a kind of awesome inevitability out of New York abstract art."[17]

Photo-Realism

By the late 1960s artists were searching for ways to get back to subject matter free of the irony or commercial associations of Pop Art. The impact of history was beginning to make itself felt on young artists who had seen a lot of art in museums and had studied art history in college. Many of them wanted to show things beyond pure existence. But the truth about the way the world looked in the 20th century could not be found in the art of Rembrandt or Manet. When people in our day speak of the truth, the artists noticed, they meant "true, as in a photograph." That led inevitably to the study of photography as a source of art.

Close. Photography had been used as a sketching medium since it was invented, but Chuck Close (b. 1940) studied the image revealed by the camera and based a painting style on it. *Frank* **[603]** is a head 9 feet (2.7 meters) tall painted in black and white on a pure white background. It records meticulously the textures of skin and hair, glasses and clothing, as the camera would see them. Even the focus of the camera lens on the front part of the face is recorded, with the farther edges of the hair and collar slightly out of focus. That shows the use of a single photograph to define the focus. Chuck Close was one of the most "photographic" of the Photo-Realists, which to his audience was a guarantee of seriousness about the search for visual realism. Close has used the air brush (a miniature spray gun) to eliminate brush strokes, or what he calls "art marks," but in another work he built up the face with finger prints, which has a different kind of non-art neutrality. Limiting the paintings to black and white reinforced the connection with photography and limited the natural illusion, keeping the work within the realm of art even without "art marks."

Goings. Many of the Photo-Realist artists relied almost entirely on the camera in place of drawing, usually developing their own photographs. They often specialized in certain subjects, preferring American car culture: cars, trailers, fast-food places, and the people around them. Ralph Goings (b. 1928) has painted several views of *Pee Wee's Diner, Warnerville, New York* **[604]**. Goings' dust-free world has been described as "not the quaint and ingratiating view of America typified by Norman Rockwell. . . . Goings paints the small town and its inhabitants as they are."[18] That statement testifies to the power of the photograph to control our idea of reality. The smooth clear colors, reduction of textural difference and concentration on reflections and highlights, not to speak of the stillness of the scene, come from the photographic sketches.

below left: 603. Chuck Close. *Frank.* 1969. Air brush, acrylic on canvas; 9 × 7′ (2.7 × 2.1 m). Minneapolis, Minnesota, Institute of Arts (John R. Van Derlip Fund).

below: 604. Ralph Goings. *Pee Wee's Diner, Warnerville, New York.* 1977. Oil on canvas, 4′ (1.2 m) square. O. K. Harris Gallery, New York.

Photo-Realist art has often been compared to Norman Rockwell's illustrations, and the comparison is a fair one. *Saying Grace* [605] was a cover picture for the *Saturday Evening Post* magazine in 1951, when Rockwell was 57 and had been a top illustrator for about thirty years. All Rockwell's work was done in oil paint, the earlier work from live models, which gave it a sculptural massiveness produced by foreshortening and **chiaroscuro**. In the later 1930s he began to work from photographs, which allowed more active and more natural poses, but tended to flatten the paintings because he was working from a flat surface. Two differences between the 1970s–1980s Photo-Realist paintings and Rockwell's are immediately apparent: in Rockwell's work textural differences are much more pronounced, and the human figures are much more expressive. *Saying Grace* is unusual in Rockwell's work for the low-key acting—over-acting was common in his early work—but all his characters exhibit more feeling in their poses, gestures, hands, and faces than Goings allows his figures to show. One suspects that a Mondrian lay in Goings' unconscious mind, suggesting strong vertical and horizontal lines, and Baroque art in Rockwell's, prompting him to find the climax of an action, when the whole meaning of the story is revealed by poses and expressions. Goings and the other Photo-Realists developed from the emotional coolness of hard-edge abstraction and Pop Art, which was reinforced by the coolness of the camera itself.

Estes. Richard Estes (b. 1936) rarely allows any human figures into his city scenes, concentrating on architecture and signs. Estes' *Central Savings* [606] also makes an interesting comparison with Goings' *Pee Wee's Diner*. Both have steel-rimmed stools and a red lunch counter in the foreground and both have the clean, smooth "photographic" surfaces. But *Pee Wee's Diner* represents entirely positive forms, while Estes elaborates the effects of plate glass. We see through it into the lunch counter, deserted at 10:15 in the morning, and out the other glass wall to the street ("tow away zone"). Reflected from the glass are the buildings

605. Norman Rockwell. *Saying Grace*. 1951. Oil on canvas, 3′7″ × 3′4″ (1 × 1 m). Cover of *Saturday Evening Post*, November 24, 1951. Collection of Mr. and Mrs. Ken Stuart.

Recognizing the Great Styles

606. Richard Estes. *Central Savings.* 1975. Oil on canvas, 3 × 4' (0.9 × 1.2 m). Nelson-Atkins Museum of Art, Kansas City, Missouri (gift of the Friends of Art).

and the street behind the observer, with the shadowy reflections of people. Estes makes many color photographs of his subjects, prints them himself, and uses them to compose an acrylic underpainting, in which each part is revised, its color adjusted, and the complexities of the design worked out. The kind of intricate natural appearance Estes creates could hardly be done without the aid of photography; imagine standing in the street with your easel while you worked out *Central Savings*.

We are not tempted to compare Estes with Rockwell, but he leads us to think of Cézanne and the Cubists. Art historian Alfred Barr, writing about the Cubist style, mentions "the cubist process of taking apart or breaking down the forms of nature . . . to analyze, to disintegrate the forms of nature in order to create out of the fragments a new form."[19] Estes lays out the main lines of his composition parallel to the edges of the canvas, like many Cubist pictures, in order to compose layers of reality and reflection which accomplish many of the aims of the Cubists. Photo-Realism is in these respects a natural heir of the early Modern styles.

Post-Modern Styles

About 1970 many people in the art world began to be alert to signs of change. The Modernist critic Harold Rosenberg surprised his readers with the first totally negative review of an avant garde exhibit in the spring of that year.[20] Charles Jencks dated "the death of modern architecture" to 3:32 p.m. on July 15, 1972, when a large housing project in St. Louis was demolished; the American Institute of Architects had given it an award when it was built in 1951.[21] It was time for a change, it seemed, but the character of the change was not clear. "Modern art" was over, but what was here in its place? Slowly, over two decades, a new period began to define itself, carrying on many elements from the Modernism of the previous hundred years, but also based on a different outlook.

Two ideas are among the most important in defining this new period: "coming to terms with history" and acceptance of the unity of the extremely varied forms of art.

Coming to Terms with History

"Coming to terms with history," a phrase that has been repeated frequently in the description of Post-Modernism, was demonstrated by a series of six lectures given by Frank Stella at Harvard in 1984. His subject was how non-objective art in our day can meet the challenge of the great art of the past. Drawing his examples from Titian, Rubens, Kandinsky, Mondrian, and many others, he discussed the problems and objectives of art by the ways artists of other times had dealt with them. That was a dramatic change from the attitude expressed by many Modern artists since 1900—that we have nothing to learn from history, but must start over. Paul Klee, for example, wrote in his diary in 1902: "I want to be as though new-born, knowing nothing about Europe, nothing, knowing no pictures, entirely without impulses, almost in an original state."[22]

Coming to terms with the past has led to very little copying from earlier art. On the contrary, the admiration for past art has mostly stimulated artists' ambitions, and when direct inspiration has come from an earlier work it is usually totally transformed into a new style. Willem de Kooning remarked in an interview in 1972:

> I am an eclectic painter by chance; I can open almost any book of reproductions and find a painting I could be influenced by. It is so satisfying to do something that has been done for thirty thousand years the world over. When I look at a picture I couldn't care less for when it was done. . . . In other words I could be influenced by Rubens, but I would certainly not paint like Rubens.[23]

The Unity of Art

It was common a few years ago to divide art into many categories, such as "minor arts," and "decorative arts," which had different levels of prestige. More and more these different categories are disappearing and their contents are merging into one general category of art. A boundary still seems to exist between art and applied design, between non-functional and functional pieces, but Post-Modern artists increasingly reject that boundary as well. The potter Virginia Cartwright has written:

> Teapots are popular right now. Collectors and gallery owners want them. But I find that despite the demand, they are not cost effective to make—at least functional handbuilt ones are not. . . . To handbuild one but keep it functional takes hours of precision work. . . . If it's functional, the price one can charge (and actually get) is limited. If it doesn't pour or hold liquid, it qualifies as "art" and the price can be doubled. This is the reality of the marketplace, and is the reason why there are more and more teapot sculptures and fewer and fewer functional teapots. . . . I haven't fully resolved this problem myself. . . . [24]

Cartwright is typical of contemporary artisans in her struggle with the problem of the relationship between function and art. That problem is faced by architects, industrial and interior designers, and a wide range of people working in art. As Cartwright implies, functional art is often more expensive to make than non-functional pieces, and less appreciated by the audience. In this respect artists and designers are still a little ahead of a large part of their audience.

Aumann.   Considering the *Cantaloupe Teapot* **[607]** by Karen Aumann, it is easy to believe that hours of precision work were required. It is a functional work of art; you can pour tea from it. It combines a wide range of techniques which show both technical skills and historical awareness. The cantaloupe is made of slip-cast porcelain, a technique with ancient roots in China and Peru which is now used for industrial production of ceramics. The spout and lid were made by throwing on the wheel, and the handle was modeled by hand. The glazes represent another whole field of expertise.

607. Karen Aumann. *Canteloupe Teapot*. c. 1985. Slip-cast porcelain. Collection of the artist, Philadelphia.

Shaw.   Richard Shaw (b. 1941) has taken the opposite approach. His porcelain *Walking Figure Jar Number 1* [608] comes down clearly on the side of sculpture. Though it is built in such a way that it could serve as a container, it is hard to imagine using it functionally. Shaw's reproduction of natural appearances with porcelain clay is amazing and has served as an influential example, especially in his home region, California. The books and paper serving as the base for *Walking Figure* are also ceramic, and the colors and textures of the can, pencils, bamboo, and pipe are faithfully reproduced.

These two examples of ceramic sculpture show the integration of the skills of the artisan and functional design with the representational and symbolic role of art. They are also characteristic of the Post-Modern style in their illusions. Abstract form, which was the principal concern of ceramic artists in earlier decades, is not the problem these artists have taken for themselves, and that sets them apart from the Modernism of the earlier part of this century.

608.   Richard Shaw.
Walking Figure Jar #1. 1978.
Porcelain with decal overglaze,
height 18½ × 10¾ × 9″
(47 × 27 × 22 cm).
Braunstein/Quay Gallery,
San Francisco (collection of
Byron Meyer).

609. Donald Judd. Desk set. 1982. Solid Douglas fir, matte varnish finish; desk 2'6" × 2'9" × 4' (0.8 × 0.8 × 1.2 m), each chair 30 × 15 × 15" (76 × 38 × 38 cm). Fabrication by Cooper/Kato, New York. Collection of James Cooper and Ichiro Kato, New York.

Judd as a Post-Modernist.   It is revealing to examine the more recent work of Donald Judd, who explained his Minimal sculpture **[601]** of the 1960s and 1970s as concrete objects without symbolism. In 1982 Judd designed a desk and chairs **[609]**. They all belong to the same family of smooth, impersonal, sharp-edged rectangular forms, but the desk and chairs are part of the real world of useful objects. They have taken on functional form, but they do not appear to be very comfortable. Aumann's teapot represents a melon, so convincingly that we might hesitate to use it, but it does function as well as represent. Shaw's *Walking Figure* is entirely representational, completely hiding the porcelain within the subject. Judd dramatizes this problem of the functional and the symbolic by making a sculpture of functional furniture, a sculpture that returns to the Modern idea that the material (wood in this case) should show. Post-Modern artists are generally convinced that a real union between functional efficiency and works of art is possible. That has always been the aim of architects and furniture designers, but recently it has been on the minds of artists in all mediums as they try to bring all the visual arts together.

Style and the Naked Truth

The painters, like the potters and the sculptors, have turned strongly toward representation, but the abstraction of earlier years still plays a powerful part. Artists look at the work of the Abstract Expressionists and Hard-Edge painters with respect and do not want to lose the ground they gained. The Post-Modern ideal is a symbolic representation in an abstract design. That ideal can appear in a variety of styles, and since no one style dominates current art, style itself has become the question.

One of the favorite subjects of Baroque artists was a female nude symbolizing "the naked truth." These days we usually think of nakedness as being truthful (sometimes "the horrible truth") and clothing as being "stylish," meaning fashionable. As Coco Chanel said, "Fashions change; style remains." Part V of this book is a history and analysis of style, which in this context means simply "a way of doing something," the emphasis, often unconscious, on certain elements of art and principles of design as we express ourselves.

In earlier times it seems that artists and their audience usually accepted the current style as simply true, and it never occurred to artists to try to develop their own personal styles. One of the outstanding features of the Modern period was the artists' search for a personal style. Now the whole idea of style is being sharply questioned. "Style is a fraud,"[25] Willem de Kooning said, implying that

A POINT IN TIME: Eric Fischl's *Cargo Cults*

In 1984 Eric Fischl gathered a set of color snapshots he had taken on the beaches in France and began to compose a large oil painting using the photographs as sketches. *Cargo Cults* [610] has the natural appearance of its photographic sources, but the mixture of figures, unrelated in the snapshots, suggests that a story full of sex and violence is about to be played out before our eyes. Cargo cults are Melanesian religions which try to obtain material riches by magic rituals; the title seems to relate to the robed figure with a mirror pendant brandishing a large knife. The mixture of clothed and nude figures also provokes the viewer to try to explain it, as Manet's audience did with *Le Déjeuner sur l'Herbe* [564]. The audience reaction to Fischl's work has been fascination with the stories.

Fischl had his first solo show in New York in 1980 when he was 32, showing a group of large oil paintings of people in normal middle-class American settings in which tragedy or sex has intervened. The nuclear family of dad, mom, brother, sister, and the family dog are the basic cast of Fischl's dramas. In *Cargo Cults* it is the gang of buddies on the beach who are caught between temptation and danger.

Very much aware of his place in the history of art, Fischl says:

> I'm related to Manet in manner perhaps [referring to his broad, free brushwork], but I'm much more interested in Degas. He's voyeuristic. He's much more involved with psychology and sexuality than Manet. Manet is someone I'm working against, because he took everything out of painting and I'm trying to put it back in. So I work within the realist tradition of meaning. I think Manet was deeply cynical. I work in the tradition of the moralism of Daumier.

Fischl brings together many contemporary currents in art: its historical awareness, its representational and story-telling side, and its use of photographic sources.

———
Source: Eric Fischl, "Figures and Fiction," *Aperture*, Winter 1985: 56–59. Quotation from Nancy Grimes, "*Naked Truths*," ArtNews Sep. 1986: 77.

610. Eric Fischl. *Cargo Cults*. 1984. Oil on canvas, 7'8" × 11' (2.3 × 3.4 m). Mary Boone Gallery, New York.

he does not cultivate a personal style, but simply tries to show the truth. Artists have often spoken of trying to make art without style, to show only the naked truth.

Every step in art in the last fifty years has been explained by the artists, their critics and patrons, and the members of the audience as a search for truth. That search has always been a part of art, but in other periods the aims of a social class or of an institution such as the government or the church often were more important than the simple truth about our experience of the world. New York museum director Thomas Hess wrote: "The classical 'look' of a painting no longer mattered for the New York artists. Art could be rough and hairy, like a Pollock; it could burst with high-velocity shapes, like a de Kooning; or, to an unfamiliar eye, seem completely empty, like a Newman. What mattered was the ethical pressure informing the work: its truth.[26]

If we all inevitably have our own personal style, is there some way to show a truth that can be shared, that is more than personal? Post-Modern solutions to this problem cover a wide range. Two painters, Avigdor Arikha and Peter Saul, exhibit opposite approaches to the search for a style which is personal and yet communicates with an audience.

Arikha. Avigdor Arikha *(ah-RE-kah)* (b. 1929), a Paris-based Israeli, had been making successful abstractions for a few years, but in 1965 he stopped painting. For the next eight years he produced nothing but drawings, all of them done from the natural scene before his eyes and completed in one sitting. *Place de la Concorde* [611], drawn with a brush and black ink on heavily textured paper, is an unpromising subject—although it shows a famous Paris square, it could be called simply "the parking lot"—but Arikha does not draw just anything. The subject must strike him "like a telephone call—when it rings, I run,"[27] he says. His drawings are an attempt to produce art without any style, a record of something *seen,* not *thought,* as his earlier abstractions had been.

In 1973 Arikha began to paint in the same style as he had been drawing, from something visible and finishing in one sitting, with no retouching. *Studio Interior with Mirror* [612] is thinly painted in oil color on a white canvas. It has a subtle and surprising composition, but it was not a composition invented in his mind; it was there before his eyes. It was also painted in one sitting, which keeps the painting true to the experience, rejecting second thoughts and "improvements."

Arikha is contemptuous of art movements—"flu epidemics," he calls them, "everyone coming down with photo-realism or neo-expressionism, and then it passes."[28] Such a remark shows that Arikha agrees with De Kooning's

611.
Avigdor Arikha.
Place de la Concorde.
1969. Ink on paper,
9⅜ × 12⅝"
(24 × 32 cm).
Collection
of the artist.

612. Avigdor Arikha. *Studio Interior with Mirror.* 1987. Oil on canvas, 5'3¾" × 4'3" (1.6 × 1.3 m). Musée Cantini, Marseilles, France.

comment on style as a fraud and considers his own work to be entirely without style. By the definition of style used in this book, everything we do inevitably has style which unconsciously reveals personality and outlook on life. The conscious adoption of a style results in affectation, which is what Arikha means by "everyone coming down" with a style.

Saul. While Arikha's drawings and paintings claim to have no style and to be impersonal records of experience, the work of Peter Saul (b. 1934) claims the opposite, to be a personal expression about experience. To understand Arikha's art you need to share a modern world that looks like his, but to understand Saul's you need to share the newspaper (the cartoons and the comics, as well as the news) and the television. Saul's paintings are not about how things look, but about how one man feels about public events. "Just put it in your own words," the interviewer says when asking your opinion about public events; Saul realizes that opinions are personal, but they are still the truth about your feelings.

613. Peter Saul. *Telephone Call.* 1988. Graphite pencil on paper, 6 × 7" (15 × 18 cm). Collection of the artist.

"Peter Saul knows exactly what he's doing," a critic wrote. "He is trying to make a painting as unbearable to look at as it is impossible to ignore, a painting one cannot like yet cannot turn away from, one that is, in his own term, 'hard core.'"[29]

Saul's style is obviously a style; he does not pretend his paintings are pure records of visual experience. His drawings, such as *Telephone Call* **[613]**, are records of thought, not vision. They are studies for paintings, a grid marked on for transfer to canvas, each square inch being enlarged to a square foot. We all recognize the source of the style in comics, an art form almost everyone shares and understands. Distortions of natural forms, which are the most striking feature of the style, express action and emotion in the comics, but Saul makes the distortions much more extreme.

Subway I **[614]**, an acrylic painting more than 13 feet (4 meters) wide, is Saul's comment on violence in the New York subways. Saul has written about the composition: "In *Subway* all the crime and punishment is there—so much there's no room for any cops to merely hold flashlights and guns. Every figure has to be used. . . . Actually, in *Subway*, the bare essentials of the full story are so much, if fully shown, that they provide a large and complex scene leaving room for very little atmosphere beyond the essential structure of the scene (subway car, seats, etc.)." Saul shares with the Baroque artists the desire to show the climax of action: "The excitement," he says, "is the actual happening, not five minutes later."[30]

614. Peter Saul. *Subway I.* 1979. Acrylic on canvas, 5'7" × 13'8" (1.7 × 4.2 m). Frumkin/Adams Gallery, New York.

Saul uses fantastic distortion to emphasize that his pictures are personal statements. They are not neutral impersonal truth, but passionate commentaries. Saul and his audience share a way of seeing the world through comic books and animated films that is *stylized*—put into a style—that does not pretend to be objective. Within that style Saul can say the truth about his own outrage, or amusement, with the way the world is going. His style has changed slowly over the years, just as Arikha's has, but neither of them has been guilty of affectation.

Even when art looks funny or unimportant, it is involved with the timeless problems of being an individual in a mass society and finding some truth that is both personal and sharable. Art plays an especially valuable role at this time in our Post-Modern world, in which the value of things is usually measured by the size of the audience or the size of the profit. Artists, and with them the whole art world, are dedicated to the proposition that the only thing that matters is the quality of the product. The definition of quality is constantly under discussion by the critics and the audience, but everyone agrees that neither the size of the profit nor the size of the audience is an important criterion of quality.

In the end it is the audience that decides what is art and how good it is, but everyone knows that the audience for an artist or a style may be small and may take years to grow. Immediate acceptance by a mass audience, such as a television show is expected to have, would be taken as proof that a work of art was too easy to be of lasting interest. The painter Jacob Lawrence told an audience, "An element which any work of art must contain if it is to endure . . . is mystery." In art the audience is expected to rise to the challenge of difficult, ambiguous, complicated experiences, which will retain an element of mystery even when they have become familiar.

Like photography, drawing and painting and the other art techniques have many uses outside art, in business, journalism, science and medicine, and countless other fields. Two features distinguish art from those other uses: its expressive aim is foremost, and the quality of the experience it provides is the only consideration. That experience belongs to everyone, to the artists, their patrons, to the critics and historians who study it, and especially to the audience. It is the audience for whom that expression was intended and for whom the experience was designed.

As members of the audience we have a special role to play. We get the kind of art and artists we ask for, and we reveal ourselves to all future generations by the things and people we choose. Our great-grandchildren will know what we saw as truth and reality by the art that belongs to us. It is no exaggeration to say that artists and their audiences create each other, and by their relationship create pleasure and understanding to be passed on as a heritage.

Summary for Review

Cubism, Expressionism, Surrealism, and non-objective art expressed a European (mainly in Paris) search for new forms of art inspired by African sculpture, spiritual ideals, and psychology. Natural appearance was replaced by mental visions as the subject of art, whether the style was geometric (Cubist or non-objective), highly colored (Expressionist), or drawn with dream-like distortion (Surrealist). After 1940, New York became a major art center. Non-objective styles (Abstract Expressionism, Hard-Edge Abstraction, and Minimalism) at first entirely dominated, but after 1958 found competition in representational styles (Pop Art, Photo-Realism, and Post-Modernism). Style has been a big question throughout the 20th century: how to make art that expresses some truth that an audience can understand, and yet remains a unique expression with a personal style? Another concern has been to merge crafts (ceramics, furniture design, etc.), which had been considered to lack symbolism, into expressive art without necessarily losing function.

TIME LINE

Ancient Styles, 25,000 B.C.–A.D. 1000

B.C. A.D.

Scale markers: 25,000 B.C., 20,000, 15,000, 10,000, 5000, 1|1 1000

Europe
- "Venus" figurines, 24,000–21,000 B.C.
- Upper Paleolithic styles, c.35,000–8000 B.C.

Americas
- Frederick Head, Oklahoma, c.18,000 B.C.?
- Cave art (Lascaux Cave), 18,000–10,000 B.C.
- Pecos style, Texas, c.6000–1000 B.C.
- Tiahuanaco, Bolivia, c.100 B.C.–A.D. 700
- Maya civilization, Mexico and Guatemala, c.100 B.C.–A.D. 900

Ancient Civilizations of the Near East, 3000 B.C.–100 B.C.

Scale markers: 3000 B.C., 2500, 2000, 1500, 1000, 500 B.C.

Mesopotamia
- Sumeria, Early Dynastic, 3000–2500 B.C.
- Ur, First Dynasty, 2500–2350 B.C.
- Akkadian Kingdoms, 2350–2150 B.C.
- Assyrian Empire, 900–612 B.C.

Egypt
- Kingdoms of the Pharaohs, 3200–332 B.C.
- Great Pyramids at Gizeh, Menkaure, 2530–2460 B.C.
- Book of the Dead of Naun, c.1000 B.C.
- Alexander's conquest, Hellenistic kingdom, 332–30 B.C.

Classical Civilizations of Greece and Rome, 500 B.C.–A.D. 300

B.C. A.D.

Scale markers: 500 B.C., 400, 300, 200, 1|1, 100, 200, 300

Greece
- Athens, "Golden Age," 480–404 B.C.
- Building of the Parthenon, 447–432 B.C.
- Sculptures of Polyclitus, c.460–420 B.C.
- Sculptures of Praxiteles, c.370–330 B.C.
- Alexander the Great, 356–323 B.C.
- Hellenistic Period, 356–146 B.C. Roman conquest of Greece
- Victory of Samothrace, 180–160 B.C.

Rome
- Reign of Augustus, 27 B.C.–A.D. 14
- Reign of Trajan, A.D. 98–117
- Pantheon built, A.D. 118–125

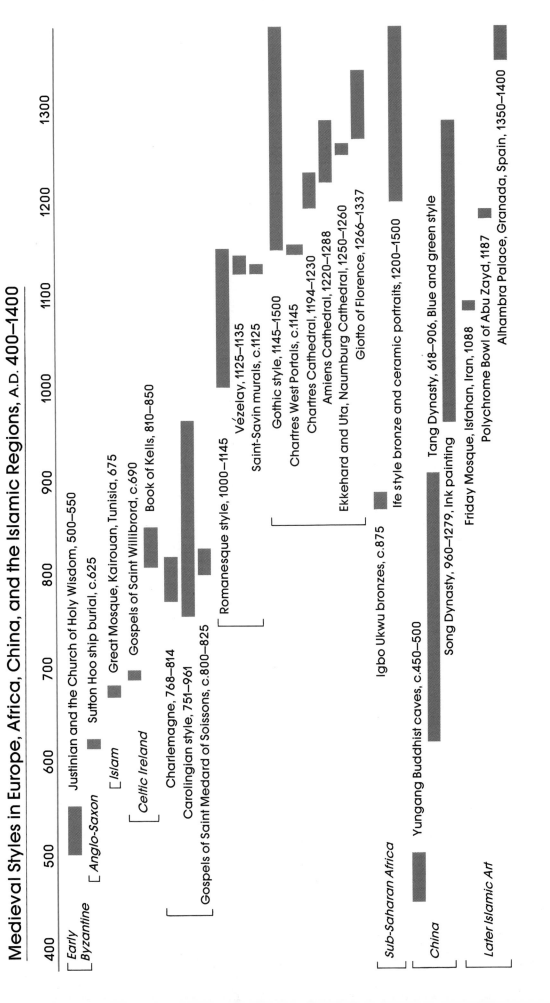

Medieval Styles in Europe, Africa, China, and the Islamic Regions, A.D. 400–1400

Early Byzantine
Justinian and the Church of Holy Wisdom, 500–550

Anglo-Saxon
Sutton Hoo ship burial, c.625

Islam
Great Mosque, Kairouan, Tunisia, 675

Celtic Ireland
Gospels of Saint Willibrord, c.690
Book of Kells, 810–850

Charlemagne, 768–814
Carolingian style, 751–961
Gospels of Saint Medard of Soissons, c.800–825

Romanesque style, 1000–1145
Vézelay, 1125–1135
Saint-Savin murals, c.1125

Gothic style, 1145–1500
Chartres West Portals, c.1145
Chartres Cathedral, 1194–1230
Amiens Cathedral, 1220–1288
Ekkehard and Uta, Naumburg Cathedral, 1250–1260
Giotto of Florence, 1266–1337

Sub-Saharan Africa
Igbo Ukwu bronzes, c.875
Ife style bronze and ceramic portraits, 1200–1500

China
Yungang Buddhist caves, c.450–500
Song Dynasty, 960–1279, Ink painting
Tang Dynasty, 618–906, Blue and green style

Later Islamic Art
Friday Mosque, Isfahan, Iran, 1088
Polychrome Bowl of Abu Zayd, 1187
Alhambra Palace, Granada, Spain, 1350–1400

400   500   600   700   800   900   1000   1100   1200   1300

461

1400–1600

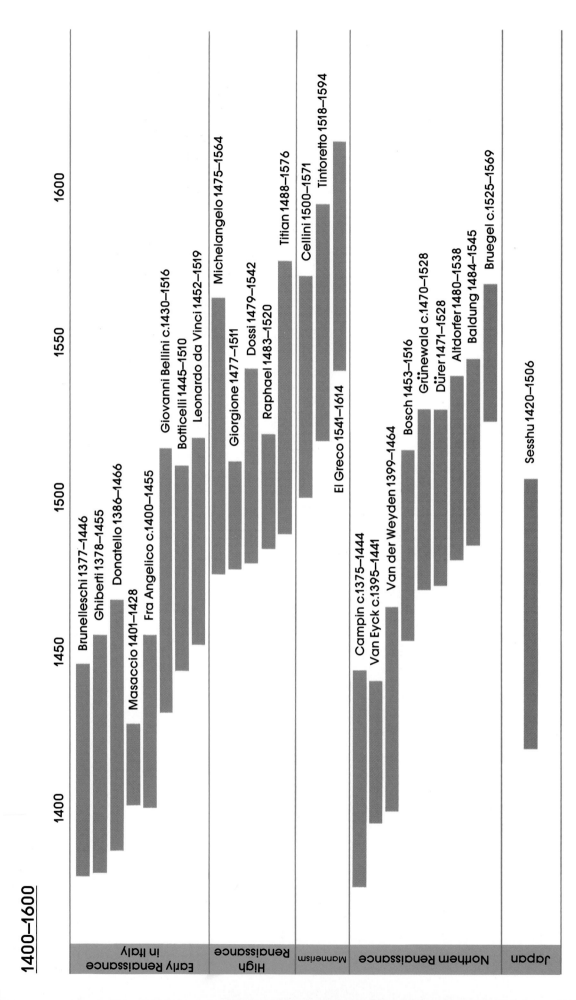

Early Renaissance in Italy
- Brunelleschi 1377–1446
- Ghiberti 1378–1455
- Donatello 1386–1466
- Masaccio 1401–1428
- Fra Angelico c.1400–1455
- Giovanni Bellini c.1430–1516
- Botticelli 1445–1510
- Leonardo da Vinci 1452–1519

High Renaissance
- Michelangelo 1475–1564
- Giorgione 1477–1511
- Dossi 1479–1542
- Raphael 1483–1520
- Titian 1488–1576

Mannerism
- Cellini 1500–1571
- Tintoretto 1518–1594
- El Greco 1541–1614

Northern Renaissance
- Campin c.1375–1444
- Van Eyck c.1395–1441
- Van der Weyden 1399–1464
- Bosch 1453–1516
- Grünewald c.1470–1528
- Dürer 1471–1528
- Altdorfer 1480–1538
- Baldung 1484–1545
- Bruegel c.1525–1569

Japan
- Sesshu 1420–1506

1600–1850

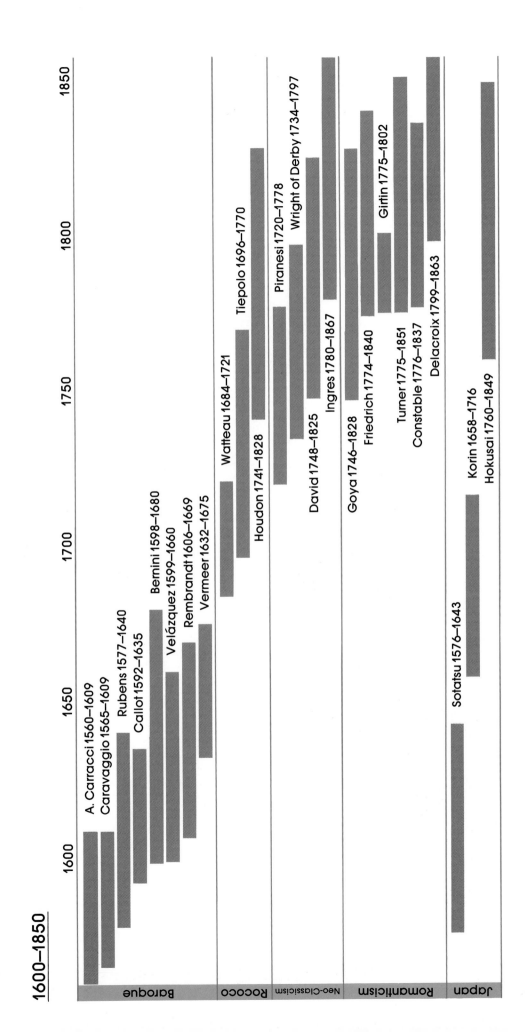

Baroque

A. Carracci 1560–1609
Caravaggio 1565–1609
Rubens 1577–1640
Callot 1592–1635
Bernini 1598–1680
Velázquez 1599–1660
Rembrandt 1606–1669
Vermeer 1632–1675

Rococo

Watteau 1684–1721
Tiepolo 1696–1770
Houdon 1741–1828

Neo-Classicism

Piranesi 1720–1778
Wright of Derby 1734–1797
David 1748–1825
Ingres 1780–1867

Romanticism

Goya 1746–1828
Friedrich 1774–1840
Girtin 1775–1802
Turner 1775–1851
Constable 1776–1837
Delacroix 1799–1863

Japan

Sotatsu 1576–1643
Korin 1658–1716
Hokusai 1760–1849

1600   1650   1700   1750   1800   1850

Realism
Millet 1814–1875
Courbet 1819–1877
Eakins 1844–1916
Repin 1844–1930

Impressionism
Pissarro 1830–1903
Manet 1832–1883
Degas 1834–1917
Monet 1840–1926
Renoir 1841–1919
Cassatt 1845–1926

Post-Impressionism
Cézanne 1839–1906
Gaugin 1848–1903
Van Gogh 1853–1890
Seurat 1859–1891

Fauvism and Expressionism
Matisse 1869–1954
Rouault 1871–1958
Kirchner 1880–1938
Chagall 1887–1985

Cubism
Picasso 1881–1973
Léger 1881–1955
Braque 1882–1963

Dada, Surrealism and related arts
Klee 1879–1940
Duchamp 1887–1968
De Chirico 1888–1978
Ernst 1891–1976
Dali 1904–1989

Non-Objective
Kandinsky 1866–1944
Mondrian 1872–1944

Modern Sculpture
Rodin 1840–1917
Brancusi 1876–1957
Boccioni 1882–1916
Calder 1898–1976
Moore 1898–1986
David Smith 1906–1965
Giacometti 1901–1966

Timeline axis: 1850 · 1875 · 1900 · 1925 · 1950 · 1975

1850–1990

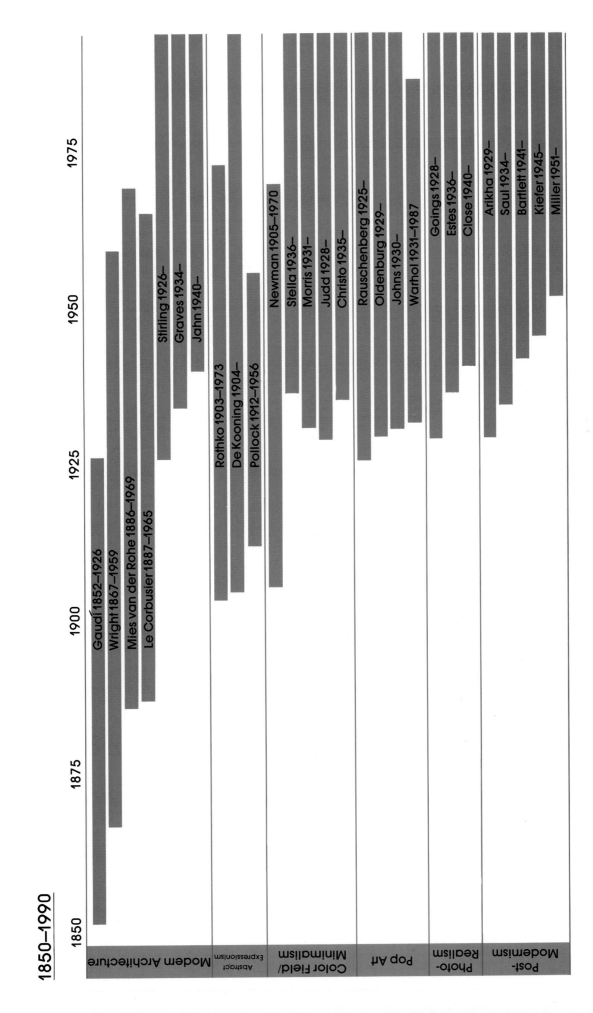

Modern Architecture

Gaudí 1852–1926
Wright 1867–1959
Mies van der Rohe 1886–1969
Le Corbusier 1887–1965
Stirling 1926–
Graves 1934–
Jahn 1940–

Abstract Expressionism

Rothko 1903–1973
De Kooning 1904–
Pollock 1912–1956

Color Field/ Minimalism

Newman 1905–1970
Stella 1936–
Morris 1931–
Judd 1928–
Christo 1935–

Pop Art

Rauschenberg 1925–
Oldenburg 1929–
Johns 1930–
Warhol 1931–1987

Photo-Realism

Goings 1928–
Estes 1936–
Close 1940–

Post-Modernism

Arikha 1929–
Saul 1934–
Bartlett 1941–
Kiefer 1945–
Miller 1951–

NOTES TO THE TEXT

Chapter 1

1. Howard S. Becker, *Art Worlds* (Berkeley: University of California Press, 1982) 34.
2. This discussion is based mainly on Elizabeth Hess, "A Tale of Two Memorials," *Art in America* April 1983: 120–128.
3. Becker 103.
4. C.K., *New Republic* Nov. 29, 1982: 42.
5. T.R.B., *New Republic* Dec. 6, 1982: 6, 39.
6. William Broyles, Jr., *Newsweek* Nov. 22, 1982: 82–83.
7. Suzanne Langer, *Feeling and Form* (New York: Scribner, 1953) 407–409.
8. T. H. Benton, *An Artist in America*, 4th ed. (Columbia: University of Missouri Press, 1983) 332.
9. Francis V. O'Connor, "The Life of Jackson Pollock, 1912–1956: A Documentary Chronology," vol. 4 of F. V. O'Connor and E. V. Thaw, eds., *Jackson Pollock: A Catalogue Raisonné of Paintings, Drawings and Other Works* (New Haven: Yale University Press, 1978) 208.
10. Benton 333.
11. Gary Schwartz, *Rembrandt: His Life, His Paintings* (New York: Viking, 1985).
12. *Gertrude Stein on Picasso*, E. Burns, ed., 1970: 18, cited in J. Alsop, *Rare Art Traditions* (New York: Harper & Row, 1982) 4.
13. Hans Kreitler and Shulamith Kreitler, *Psychology of the Arts* (Durham, N.C.: Duke University Press, 1972) 5–6.
14. Eloise Spaeth, *American Art Museums*, 3rd ed. (New York: Harper & Row, 1975).
15. Karl E. Meyer, *The Art Museum* (New York: Morrow, 1979) 13.
16. The Frick Collection, *Masterpieces of the Frick Collection*, text by E. Munhall (New York: The Frick Collection, 1970) 4.
17. Robert Coles, "The Art Museum and the Pressures of Society," *On Understanding Art Museums*, S. E. Lee, ed. © American Assembly, Columbia University (Englewood Cliffs, N.J.: Prentice-Hall, 1975) 200.

Chapter 2

1. Paul Cézanne, letter quoted in Fleming, *Art, Music and Ideas* (New York: Holt, Rinehart and Winston, 1970) 325.
2. Charles Sterling, *Still Life Painting*, 2nd ed. (New York: Harper & Row, 1981) 126.
3. B. Conrad, III, "Wayne Thiebaud," *Horizon*, Jan.–Feb. 1986: 6–8.
4. A good discussion of this subject is in Kenneth Clark, *The Nude* (New York: Pantheon, 1956).
5. Sherman E. Lee, *A History of Far Eastern Art*, 4th ed. (Englewood Cliffs, N.J.: Prentice-Hall, 1982) 343.
6. Malcolm Cormack, *Constable* (Cambridge; New York: Cambridge University Press, 1986) 20.
7. Cormack 111.
8. Frank H. Goodyear, Jr., *Welliver* (New York: Rizzoli, 1985) 127.
9. Goodyear 13.
10. Hayden Herrera, *Frida Kahlo* (Chicago: Museum of Contemporary Art, 1978).

Chapter 3

1. John Golding, Introduction, in John Elderfield, *The Drawings of Henri Matisse* (New York: Thames & Hudson, 1985) 17.
2. Golding 10.
3. *The Elder Pliny's Chapters on the History of Art*, trans. K. Jex-Blake (Chicago: Argonaut, 1968; reprint of 1896 edition) Book XXXV: 67–68.
4. Golding 15.
5. Rudolf Arnheim, *Art and Visual Perception* (Berkeley: University of California Press, 1954) 140.
6. Judy Pfaff, "Sculptors' Interviews," *Art in America* Nov. 1985: 131.
7. Guo Xi (Kuo Hsi), *An Essay on Landscape Painting*, trans. Shio Sakanishi (London: John Murray, 1959). For a modern analysis see Fritz van Briessen, *The Way of the Brush* (Rutland, Vt.: Charles E. Tuttle, 1962) 125–129.
8. Zong Bing (Tsung Ping), "Introduction to Landscape Painting," *The Spirit of the Brush*, trans. Shio Sakanishi (London: John Murray, 1939) 38.
9. Ted Castle, "Nancy Holt, Siteseer," *Art in America* Mar. 1982: 88.

Chapter 4

1. Alfred H. Barr, Jr., *Matisse: His Art and His Public* (New York: Museum of Modern Art, 1951) 552.
2. Lawrence Alloway, *Agnes Martin* (Philadelphia: Institute of Contemporary Art, University of Pennsylvania, Philadelphia, 1973) 9; cited in Hermann Kern, *Agnes Martin* (Munich: Kunstraum, 1973) 9, note 7.
3. Martica Sawin, "Kenneth Snelson: Unbounded Space," *Arts Magazine* Sep. 1981: 171–173.
4. Piet Mondrian, *The New Art—The New Life: The Collected Works of Piet Mondrian*, ed./trans. Harry Holtzman and Martin S. James (Boston: G. K. Hall, 1986) 224.
5. Mondrian 201.
6. Calvin Tomkins, "Profiles: Getting Everything In" (Jennifer Bartlett). *The New Yorker* Apr. 15, 1985: 66.

Chapter 5

1. Seymour Chwast, *The Left-Handed Designer*, ed. Steven Heller (New York: Harry N. Abrams, 1985) 8.
2. Jerry N. Uelsmann, *Uelsmann: Process and Perception* (Gainesville: University Presses of Florida, 1985) 3.
3. Barbara London, *National Video Festival* (Washington, D.C.: American Film Institute, 1982) 85.
4. Nam June Paik, "La Vie, Satellites, One Meeting—One Life," *Video Culture, A Critical Investigation*, ed. J. G. Hanhardt (New York: Visual Studies Workshop, 1986). From exhibition catalogue *Nam June Paik—Mostly Video*, Tokyo Metropolitan Art Museum, 1984.
5. Robert Edmonds, *The Sights and Sounds of Cinema and Television* (New York: Teachers College Press, 1982) 3.
6. Carol Littleton, quoted in David Chell, *Moviemakers at Work* (Redmond, Wash.: Microsoft Press, 1987) 49–65.

7. Nam June Paik, "Input-Time and Output-Time," *Video Art, An Anthology*, comp. and ed. I. Schneider and B. Korot (New York: Harcourt Brace Jovanovich, 1976) 98.

8. Edmonds 22–29.

9. Tracy Biga, "Blue Velvet," *Film Quarterly*, Fall 1987: 44–49.

10. Bill Lundberg, quoted in *Film Installations*. Exhibition catalogue at Emily Davis Gallery, University of Akron, 1987 (Michael Jones, curator) 48.

Chapter 6

1. The Rev. William Gilpin, quoted in Michael Clarke, *The Tempting Prospect* (London: British Museum, 1981) 53.

2. Gilpin in Clarke 49.

3. Wanda Corn, *The Art of Andrew Wyeth* (San Francisco: Fine Arts Museums of San Francisco, 1973) 130.

4. *Siqueiros, 70 Obras recientes* (Mexico City: Instituto Nacional de Bellas Artes, 1947). Quoted in English in Antonio Rodriguez, *A History of Mexican Mural Painting* (New York: Putnam, 1969) 378.

Chapter 7

1. In Spanish it has a certain ring to it: "La escultura tiene el ser y la pintura el parecer." Francisco Pacheco, *Arte de la pintura* (1649) (Madrid: Instituto de Valencia de Don Juan, 1956) 44.

2. A. Giacometti, letter to Pierre Matisse, 1947, *Alberto Giacometti* (New York: Museum of Modern Art, 1965) 28.

3. Quoted in Magdalena Abakanowicz (Chicago: Museum of Contemporary Art; New York: Abbeville Press, 1982) 147.

4. Quoted in David Bourdon, "The Razed Sites of Carl Andre . . . ," *Artforum* Oct. 1986: 15.

5. Robert Irwin, *Being and Circumstance* (Larkspur Landing, Calif.: Lapis Press, 1985) 67.

6. Dan Flavin, *Three installations in fluorescent light* (Koln: Wallraf-Richartz Museums, 1973) 14.

7. Quoted in M. Mathews, "Duane Hanson Super Realism," *American Artist* Sep. 1981: 97, 104.

Chapter 8

1. Le Corbusier, *Towards a New Architecture*, trans. F. Etchells (New York: Praeger, 1960) 114.

2. Le Corbusier 190.

3. Charles Jencks, *Le Corbusier and the Tragic View of Architecture* (Cambridge: Harvard University Press, 1973) 152–153.

4. Le Corbusier 165.

5. Christopher Alexander, *A Pattern Language* (New York: Oxford University Press, 1977).

6. Tony Hiss, "Experiencing Places," *The New Yorker* June 22, 1987: 45 ff.

7. Hiss 52.

8. Hiss 65.

9. Hiss 60.

10. Henry N. Wright, "Radburn Revisited," *Architectural Forum* July–Aug. 1971: 53.

11. Guy Davenport, quoted in R. J. Onorato, "Richard Fleischner," in *Sitings* (La Jolla, Calif.: Museum of Contemporary Art, 1986) 66.

12. Peter Blake, *The Master Builders* (New York: Knopf, 1970) 95, 379.

Chapter 9

1. Bauhaus brochure, quoted in Walther Scheidig, *Crafts of the Weimar Bauhaus* (New York: Reinhold, 1967) 6.

2. Bauhaus brochure 6.

3. Bauhaus brochure 6.

4. François Boucher, *20,000 Years of Fashion* (New York: Abrams, 1966) 108.

5. Bernard Leach, "Belief and Hope," *50 Years a Potter* (London: Arts Council of Great Britain, 1961), quoted in Garth Clark, *American Potters* (New York: Watson–Guptill, 1981) 21–22.

6. Dimitri Gerakaris, "Eagle Square Gateway," *American Craft* Dec. 1983–Jan. 1984: 12.

7. Gerakaris 12.

Chapter 10

1. T. Grieder, *Origins of Pre-Columbian Art* (Austin: University of Texas Press, 1981) 7–15.

2. Shana Alexander, "Feminine Eye: Visit to Lascaux Cave," *McCall's* Sep. 1970: 6.

3. Elias Howard Sellards, "Stone Images from Henderson County, Texas," *American Antiquity* 1941, vol. 7: 29–38.

4. George M. A. Hanfmann, *Classical Sculpture* (Greenwich, Conn.: New York Graphic Society, 1967) 29.

5. Ernst H. Gombrich, *Art and Illusion*, 2nd ed. (Princeton, N.J.: Princeton University Press [Bollingen Series XXXV.5], 1961) 141.

6. Suetonius Tranquillus, Gaius, *The Twelve Caesars*, trans. Robert Graves (Harmondsworth, England: Penguin, 1957) chap. 79, p. 94.

7. Eleanor Winsor Leach, "Patrons, Painters, and Patterns: The Anonymity of Romano-Campanian Painting and the Transition from the Second to the Third Style," in *Literary and Artistic Patronage in Ancient Rome*, ed. Barbara K. Gold (Austin: University of Texas Press, 1982) 135–173.

Chapter 11

1. Procopius, 6th-century Byzantine writer, quoted in Steven Runciman, *Byzantine Style and Civilization* (Baltimore: Penguin, 1975) 53.

2. Wang Wei, *The Spirit of the Brush*, ed. and trans. Shio Sakanishi (London: John Murray, 1939) 44.

Chapter 12

1. Kenneth Clark, *Leonardo da Vinci* (London and Baltimore: Penguin, 1958) 118.

2. Michael Baxandall, *Painting and Experience in Fifteenth Century Italy*, 2nd ed. (Oxford: Oxford University Press, 1972) 2.

3. Baxandall 34.

4. Benvenuto Cellini, *Memoirs*, trans. J. A. Symonds (New York: Random House, c. 1945) Book II, XC: 439.

5. Giorgio Vasari, *Lives of the Artists*, ed. B. Burroughs (New York: Simon & Schuster, 1946) 67.

6. Kenneth Clark, *The Nude* (New York: Pantheon, 1956) 413.

7. Michael Cooper, ed., *They Came to Japan: An Anthology of European Reports on Japan, 1543–1640* (Berkeley: University of California Press, 1965) 260–261.

8. Shuichi Kato, *Form, Style, Tradition: Reflections on Japanese Art and Society* (Berkeley: University of California Press, 1971) 137.

9. Cooper 254–255.

10. Cooper 253.

11. Alexander Soper in R. T. Paine and A. Soper, *The Art and Architecture of Japan* (Harmondsworth, England: Penguin, 1955) 263.

12. Donald Keene, "Japanese Aesthetics," *Philosophy East and West* (Honolulu) July, 1969: 294.

13. John Evelyn, Diaries, ed. E. S. de Beer (Oxford: Clarendon Press, 1955) vol. II: 261. Irving Lavin, *Bernini and the Unity of the Visual Arts* (New York: Oxford, 1980) 146.

14. Frans Baudouin, *Peter Paul Rubens* (New York: Abrams, 1977) 253–257.

Chapter 13

1. Charles Baudelaire, "The Salon of 1846," *The Mirror of Art*, trans. and ed. J. Mayne (New York: Doubleday, 1956) 44.

2. William Bartram, *Travels Through North and South Carolina, Georgia, East and West Florida* (Savannah, Ga.: Beehive, 1973; first ed. 1791) 341.

3. Richard Shiff, *Cézanne and the End of Impressionism* (Chicago: University of Chicago Press, 1984) 2.

4. Clement Greenberg, "The Later Monet," *Art News Annual*, 1957: 132.

5. L. E. Duranty, *La Nouvelle Peinture*, ed. M. Guérin (Paris: H. Floury, 1946; first ed. 1876).

6. Anne Coffin Hanson, *Manet and the Modern Tradition* (New Haven: Yale University Press, 1977) 92.

7. A. E. Elsen, S. C. McGough, and S. H. Wander, *Rodin and Balzac* (Beverly Hills, Calif.: Cantor, Fitzgerald, 1973) 12.

8. H. de la Croix and R. G. Tansey, *Art Through the Ages* (New York: Harcourt Brace Jovanovich, 1980) 783.

9. Ronald Pickvance, *Van Gogh in Saint–Rémy and Auvers* (New York: Metropolitan Museum of Art; Abrams, 1986) 189.

10. W. H. Auden, ed., *Van Gogh, A Self-Portrait* (Greenwich, Conn.: New York Graphic Society, 1961) 313.

11. John Rewald, *Paul Gauguin* (New York: Abrams, 1952) 14.

12. Rewald 14.

Chapter 14

1. Pablo Picasso, "Picasso Speaks. A Statement by the Artist," *The Arts*, May, 1923: 326.

2. Statement by Picasso from *Cahiers d'Art*, 1935, vol. 10, no. 10: 173–178; reprinted in A. H. Barr, Jr., *Picasso: 50 Years of His Art* (New York: Museum of Modern Art, 1946) 272–274 (trans. Myfanwy Evans).

3. Robert Rosenblum, *Cubism and Twentieth-Century Art* (Englewood Cliffs, N.J.: Prentice-Hall, 1966) 130.

4. M. Fagiolo dell'Arco, in *De Chirico*, ed. W. Rubin (New York: Museum of Modern Art, 1982) 11–34.

5. W. S. Lieberman, ed., *Max Ernst* (New York: Museum of Modern Art, 1961) 10.

6. Ignacio Gómez de Liaño, *Dalí* (New York: Rizzoli, 1984) 29.

7. Wassily Kandinsky, *Concerning the Spiritual in Art* (New York: G. Wittenborn, 1947) 59, 60, 70.

8. Piet Mondrian, *The New Art—The New Life: The Collected Works of Piet Mondrian*, ed. and trans. Harry Holtzman and Martin S. James (Boston: G. K. Hall, 1986) 370, 17.

9. Harold Rosenberg, *Artnews* Dec. 1952: 22.

10. Hans Namuth and Barbara Rose, *Pollock Painting* (New York: Agrinde, 1978) "Statements by Jackson Pollock" (no page numbers).

11. Clement Greenberg, "The 'Crisis' of Abstract Art," *Arts Yearbook: New York: The Art World*, No. 7 (1964): 91.

12. Robert Rosenblum, "Introduction," in Lawrence Rubin, *Frank Stella* (New York: Steward, Tabori and Chang, 1986) 10.

13. Donald Judd, "Black, White and Gray," *Arts Magazine* Mar. 1964: 37.

14. *Perspecta 11*, 1967, in W. C. Agee, *Don Judd* (New York: Whitney Museum, 1968) 16.

15. J. Goldman, *James Rosenquist* (New York: Viking, 1985) 22.

16. Goldman 27–28.

17. Goldman 33.

18. J. Arthur, *Realism/PhotoRealism* (Tulsa, Okla.: Philbrook Art Center, 1980) 68.

19. Barr 66–68.

20. Harold Rosenberg, "The Art World," *The New Yorker* May 9, 1970: 54.

21. Charles Jencks, *The Language of Post-Modern Architecture*, 4th ed. (New York: Rizzoli, 1984) 9.

22. W. Haftmann, *Paul Klee* (New York: Praeger, 1954) 53.

23. Harold Rosenberg, "Interview . . . ," *ArtNews* Sep. 1972: 54.

24. Virginia Cartwright, "The Market for Teapots," *Ceramics Monthly* Oct. 1986: 45.

25. *Willem de Kooning: The North Atlantic Light* (Amsterdam: Stedelijk Museum, 1983) 67.

26. Thomas B. Hess, *Barnett Newman* (New York: Walker, 1969) 32.

27. Dan Hofstadter, "Profiles: A Painting Dervish," *The New Yorker* June 1, 1987: 49.

28. Hofstadter 49.

29. Robert Storr, "Peter Saul: Radical Distaste," *Art in America* Jan. 1985: 92.

30. *Peter Saul: New Paintings and Works on Paper* (New York: Alan Frumkin Gallery, 1987).

31. E. H. Wheat, *Jacob Lawrence, American Painter* (Seattle: University of Washington Press; Seattle Art Museum, 1986) 108.

SUGGESTED READINGS

1 The Art World

Becker, Howard S. *Art Worlds.* Berkeley: University of California Press, 1982.

Hess, Elizabeth. "A Tale of Two Memorials." *Art in America.* April, 1983: 120–128.

Kranz, Stewart. *Science and Technology in the Arts.* New York: Van Nostrand-Reinhold, 1974.

Kreitler, Hans, and Shulamith Kreitler. *Psychology of the Arts.* Durham: Duke University Press, 1972.

Meyer, Karl E. *The Art Museum: Power, Money, and Ethics.* New York: Morrow, 1979.

Munhall, E. *Masterpieces of the Frick Collection.* New York: The Frick Collection, 1970.

Rivera, Diego. *My Art, My Life.* New York: Citadel Press, 1960.

Diego Rivera: A Retrospective. New York: Founders Society, Detroit Institute of Arts; Norton, 1986.

Spaeth, Eloise. *American Art Museums,* 3rd ed. New York: Harper & Row, 1975.

2 Interpreting Works of Art

Clark, Kenneth. *Landscape into Art.* London: John Murray, 1952.

———. *The Nude, a Study in Ideal Form.* New York: Pantheon, 1956.

Herrera, Hayden. *Frida Kahlo.* Chicago: Museum of Contemporary Art, 1978.

Loehr, Max. *The Great Painters of China.* New York: Harper & Row, 1980.

Sterling, Charles. *Still Life Painting: From Antiquity to the Twentieth Century,* 2nd ed. New York: Harper & Row, 1981.

3 The Elements of Art

Arnheim, Rudolf. *Art and Visual Perception.* Berkeley: University of California Press, 1954.

Elderfield, John. *The Drawings of Henri Matisse.* New York: Thames & Hudson, 1985.

Gill, Robert W. *Basic Perspective.* London: Thames & Hudson, 1980.

Lauer, David A. *Design Basics,* 3rd ed. Fort Worth: Holt, Rinehart and Winston, 1990.

4 Understanding Design

Bartlett, Jennifer. *In the Garden.* New York: Harry N. Abrams, 1982.

Bevlin, Marjorie Elliot. *Design Through Discovery,* 5th ed. Fort Worth: Holt, Rinehart and Winston, 1989.

Herter, Christine. *Dynamic Symmetry: A Primer.* New York: Norton, 1966.

5 The Graphic Mediums

Chell, David. *Moviemakers at Work.* Redmond, Wash.: Microsoft Press, 1987.

Chwast, Seymour. *The Left-Handed Designer.* Ed. by Steven Heller. New York: Harry N. Abrams, 1985.

Edmonds, Robert. *The Sights and Sounds of Cinema and Television.* New York: Teachers College Press, 1982.

Edwards, Betty. *Drawing on the Right Side of the Brain.* Los Angeles: Tarcher, 1979.

Hanhardt, John G. *Nam June Paik.* New York: Whitney Museum of American Art, 1982.

Saff, Donald, and Deli Sacilotto. *Printmaking: History and Process.* Fort Worth: Holt, Rinehart and Winston, 1978.

6 Painting

Clarke, Michael. *The Tempting Prospect.* London: British Museum, 1981 (on English watercolor painting).

Horgan, Paul. *Peter Hurd: A Portrait Sketch from Life.* Austin: Amon Carter Museum, Fort Worth, and University of Texas Press, 1965.

Mayer, Ralph. *The Artist's Handbook of Materials and Techniques.* New York: Viking Press, 1981.

Rodriguez, Antonio. *A History of Mexican Mural Painting.* New York: Putnam, 1969.

7 Sculpture

Davies, Hugh M., and R. J. Onorato. *Sitings.* La Jolla, Calif.: Museum of Contemporary Art, 1986.

Gray, Cleve, ed. *David Smith by David Smith.* Fort Worth: Holt, Rinehart and Winston, 1968.

Krauss, Rosalind E. *Passages in Modern Sculpture.* New York: Viking Press, 1977.

8 Styles and Structures in Architecture and the Environment

Alexander, Christopher. *The Timeless Way of Building.* New York: Oxford University Press, 1979.

Blake, Peter. *The Master Builders.* New York: Knopf, 1970.

Hiss, Tony. "Experiencing Places." *The New Yorker.* June 22, 1987.

Jencks, Charles A. *The Language of Post-Modern Architecture,* 4th ed. New York: Rizzoli, 1984.

———. *Le Corbusier and the Tragic View of Architecture.* Cambridge, Mass.: Harvard University Press, 1973.

Wright, Frank Lloyd. *Frank Lloyd Wright: Writings and Buildings.* Selected by E. Kaufmann and B. Raeburn. New York: Meridian, 1960.

9 Design Applications

Boucher, François. *20,000 Years of Fashion.* New York: Harry N. Abrams, 1966.

Clark, Garth. *American Potters.* New York: Watson-Guptill, 1981.

Kemp, Gerald van der. *Versailles: A Complete Guide.* New York: Vilo, 1981.

Rowe, Ann P., ed. *The Junius B. Bird Conference on Andean Textiles.* Washington, D.C.: The Textile Museum, 1986.

Silk, Gerald. *Automobile and Culture.* New York: Harry N. Abrams; Los Angeles: Museum of Contemporary Art, 1984.

Whitney Museum of American Art. *High Styles: Twentieth-Century American Design.* Intro. by Lisa Phillips. New York: Whitney Museum, 1985.

10 Ancient Styles

Brilliant, Richard. *Roman Art.* London: Phaidon, 1974.

Hanfmann, George M. A. *Classical Sculpture.* Greenwich, Conn.: New York Graphic Society, 1967.

Lange, Kurt, and Max Hirmer. *Egypt: Architecture, Sculpture, Painting in Three Thousand Years.* London: Phaidon, 1968.

Pollitt, J. J. *Art and Experience in Classical Greece.* Cambridge, U.K.: Cambridge University Press, 1972.

Ruspoli, Mario. *The Cave of Lascaux: The Final Photographs.* New York: Harry N. Abrams, 1988.

Schele, Linda, and Mary Ellen Miller. *The Blood of Kings.* Fort Worth: Kimbell Art Museum, 1986.

Shafer, Harry. *Ancient Texans.* Austin: Texas Monthly Press, 1986.

11 Styles of the Middle Ages, 400–1400

Lee, Sherman E. *A History of Far Eastern Art,* 4th ed. Englewood Cliffs, N.J.: Prentice-Hall, 1982.

Ry, Carel J. du. *Art of Islam.* New York: Harry N. Abrams, 1970.

Stokstad, Marilyn. *Medieval Art.* New York: Harper & Row, 1986.

Swaan, Wim. *The Gothic Cathedral.* Garden City, N.Y.: Doubleday, 1969.

Willett, Frank. *African Art.* New York: Thames & Hudson, 1971.

12 Styles of the Columbian Age, 15th–18th Centuries

Baudouin, Frans. *Peter Paul Rubens.* New York: Harry N. Abrams, 1977.

Baxandall, Michael. *Painting and Experience in Fifteenth Century Italy.* Oxford: Oxford University Press, 1972.

Brown, Jonathan. *Velázquez, Painter and Courtier.* New Haven: Yale University Press, 1986.

Clark, Kenneth. *Leonardo da Vinci.* London and Baltimore: Penguin, 1958.

Cooper, Michael, ed. *They Came to Japan: An Anthology of European Reports on Japan, 1543–1640.* Berkeley: University of California Press, 1965.

Hartt, Frederick. *Michelangelo: The Complete Sculpture.* New York: Harry N. Abrams, 1968.

Swann, Peter C. *An Introduction to the Arts of Japan.* Oxford: Bruno Cassirer, 1958.

Vasari, Giorgio. *Lives of the Painters, Sculptors, and Architects.* New York: E. P. Dutton, 1927.

13 From Neo-Classicism to Post-Impressionism, 1750–1900

Hanson, Anne Coffin. *Manet and the Modern Tradition.* New Haven: Yale University Press, 1977.

Herbert, Robert L. *Impressionism: Art, Leisure and Parisian Society.* New Haven: Yale University Press, 1988.

Rewald, John. *A History of Impressionism,* 4th ed. New York: Museum of Modern Art, 1973.

———. *Post-Impressionism,* 3rd ed. New York: Museum of Modern Art, 1978.

14 Styles of the 20th Century

Arnason, H. H. *History of Modern Art: Painting, Sculpture, Architecture, Photography.* New York: Harry N. Abrams, 1986.

Rosenblum, Robert. *Cubism and Twentieth-Century Art.* Englewood Cliffs, N.J.: Prentice-Hall, 1966.

Rubin, William, ed. *Pablo Picasso: A Retrospective.* New York: Museum of Modern Art, 1980.

Sandler, Irving. *The Triumph of American Painting: A History of Abstract Expressionism.* New York: Harper & Row, 1976.

Seitz, William C. *Abstract Expressionist Painting in America.* Cambridge, Mass.: Harvard University Press, 1983.

GLOSSARY

Terms italicized within the definitions are themselves defined in the Glossary, except the term "art," which is in italic type only when the definition is relevant to the definition of art.

abstract A *composition* of forms which exist in the mind and in *art*, but not in nature, though they may derive from nature.

Abstract Expressionism Art movement of the 1940s and 1950s, especially in the United States.

academy Art school in which art is taught as an intellectual discipline, first established in Italy in the 16th century.

acrylic A painting *medium* in which the *binder* is a synthetic resin.

aerial perspective System of representing masses and spaces by the relative distances colors seem to have, warm colors seeming closer than cool ones.

aesthetics Philosophy concerned with the questions: what is beauty? why is it a cultural value?

alla prima All at once, or wet-into-wet, *oil painting* technique; in contrast to *impasto-glaze* technique.

altarpiece A painting or sculpture placed on or behind an altar.

aquatint A printmaking technique, to make areas of tone in *etching* by dusting the plate with resin dust. The acid bites through the resin making a rough area which prints a gray tone.

arcade A series of arches.

arch A curved construction of brick or stone which spans an opening above a room or doorway, with wedge-shaped blocks held in place by their pressure against each other and by *buttresses*.

art A symbolic communication of more than instrumental value (that is, it must have more than a practical use) by a human being.

artisan A person who works at a *craft*.

art world All the people whose activities are necessary to the production of a particular kind of art.

assemblage A constructed sculpture of found objects, a three-dimensional form of *collage*.

asymmetry Not symmetrical; a design in which the two halves are different, not mirror images.

Autochrome The first commercially available (1907) color photography process.

automaton A robot or mechanized kinetic sculpture.

balance *Principle of design* requiring the parts of a *composition* to appear in equilibrium around some axis.

Baroque A European style of the 17th century: dramatic, energetic, sensuous style; applied (small "b") to any style with those qualities.

barrel vault A semicircular *arch* repeated to make a *vault*.

bay One of a set of equal spaces in a building, such as a *Gothic* church, usually formed by four columns or *piers* at the corners of a rectangular floor, supporting a *groin-vaulted* ceiling.

Benin Ancient kingdom in West Africa, now part of Nigeria.

binder A glue or glue-like substance in paint which binds *pigment* together and attaches it to a surface.

bronze Alloy of copper and tin, the commonest metal for *casting*.

burin The small steel chisel used to make *engravings*.

buttress A mass of masonry used to support a building—usually an *arch, vault,* or *dome*—by opposing the outward thrust of the arches.

calligraphy The art of writing; writing as an art form.

camera obscura A drawing tool composed of a box with a lens which projects a view onto a ground glass or paper, a camera without film.

canon A rule or set of principles or standards, most commonly for the forms or *proportions* of architecture or the human body.

cantilever A structural technique in architecture in which a beam that projects beyond its support has a balancing weight on the other end.

cartoon (1) A preparatory drawing (*study*) in full scale; (2) a satirical or humorous drawing.

cast or **casting** The process of duplicating a model by making a mold of it and filling the mold with another material; commonly the mold is plaster, the casting bronze.

cella The chamber of a *Classical* temple.

ceramics Objects made of fired clay, including pottery, *porcelain*, and *terra-cotta* sculpture.

chase The application of finishing touches with tools to a metal *casting*.

chiaroscuro Light and shadow represented in art; a way of drawing with black and white on a gray or middle-value ground to show light and *shade*.

Classical Referring to Greek culture of the 5th century B.C. and its influence on *Hellenistic* and Roman cultures in the following eight centuries; small "c" (classical or classic): any style based on strict *canons* of *form*.

collage Two-dimensional art made by pasting shapes of paper or other materials onto a flat surface, usually with painting or drawing.

color wheel The arrangement of primary colors in a circle to show how they can be mixed to produce secondary and tertiary colors.

complementary colors Colors on opposite sides of the *color wheel* that make gray when mixed equally, such as red and green.

composition Arrangement of art *elements* according to the *principles of design*.

conceptual art Art movement of the 1970s showing diagrams and written proposals or descriptions ("concepts") of *forms* or actions, rather than forms themselves.

concrete art   A work of art interpreted (by its creator or by its audience) as a material thing without symbolism, *subject,* or *representation.*

content   The meaning, message, or idea expressed by the *form* and *subject.*

contour   Line showing the boundary of a three-dimensional mass.

contrapposto   Natural action pose of the human figure as if walking, especially in sculpture. Opposite of *frontality.*

Corinthian   Fanciest of the Greek Classical *orders;* the capital is ornamented with acanthus leaves.

craft   The skill and knowledge to make some kind of material object; basic to *art,* which is considered to transcend craft by its expression of mental or spiritual powers usually defined as "genius."

critic   A writer on art who is an expert on cultural value.

Cubism   Art movement of 1907 and later emphasizing *abstractions* based on geometric analysis of natural forms; begun by Picasso and Braque.

Dada   Art movement that originated in Germany in 1914 in the anti-war movement showing the absurd, shocking irrationality of life.

Dogon   African tribe in Mali.

dome   A circular *vault,* usually a portion of a sphere, used as a ceiling.

Doric   Classical architectural *order;* the capital has a block (abacus) and curved molding (echinus).

drawing   Marks on a surface produced by hand; a **finished drawing** is distinguished from a *sketch* and a *study* or *cartoon* by being a final work of art.

drypoint   A technique in *intaglio* printing in which lines are cut into the plate by hand with the sharp point of a steel etcher's needle. Drypoint is often used to add details to an *etching* or *engraving.*

edition   A set of prints made from the same plate, block, or stone. A "limited edition" does not exceed a predetermined number of prints.

elements of art   The artist's marks: lines, shapes, masses, spaces, colors, values, textures.

elevation   A drawing of a building showing its appearance from one side as it "elevates" from the ground (cf. *plan*).

emphasis   *Principle of design* showing relative importance of parts by size, color, contrast, and so on. Parts may be equal or different in emphasis.

enamel   A colored glass, usually forming a design, fused onto a metal or ceramic surface by fire. Paint that has a thick, shiny appearance may be called enamel because it looks like true enamel.

encaustic   Painting medium; the *pigment* is mixed with wax, which is dissolved by heat.

engraving   Printmaking medium in which a copper plate is cut with a *burin* to make an *intaglio* print.

etching   Medium in which a copper (or zinc) plate is cut with acid to make an *intaglio* print.

Expressionism   Group of 20th-century art movements stressing individual emotional expression.

Fauvism   Art movement in France beginning about 1903 based on vivid color.

figure   The solid or positive shape set against a background area in a two-dimensional art form; see *ground.* Often refers to "human figure."

flying buttress   An *arch* used to span a space between an arch or *vault* which needs external support and the *buttress* which provides the support. In *Gothic* churches the space under the flying buttresses was used for aisles and chapels.

foreshortening   Depiction of three-dimensional forms on a two-dimensional surface with the third dimension diminished to emphasize depth; a *perspective* method for irregular forms such as human bodies.

form   All the things that are presented (as opposed to represented) in a work of art: canvas or stone, brush or chisel marks, colors, a design of lines and shapes, and so on.

frontality   In sculpture, a figure in a *symmetrical* pose facing the front; a pose used for beings in eternity. Opposite of *contrapposto.*

forum   A public mall in ancient Roman cities.

fresco   Painting medium using *pigment* mixed with water on a wet lime plaster ground, usually used as a mural medium. Work must stop when the plaster begins to dry. Painting on dry plaster is called **fresco secco**; it is less durable than fresco.

frieze   A strip of ornament on a building.

functionalism   Aesthetic theory that utility is the ruling factor in design.

Futurism   Art movement in Italy beginning in 1909 which glorified speed and machines.

geodesic   *Dome* form made of trusses, an invention of Buckminster Fuller.

gesso   Italian for gypsum, or "plaster of Paris," applied to paper or wooden panels as a *ground* for *tempera* painting or silverpoint drawing.

glaze   Any glass-like surface: the finish coat of glass on *ceramics* or a thin transparent coat of *oil paint.*

Golden Mean   An ancient *proportional* system which proposes that the most beautiful division of a line is: the shorter segment is to the longer as the longer is to the whole line—a proportion of 1 to 1.618. Those proportions can be used as the sides of a rectangle. Also called the Golden Section.

gouache   Painting *medium;* the *pigment* is mixed with water-soluble glue forming an opaque watercolor. Paper is the usual *ground.*

Gothic   Art movement mainly in northern Europe, c. 1150–1500.

groin vault   A *vault* formed of intersecting *barrel vaults.*

ground   The surface on which a two-dimensional work of art is made. In "**figure and ground**" the word refers to background or space around the part of the design considered positive or solid. Also, in *etching,* the acid-resistant material applied to the surface of the metal plate.

hatching   Parallel lines used as shading in a drawing; **crosshatching** (sets of parallel lines that cross) gives a darker shade.

Hellenistic   Period c. 350–31 B.C. of Greek culture after Alexander the Great.

hieroglyphic writing A system of writing incorporating pictures of objects as symbols, along with conventional and/or phonetic signs; Egyptian and *Maya* are among the best-known systems of hieroglyphic writing.

hue A named color for a specific wave length of light reflected from a surface.

iconography Symbolism in art, either personal symbols or those of a culture.

impasto Thick paint, usually oil paint. Traditionally used for highlights in the *impasto-glaze* technique.

Impressionism Art movement, originating in France c. 1872, based on painting outdoors to record color as light is received by the eye.

intaglio Printmaking techniques (mainly *etching* and *engraving*) in which the design is cut into a metal plate. Opposite of *relief*.

intensity The purity and strength, or saturation, of a color.

International Style The 20th-century architectural style developed by Le Corbusier, Gropius, Mies van der Rohe, and others characterized by simple rectangular forms of reinforced concrete and glass.

in the round Sculptural form that can be seen from all sides, which has no background plane. Opposite of *relief* sculpture.

Ionic Classical architectural order; the capital has a volute (scroll).

isometric perspective System in which parallel lines are parallel, but angles are drawn to a standard, usually 60/30° for 90°.

kinetic art Art that employs actual movement, using wind, water, a motor, or some other power source. See *mobile*.

krater Ancient Greek jar used for mixing wine and water.

line A long narrow mark which may record a gesture of the artist's hand or be the boundary of a *shape*, the *contour* of a mass, or an *abstract* symbol or sign.

linocut A *relief* print made from a linoleum surface.

lithography Printing from stone using the chemical opposition of grease and water to make the design.

lost wax In French *cire perdue*, method of making a metal sculpture by *casting* it from a wax model that is melted out of the mold.

mandala Ancient design composed of a circle in a square (or a square in a circle) symbolizing the universe.

Maya Native American civilization in Mexico and Central America.

medium The material or technical means used for artistic expression (plural *mediums* or *media*). In painting, a process characterized by a specific *binder*, *solvent*, and *ground*.

Minimalism A non-objective art style of the period 1960s to 1980s using the simplest possible geometric shapes and forms.

mobile A kinetic sculpture, particularly Alexander Calder's wind-powered suspended sculptures.

Modernism, or **Modern movement** The art movement which emerged from the self-conscious break with past theory and practice in art that occurred at the beginning of the 20th century and lasted until about 1970. *Cubism, Expressionism, Futurism,* and *Surrealism* are styles within the Modern movement.

mosaic An art medium in which small pieces of colored stone or glass (*tesserae*) are embedded in a plaster or cement background.

mosque A Muslim, or Islamic, temple.

mural Any decoration on a wall; *fresco* is usually used for murals.

naturalistic Art depicting natural forms as they appear in nature.

nave The main space in a medieval church, where the congregation is accommodated.

non-objective Art representing no material object; usually used as a synonym for *abstract*.

non-representational Synonym for non-objective.

occult balance "Hidden" balance, asymmetrical balance.

oil painting A painting *medium* in which colored *pigments* are mixed with linseed oil used as the *binder*, which has turpentine as its *solvent*; usually applied to a canvas *ground*.

order A set of architectural forms and proportions, usually referring to the *Doric, Ionic,* and *Corinthian* columnar temple architecture invented by the ancient Greeks.

painting A work of art produced by applying *pigments* mixed with a *binder* to a *ground*.

pastel *Pigment* mixed with glue formed into a stick for *drawing*.

patina The natural or artificial oxidation of a metal sculpture as a surface finish.

patron The person who provides financial support for a work of art and usually sets certain requirements.

pediment The gable of a Classical temple.

pentimenti Italian for "repentances"; changes and corrections in a work of art which are still visible in the finished work.

peristyle A set of columns (called a colonnade) surrounding an open space or a building, most commonly used on the exterior of *Classical* temples.

personification A human figure representing an idea, such as Mother Nature.

perspective Any system for depicting in two dimensions the relative positions of three-dimensional forms in space. Compare *aerial perspective, foreshortening, isometric perspective*.

picture plane The actual surface of a two-dimensional work of art—the paper or canvas, for example—as opposed to the illusion of space.

pier A masonry (brick, stone, or concrete) pillar used as the support for a building; usually given the form of a cluster of columns in *Gothic* churches.

pigment Powdered color, usually of a mineral substance, used to make paint by mixing it with a *binder*.

pixel Word coined from "picture element," the dot that forms a computer or electronic image on a cathode ray tube screen.

plan A drawing of the shape a building makes on the ground, showing its architectural features (cf. *elevation*).

pointillism A late-19th-century painting style using dots of pure color, also called divisionism.

polyptych A work of art made of more than three separate panels or canvases.

Pop Art A 1960s style based on popular commercial art.

porcelain Fine-grained white translucent pottery fired at a high temperature.

post-and-lintel A system of building using beams (of wood, stone, steel), some set vertically as posts to support others (lintels) laid horizontally across their tops.

Post-Modernism Art movement that began about 1970 characterized by renewed interest in the European art traditions, new attempts to incorporate varied mediums (for example, furniture) into the art tradition, and a search for styles independent of *Modernism*; important in architecture.

principles of design The fundamental considerations for the organization of visual art to produce understandable compositions. See *unity, variety, balance, rhythm, emphasis.*

proportion Relationships of size reflecting significance or function.

relief The projection of a design from a background plane, as in sculpture (opposite of *in the round*) and printmaking. Low relief in sculpture barely projects above the plane; high relief is barely attached to the background plane. In relief printing, such as woodcut, the ink is applied to the projecting parts, which are stamped on paper (opposite of *intaglio*).

repoussé Metal worked by hammering to make *relief* decorations.

representational Depiction of forms that have material existence.

rhythm Principle of design referring to repetition of an element of art according to a rule of location or spacing.

Romanesque A style of architecture and other arts in western Europe from about 1000 to about 1145 characterized by massive structures, semicircular *arches*, and sculpture and painting in expressive linear styles.

scumbling The process of partly covering a color with a thin coat of fairly dry, opaque paint of another color to allow traces of the first color to show; used as a way to blend or model colors.

serigraphy *Silkscreen printing,* using a stencil on a silk backing.

shade A color (*hue*) to which black has been added, or shadow, as in "light and shade."

shape A two-dimensional surface with a definite boundary or edge.

silkscreen printing See *serigraphy.*

sketch A drawing made as a note of something seen or thought.

solvent A liquid that dissolves the *binder* in a paint.

stela (plural *stelae*) An upright slab of stone used as a monument, usually bearing an inscription and/or a design; *stela* is used for Maya and other New World examples; *stele* is the common spelling for other regions (Egypt and Greece, for example).

still life A work of art, usually a painting, representing household objects and/or flowers, traditionally considered a *representation* of the pleasures of life.

study A drawing done to plan another work of art.

style Emphasis on certain elements of art or principles of design for expressive purposes. Period style represents a place and time; personal style represents an individual.

subject All the things that are represented in a work of art; the things in the picture or sculpture. Compare *form, content.*

Surrealism European art movement beginning about 1921 which emphasized psychology and the unconscious mind.

symmetry Term for a design in which the two halves are mirror images, meaning "same measure."

tapestry A decorated cloth hanging, usually made by weaving a design with weft (horizontal) into plain warp (vertical) threads.

tempera Painting medium in which *pigment* is mixed with egg yolk, whose *solvent* is water. The *ground* is usually paper or a *gesso* panel.

terra cotta Italian for "baked earth"; fired pottery clay.

tessera (plural *tesserae*) The small pieces of stone or glass used to make a *mosaic.*

tint A color to which white has been added.

transept The wings of a cross-plan medieval church.

triptych A work of art composed of three separate panels or canvases.

trompe l'oeil "Fool the eye" in French, referring to a style of painting in which the observer might actually mistake the painted image for reality.

truss In architecture; a triangle of wood or metal; a rigid form, it can be combined in multiple triangles to make roofs, bridges, *geodesic domes.*

tympanum An arched area above the lintel of a door in a medieval church, often decorated with relief sculpture.

unity Oneness; the perception by an observer that a group of *elements* of art are parts of one *composition.*

value Light and dark as an element of art, the range of tones from white to black. Monetary value of art is market value. Beauty is a cultural value.

vanishing point A point on the horizon, or eye level, in a linear perspective drawing at which parallel receding lines meet.

variety Differences among *elements of art* in a *composition.* Variety opposes *unity* and offers contrast and change, but must be subordinate to unity.

vault A ceiling or roof made of *arches.*

watercolor Painting *medium* in which *pigment* is mixed with gum arabic, whose *solvent* is water, usually applied to paper.

woodcut A *relief* print made from a block of wood.

ziggurat Ancient Akkadian for "mountaintop" or "pinnacle"; an ancient Mesopotamian temple tower topped by a shrine reached by a stairway.

INDEX

Photographic credits and acknowledgments. The author and publisher thank the custodians of the works of art for supplying photographs and granting permission to use them. Photographs have been obtained from sources noted in the captions, unless listed below.

A/Ar: Alinari/Art Resource, NYC. AF: Alison Frantz, Princeton, NJ. AFK: A. F. Kersting, London. BPK: Bildarchiv Preussicher Kulturbesitz, West Berlin. CAISSE: Caisse Nationale des Monuments Historiques et des Sites, Paris. G/AR: Giraudon/Art Resource, NYC. H: Hirmer Verlag, Munich. HB: Hedrich-Blessing, Chicago. HRV: H. Roger-Violett, Paris. LVM: Leonard von Matt, Basel, Lucerne, Switzerland. M/AR: M/Art Resource, NYC. MAS: MAS, Barcelona. RMN: Service de Documentation Photographique de la Réunion des Musées Nationaux, Paris. S/AR: Scala/Art Resource, NYC. WS: Wim Swaan, NYC.

PART I   **1:** courtesy of the artist.

CHAPTER 1   **3, 4, 7, 8:** Dolores Neuman, Washington, D.C. **5:** John McDonnell/The Washington (D.C.) Post. **6:** Dept. of Defense (Marine Corps), Washington, D.C. **11:** Lucienne Block, Gualala, CA. **13:** Subdirreccion de Documentacion e Informacion; CENIDIAP, Mexico City. **15:** BPK. **18:** Laboratoire de Recherche des Musées de France, Paris; © LRMF. **21:** CEA (Atomic Energy Commission), Grenoble, France. **24:** Adam Bartos, courtesy of the Museum of Modern Art, NYC. **25:** Leonard McCombe, LIFE Magazine, © Time, Inc. **26:** Press and Information Office, Tate Gallery, London.

CHAPTER 2   **27:** Rudolph Burckhardt, NYC. **35, 42, 46, 49, 50:** RMN. **44:** Allan Stone Gallery, NYC. **45, 47:** A/AR. **48:** S/AR. **58:** A.C.L. Brussels. **59:** MAS. **60:** Mary-Anne Martin/Fine Art, NYC.

CHAPTER 3   **64:** Dmitri Kessel, LIFE Magazine, © 1984 Time, Inc. **65:** Chiang Lee, *Chinese Calligraphy*, Harvard Univ. Press, Cambridge, MA; © 1973. Reprinted by permission of The President and Fellows of Harvard College. **69:** Courtesy of the Wellington Galleries, Ltd., London; © Succession H. Matisse/1942; Photo Archives Matisee (D.R.). **70:** Jack Flam, NYC. **75:** RMN. **77:** CAISSE. **79:** Rudolph Arnheim, *Art and Visual Perception*, The Univ. of California Press, Berkeley. **81:** George Holmes, Archer M. Huntington Art Gallery, Austin, TX. **86:** Jorg P., Anders/Staatliche Museen Preussischer Kulturbesitz, Kupferstichkabinet, West Berlin. **88:** John Bigelow Taylor, NYC. **89:** From *The Woodcuts of Aristede Maillol* by John Rewald. Pantheon Books, p. 168. Paula Cooper Gallery, NYC. **96, 115:** S/Ar. **97:** Pedro E. Guerrero, New Canaan, CT. **98:** Courtesy of the Board of Trustees of the Victoria and Albert Museum, London.

102, 111: A/AR. **106:** Gemma Levine, London. **109:** Courtesy of Pierre Matisse Gallery, NYC.

CHAPTER 4   **133:** Marlborough Art Gallery, NYC. **138:** © Cervin Robinson 1989, NYC. **139:** Wayne O. Attoe, University of Texas, Austin. **140, 153, 154:** MAS. **157:** A/AR. **166, 167, 169:** Paula Cooper Gallery, NYC. **170:** H. **173, 176:** S/AR.

CHAPTER 5   **203:** Push Pen Group, NYC. **204:** Reale Fotografia Giacomelli, Venice. **209:** Wide World Photos, Inc., NYC. **210:** Collection of Josephus Daniels Gallery, Carmel, CA. **211:** Uelsman, *Process and Perception* (Gainesville: Univ. of Florida Press, 1985). **212:** Commerce Graphics Ltd., Inc. East Rutherford, NJ. **214:** The Image Bank, NYC. **215:** Magnum Photos Inc., NYC. **220:** Elliot Caplan, photos, courtesy the Whitney Musuem of American Art, NYC. **221:** Film Stills Archive, Museum of Modern Art, NYC. **223:** Photofest, NYC. **226:** Leo Castelli Gallery, NYC.

CHAPTER 6   **228, 229, 231:** A/AR. **230:** S/AR. **232–235:** VEB Verlag der Kunst, Dresden. **251:** Hans Namuth, Ltd., NYC. **254–255:** VEB Verlag der Kunst, Dresden. **259:** Robert Lorenzon.

CHAPTER 7   **260, 261:** Donald M. Stadtner. **260, 262 (both), 272, 289:** A/AR. **269:** Audrey Topping. **274:** Lee Boltin Picture Library, Croton-on-Hudson, NY. **276:** Hamburgisches Museum fur Völker Kunde, Hamburg. **280:** Dirk Bakker, Huntington Woods, MI. **281:** © 1990 Henry Moore Foundation. **283:** John F. Gorgoni, NYC. **282:** © Christo 1989. Wolfgang Volz, Dusseldorf. **286:** Pedro E. Guerrero, New Canaan, CT. **290:** MAS. **291:** © 1981 Harvey Stein, NYC. **292:** Courtesy of Sidney Janis Gallery, NYC. **284:** Pace Gallery, NYC. **285:** Edmund B. Thornton Foundation, Ottawa, IL.

PART IV   **293:** HB.

CHAPTER 8   **294:** John Weber Gallery, NYC. **295:** Roger Violett, © Collection Violett, Paris. **297:** Claus-Dieter Brauns, Bad Liedinaell-u, West Germany, courtesy of National Geographic Society, Washington, D.C. **298, 308b:** H. **299, 301, 330:** HB. **303:** Russ Kinne/Comstock. **304, 305, 307b:** AF. **309b, 324–326:** A/AR. **311:** Joan Lebold Cohen, NYC. **313:** AFK. **314:** A/AR. **316:** LVM. **317:** French Government Tourist Office, NYC. **318:** WS. **322:** S/AR. **329:** Library of Congress. **331:** © Frank Lloyd Wright Foundation, 1987. **332:** Henry Fuermann & Sons, courtesy the Art and Architecture Library, Univ. of Michigan, Ann Arbor. **335:** © Frank Lloyd Wright Foundation, 1987, Scottsdale, AZ. **337:** Courtesy the Museum of Modern Art, NYC. **338, 399:** Lucien Hervé, Paris. **343:** Eddie Hiromaka/The Image Bank, NYC. **346, 353, 354:** Helmut Jahn Architectural Firm, Chicago. **350:** Museum of the City of NY. **351:** German Information Center, NYC. **352:** Vancouver (Canada) Tourist Commission. **355:** Balthaxar Korab, Troy, MS. **356:** Michael Graves, Princeton, NJ. **357, 358:** Waltraud Krase, Frankfurt, W. Germany.

CHAPTER 9   **362:** Giraudon/AR. **366:** Tim Street-Porter, Hollywood, CA. **368:** H. **370:** © 1981 Laura Gilpin Collection, Amon Carter Museum, Fort Worth, TX. **373:** S/AR. **375:** HRV. **377:** Staley Wise Gallery, NYC. **382:** Langdon Clay, Sumner, MS. **383:** Courtesy the National Gallery of Art, Washington, D.C. **386:** Reale Fotografia Giacomelli, Venice. **387:** Courtesy Bauhaus Archiv, W. Berlin. **388:** Dennis Griggs, Topsham, ME. **389:** George Erml, Forest Hills, NY. **390:** Courtesy the artist. **391:** John Lamm, courtesy Alfa Romeo Distributors of N. America, Englewood Cliffs, NJ. **392:** Henry Wolf, NYC. **394:** Chrysler Corporation Historical Archives, Detroit.

CHAPTER 10   **397:** André Koti, Paris. **398:** David Heald. **400, 414:** CAISSE. **402:** Werner Forman Archive, London. **406:** Jim Zintgraff, San Antonio, TX. **407, 412, 425–427:** H. **418:** André Held, Paris. **423:** Photo Archives, Univ. Museum, Philadelphia. **424:** Merle Green Robertson, San Francisco. **432, 436, 439, 441:** A/AR. **433:** S/AR. **434:** RMN.

CHAPTER 11   **443:** A/AR. **449, 451:** AFK. **452:** Joan Evans, *The Romanesque Architecture of the Order of Cluny*, Cambridge Univ. Press, NYC., 1938. **453:** CAISSE. **455:** AFK. **456:** Marburg/Art Resource. **457:** German Information Center, NYC. **459:** Hans Hinz, Allschwil, Switzerland. **460:** S/AR. **461:** Roger Wood, London. **465:** MAS. **466:** Ancient Art & Architectural Collection (Ronald Sheridan's Photo Library, London). **471, 472:** Frank Willet, Glasgow. **473:** Museum of Mankind, London. **474:** Jerry L. Thompson, Amenia, NY. **475:** Herbert M. Cole, Santa Barbara, CA. **476:** Walt Disney Imagineering, Los Angeles. **481:** Seiichi Mizuno. **485, 486:** Sekino Masaru, Tokyo Univ.

CHAPTER 12   **490, 491, 495–497, 499–501, 504, 525, 527, 528:** S/AR. **493, 526, 534, 535:** A/AR. **508, 509:** WS. **511, 533:** MAS. **536:** Collecion Hancock Sandoval, Centro de Estudios de Histriade Mexico Condumex, 1985. Judith Hancock Sandoval, Bonanza Productions, Inc., NYC. **540:** RMN.

CHAPTER 13   **542, 543:** RMN. **545:** Richmond (VA) Chamber of Commerce. **555:** Sovfoto, NYC.

CHAPTER 14   **575:** RMN. **576:** Hans Hinz. **578:** Malcolm Varon, NYC; © 1982. **593, 594:** Harry Shunk, NYC. **605:** The Saturday Evening Post. **607:** John Carlano, Philadelphia. **609:** eeva-inkeri, NYC. **611, 612:** Courtesy Marlborough Gallery, NYC.